COUNTRY INNS

and SELECTED HO

GREAT BR

and IRELAND

2000

PELICAN PUBLISHING COMPANY
Gretna 1999

First Pelican edition, 1985
Second edition, 1986
Third edition, 1987
Fourth edition, 1988
Fifth edition, 1989
Sixth edition, 1990
Seventh edition, 1991
Eighth edition, 1992
Ninth edition, 1994
Tenth edition, 1995
Eleventh edition, 1996
Twelfth edition, 1997
Thirteenth edition, 1998
Fourteenth edition, 1999
Fifteenth edition, 2000

ISBN 1-56554-733-0

Manufactured in Great Britain

Published by Pelican Publishing Company, Inc.
1000 Burmaster Street, Gretna, Louisiana 70053

Contents

PAGE

The regions

Map of the regions

Welcome to the 61st edition of **Signpost** - *the definitive guide to 225 of the finest hotels in Great Britain and Ireland.*

Signpost founder, Gordon 'Mac' McMinnies, late grandfather of the present publisher, leaving Sheffield for the English Six Days Hill Climb in March 1913.

Our inspectors have checked every single hotel personally, and we believe our standards are second to none. Motoring conditions may have changed since the founder of *Signpost* first took to the road, but inspectors' standards are still the same: individual style, value for money, friendly service and a personal welcome.

The Signpost sign. Your guarantee of a top quality hotel.

So whether you're looking for a quiet weekend away, or a two-week family holiday, *Signpost* has a wide variety of hotels to choose from - magnificent country hotels set in beautiful grounds, small hotels with log fires and cosy bedrooms deep in the heart of quiet country villages, as well as modern city hotels with full leisure and business facilities.

Irish Inspector John Paxman (left) with Frank Slattery, owner of Carrig House, County Kerry, Ireland.

Signpost Inspector Fiona Davison (right) with owners Peter Butterfield and Jackie Gainsford at Redcoats Farmhouse Hotel, near Hitchin, Hertfordshire.

Signpost *(1935 - 2000)*

Reproduced from original 1930's drawings by the founder of Signpost, W.G. McMinnies A.F.C. B.A. Oxon.

The following hotels appeared in the first edition of Signpost and are also in this Millennium edition

St Austell Hotel
(now Carlyon Bay Hotel) (page 18)
Hoops Inn *(page 24)*
Saunton Sands Hotel *(page 32)*
Knoll House Hotel *(page 48)*
Beauport Park Hotel *(page 71*)*
Oatlands Park Hotel *(page 80)*
Peacock, Rowsley *(page 106*)*
Hare & Hounds *(page 110)*
The Old England *(page 114)*
Armathwaite Hall *(page 126)*
Netherwood Hotel *(page 128*)*
St Mellons *(page 164)*
Formerly a Country Club
* LINE ENTRIES ONLY IN 1935 EDITION

In November 1998, *Signpost* celebrated its Diamond Jubilee. Happily many hotelier friends and colleagues were able to attend the celebration at the Cavendish St James Hotel in London's West End.

The 2000 edition is also something of a milestone. *Signpost,* which has had several imitators, has been published continuously since 1935, with the exception of the war years. In that time its ownership, like many of the hotels whom it represents, has only been in two families.

We hope today's readers enjoy *Signpost* as much as their parents and grandparents did and we hope that they will continue to inform us, the publishers, about any particularly good (or bad) experiences they have had staying in one of the *Signpost* family of hotels, as well as recommending to us any potential new entrants which they would like us to inspect. Forms are included at the back of the book for this purpose.

Publisher Malcolm Orr-Ewing (left) with past owner and continuing consultant, Christopher Carney-Smith.

The original logo adopted by the founder of Signpost 60 years ago - WG 'MAC' MCMINNIES

Our standards

Signpost Inspector Peter Lloyd (right) with General Manager, Jill Peterson, outside Simonstone Hall, North Yorkshire.

Today our inspectors still set the highest standards and expect every hotel to live up to them. We demand fine cuisine, using the best fresh produce. Bedrooms should be furnished with style and have all the comforts you need away from home. The hotel should be located in an interesting area, with plenty of opportunity for sport and leisure. Above all hotels should be welcoming, places you want to return to again and again.

Devon Inspector Olof White (right) with new owner Mark Trumble outside Buckland-tout-Saints Hotel, Kingsbridge.

Bonus

Once again this year the majority of our approved establishments have agreed to an *extra bonus* for Signpost readers. By presenting one of the vouchers at the back of this book, Signposters are entitled to a £5 reduction off the cost of their stay - at least the equivalent of a free bottle of wine!

Competition

In 2000 we again have a FREE weekend for two to be won. The prize is two nights bed and breakfast at a Country House Hotel. See page 283 for full details.

How to use the guide. The guide is divided into 11 regional sections.

Regional Section

There is a map of the regions at the beginning of the guide. If you want to look up the hotels in a particular region, simply turn to the relevant regional colour-coded section. Alternatively, turn to the colour maps starting on page 290. The numbers on the maps refer to the pages in this guide on which **Signpost** approved hotels are described.

The guide is divided into 11 regions. Each region has its own selection of hotels as well as a FactFile of useful information.

Fact File

Each regional section is prefaced by an illustrated guide to places of interest, walks, and historic houses and museums in the area together with a unique diary of events that take place. All designed to give you a feel for the area.

The factfile shows you places to go, gardens open, and a diary of events that take place in the area.

Hotel entry

The hotel entries for each region follow and most hotels have a page to themselves. There is a large colour photograph of each hotel and a detailed description of all the features of the hotel -

number of bedrooms standards of comfort, cuisine, leisure and sport facilities etc. There is also a description of the location and general ambience of the hotel to give you an idea of its character. **Signpost** member hotels make an annual contribution towards the costs of our inspections and a range of member services we provide.

Each hotel has a page to itself, with a large colour photograph and full details of rooms.

Room rates

Room rates are clearly shown as well as details of any special offers for weekend breaks etc.

***Single** room including breakfast from £31.00*
***Double** room including breakfast from £62.00*
Leisure Breaks:
2 day breaks or longer from £36.00 pp per night b & b; £46.00 p.p including dinner.

Room and room rates are clearly marked as well as full details of special rates for weekend breaks etc.

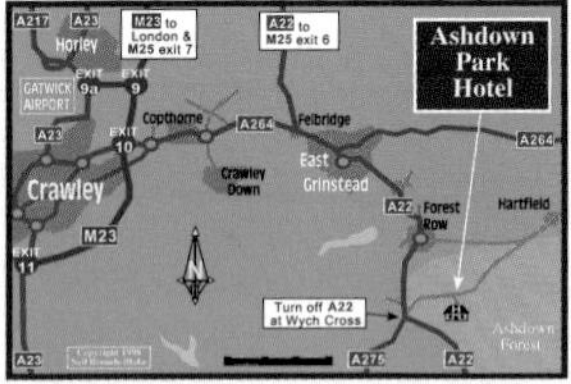

A location map shows the position of each hotel.

How to get there

To help you find the hotel, there is an area map which shows the hotel location and the surrounding roads and motorways.

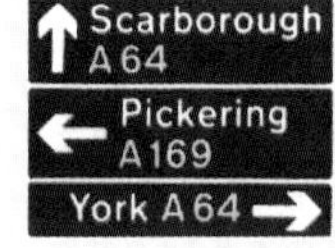

Listings and Maps

Internet

Reservations and enquiries can now be made directly via our INTERNET site on **http://www.signpost.co.uk.** Watch this site also for special offers from individual hotels throughout the year.

Historic Houses, Gardens & Parks

Bath & North-East Somerset
Sally Lunn's House, Bath

Cornwall
Cotehele House, St Dominic, Saltash
Glendurgan Garden, Mawnan Smith
Kit Hill Country Park, Callington
Lanydrock House, Bodmin
Mount Edgcombe House & Park, Torpoint
Trebah Garden, Mawnan Smith
Trelissick Garden, Truro
Trengwainton Garden, Penzance
Trerice, Newquay

Devon
Arlington Court, Barnstaple
Bicton Park & Gardens, E Budleigh
Overbecks Museum & Garden, Salcombe
Rosemoor Garden, RHS Garden, Gt Torrington
Saltram House, Plympton
Ugbrooke House & Park, Newton Abbot

Somerset
Barrington Court Gardens, Ilminster
Clapton Court Gardens
Clevedon Court, Clevedon
Fyne Court, Broomfield, Bridgwater
Hestercombe Gdns, Fitzpaine, Taunton
Lytes Carey Manor, Charlton Mackrell, Somerton
Montacute House
Tintinhull House Garden, Nr Yeovil

Walks & Nature Trails

Cornwall
The Camel Trail, runs along the river Camel from Padstow to Poley's Bridge
The North Cornwall Heritage Coast

Devon
Dartmoor National Park Guided Walks
The Tarka Trail

Somerset
West Mendip Way, starts at Uphill, following the crest of the Mendip Hills
Exmoor National Park Country Walks
West Someerset Mineral Railway, from Watchet to Washford

Historical Sites & Museums

Bath & North-East Somerset
Museum of Costumes, Bath
Pump Room, Bath
Roman Baths Museum, Bath

Bristol
Bristol City, Museum & Art Gallery
Harveys Wine Museum, Bristol

Cornwall
Launceston Castle
Restormel Castle, Lostwithiel
St Catherine's Castle, Fowey
St Mawes Castle
St Michaels Mount, Marazion
Tintagel Castle

Devon
Buckfast Abbey, Buckfastleigh
Buckland Abbey, Yelverton
Castle Drogo, Drewsteignton, Exeter
Compton Castle, Marldon, Paignton
Dartmouth Castle
Okehampton Castle
Powderham Castle, Kenton, Nr. Exeter
Watermouth Castle, Berrynarbor, Ilfracombe

Dorset
Corfe Castle
Dorset County Museum, Dorchester
Maiden Castle, Dorchester
Portland Castle
Sherborne Castle

Somerset
Cleeve Abbey, Washford, Watchet
Dunster Castle
Glastonbury Abbey
Nunney Castle
Taunton Cider Mill
Wells Cathedral

Entertainment Venues

Bristol
Bristol Zoological Gardens

Cornwall
Cornish seal Sanctuary, Gweek, Helston
Flambards Victoria Village Theme Park, Helston
Land's End, Penzance
Newquay Zoo
Paradise Park, Hayle
World in Miniature, Truro

Devon
City Museum & Art Gallery, Plymouth
Combe Martin Wildlife & Dinosaur Pk
Dartmoor Wildlife Park & West Country Falconry Centre, Sparkwell, Plymouth
Kents Cavern Showcaves, Torquay
Paignton & Dartmouth Steam Railway
Paignton Zoological & Botanical Gdns
Plymouth Dome, Plymouth
Railway Museum, Newton Abbot
Riviera Centre, Torquay
Torquay Museum

Somerset
Cheddar Showcaves, Cheddar Gorge
Haynes Motor Museum, Sparkford
Tropical Bird Gardens, Rode
West Somerset Railway, Minehead
Wookey Hole Caves & Papermill

DIARY OF EVENTS

January

30.12.99-2 Jan. **Greenbank Festival of Light**, Falmouth.

March

9. **Racing at Wincanton.**
13. **Racing at Taunton**.
15. **Racing at Newton Abbot.**

April

23. **Bournemouth Easter Parade.** From Boscombe Pier to Bournemouth Pier, Dorset.
29-30. **SW Custom & Classic Bike Show**,Royal Bath & West Showground, Shepton Mallet.
29-1 May. **Bath Annual Spring Flower Show.**
30-1 May. **Weymouth Intl Beach Kite Festival**, Weymouth.
30-1 May.**North Somerset Show** Ashton Court Est, Long Ashton

May

6. **Helston Flora Day.** Helston, Cornwall.
18-22*. **Devon County Show.** 105th Show. Westpoint Showground, Clyst St. Mary,Devon
19-June 4. **Bath International Music Festival.** Various venues in & around Bath, Somerset
19-Sept 13***The Minack Drama Festival.**The Minack, Porthcurno, Penzance, Cornwall.
26-June 11. **Bath Fringe Festival.** Various venues, Bath.
20-4 June*. **English Riviera Dance Festival.** Victoria Hotel Ballroom and Town Hall, Torquay, Devon.
20-23***.Intl Festival of the Sea** Bristol Historic Harbour.

June

7-10*. **Royal Bath & West Show.** RB&W Showground, Shepton Mallet.
8-10. **Royal Cornwall Show.** Royal Cornwall Showground, Wadebridge, Cornwall
23-25. **The Glastonbury Festival of Performing Arts.** Worthy Farm, Pilton, Somerset
30-16 July. **Exeter Festival.** Various venues, Exeter.

July

2-7. **National Youth Arts Festival.** Various venues, Ilfracombe, Devon.
2-11*. **Newquay 1900.** Presents *Celebrate the Century*, various venues, Newquay.
6-13*. **'Ways with Words' Literature Festival.** Dartington Hall Gardens, Dartington, Devon.
15. **Yeovilton International Air Day.** RNAS Yeovilton, Ilchester, Somerset.
10*. **Countryside Cavalcade**. Royal Bath & West Showground, Shepton Mallet, Somt17*. **Tolpuddle Rally.** Trade Union March.
22-2 Aug*. **World Professional Surf Festival.** Fistral Beach, Newquay, Cornwall.
29-5 Aug*. **Sidmouth International Festival of Folk Arts.** Devon. Various venues.

August

3*. **RAF St Mawgan Air Day.** RAF St Mawgan, Newquay, Cornwall. International air show with flying displays, stalls, funfair, helicopters etc.
5. **Stoke Gabriel Grand Carnival**. Nr Totnes, Devon.
11-12. **Bristol Balloon Fiestas Night Glow.** Ashton Court Estate, Long Ashton, Bristol.

The West Country

19-23. **Torbay Royal Regatta.** The Harbour, Torquay, Devon
3. **Honiton Agricultrural Show** The Showground, Honiton.
6-12. **Falmouth Regatta Week** Helford river, Carrick Roads and Falmouth Bay.
7. **Racing** at Newton Abbot.
9*. **Wadebridge Carnival.** The Seafront, Wadebridge, Cornwall Folk concerts, dances, ceilidhs, workshops, entertainment &c.
14-19*.**Celtic Art 2000**. Stuart House, Barras Street, Liskeard
26-29*. **Glastonbury Children's Festival.** Abbey Park Playground, Fisher's Hill, Glastonbury, Somerset. 20 different performances for children each day plus many participative workshops.
27-3 Sept*. **Bude Jazz Festival.**Various venues, Bude,Cnwl
28*. **Newlyn Fish Festival.** Newlyn Harbour & Fish Market. Newlyn, Cornwall.

September

1-3. **The National Amateur Gardening Show**. Royal Bath & West Showground, Shepton Mallett, Somerset.
3. **Racing.** Bath racecourse.
13.**Widecombe Fair.** OldField, Widecombe-in-the-Moor, Devon
13-17*. **Millennium Celebrations.** Voices of G lastonbury, Glastonbury Abbey, Somerset

October

7-8*. **Tudor Experience**. Buckland Abbey, Yelverton. Period entertainment etc.
8*. **Exeter Carnival.** Various venues, Exeter, Devon.
11. **Tavistock Goose Fair.** Town Centre. Street stalls, fun fair, livestock market.
18. **Trafalgar Day Service.** Exeter Cathedral, Devon.
24-1 Nov. **Halloween Magic Lanterns Day.** Crealy Park, Sidmouth Rd, Clyst St Mary, Devon. Witches Halloween Party on 31 Oct. Pumpkins &c

November

4. **Old Custom - Rolling of the Tar Barrel.** Town Centre, Ottery St Mary, Nr Exeter.
6. **Hibridge & Burnham-on-Sea Guy Fawkes Carnival**
10. **Collaton Guy Fawkes Festival.**
13. **Glastonbury Guy Fawkes Festival.**
16*. **Weston-super-Mare Guy Fawkes Festival.**
17-Dec 5. **Plymouth Christmas Crafts Festival.** City Centre, Plymouth, Devon.

December

1. **National Hunt Horse Racing.** Exeter racecourse.
26. **National Hunt Horse Racing**. Newton Abbot.
26. **National Hunt Horse Racing**. Wincanton.

** denotes provisional dates. The Tourist Board had not informed us of further events at press time. For further information, please contact:*

TOURIST BOARD

The West Country Tourist Board. 60 St Davis Hill, Exeter, Devon EX4 4SY.
Tel: (01392) 276351

England's West Country

The counties of Cornwall, Devon, Somerset, Dorset and Wiltshire comprise England's West Country, the great southwestern peninsula stretching out into the Atlantic Ocean.

The popularity of the region owes much to its geography and landscape. The coastline alone offers great variety and choice for the holiday maker. Around the coast you can also seek out the little ports and villages where visitors rub shoulders with the fishermen. If imposing scenery and bracing cliff walks are for you, then make for North **Cornwall**. The north coast is famous for its surfing beaches, whereas the south coast has the picturesque tree-lined Helford River and its subsidiary Gillan Creek. There is the historic county town of Bodmin, the cathedral city of Truro and Launceston, once the ancient capital of Cornwall.

Plymouth, the largest city in **Devon**, is a happy blend of holiday resort, tourist centre, historic and modern city. The famous Hoe has its associations with Sir Francis Drake and the Barbican with the Pilgrim Fathers. Exeter is the cultural capital of the county with its university, theatre, medieval cathedral and Maritime Museum. 19th-century dramatist Richard Ford wrote: "This Exeter is quite a capital, abounding in all that London has, except its fog and smoke".

Inland are the two magnificent National Parks of Dartmoor and Exmoor. Dartmoor lies in the south of Devon, 365 square miles of great natural beauty and rugged grandeur where you can sense the history and legend and discover peace and quiet. From the sparkling streams of the outskirts to the starker granite tors of the *high moor*, new pleasures unfold. The wild heather moorland and deep, wooded valleys are the home of red deer and of the legendary Doones of R D Blackmore's novel.

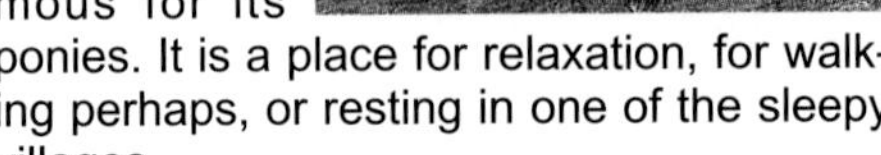

Exmoor, in the north of Devon is famous for its ponies. It is a place for relaxation, for walking perhaps, or resting in one of the sleepy villages.

The West Country also suits those who look for activity on their holiday. Fishing, for example - whether sea, game or coarse, is available in the five counties. The varied coastline is ideal for all watersports, with much opportunity for surfing, windsurfing, sailing and diving. Golf, with over 80 courses on breezy cliffs, amid the dunes, in parkland or on the moor, the West Country is a paradise for the golfer, The walker can choose to follow part of the Southwest Peninsula Coast Path, 515 miles of the finest coastal scenery, or try a long distance path like the Ridgeway in Wiltshire or the West Mendip Way, from Weston-super-Mare along the Mendips down to Wells in Somerset. Details of shorter nature trails and walks around historic cities are available from Tourist Information Centres.

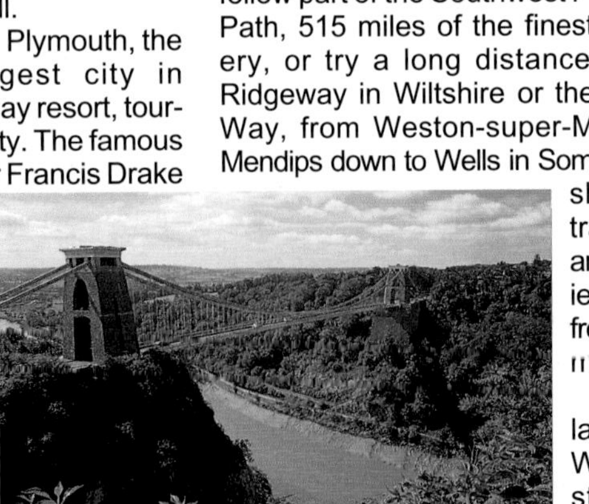

Bristol, the largest city in the West Country, is steeped in history. You can stroll down cobbled King Street, famous for its Theatre Royal, Almshouses and Llandoger Trow. The city docks are of great interest, providing a home for the SS Great Britain, Brunel's famous iron ship, the Industrial Museum and The Watershed shopping area.

A few miles up the river Avon is Britain's oldest and most famous spa, the City of Bath. Bath's 2000-year old fame started with its popularity as a resort for the Romans, who discovered its hot springs, still operative today. A second great era dawned in the 18th century Regency period, characterised by the Assembly Rooms, Royal Crescent, Circus, Lansdowne Crescent and other notable architecture.Tea in the Regency *Pump Room*, with a string quartet playing, should not be missed.

The county town of **Dorset** is Dorchester, founded by the Romans and later to become the fictional "Casterbridge" of Thomas Hardy's novels. Judge Jeffreys lodged in High West Street during his Bloody Assize. There are fine walks around Chesil Beach and on the Studland peninsula, part of the 7000-acre Corfe Castle estate. Bournemouth, with a population of 160,000 is the largest town in Dorset, representing a quarter of the county's population, is famous for its multitude of hotels and guesthouses, its theatre and concert hall with one of the few permanent non-Metropolitan orchestras of Britain in residence, its exhibition centre, its English Language Schools and for some reason often the highest priced fruit and vegetables in National comparative surveys!

In **Somerset**, visit the city of Wells, dominated by the great cathedral, with its magnificent west front. And do not miss Vicar's Close, one of the oldest medieval streets in Europe, and the moated Bishop's Palace. On the West coast of he county are the resorts of Weston-super-Mare and Minehead. Cheddar Gorge and the Wookey Hole caves in the Mendip Hills should not be missed. Glastonbury Tor, another Druidic site and now home to an annual popular music festival, is also striking.

Also dominated by its cathedral with its 404 ft spire, is Salisbury in **Wiltshire,** and around it, set back from the close, are many fine historic buildings. 20 miles north of the city is Stonehenge, one of the most visited Druidic sites of Britain, dating back 3000 years. Amesbury, with its Roman burial mound and seemingly random stones, dates form the same period.

Every county in the West Country has its share of stately homes and gardens (see *Historic Houses, Gardens and Parks* on page xi). With a coastline of 650 miles, the West Country is to this day strongly influenced by the sea.

England is a nation of garden lovers and the mild climate, which makes the West Country so popular with tourists, offers a long growing season. Some gardens, like Abbotsbury and Tresco (in the Scillies) specialise in subtropical plants. Spring is the best time for visiting the gardens of the Southwest. Few sights can compare with the flowering of the rhododendrons and azaleas across the lake at Stourhead. At gardens like Killerton, with its hardwood trees, the warm tones of Autumn create another riot of colour to reward the late visitor.

Photographs reproduced by kind permission of the West Country Tourist Board. This page, top to bottom: Roman Baths at Bath, Wells, Westbury White Horse. Previous page Bowormans Nose, Hells Mouth,Clifton Suspension Bridge, Bristol.

Royal Duchy Hotel

Falmouth, South Cornwall TR11 4NX
Tel: (01326) 313042; Fax: (01326) 319420
E-mail: info@royalduchy.co.uk
Internet: http://www.royalduchy. co.uk

Set in the historic maritime resort of Falmouth on the riviera coastline is the Royal Duchy Hotel. This seafront hotel is just a short, level walk from the town centre and harbour, and with its beautiful gardens and terraces, has fantastic views across Falmouth Bay to Pendennis Castle. The Royal Duchy Hotel is part of the Brend Hotel Group, the West Country's leading hoteliers (see also Carlyon Bay Hotel, near St Austell on page 18). The hotel is expertly managed by Darryl Reburn and his staff, whose friendly, attentive service is second to none. The reception rooms and most bedrooms enjoy spectacular sea views and all are well furnished to create a relaxing, comfortable atmosphere. The recently refurbished restaurant has a renowned reputation and boasts two AA rosettes for cuisine. The interesting selection of dishes is beautifuly cooked, well presented and is complemented by an extensive selection of fine wines. I can thoroughly recommend a stay at the Royal Duchy in any season. Whether you opt for a quiet relaxing break or a more active fun-filled holiday, you will always enjoy the best in accommodation and cuisine with impeccable service. Please write for their brochure or for details of special seasonal breaks.

Rates: *Room and breakfast from £58.00 single, £54.00 double/twin, per person inc. VAT.* V
Dinner, room and breakfast *from £70.00 single, £66.00 double/twin, per person inc. VAT.*
Bargain breaks. *Winter breaks from £90; Autumn breaks from £116; special June and July breaks from £128 and special July breaks from £124. All prices are per person for a minimum stay of two nights and include dinner, room and full English breakfast.*

● *43 en suite bedrooms, all with direct dial telephone and satellite TV; room service; baby listening; night service; lift.* ● *Last dinner orders 9.00 p.m, bar meals available lunchtime, à la carte and table d'hôte menu.* ● *Children welcome; dogs accepted at manager's discretion; conferences max. 40.* ● *Open all year.* ● *Small snooker/billiards table, table tennis; indoor heated swimming pool; sauna; solarium; spa pool; sea bathing; free golf to hotel residents at Carlyon Bay; sailing, boating, riding, shooting and fishing.*
Redruth 10, Truro 11, Lizard 20, Penzance 25, Bodmin 34, London 267.

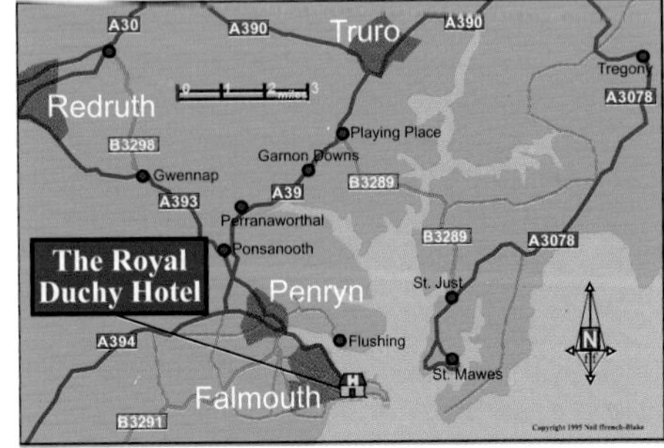

The Greenbank Hotel & Retreat

Harbourside, Falmouth,
Cornwall TR11 2SR
Tel: (01326) 312440; Fax: (01326) 211362
E-mail: sales@greenbank-hotel.freeserve.co.uk
Internet: http://www.greenbank-hotel.com

The Greenbank is Falmouth's only hotel situated on the banks of one of the world's deepest natural harbours. With its own private 17th century listed granite quay, it is Falmouth's oldest hotel - originally having catered for the packet ship captains of the 17th century. More recently Kenneth Graham stayed at the hotel whilst writing the *Wind in the Willows* stories. During 1999 new owners put in hand a refurbishment programme to transform the Greenbank into Cornwall's most stylish and imaginative facility. Their ambition was to blend contemporary style, service and technology with a spectacular location and Cornish culture. Bedrooms have been reappointed in Georgian style. All have ISDN lines, voicemail and high security lock systems. The hotel restaurant specialises in seafood which is landed daily on the quayside. Moneta's Bar is open for alcoholic refreshments, coffee, tea and pastries and serves lighter dishes until late in the evening. The Working Boat Pub has been the scene of tale-telling for over 200 years. Yacht charters, tours, sailing and fishing trips start from the hotel's quay. Cornwall's walks and tropical gardens are nearby.

Rates: *Single inc. breakfast from £45; double/twin from £75.* V
Bargain breaks*. 2 nights, dinner, b & b from £58.50 pppn; 3 nights from £49.50 pppn. Stay 10 nights d, b & b basis and hotel pays train fare to Falmouth from anywhere in UK and provides a hire car (ins. extra)*

- *59 en suite bedrooms, all with direct dial telephone and satellite TV, modem hook-up points, ISDN & voicemail, laundry service; tea/coffee making, 24 hr room/meal service; safety deposit box, radio/alarm clock. Non-smoker rooms available*
- *Table d'hôte £17.95; à la carte also available; last orders 2145; also Moneta's Bar, Working Boat Pub.*
- *Business services inc 5 meeting rooms to 100.*
- *Snooker, fishing, beauty salon, sauna, boating, sailing, diving. Shooting, 12 miles, riding nearby.*
- *Open all year. All major credit cards accepted.*

Truro 11, Penzance 26, Plymouth 65, London 308

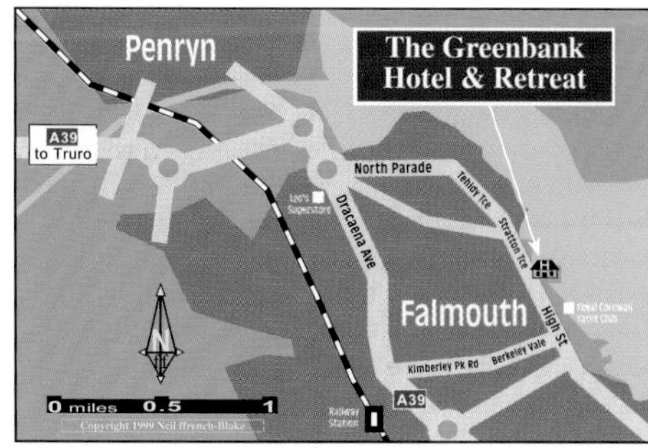

Meudon Hotel

Mawnan Smith, Falmouth,
Cornwall TR11 5HT
Tel: (01326) 250541; Fax: (01326) 250543

In many ways Meudon is a hotel of contrasts. Originally a country mansion built at the turn of the century, it then incorporated two 17th-century former coastguards' cottages and now has a large modern wing. Furnished with many antiques and fine paintings, it also has every modern comfort that a guest could want. Most bedrooms and public rooms overlook the fantastic gardens. These contain rare shrubs and trees such as Australian tree ferns, Chilean flame trees, lantern bushes, gunnera (giant rhubarb), mimosa, eucalyptus and rare rhododendrons. The award winning restaurant, under the supervision of chef Alan Webb, specialises in local seafood, oysters and crab which are delivered daily by local fishermen. Mr & Mrs Harry Pilgrim developed the hotel and their son, Mark, now manages it, representing the third generation - a true Pilgrim's Progress of fine Cornish family hotel-keeping. By car it is possible to reach Cornwall's many resorts, castles and gardens with Falmouth, the third largest deep water harbour in the world, on the doorstep. Local golf on eight courses is free to residents and riding, sailing, Cornwall's coastal footpath and many attractions are nearby.

***Rates:** Single, inc. breakfast and dinner from £105; double from £190.* V
***Impulse Breaks:** Minimum two days, dinner, b & b and free golf, from £160 per head.*

- *29 en suite bedreooms (inc 3 suites), all with colour TV, direct-dial telephone, hairdryer, laundry service, tea/coffee making, radio/alarm clock, safety deposit box & trouser press. Disabled rooms available. Separate cottage, sleeping 4/5 available from £200 (Winter, exc Xmas/New Year) to £650.*
- *5 course table d'hôte dinner £25. A la carte, lunch & special diets available. Last orders 9 pm.*
- *Snooker, fishing, golf, sea bathing from hotel. Watersports, sailing, boating, squash four miles; tennis one mile; shooting 10 miles.*
- *Barber shop; car parking 50; car rental; taxi service.*
- *Open all year. Visa, Amex, Diners cards accepted*

Falmouth 5, Helston 8, Redruth 12, Truro 13, Lands End 50, London 259.

Penhallow Manor Country House Hotel

Altarnum, Nr. Launceston,
Cornwall PL15 7SJ
Tel: (01566) 86206; Fax: (01566) 86179
Internet: http://www.cornwall-online.co.uk/penhallow

Penhallow Manor lies next to the church of St Nonna, known as the 'Cathedral of the Moor', in the award winning village of Altarnum. Originally the vicarage and now Grade II listed, it featured in *Jamaica Inn* as the home of the notorious vicar, Francis Davey, after a visit by Daphne du Maurier. With its Georgian proportions, the hotel retains many of its period features: fireplaces, windows and lantern hallway. The six individually presented bedrooms overlook the church and gardens, whilst the public rooms, with their decorative antiques and furnishings, provide the ideal setting for those seeking comfort and tranquillity. There are a further three bedrooms in the original coach house. With the sea only 30 minutes away, numerous gardens, National Trust properties and access to golf courses and fishing nearby, Penhallow is an ideal place to stay whether as a stopping off point or for an extended break. Freshly prepared local food is an important feature of the Manor and complements the personal attention new owners Val and Peter Russell have brought to Penhallow Manor.

Rates: *Single inc. breakfast from £35.00; double room inc. breakfast £70-100.*
Spring and Autmun Breaks: *discount for din ner, bed & breakfast 3 nights 10%, 5 nights 15%.*

- *6 en suite bedrooms (3 in coach house), all with direct dial telephone, colour TV, radio/alarm clock, tea/coffee making facilities, hairdryer, trouser press. Non-smoking.*
- *Four-course à la carte dinner £20 (residents); special diets available. Last orders 8.45 pm. AA ® Restaurant.*
- *Children over 12 welcome; well-behaved dogs by arrangement. Car parking for nine.*
- *Golf 15-25 miles; riding 5 m; birdwatching nearby; fishing, bathing, watersports 15 miles.*
- *Closed January. Visa, Mastercard, Switch, Delta cards accepted.*

Launceston 7, Bodmin 12, Okehampton 26, Exeter 48, Plymouth 34, London 218.

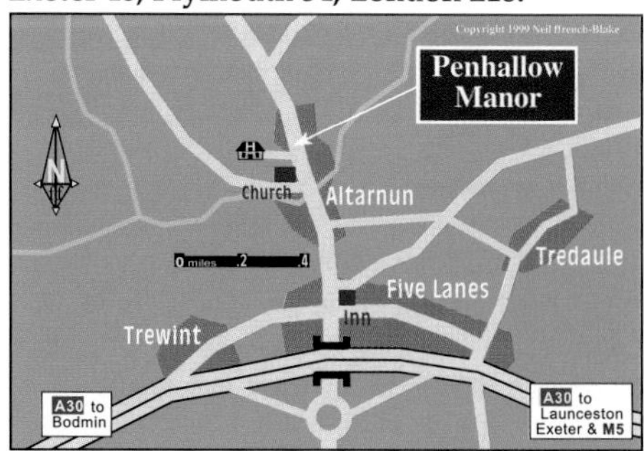

Polurrian Hotel

Mullion, Lizard Peninsula, Cornwall
TR12 7EN
Tel: (01326) 240421;
Fax: (01326) 240083

Three hundred feet above Polurrian Cove and surrounded by wonderful National Trust coastline, the Polurrian Hotel enjoys an enviable position overlooking some of Cornwall's loveliest scenery. Steps lead down from the hotel to the sandy beach where bathing is safe and clean, or there is an alternative of indoor swimming or outdoor heated swimming pools. The hotel's leisure club includes a hairdressing and beauty salon, sauna and solarium, a gym for the more energetic, a tennis court and light snacks can be enjoyed in the Aqua Bar. An inviting 18-hole golf course is nearby. Small children can enjoy a safe play area within the hotel's gardens, an indoor activity room, and, during my visit, a conjuror! The attractive restaurant romantically overlooks the sea. The dishes are expertly cooked and presented and seafood is a speciality. Early rising guests can help with the catch! The bedrooms are luxurious, some having four-posters. The Polurrian Hotel also has its own self-catering apartments and bungalows. A great place for a family holiday.

Rates: *Dinner, room & breakfast from £55 + VAT*
Bargain Breaks: *For a special occasion or a break from the stress of life, our Feature Breaks and Leisure Breaks in this unspoiled part of Cornwall will provide you with a memory to treasure. 3-day breaks - dinner, bed & breakfast from £120 per person* V

- *39 en suite bedrooms (8 ground floor), all with direct dial telephone and TV, room service, baby listening, night service.*
- *Last dinner orders 9.00 pm; diets catered for.*
- *Children welcome; dogs accepted, conferences to 100*
- *Games room, snooker/billiards, outdoor & indoor heated swimming pools, leisure centre, sauna, solarium, spa pool, gymnasium, squash, tennis, sea bathing 200 yards, golf ½ mile, shooting/fishing ½ mile, sailing & boating 5 miles.*
- *Open all year; all major credit cards accepted.*

The Lizard 4½, Helston 4, Penzance 22, Truro 26, London 323

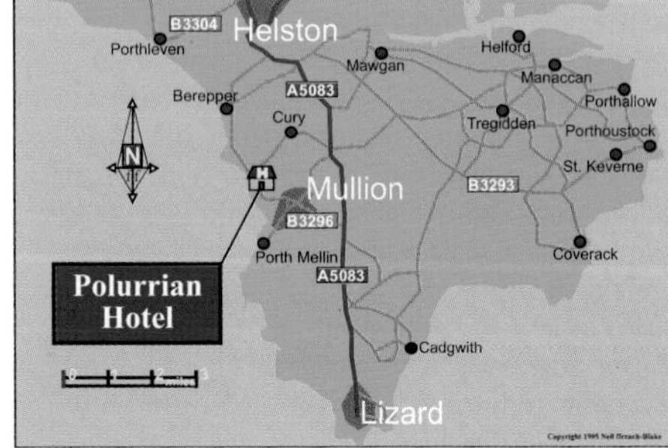

Coombe Farm

Widegates, Nr. Looe,
Cornwall PL13 1QN
Tel: (01503) 240223; Fax: (01503) 240895
E-mail: martin_eades@hotmail.com
Internet: http://www.coombefarmhotel.co.uk

This award-winning small hotel is the epitome of what we, as inspectors, are always looking for. Using the time-honoured Signpost criterion of "Would we stay here again?", the answer is an emphatic 'YES'. Coombe Farm is a delightful 10-bedroomed country house superbly situated in 10½ acres of lawns, meadows, woods and streams with magnificent views down an unspoiled wooded valley to the sea. It offers extremely comfortable lounges and bedrooms together with beautifully prepared and presented food in a pretty dining room. There are acres of gardens with woods, swimming pool, croquet etc and a games room - a converted stone barn - with snooker and ping-pong tables, card and board games for inclement weather. Whilst not a working farm, a further attraction for children are the family dogs, cats, ducks, horses, peacocks and rabbits. For the holiday-maker, almost every historic house, garden, beach and tourist attraction in Devon and Cornwall is within an easy drive. Truly this is an excellent venue from which to get to know this idyllic area.

Rates: *Room with breakfast from £30 per person; room, breakfast and dinner from £46 pr person.* V
Short breaks: *Terms available.*

- *10 en suite bedrooms, (4 double, 2 twin, 4 family) all non-smoking and with direct dial telephone, satellite colour TV, hairdryer, music/radio/alarm clock, tea/coffee making.*
- *Table d'hôte dinner from £16.*
- *Billiards/snooker; table-tennis; heated outdoor swimming pool, indoor games; golf two miles; watersports and tennis three miles, squash six miles.*
- *Open 1st March-31st October; All major credit cards accepted.*

Looe 3, Liskeard 6, Plymouth 15, Bodmin 16, Saltash 13, Fowey 22, St Austell 27, London 224.

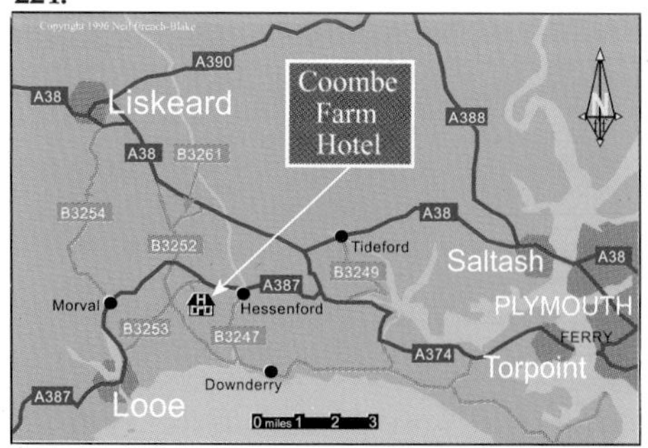

Hannafore Point Hotel

Marine Drive, West Looe, Cornwall
PL13 2DG
Tel: (01503) 263273; Fax: (01503) 263272
E-mail: hannafore@aol.com

Marine and Hotel Leisure, a small family owned West Country Hotel Group who also own the Berry Head (page 22) and The Polurrian (page 10) hotels, took over this spectacularly situated hotel in 1999. With panoramic views of sea, cliffs and St George's Island, the hotel is conveniently placed for sandy beaches, the town of Looe, and, naturally, the facilities for deep sea fishing for which the area is famous. Should the weather not be conducive for indulging these activities, the hotel has comfortable public rooms in which to relax, a complete leisure centre with indoor heated swimming pool, a restaurant offering à la carte and table d'hôte menus and two bars. The public rooms can accommodate 100 for a conference or 160 for a wedding or private function. Hannafore Point is an excellent venue for a family holiday. Golf can be booked at discounted rates at St Enodoc, Lanhydrock and Looe courses. Hannafore is on the southwest coastal path and there are several gardens nearby including the Lost Gardens of Heligan, the Eden Project and Cotehele. In addition the famous Looe to Polperro walk starts just outside the hotel.

Rates: *Room with breakfast from £38 per person;* V *room, breakfast and dinner from £45 per person.* ***Bargain breaks:*** *Two nights, dinner, bed & breakfast from £75*

- *37 en suite bedrooms, all with colour TV, hairdryer, trouser press, tea/coffee making.*
- *Headland restaurant with table d'hôte and à la carte menus; last orders 9pm. Lunch & special diets available. Raffles Lounge Bar and Island Bar.*
- *Heated indoor swimming pool, sauna, steam room, spa pool, squash court, gymnasium, indoor games. Massage & hydrotherapy by appt. Golf, diving, fishing, watersports & sailing nearby.*
- *Conferences to 100; receptions to 160.*
- *Open all year; All major credit cards accepted.*

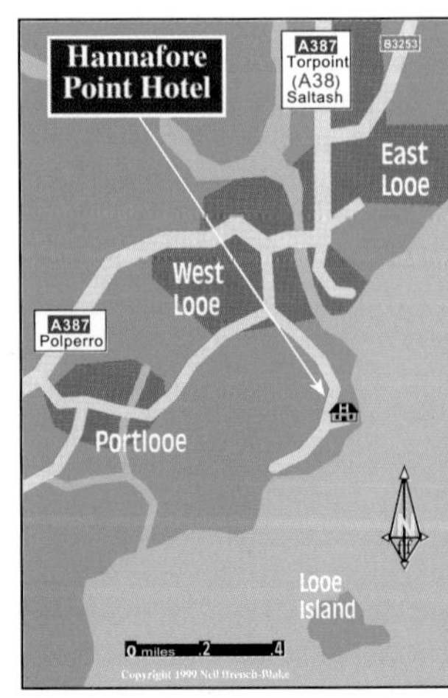

Liskeard 9, Plymouth 19, Bodmin 16, Fowey 18, St Austell 23, London 228.

Talland Bay Hotel

Talland by Looe, Cornwall PL13 2JB
Tel: (01503) 272667; Fax: (01503) 272940

Imagine a beautifully furnished Cornish country house with superb gardens overlooking the sea, situated between picturesque Polperro and Looe, and you begin to understand what award-winning Talland Bay has to offer. Barry and Annie Rosier, your hosts, are experienced hoteliers and their attention to detail is legendary. Talland was first mentioned in the Domesday Book in 1089 but the present house dates back some four hundred years.
Each of the 19 bedrooms is individually furnished to a high standard. Public rooms are comfortable and service is unashamedly 'old-fashioned', presided over by a friendly and hard-working staff. Little touches such as free afternoon buffet teas and morning newspapers enhance the picture.
The food, for which the hotel has an AA rosette, is superb. The menu specialises in seafood from Looe - locally caught lobster, crab and scallop, West Country cheeses and tender Cornish lamb - all complemented by a fine 100+ bottle wine list. If you are looking for a venue in which to relax away from the crowds, where comfort and service are second to none, then the Talland Bay represents one of those far too rare hotels.

Prices *from £62 per person dinner, bed and breakfast, inc. VAT and service.* V
Bargain breaks *available - details on request.*

- *19 en suite bedrooms all with direct dial telephone, colour TV; haidryer, laundry service, tea/coffee making facilities, trouser press, music/radio/alarm clock*
- *Table d'hôte dinner £22; à la carte, bar snacks and special diets available; last orders 9 p.m*
- *Games room, croquet, sauna, outdoor heated swimming pool. Fishing, golf, watersports, riding, squash and tennis nearby.*
- *Meeting rooms to 20; car parking (20); car rental by arrangement.*
- *Major credit cards accepted. Open all year*

Fowey 14, Saltash 18, Bodmin 24, Plymouth 25, Truro 35, London 268

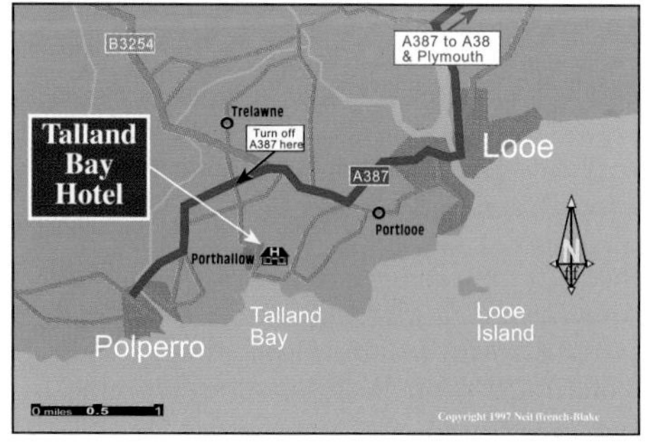

Crantock Bay Hotel

Crantock, Newquay, Cornwall TR8 5SE
Tel: (01637) 830229; Fax: (01637) 831111
E-mail: stay@crantockbayhotel.co.uk

The charming owners of this hotel, Mr & Mrs Eyles, have been here for over 40 years and in that time have continuously upgraded the hotel. It is now one of the foremost establishments in the area and, as a venue for either a family holiday or a conference, I cannot recommend it more highly. It is situated high above Crantock Bay, commanding the most stunning views over the sea and cliffs. Beautifully tended gardens merge into and complement the natural landscape. There are numerous sporting and fitness facilities and, for those who hanker after more sophisticated entertainment, Newquay is but five miles away. Beware, however, lest any benefit gained in the leisure complex is quickly eroded in the dining room! Cooking at its best, using locally produced ingredients where possible and with a well chosen wine list from which to select a suitable vintage, is a temptation too strong to withstand.
The North Cornwall Coastal Path runs through the hotel grounds and gives access to miles of spectacular coastline. The Gannel estuary nearby is famous for walking, riding and windsurfing. Wild flowers abound in May and June.

Rates: *Single room, dinner, bed & breakfast from £51.50; double room, dinner, b & b from £103.* V
Bargain breaks: *Various available. including special interest weekends. prices on application.*

- *33 en suite bedrooms, all with colour TV, direct-dial telephone, laundry service, tea/coffee making facilities, radio/alarm clock.*
- *Table d'hôte dinner £18.95; lunch & special diets available; last orders 8.30 pm.*
- *Heated indoor swimming pool, saunas, jacuzzi, childrens' pool, all-weather tennis court, gymnasium, indoor games, watersports.*
- *Business serviecs inc. conferences up to 50 pax.*
- *Open all year; All major credit cards accepted.*

Truro 16, Wadebridge 16, Bodmin 20, Penzance 38, London 255.

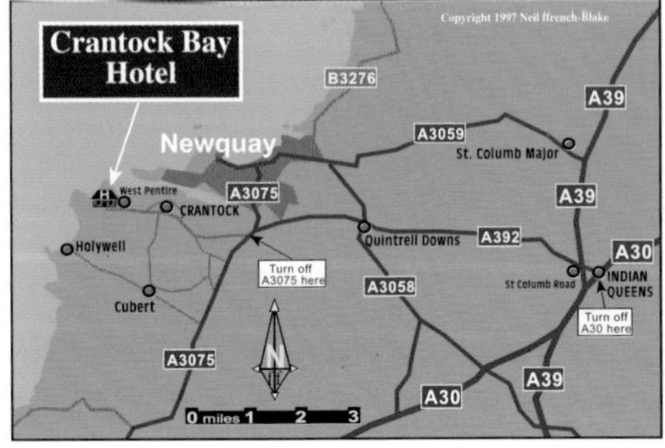

Cross House Hotel

Church Street, Padstow,
Cornwall PL28 8BG
Tel: (01841) 532391;
Fax: (01841) 533633
E-mail: info@crosshouse.co.uk
Internet: http://www.crosshouse.co.uk

My visit to Cross House was the discovery of a new oasis in Cornwall. The Grade II Listed Georgian building was once owned by John Tredwen, the last of the local sailing ship builders. It is located slightly away from the bustling port in an area of quiet tranquility. The recent refurbishment and expansion shows a quality of taste and luxury normally only seen and enjoyed in much larger hotels and in more exotic locations. It is difficult to leave the comfort of the hotel for the short walk to the harbour, but leave one surely must in order to explore the colourful tableaux there or possibly to sample Padstow's many fine restaurants including the famous Seafood Restaurant. The more energetic can take a walk along the coastal footpath with its breath-taking views of the North Cornwall coast or hire bikes and follow the Camel Estuary to the town of Wadebridge. The estuary is also an ideal spot for many watersports and two excellent 18-hole golf courses are nearby - Trevose and St Enodoc at Rock. Riding and fishing are also available as are pleasure trips from the harbour.

Rates: *Single room with breakfast £60; double room £80-120.* V
Bargain Breaks: *For three-day stays or more we offer a reduction in tariff of £20 per room per night.*

- *9 en suite bedrooms with airconditioning, colour TV + video, direct-dial telephone, hairdryer, tea/coffee making facilities; all rooms non-smoking; smoking lounge available.*
- *No restaurant. Car parking for five cars*
- *Fishing, golf, watersports, massage, sailing/boating, riding all available locally*
- *Open March to January. Major credit cards accepted.*

Wadebridge 7, Newquay 14, St Austell 18, Truro 23, London 246

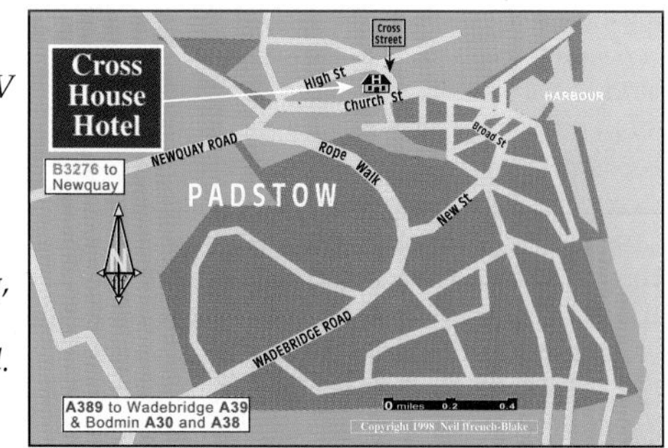

Port Gaverne Inn

Port Gaverne, Nr. Port Isaac,
Cornwall PL29 3SQ
Tel: (01208) 880244; Fax: (01208) 880151
E-mail: pghotel@telinco.co.uk

This charming 17th century inn, situated in an unspoilt North Cornish coastal cove 1/2 mile from Port Isaac, has been welcoming travellers for nearly 400 years. Today your hostess Midge Ross, who has owned Port Gaverne for 30 years, and her caring staff continue this tradition. The public rooms retain their period charm - the old baking oven is still to be seen - and many paintings and interesting objects will catch your attention in the public rooms. Bedrooms are well appointed with restful, soft colour schemes. The hotel has a fine reputation for good food, served in an attractive candlelit dining room. Here you will enjoy local beef and lamb, fresh garden produce and locally landed fish, lobster and crab in season, augmented by the chef's daily specialities and accompanied by a well-chosen wine list. Across the lane from the hotel are eight *Green Door* self-catering cottages. The hotel also has *Upper and Lower Tregudda,* two self-catering apartments, each for up to 8 people. Port Isaac is a charming sheltered cove on the North Cornish Heritage Coast. Much of its surrounding land is owned by the National Trust.

Rates: *Single room with breakfast from £49.50; double room inc. breakfast from £99.* V
Bargain Breaks: *Breathers. Low season min 2 nights, dinner, b & b from £56.50 pp per night; Summer Tourer Breaks min 2 nts from £65 pp per night, dinner b & b, according to availability.*

- *17 en suite bedrooms, all with direct dial telephones, colour TV, radio/alarm clock, hairdryer, laundry service, tea/coffee making facilities. 10 self-catering cottages/apartments.*
- *AA ® Restaurant, last orders 9.30 pm; bar and packed lunches, special diets available. Childrens' early sitting. Car parking for 40.*
- *Sheltered beach by hotel; golf, fishing, riding, sailing all within 5 miles.*
- *Closed early January to mid February. All major credit cards accepted.*

Camelford 7½, Wadebridge 10, London 235.

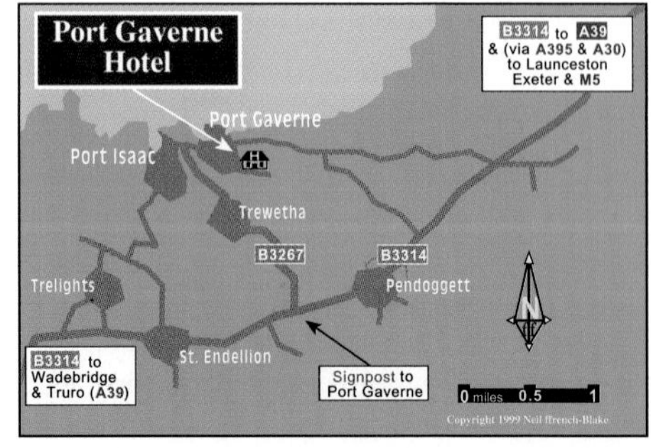

Trevaunance Point Hotel

Trevaunance Cove, St Agnes,
Cornwall TR5 ORZ
Tel: (01872) 553235; Fax: (01872) 553874

For a decade or more I have walked from Chapel Forth over the coastal path past defunct tin mines and down the hill to St Agnes. Each year, tired and dishevelled, I have passed the Trevaunance Point Hotel fearing that my appearance and muddy boots would not be welcome within such august portals. This year I decided to risk embarrassment and what a wise decision this was! The welcome, liquid refreshment and open fire showed the warmth of a bygone age. On entering the hostelry, you surrender to a tempo far removed from the 20th century. There is no reception desk or chattering typewriter to greet you, but a smiling face behind the bar. The hotel hangs to the cliff face, with some of the quaint bedrooms, all of which overlook the sea, below ground floor level. The loudest noise is the lapping of waves on the beach 60 feet below. Food is given a high priority with three chefs preparing a variety of fresh fish, meat and vegetarian dishes. Your hosts will be able to suggest visits to local country houses and gardens. For the energetic there is surfing, sailing and sailboarding tuition available in St Agnes with riding, golf, flying and gliding all in the vicinity.

***Rates:** Single room inc breakfast from £50; double inc. breakfast from £75.* V
***Bargain breaks:** 2 or 3 nights, dinner, b & b from £60 per person per night (inc. full board & 3- course dinner). 4 or 5 night breaks (Sun-Thurs only) from £40 pppn.*

● *8 en suite bedrooms, all with direct dial telephone, colour TV, hairdryer, laundry/valet service, music/radio/alarm clock, tea/coffee making.*
● *Table d'hôte dinner £21.50; à la carte, lunch & special diets available; last orders approx. 21.00. Junior menu available.*
● *Fishing, sea bathing, garden, watersports; riding one mile; golf four miles.*
● *Car parking for 20. Airport pickup by arrangement. Dogs accepted.*
● *Open all year. Amex, Visa, Mastercard, Diners accepted.*

Truro 8, Redruth 8, Helston 10, Newquay 11, Penzance 26, Bodmin 26, London 269

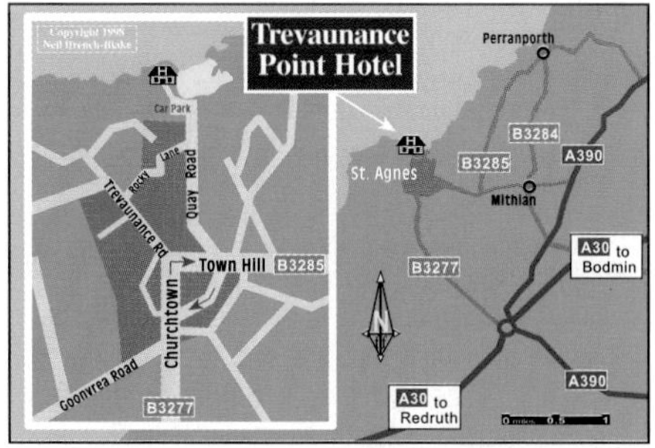

The Carlyon Bay Hotel

Nr. St Austell,
Cornwall PL25 3RD
Tel: (01726) 812304;
Fax: (01726) 814938
E-mail: info@carlyonbay.co.uk
Internet: http://www.carlyonbay.co.uk

The Carlyon Bay Hotel, which 61 years ago was called the St Austell Bay Hotel, featured in the first edition of SIGNPOST in 1935 and was then described as an "entirely modern hotel". Today the hotel maintains its fine, art déco features, combined with every luxury that you would expect from a four star hotel. The hotel's setting is truly unique, positioned in 250 acres of beautiful secluded gardens on the cliff top overlooking St Austell Bay. As part of the Brend Group, the West Country's leading hoteliers, the hotel is operated under the personal supervision of the Brend family. It is a place of character and luxury with the public rooms and most bedrooms having unsurpassed sea views and all comfortable and stylish. In the Bay View Restaurant you can take in the wonderful view and be assured of fine cuisine, presented with skill and imagination. The wine list is well chosen and extensive, and perfect compliments the table d'hôte and special reserve menu. Carlyon Bay is a sportsman's paradise with its renowned 18-hole, 6500-yard golf course, 9-hole approach course set in the secluded palm-fringed gardens, indoor and outdoor heated swimming pools, two tennis courts and a lovely children's play area. Whether embarking on sport or leisure, the hotel offers a superb family holiday throughout the year. And with a full children's entertainment programme available during the school holidays, you are free to enjoy the extensive facilities which the hotel has to offer.

Rates: *Single room with breakfast from £76;* V *double/twin from £73 per person. Dinner, bed & breakfast £88 single; £85 double/twin per pers.* ***Bargain Breaks:*** *Minimum 2-night stay Winter (Nov-Feb) from £100; Spring (April-May exc. Easter) from £146. All prices are per person for 2 nights and include room, dinner, bed & full English breakfast.*

● *72 en suite bedrooms, all with direct-dial telephone and satellite TV with Guest Link facility, room service, baby listening, night service & lift*
● *Last orders for dinner 9 pm; bar lunches, special diets available; children welcome; conferences max. 125.*
● *2 snooker tables, indoor and outdoor heated swimming pools, sauna, solarium, spa bath, sea bathing, golf free to residents, 2 tennis courts, health & beauty room and playroom. Sailing, boating, riding, shooting and fishing all nearby.*
● *Open all year. All major credit cards accepted*

Bodmin 11, Truro 14, Falmouth 25, Exeter 75, Bristol 147, London 242

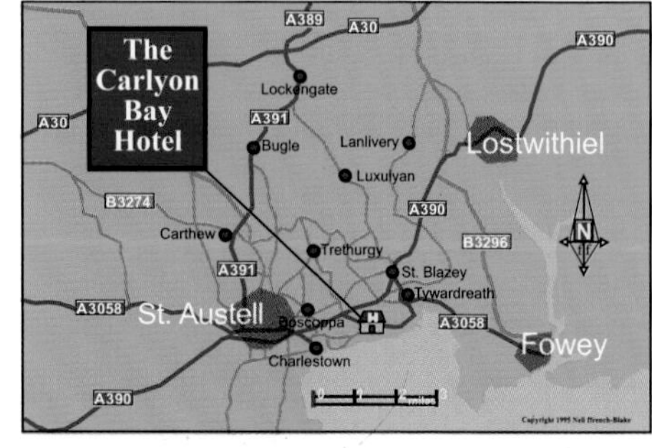

Boskerris Hotel

Carbis Bay, Nr. St Ives, Cornwall TR26 2NQ
Tel: (01736) 795295; Fax: (01736) 798632

Boskerris stands in attractive gardens above the safe golden sands of Carbis Bay, with fine views across St Ives Bay. This delightful hotel was bought by the Sparks family in 1999 who are continuing the friendly, happy atmosphere which the hotel imbues. The public rooms are attractive and furnished to a high standard and together with the Cocktail Bar have extensive views over the Bay. In the dining room a carefully chosen menu is offered. The dishes are interesting, well presented and nicely served. Similar care is given in the selection of wines, which is excellent. The majority of the comfortable and well appointed bedrooms, all with private bathrooms, enjoy sea views and overlook the well kept gardens. Boskerris is an ideal centre for a wide range of activities, including a golfing package which enables you to play at 14 major golf courses in Cornwall, all within easy distances, plus the many beautiful moorland and coastal walks.

Room and breakfast *from £38.50 per person, or with dinner £51.00, including VAT. Other terms on application. Open Easter till November.* ***Bargain breaks****: Low season breaks from two to four days - prices on application. Golfing packages available.* V

- *16 en suite bedrooms (some ground floor), with remote control colour TV, direct dial telephone and tea/coffee making facilities, hairdryer.*
- *Diets available; children welcome.*
- *Drying and games rooms; heated outdoor swimming pool; putting green; sea bathing, boating, surfing, rock climbing and tennis all nearby, ample car parking facilities.*

St. Ives 1, Penzance 8½,, Helston 13 , Redruth 14, London 277

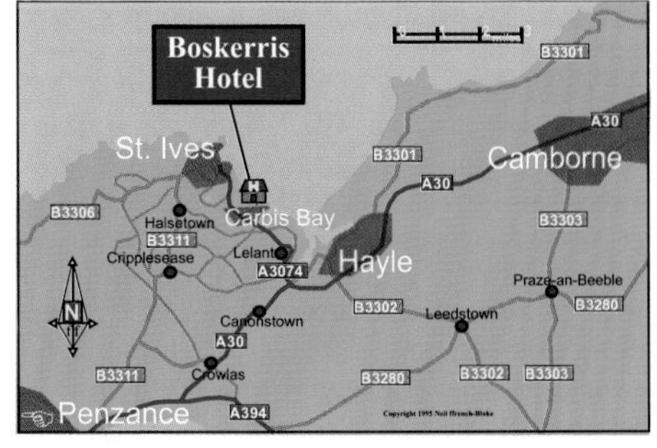

The Garrack Hotel & Restaurant

Burthallan Lane, St. Ives, Cornwall
TR26 3AA
Tel: 01736 796199; Fax 01736 798955
E-mail: garrack@accuk.co.uk

The discerning traveller seeking a classic small country house hotel could hardly do better than to stay in the family-run Garrack with its spectacular views over the old town of St. Ives and the sea. It has two acres of gardens , is near a coastal footpath and its excellent leisure centre caters for most eventualities. The personal touch and friendliness of the Garrack is reflected in the main lounge with its log fire in winter, books, magazines and board games. In addition there is a small TV lounge and a bar lounge. Whilst the bedrooms in this the main house are traditional as befits the build ing, an extension houses additional rooms of more modern design and equally comfortable. Some rooms have four posters, others whirlpool baths. There are family rooms and a room for the disabled. The hotel restaurant is justifiably renowned for its seafood with lobsters fresh from the hotel's storage tank, as fresh as is the other locally produced food with many of the vegetables coming from the garden. It would take several weeks to work through the wine list. The Garrack is a rarity - one of those places which it was a delight in itself to visit - and so hard to leave.

Single room *including breakfast from £60.00.* V
Double room *with breakfast from £50.00 p.p.*
Bargain breaks *available November to end March*

- *18 en suite bedrooms with TV, direct-dial telephone, hairdryer on request. Morning tea service. One room for disabled. Baby monitoring.*
- *AA 2 Rosetted Restaurant. Last dinner orders 21.00.*
- *Conferences for up to 25 guests.*
- *Indoor swimming pool, sauna, solarium and fitness area. Access to fishing, riding, shooting (clay),golf, water sports, squash and tennis.*
- *Airport pick-up and car rental by arrangement. Car parking for 30 cars.*
- *Open all year. All major credit cards accepted.*

Penzance 10, Redruth 14, Truro 25, London 319.

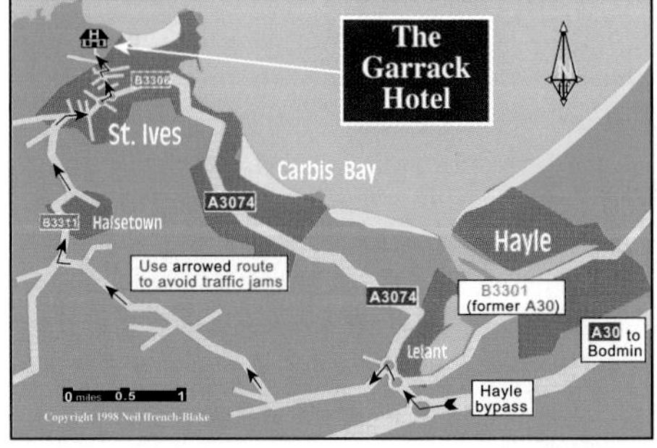

Alverton Manor Hotel

Tregolls Road, Truro, Cornwall TR1 1XQ
Tel: (01872) 276633; Fax: (01872) 222989
E-mail: alverton@connexion.co.uk

Alverton Manor is a splendid Grade II listed building of special historical interest, set high on a hillside in the heart of Truro, one of England's most beautiful cathedral cities. The house was built for the Tweedy family in 1840, and was acquired by the Bishop of Truro in the late 1880s. It later became a convent and today exhibitions and conferences may be held in the Gothic style former chapel. All the bedrooms are spacious, individually and beautifully decorated and include several luxury suites. Some single bedrooms, which have showers, are in the tower. I admired the mahogany lined stairwells and the quiet and tasteful furnishing of the rooms, expressing the feel of the country house it once was. The elegant Terrace restaurant offers diners a wonderful range of meals in English style, including a superb array of seafood. Local produce is used whenever possible and all meals are beautifully cooked and presented. The staff are charming and helpful, nothing seeming to be too much trouble. Alverton Manor is the perfect place from which to explore the magic of Cornwall - Trelissick Gardens, St Michael's Mount, the villages of Gweek and Penberth, the Mynack Theatre, to name but a few nearby.

***Single room** including breakfast from £67.* V
***Double room** with breakfast from £99.*
***Bargain breaks:** Cornish garden breaks to include Isles of Scilly; golfing breaks on our own course Killiow; champagne weekends half board to include a box of chocolates, red rose & champagne.*

- *34 en suite bedrooms with TV+ satellite, direct-dial telephone, hairdryer, laundry service, tea/coffee making, trouser press. Facilities for the disabled.*
- *Table d'hôte £21.95; à la carte, lunch & special diets available; last orders 9.30 pm. Parking for 120.*
- *Full business services inc 5 meeting rooms to 450*
- *Snooker, golf (own course), riding. Watersports, fishing, sailing, shooting all within 4 miles.*
- *Open all year. All major credit cards accepted.*

Falmouth 11, St Austell 14, Newquay 18, Wadebridge 23 Exeter 100, London 246.

Alverton Manor
A39 to A30 Bodmin
A390 to St Austell
City of Truro
Church
Tregolls Road
Police Station
A39 to Falmouth
0 miles 2 4
Copyright 1999 Neil French-Blake

The Berry Head Hotel

Berry Head Road, Brixham,
Devon TQ5 9AJ
Tel: (01803) 853225; Fax: (01803) 882084

The Berry Head Hotel is set in a superb water's edge position in six acres of its own gardens and woodland, in the seclusion of the Berry Head Country Park, which is noted for its bird life and rare wild flowers. The hotel is steeped in history. It was built as a military hospital in the Napoleonic Wars, and was later the home of the Reverend Francis Lyte, who wrote the famous hymn *Abide with Me* at the hotel, no doubt inspired by the glorious sunsets. The historic fishing port of Brixham, where William of Orange first landed on English soil, is only a short walk away. The hotel offers relaxing accommodation and all the en suite bedrooms have colour television, radio and tea and coffee making facilities. The comfortable lounge and the restaurant, which overlook the terrace, enjoy spectacular views of Torbay and the Devon coast. The emphasis here is upon good food, wine and company in a very special setting. Set in national parkland at the water's edge, with miles of coastal walks, fishing, birdwatching and sailing, yet close to the major resort of Torquay, this is an ideal hideaway for a short break.

***Room** and breakfast from £38.00, and dinner, room and breakfast from £45.00 including VAT.*
***Bargain breaks:** Two nights, dinner, bed and breakfast from £75.00* V

- *32 en suite bedrooms all with direct dial telephone, TV; hairdryer; tea/coffee facilities; room service; baby listening; night service.*
- *Last orders for dinner 9.30p.m; bar meals until 9.30p.m; special diets; children welcome.*
- *Dogs accepted; conferences 100 max.*
- *Boules; sea bathing 30 yds; indoor heated swimming pool; outdoor seawater pool 200 yds; squash courts 1/2 mile; sailing and boating, shooting and fishing 1/4 mile; tennis one mile; golf and riding two miles.*
- *Open all year. Amex, Visa and Mastercard accepted.*

Torquay 8, Exeter 30, Plymouth 32, Bristol 100, Birmingham 200, London 230

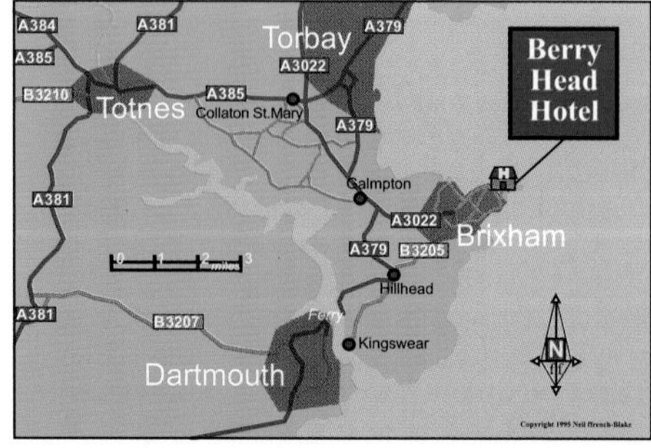

Quayside Hotel

King Street, Brixham,
Devon TQ5 9TJ
Tel: (01803) 855751;
Fax: (01803) 882733
E-mail: quayside.hotel@virgin.net

With views right across the harbour, the Quayside hotel offers the best opportunity to watch the comings and goings of the fishing fleet, the trip boats and the yachts in the marina. This picturesque town has so much going on all the time bit it is all within easy walking distance of the hotel. The car can be forgotten during your stay here as there is private parking, almost unheard of in Brixham! This friendly and welcoming hotel, which has been built up over the years out of six quayside cottages, has comfortable public rooms and bedrooms furnished with all the comforts that today's traveller requires.
The restaurant offers both French and English cuisine and uses a variety of local produce, including the famous fresh Brixham fish, straight from the decks of local fishing boats, along with a wine list to suit all tastes. If you must use the car, the Quayside makes an excellent base from which to explore Torquay, Exeter, Dartmouth and all the pretty villages in and surrounding Dartmoor. The keen birdwatcher will want to observe the 'Seabird Watch', televised daily from the cliffs of nearby Berry Head in season.

Rates: *single room with breakfast from £60; double room inc. breakfast from £75.* V
Bargain breaks: *Three-day breaks from £120 per person inc. 4-course alc dinner, b & b.*

- *29 en suite bedrooms all with direct dial telephone, colour TV; hairdryer; tea/coffee facilities; radio/alarm clock, trouser press.*
- *A la carte restaurant; last orders for dinner 9.30p.m; special diets available.*
- *Parking for 30 cars; meeting room for up to 16*
- *Sea bathing, sailing, boating, golf, water-sports, bowls, tennis nearby.*
- *Open all year. Major credit cards accepted.*

Torquay 8, Exeter 30, Plymouth 32, Bristol 100, Birmingham 200, London 230.

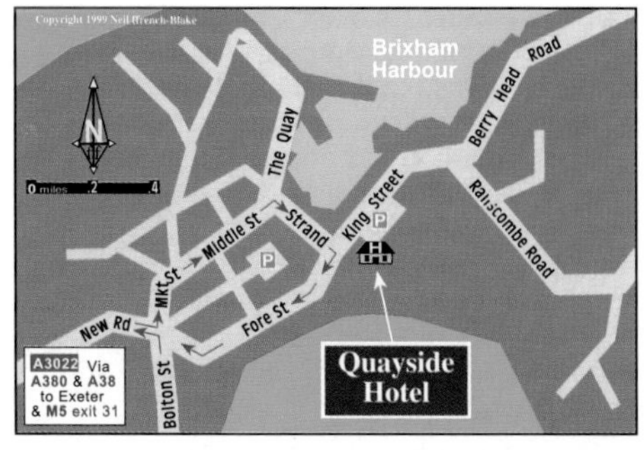

Hoops Country Inn & Hotel

'Hoops'. Nr. Clovelly, Bideford,
Devon EX39 5DL
Tel: (01237) 451222; Fax: (01237) 451247
E-mail: hoopsinn@webleicester.co.uk
Internet: http://www.hoopsinn.co.uk

The Hoops Inn has often been used as a film location and is the choice of many well known figures in politics, media and business when looking for a base in North Devon. If you are looking for something a bit different, where the food, wine, ambience and welcome are matched by the style of your accommodation, then the Hoops is for you. Whether it is for a special occasion, on business or on holiday, Gay Marriott and her staff will do their utmost to make your stay memorable. Dating from the 13th century, the Hoops was notorious as a meeting place for smugglers and local seafarers. Ensconced within the five foot thick walls, sitting by a roaring log fire, travellers from around the world can today find a cosy haven and can choose to stay in either the Coach House or the original part of the inn. In each the best traditional values have been combined with modern conveniences to meet the individual needs of each guest.
Set in some of the most unspoiled Devon countryside, the Hoops is an excellent centre for touring Exmoor and the rugged North Devon coast. Golf, fishing, sailing and cycling are available nearby and walkers and birdwatchers can explore the Coastal Path.

Rates: *Single room with breakfast from £47. Double room inc. breakfast from £70.* ***Bargain Breaks:*** *2 night break inc à la carte dinner each night from £92 per person - avail. until April 2000.* V

● *12 en suite bedrooms, all with colour TV, direct-dial telephone, hairdryer, laundry service, tea/coffee making, 12-hr room/meal service, radio/alarm, safety depoit box. Non-smoker bedrooms available.*
● *Dining (alc) either in Restaurant or less formal Bar/Restaurant. Real ales served. Lunch available. Last orders 2130. Vegetarian dishes a speciality.*
● *Billiards/snooker, croquet, jogging track, tennis, jacuzzi (some rooms). Fishing, golf, bathing, watersports, sailing, shooting, indoor swimming pool, riding, walking coastal path, cycling, Tarka Trail, gardens of North Devon all nearby.*
● *Full business services inc 2 meeting rooms to 50*
● *Open all year. Mastercard, Visa, Amex, Diners, Switch, Delta cards accepted.*

Bideford 10, Bude 15, Barnstaple 18, Exeter 52, Penzance 92, London 179.

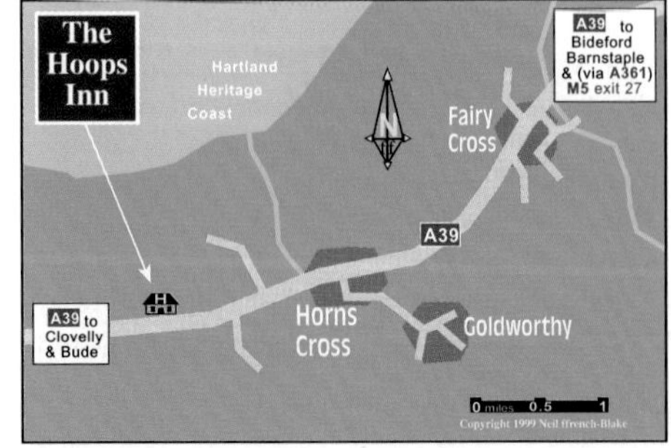

The Cottage Hotel

Hope Cove, Kingsbridge, South Devon
TQ7 3 HJ
Tel: (01548) 561555; Fax: (01548) 561455

__Rates:__ Dinner, room and breakfast from £47.50. ***Bargain breaks*** *are available from 1st November to April inclusive.2-night stay £29.00-£44.75; 7-night stay from £28.00-£43.75 according to room. Prices are per person per night and include accommodation, 6-course dinner plus coffee, full English breakfast, service and VAT.* V

The Cottage Hotel enjoys a superb position, overlooking the picturesque harbour and cove, with spectacular sea views and sunsets. The gardens descend to the beach, where you can bathe in safety. The hotel is delightful and has 35 beautifully furnished bedrooms, with 23 of them having private bathrooms / showers. I always enjoy visiting The Cottage; it has a happy and relaxing atmosphere thanks to the owners, John and Janet, Sarah and William Ireland, who, with Patricia Bazzano personally care for this pleasant and comfortable haven. The enticing dining room, which has lovely views of the cove and coast, offers table d'hôte and à la carte menus. I chose the former, which was excellent, cooked with great interest and attention, served by cheerful, efficient and courteous staff of many years' standing. The meal was supported by a selective wine list. This hotel still remains one of the best family hotels I visit, well illustrated by the preponderance of sun-tanned, well-fed families.

● *25 en suite bedrooms (7 ground floor), all with direct-dial telephone and colour TV, room service, baby listening. 12 other bedrooms.*
● *Last orders for dinner 8.30 pm; bar meals 12-1. 30 pm.* ● *Conferences, max. 50*
● *Children welcome; dogs accepted.*
● *Games room, sea bathing, sailing/boating, riding three miles, golf four miles, tennis & squash six miles.*
● *Hotel closed 2-30th January. No credit cards.*

Totnes 18, Torquay 21, Plymouth 25, Exeter 36, London 236

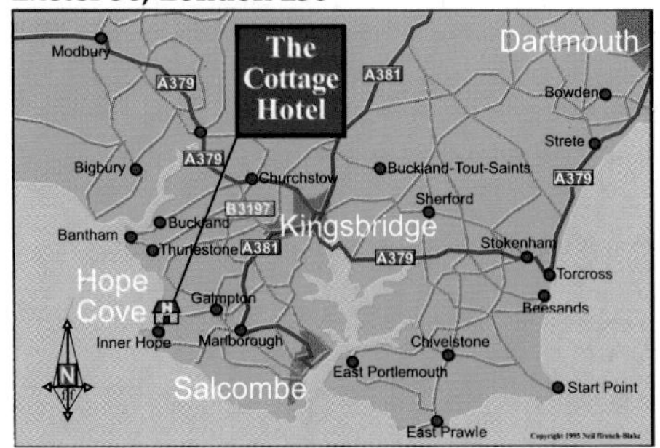

Buckland-Tout-Saints Hotel

Goveton, Nr. Kingsbridge,
Devon TQ7 2DS
Tel: (01548) 853055; Fax: (01548) 856261
E-mail: buckland@tout-saints.co.uk
Internet: htp://www.tout-saints.co.uk

Under the new ownership of Mark and Julia Trumble, Buckland-Tout-Saints has been renovated and refurbished at a cost running into seven figures. However the ambience and character of the old Queen Anne manor house remain and many of the antique furnishings are still here and have indeed been added to. The chef, Jean-Philippe Bidart, who has built up such a well-deserved reputation for classic English and French cuisine, using only the best of local produce, has selected a dynamic new team in the kitchen. Many of the old staff quarters have been replaced by a stunning looking, purpose-built suite of rooms called the *Kestrel Rooms*. These access directly onto the terrace and are suitable for wedding receptions or business seminars for up to 150. The Queen Anne dining-room and the Lavender room are both licensed for the celebration of civil matrimony. Buckland-Tout-Saints has regained its position as one of the premier hotels of Britain and as such, I can wholeheartedly recommend it to anyone visiting this beautiful area.

Rates: *Single room with breakfast from £95; Double/twin from £190, both prices inc. VAT.* V
Special interest breaks *: e.g. shooting, golfing, sailing, flower-arranging, music or murder and mystery - all prices on application.*

- *12 en suite bedrooms (inc two suites), all with colour TV, direct dial telephone, hairdryer, laundry service, radio/alarm clock, trouser press. Non-smoker rooms available. Car parking for 40.*
- *Table d'hôte £25. A la carte, lunch & special diets available. 2 restaurants, bar, function suite.*
- *Full business services inc. 3 meeting rooms to 210. Helicopter landing pad and charter. Car rental.*
- *Croquet. Bathing, tennis, riding, squash, sailing nearby. Fishing 15 miles; golf 8 miles, watersports 10 miles, shooting by arrangement.*
- *Open all Year. Mastercard & Visa accepted.*

Salcombe 9, Dartmouth 10, Plymouth 20, Exeter 30, London 203.

Thurlestone Hotel

Thurlestone, Nr. Kingsbridge,
South Devon TQ7 3NN
Tel: (01548) 560382; Fax: (01548) 561069
E-mail: enquiries@thurlestone.co.uk
Internet: http://www.thurlestone.co.uk

AA ★★★★RAC ETB 👑👑👑👑👑 ⊛ Food
Voted Best West Country Hotel for *England for Excellence* (ETB)
RAC Merit Awards for hospitality, service and comfort.

This luxurious hotel has been owned and run by the Grose family for over 100 years and during that time they have gained a 72% AA 4-star award - the highest graded hotel in the district. The standard of rooms, especially the beautifully appointed suites, testify to this. The AA have also awarded a rosette for their cooking and Hugh Miller, the chef, is striving for a second one. The food is balanced, well presented and simply delicious and the menu is accompanied by a comprehensive wine list. The staff, many of whom are long serving members, are courteous, discreet and efficient. The hotel caters for everyone in that conferences can be arranged for the business traveller, there are all manner of facilities for the sportsman and there is something for every member of the family, whatever the weather. Even the dog is welcome.
The hotel has its own golf course, which was the venue for the British Professional Shortcourse Championship in 1980 and which brought Edward VIII, when Prince of Wales, to Thurlestone on a number of occasions.

Single room *including breakfast £39-100.* V
Double room *including breakfast £76-200.*
Bargain breaks *Dinner, b&b from £49 per person per night Nov-March. Others on application.*

- *64 en suite bedrooms (inc 4 suites & 19 deluxe), all with colour TV (+Sky), direct-dial telephone, music/radio/alarm clock, hairdryer, laundry/valet service, tea/coffee making facilities, 24-hr room service, trouser press.*
- *Table d'hôte dinner £28; à la carte, lunch & special diets available; last orders 2100 hrs.*
- *Outdoor & indoor swimming pools; continental terrace; billiards/snooker, croquet, fitness centre, 9-hole golf course, indoor games, jacuzzi, massage/sauna, squash, tennis, children's playrooms. Fishing, watersports, riding, sailing/boating nearby.*
- *Hairdressing/beauty salon. Conferences to 120.*
- *Open all year. Mastercard, Visa & Amex accepted*

Kingsbridge 4, Plymouth 20, Torquay 21, Exeter 36, London 236.

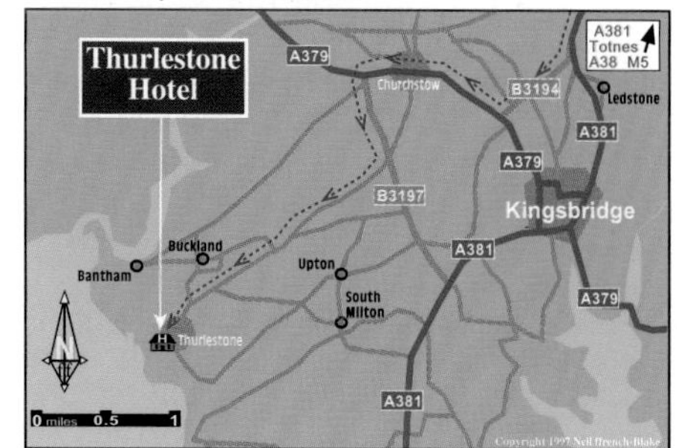

Collaven Manor Hotel

Sourton, Okehampton,
Devon EX20 4HH
Tel: (01837) 861522; Fax: (01837) 861614
Internet: http://www.trevean.c om/collaven

Those readers looking to stay in a small country manor house need look no further. Collaven is a picturebook Devon Manor both externally and internally. Dating from the 15th century, it stands in four acres of picturesque gardens and paddocks. It has been sympathetically restored to cater for discerning guests as it would have done in the days of its earlier owners. Notable amongst these are the Hamilton family (of Nelson fame) and the house positively exudes Devon history. On entering the manor via the Baronial Reception Hall, the visitor is greeted by a feeling of warmth and comfort, enhanced by log fires in winter and cooled by medieval thick walls in summer. The Hamilton Restaurant offers a 4-course dinner, changing daily, with the emphasis on the Best of British cuisine, with Continental and Oriental influences. A vegetarian speciality is always on the menu. Here the atmosphere is serene, the setting tranquil but, for the adventurous, the moors are on the doorstep, to delight the walker, naturalist or outdoor sportsman.

***Single**: inc. breakfast from £53; **double** from £78.*
***Bargain Breaks:** Oct 4-mid Dec, Jan to end March, for a two nights+ stay, dinner b & b is at 20% discount.* V

- *9 en suite bedrooms (inc one family room & 2 four-posters), all with direct dial telephone, colour TV, hairdryer, laundry/valet service, tea/coffee making facilities, trouser press, music/radio/alarm clock.*
- *Table d'hôte £19.50 non-residents/£17 residents; lunch available; vegetarian dishes a speciality; last orders 20.30.*
- *Croquet, bowls, badminton.*
- *Meeting room to 28. Car parking for 30.*
- *Mastercard, Visa, Delta, Switch accepted. Open all year.*

Okehampton 7, Tavistock 16, Crediton 17, Exeter 22, Plymouth 25, London 192

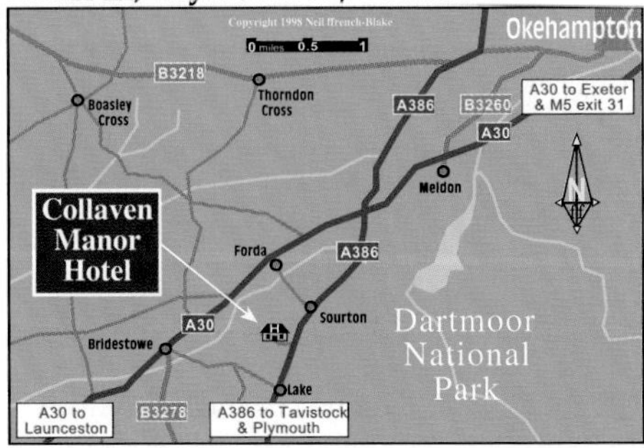

Heddon's Gate Hotel

Heddon's Mouth,
Parracombe, Barnstaple,
North Devon EX31 4PZ
Tel: (01598) 763313;
Fax: (01598) 763363;
E-mail: info@hgate.co.uk
Internet: http://www.hgate.co.uk

When the English poets discovered this corner of Exmoor, they named it the 'Switzerland of England'. The wealthy soon followed, choosing all the best sites for their country estates and building in the 'Swiss-Victorian' style. Heddon's Gate was no exception to this fashion and in 1890 a single storey lodge was built high above the stunningly beautiful Heddon Valley. Bob De Ville bought it in 1967 with the intention of turning it into an hotel. In fact a Country House has been created which guests feel they can call 'home' during their stay. Accommodation at Heddon's Gate is divided into individually designed bedrooms or free-standing cottages below the hotel. The proprietor supervises the cuisine which is modern English with a Mediterranean bias. West Country Farmhouses Cheeses abound and fresh local fish and game are used. Even the hotel's water supply comes from a natural spring rising on the hill behind. Exmoor and North Devon contain a wide choice of places to visit: stately old homes and castles, fine churches and craft centres including the famous Dartington Glass Works where 'seconds' can be bought cheaply. Sheepskin goods and antiques can also be picked up reasonably in the area. There are spectacular walks from the hotel and a further 700 miles of marked Exmoor footpaths are on the doorstep.

- *14 en suite bedrooms with colour TV, direct-dial telephone, hairdryer, tea/coffee making facilities*
- *Table d'hôte dinner £25; picnic lunch & special diets on request. Last orders 8 pm. Car parking for 20*
- *Walking the southwest footpath from hotel; fishing; golf ten miles; riding three miles.*
- *Open Easter-end November. Mastercard, Visa, Switch accepted.*

Rates: *Single room with breakfast, afternoon tea, 5-course dinner, VAT & service £70; double room, as above, from £132.* ***Bargain Breaks:*** *available for stays of three nights or more, from £60 per person per night. Weekly rate also available.* V

Lynmouth 5, Ilfracombe 11, Barnstaple 12, South Molton 15, Dunster 24, London 188

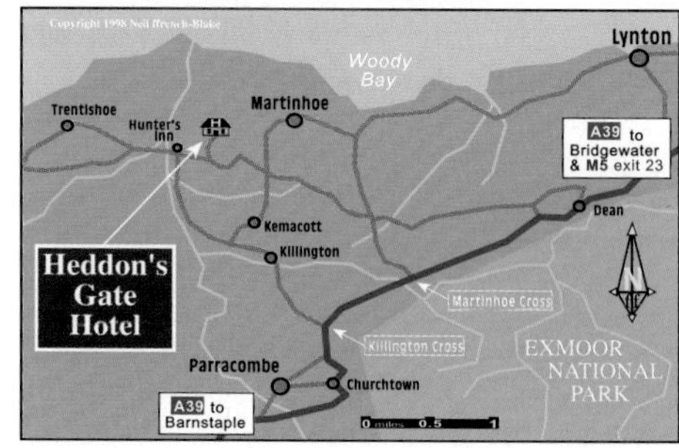

The Bolt Head Hotel

Salcombe, South Devon TQ8 8LL
Tel: (01548) 843751; Fax: (01548) 843061
E-mail: info@bolthead-salcombe.co.uk
Internet: www.bolthead-salcombe.co.uk

Blessed with a climate that is said to be the mildest in Devon, and set amid imposing scenery that ends with the fantastically shaped black rocks of mighty Bolt Head, this most southerly hotel in Devon commands a marvellous view of the Salcombe Estuary and coastline, and overlooks the sheltered golden cove of South Sands Beach. There are always yachts and fishing boats to be seen in this unspoilt estuary. The hotel has been completely refurbished to a very high standard under the ownership of Mr. Colin Smith. A sun terrace leads off the main lounge. The bedrooms are also very comfortable and equipped as one would expect of this well run hotel. The hotel is renowned for its warm welcome and friendly service and the staff are courteous, attentive and cheerful. The table d'hôte menu with specialities, is interesting and provides a splendid choice carefully served, in an attractive restaurant which has panoramic views of the estuary. In spite of all that is offered at this first class establishment, it also provides peace and quiet with lovely walks in the National Trust property adjoining the grounds.

***Rates**: Bed and breakfast from £69.00 per person per night inclusive of VAT.* V
***Getaway Breaks** available; details on request.*

● *29 en suite bedrooms (four ground floor), all with direct dial telephones, remote control colour TV, radio, tea/coffee making facilities; full central heating.*
● *Meals to 9p.m.; diets available.*
● *Children welcome, baby listening; dogs at manager's discretion.*
● *Games room; outdoor heated swimming pool; sailing, boating, private moorings; sea fishing; tennis 1/4 mile; riding seven miles; golf eight miles.*
● *Closed mid November to mid March, but office open. A Best Western Hotel. Major credit cards accepted.*

Kingsbridge 7, Totnes 18, Exeter 43, Plymouth 25, London 214

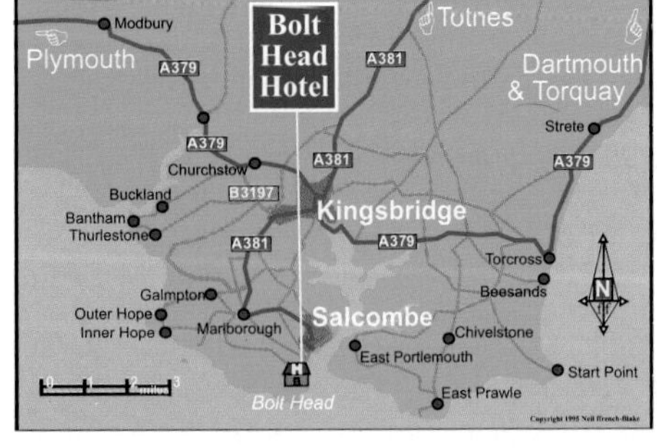

Tides Reach Hotel

South Sands, Salcombe, South Devon
TQ8 8LJ
Tel: (01548) 843466; Fax: (01548) 843954
E-mail: enquiries@tidesreach.com
Internet: http://www.tidesreach.com

The position of Tides Reach is perfect - a beautiful secluded sandy cove. The quiet luxury of the hotel strikes you as you enter the conservatory-style hall with its indoor water garden and the flower garden lounge-hall so full of sunshine and scented blooms. The décor throughout was chosen and supervised by Mrs. Edwards and the colours are wonderfully vibrant and original. The indoor heated swimming pool, around which has been built a new bar and coffee shop, is as glamorous as a Hollywood film set - there is an outdoor sun patio and sun deck leading off and below, a new hairdressing and beauty salon, multi gym, sunbed, Whirlpool Spa bath, sauna, steam baths and squash court. In addition to the new facilities the dining room has been extended and the bedrooms and public rooms have been refurnished throughout in a most comfortable and luxurious manner. The food is superb, both à la carte and table d'hôte dishes being really first class.

Rates: *Dinner, room and breakfast from £62.00 to £120.00 per person including VAT according to season and length of stay.* V
Bargain Breaks *available from mid February - 22nd May 1999 (excluding Easter) and Oct,Nov 1999. 2-day breaks from £136 for dinner, bed and breakfast. 4-day breaks from £260 for dinner,bed and breakfast. Extra days pro rata.*

- *40 en suite bedrooms with colour TV, radio, direct dial telephone; some family suites.*
- *Lift; children over eight welcome; dogs by arrangement; some diets available.*
- *Games room; snooker room; indoor heated pool; solarium; sauna; spa bath; squash; indoor and outdoor water gardens; drying room; golf, tennis, riding nearby; sea bathing; boating; fishing, windsurfing, water sports from own boathouse.*
- *Closed 2nd December-mid Febryary*
- *Resident proprietor - Roy Edwards FHCI*

Kingsbridge 7, Totnes 19, Plymouth 26, Exeter 43, London 214

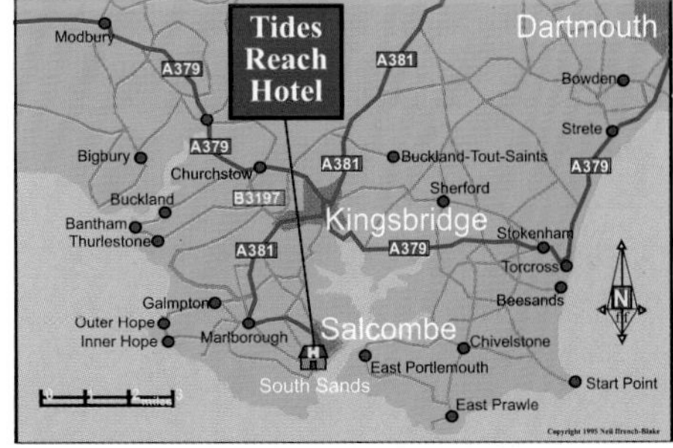

The Saunton Sands Hotel

Saunton Sands, Nr. Braunton, Devon
EX31 lLQ
Tel: (01271) 890212; Fax: (01271) 890145

Lots of sun, miles of golden sands and tiered silvery waves advancing eagerly up the beach is what you look down on from the warm and luxurious rooms of The Saunton Sands, a member of the Brend Group of Exclusive Hotels. The hotel is light and sunny as most of the rooms face the south, the sea and the sands, and there are panoramic views from most. All the staff are efficient and attentive, creating an air of warmth and friendliness. The furnishings are elegant and comfortable, and the bedrooms have all the modern facilities that you could want. Food is of a very high standard and the wine list is well chosen. Other seafront hotels in the Brend Group include *Carlyon Bay* near St. Austell and The *Victoria Hotel* in Sidmouth (see pages 00 and 00). This splendid hotel provides a truly outstanding holiday for all the family, all year round.

Rates: *Room and breakfast from £65.00 single, £60.00 per person double, all inclusive of VAT.*
Bargain Breaks: *A Luxury Breaks tariff is available in addition to the hotel's main tariff, with reduced rates for stays of two nights or more. Spring, June and Autumn Breaks represent excellent value with prices from £56 per person per night for dinner, room and breakfast. Child reductions are also available. Telephone the hotel and ask for the Luxury Breaks Tariff.* V

- *92 en suite bedrooms, all with telephone, satellite TV, tea/coffee making facilities; lift; 24-hour room service; baby listening; no dogs*
- *Last orders 9.30 pm; bar meals (lunch); afternoon teas; vegetarian and vegan diets.*
- *Children welcome. Conferences max. 200.*
- *Games room; dancing frequently; full size snooker table; children's paddling pool; supervised nursery; heated indoor and outdoor swimming pools; sauna/solarium; hairdressing salon; gym; miles of beach below; sailing; tennis; squash; riding; shooting; fishing; helipad; golf nearby.*
- *Open all year. Mastercard, Amex, Diners, Visa credit cards accepted.*

Barnstaple 8, Ilfracombe 8, Bideford 17, Exeter 48, London 203.

Eleven exclusive Westcountry Hotels and they're just a phone call away.

THE SAUNTON SANDS HOTEL
NR. BRAUNTON, NORTH DEVON
AA ★★★★ RAC
92 bedrooms and 20 self contained apartments. Large Indoor and Outdoor Heated Pools, Sauna and Solarium, Tennis and Squash Courts, Billiards and Games Rooms, Shop and Health & Beauty Salon, Restaurant and Bars open to non-residents.
Tel: (01271) 890212

THE IMPERIAL HOTEL
TAW VALE, BARNSTAPLE, N. DEVON
AA ★★★★ RAC
55 bedrooms all with private bath, colour TV, radio, direct dial telephone. Large Restaurant offering Table d'Hote and A La Carte menus daily. Comfortable Lounge Bar. Many rooms overlooking the River Taw.
Tel: (01271) 345861

THE ROYAL DUCHY HOTEL
FALMOUTH, CORNWALL
AA ★★★★ RAC
50 bedrooms. Indoor Leisure Complex, including Heated Pool, Sauna and Solarium, Restaurant and Bars open to non-residents.
Tel: (01326) 313042

THE VICTORIA HOTEL
SIDMOUTH, DEVON
AA ★★★★ RAC
63 bedrooms. Indoor and Outdoor Heated Pools, Sauna and Solarium, Spa-bath, Tennis Courts, Billiards Room, Hairdressing Salon, Restaurant and Bars open to non-residents.
Tel: (01395) 512651

THE ROYAL & FORTESCUE HOTEL
BOUTPORT ST., BARNSTAPLE, N. DEVON
AA ★★★ RAC
50 bedrooms Two comfortable Bars, Coffee Lounges and Restaurant, open to non-residents. Lift to all floors. Function Suites. Under cover car parking.
Tel: (01271) 342289

THE CARLYON BAY HOTEL
NR. ST. AUSTELL, SOUTH CORNWALL
AA ★★★★ RAC
74 bedrooms. Indoor and Outdoor Heated Pools, 18-hole Golf Course (6500 yds) and 9 hole Approach Course FREE TO RESIDENTS, Sauna and Solarium, Tennis Courts, Billiards and Games Rooms, Spa-Bath, Health & Beauty Room, Restaurant and Bars open to non-residents.
Tel: (01726) 812304

THE DEVON HOTEL
MATFORD, EXETER, DEVON
AA ★★★ RAC
42 bedrooms, Carriages Bar & Brasserie open to non-residents, Regency Function Suite. Children's Outdoor Adventure Playground.
Tel: (01392) 259268

THE BELMONT HOTEL
SIDMOUTH, DEVON
AA ★★★★ RAC
55 bedrooms all with private bath, colour TV, radio, direct dial telephone. Large Restaurant offering Table d'Hote and A La Carte menus daily. Function Suite suitable for large or small parties. Lounge Bar and comfortable sea-facing Lounges.
Tel: (01395) 512555

THE BARNSTAPLE HOTEL
BRAUNTON ROAD, BARNSTAPLE, N. DEVON
AA ★★★ RAC
57 bedrooms. Leisure Complex including Outdoor and Indoor Heated Pool, Sauna and Solarium. Large air-conditioned Function Suites. Restaurant and Bars open to non-residents.
Tel: (01271) 376221

THE PARK HOTEL
TAW VALE, BARNSTAPLE, N. DEVON
AA ★★★ RAC
44 bedrooms. Park View Bar and Restaurant open to non-residents, Function Suites and Bar. Parking for 100 cars.
Tel: (01271) 372166

THE ROYAL HOTEL
BIDEFORD, NORTH DEVON
AA ★★★ RAC
30 bedrooms. Bars, Restaurant and Kingsley Room open to non-residents, luxury accommodation. Ample parking.
Tel: (01237) 472005

Central Information & Group Sales

CONTACT CENTRAL RESERVATIONS (01271) 344496

The Victoria Hotel

Sidmouth, Devon EX10 8RY
Tel: (01395) 512651; Fax: (01395) 579154
E-mail: info@victoriahotel.co.uk
Internet: http://www.victoriahotel.co.uk

Sidmouth was discovered as a resort by the affluent in Queen Victoria's day - hence the name of this imposing hotel which dominates the west end of the promenade, and has an uninterrupted view of the wide sweeping bay. The Victoria is owned by the Brend family who own other luxurious hotels, including the Royal Duchy at Falmouth (see page 6), Carlyon Bay at St. Austell (see page 18) and The Saunton Sands Hotel at Saunton Sands (see pages 32) . Mr. John Brend, Managing Director, is very much in evidence looking after the needs of the guests, with the help of his efficient and friendly staff. The ground floor creates an impression of space and good taste; everything is planned for your comfort and well-being. The restaurant has a first class reputation for its cuisine, the table d'hôte and à la carte menus reaching high levels in quality, presentation and service. The wine list is comprehensive and well chosen. Upstairs, the well appointed bedrooms are comfortable and pleasantly furnished. The Victoria is set in 5 acres of landscaped gardens, with many outside attractions. I can recommend it to all ages.

***Single** room and breakfast from £66.00 single,* V
***Double** per person from £61 (including VAT).*
***Bargain Breaks** available at various times of year. Winter, Spring and Autumn breaks are particularly good value with single rooms from £62 and doubles from £52 per person, dinner, b & b, min. two nights.*

- *61 en suite bedrooms, all with telephone and TV; lift; night service.*
- *Meals to 9 p.m.; diets & vegeterian menus available.*
- *Children welcome; no dogs; conferences max. 100; hairdressing salon.*
- *Entertainment; snooker room, indoor and outdoor heated swimming pools and lido, sauna, solarium, spa bath, tennis court, 18 hole putting course, sea bathing, sailing and fishing by arrangement; squash, badminton and riding all nearby.*
- *Major credit cards accepted.*

Honiton 9, Exeter 15, Torquay 35, Bristol 70, Birmingham 159, London 161

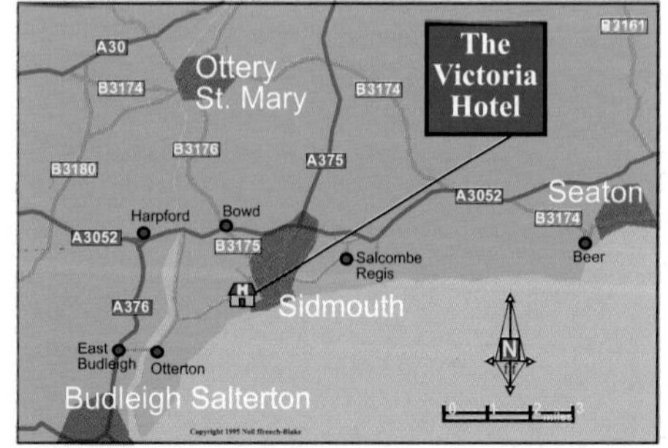

The Royal Glen Hotel

Sidmouth, Devon EX10 8RW
Tel: (01395) 513221/513456;
Fax: (01395) 514922

***Rates** start from £30.00 per night for bed and breakfast, and from £43.50 dinner, bed and breakfast in the winter.*
***Bargain breaks** available November until the end of April, excluding Christmas and Easter. Details on application.* V

Originally built in 1700 as a farmhouse, the Royal Glen Hotel has been managed by a member of the Crane family for over 100 years. This historic and lovely hotel stands in its own grounds, 200 yards from the sea-front at Sidmouth. The cricket club is nearby as well as the golf course and shopping centre. Mr. Orson Crane proudly showed me around his lovely hotel, with its wonderful antique furniture and memorabilia from the time of Queen Victoria, whose family, the Kents, used it as a holiday cottage until the untimely death of the Duke. During the course of the young Victoria's stay, she came close to death when an apprentice boy who was shooting at birds in the garden, hit a window in the nursery, narrowly missing the future Queen. The hotel has a great deal of old world charm; the upstairs drawing room is oval with period furniture, and the dining room of the same shape houses an intriguing collection of period chairs. The food is excellent, including a superb selection of puddings and an extensive wine list. It is possible for visitors to the hotel to stay in a Royal bedroom or Princess Victoria's nursery.

- *32 bedrooms with bathroom/shower, three on ground floor; all with colour TV, radio, tea-making facilities, telephone and full central heating.*
- *Dinner - last orders 8.30 p.m.*
- *Special terms for children; dogs allowed.*
- *Indoor heated swimming pool; sea bathing; golf and tennis nearby.*
- *Open February 1-January 2nd. Mastercard and Visa accepted.*

Torquay 35, Birmingham 159, London 161.

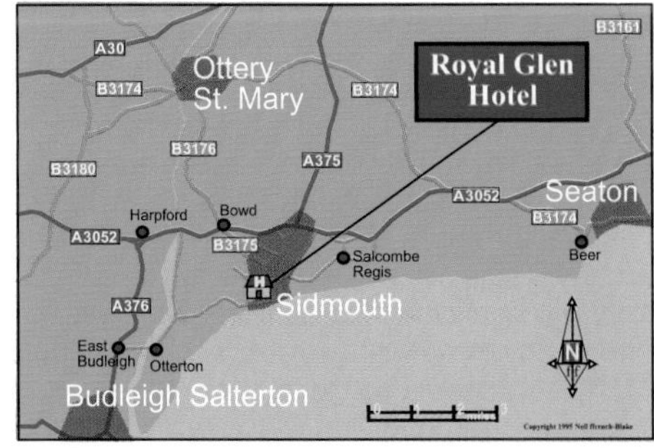

The Osborne Hotel

Hesketh Crescent, Meadfoot, Torquay, Devon TQ1 2LL
Tel: (01803) 213311; Fax: (01803) 296788

The Osborne Hotel, known by the discerning as "the country house hotel by the sea", is the centrepiece of an elegant Regency crescent. Rooms provide a panoramic view of five acres of hotel gardens and the broad sweep of Torbay, yet the neighbouring woodland is a reminder that the countryside is just a few minutes away. There are two hotel restaurants: the gourmet *Langtry's* which combines innovative dishes with tempting regional specialities and the more informal *Brasserie*, open all day for lighter meals, coffee and Devon cream teas. The hotel has a fully equipped gymnasium and many other sporting facilities in the grounds. Conferences are catered for in the library and social occasions such as weddings and birthdays take place in the elegant Drawing Room. Most of the luxurious bedrooms have sea views and are individually designed with every modern convenience. The Osborne is a hotel big enough to be luxurious and small enough to be able to care for every guest individually. Torquay is an ideal touring centre, easily accessible via the motorway network and within easy reach is Dartmoor, Exeter and the romantic West Country coasts, with their picturesque harbours and cliff walks.

Rates: *Single inc. breakfast from £52; double/twin from £104. Dinner, room and breakfast from £68 per head per night.*
Bargain Breaks: *2 nights or more from £50 per person, dinner, b & b.*

- *29 en suite bedrooms, all with colour TV+ satellite, direct dial telephone, hairdryer, laundry/valet service, music/radio/alarm, trouser press, tea/coffee making facilities, 24-hr room/meal service.*
- *Table d'hôte dinner £17.95; à l carte & special diets available; last orders 9.45 pm.*
- *Conference room - cap. 25. Car parking for 90.*
- *Billiards/snooker, gymnasium, sea/river bathing, sauna/solarium, indoor & outdoor swimming pools, tennis, putting green. Fishing & watersports 1 mile; golf 5 miles.*
- *Open all year. All major credit cards accepted.*

Newton Abbot 6, Totnes 8, Exeter 23, Plymouth 32, Bristol 106, London 223

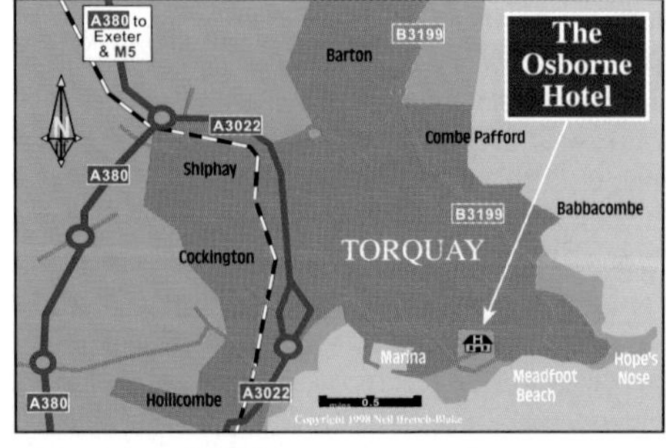

Woolacombe Bay Hotel

Woolacombe, Devon EX34 7BN
Tel: (01271) 870388; Fax: (01271) 870613

Rugged moors, rocky tors, endless National Trust walks on beach and headland; picturesque villages of "olde worlde" charm are the feel and freedom of Devon. Set amidst six acres of quiet gardens running to three miles of golden sand is the luxurious Woolacombe Bay Hotel, built in the halcyon days of the mid 1800's. It exudes a relaxed air of friendliness, good living, comfort and traditional service. The hotel has been extensively but sensitively modernised, combining discreet old fashioned ambience with modern charm. Dining is simply a delight, the best of English and Continental cooking, using the freshest local produce with special diets catered for. Complementing the menus is an interesting wine list, and you can also enjoy a drink in one of the relaxed bars. Guests have unlimited use of the extensive leisure and sporting amenities (see facilities below), and the hotel's *MV Frolica* boat is available for charter.
A magnificent ballroom and spacious lounges, combined with the outstanding facilities at the Woolacombe Bay Hotel, enables everyone to have the holiday of their choice. Energetic or relaxed - the decision is yours.

Rates: *room and breakfast from £62 per person,* ***Dinner****, room and breakfast from £82 per person including VAT.* V
Bargain breaks: *Special seasonal offers available. Please enquire for details.*

● *64 en suite bedrooms, all with telephone and TV, room/night service; baby listening, lift.*
● *Last orders for dinner 9 p.m; bar meals in bistro; special diets; children welcome; conferences max. 200.*
● *Games room; snooker/billiards; short mat bowls; tennis coaching; indoor and outdoor heated swimming pools; the 'Hot House' fitness centre with aerobics studio, fitness room, beautician, masseur, trimtrail; 2 squash courts; 9 hole approach golf course; 2 floodlit all-weather tennis courts; sea bathing (blue flag beach); sailing/boating; own motor yacht; riding, shooting and fishing nearby.*
● *Hotel closed Jan.-mid Feb.; all credit cards accepted.*

Barnstaple 14, Exeter 56, Taunton 62, Bristol 79, London 203

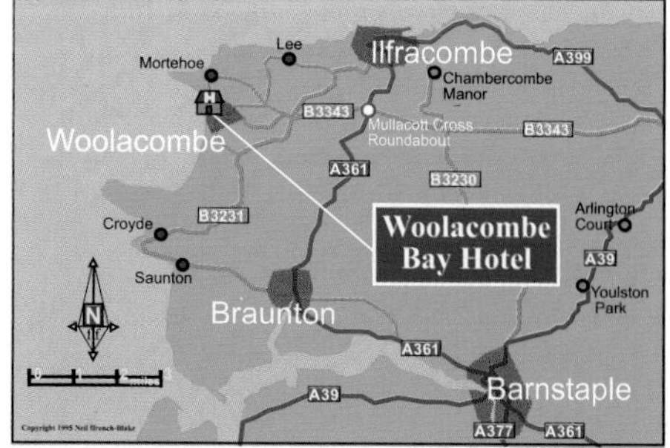

Kitley House Hotel

Kitley Estate, Yealmpton, Plymouth, Devon PL8 2NW
Tel: (01752) 881555; Fax: (01752) 881667
E-mail: sales@kitleyhousehotel.com

Approached by a mile long drive through a 300-acre estate of wooded parkland along the Yealm estuary, Kitley House is an oasis of quiet luxury, providing a relaxing alternative to urban Plymouth. The Grade 1 listed country house is one of the earliest Tudor Revival houses in England and has now been restored to its former glory. A sweeping staircase leads to the 20 spacious bedrooms and suites, most of which overlook the estate. All are richly appointed to reflect the traditional elegance of the period. A grand piano greets you in the hall whilst the book-lined dining room is welcoming. The restaurant has an AA rosette and specialises in English and French cuisine. There is fishing in the hotel's private lake, other sports nearby and, if you over-indulge, you can burn off some of the calories in the hotel's newly refurbished gym, complete with cardiovascular fitness equipment. Kitley, home of the National Shire Horse Centre, is an excellent base from which to explore Dartmoor, the maritime city of Plymouth and the Dart Valley. The South West Coast Path, Wembury Church and Bay, a marine conservation area, and Burgh Island are within 5 miles.

Rates: *Single room with breakfast from £95; double inc. breakfast from £110.* V
Bargain Breaks: *Kitley Leisure Breaks from £45 pppn b & b; Romantic Breaks from £65, available all year round, weekday & weekend.*

- *20 en suite bedrooms (inc 7 suites), all with colour TV+satellite, direct-dial telephone, hairdryer, laundry service, minibar, tea/coffee making facilities, radio/alarm clock, safety deposit box, trouser press. Non smoker & disabled rooms available.*
- *Table d'hôte £24.50; lunch & special diets available; last orders 9.30 pm. Car parking for 60.*
- *Full business services inc. 4 meeting rooms to 100; airport pickup, car rental by arrangement.*
- *Fishing, fitness centre/gym, jogging track, river bathing, clay shooting. Golf, water-sports, sailing, squash, tennis, riding within 5 miles*
- *Open all year. All major credit cards accepted.*

Newton Ferrers 4, Plymouth 6, Kingsbridge 14, Torquay 21, Exeter 42, London 205.

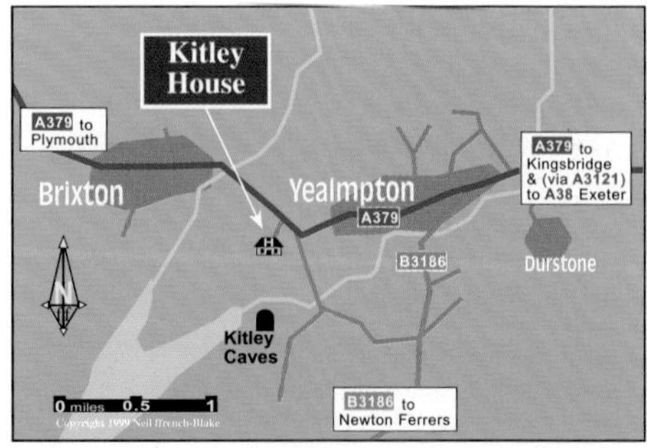

Dukes Hotel

Great Pulteney Street, Bath, Somerset
BA2 4DN
Tel: (01225) 463512; Fax: (01225) 483733

Rates: *Single room inc breakfast £55-70; double room inc. breakfast £70-100.* V
Bargain Breaks: *rates on application.*

Dukes Hotel is situated in one of Bath's most elegant boulevards, and yet is just a few minutes' stroll from the city centre. The architecturally important Grade I listed Georgian building has been fully restored externally and modernised internally. Mouldings, cornices and other original Georgian features have been retained and the magnificent staircase, cosy fully licensed bar and relaxing drawing room instill a sense of well-being as soon as you set foot in the hotel. The varied dinner menu is prepared from the finest local produce and the reasonably priced wines have been selected by a Master of Wine. Breakfast is complemented by Duke's own marmalade. Bedrooms are individually furnished to a high standard.
Bath is one of only three World Heritage Centres in Europe and as well as the many places to visit - the Roman Baths, Pump Room, Assembly Rooms, Museum of Costume, Theatre Royal, Royal Photographic Society etc, it is also a renowned shopping and artistic centre and a good jumping-off point for touring the Mendips and Cotswolds.

- *24 en suite bedrooms, all with colour TV + satellite, direct-dial telephone, hairdryer, tea/coffee making facilities.*
- *Table d'hôte dinner £15.95; special diets available; last orders 9 pm.*
- *Open all year. Mastercard, Visa, Amex credit cards accepted.*

M4 (junc 18) 9, Bristol 12, Chippenham 13, Frome 13, Wells 19, London 104

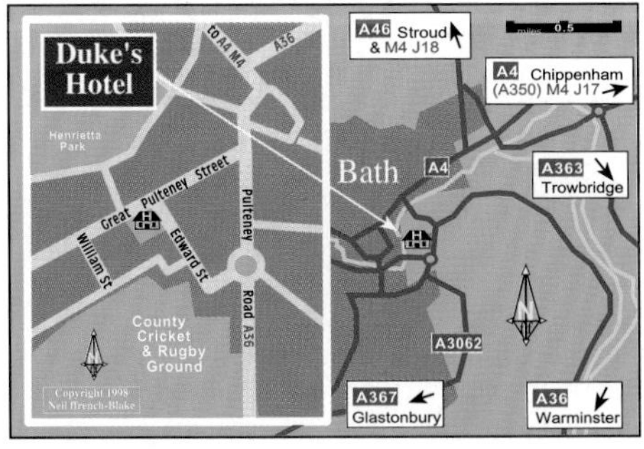

Hunstrete House

Hunstrete, Chelwood, Nr. Bath,
Somerset BS39 4NS
Tel: (01761) 490490; Fax: (01761) 490732
E-mail: info@hunstretehouse.co.uk
Internet: http://www.hunstretehouse.co.uk

This elegant 18th century country house has been carefully and thoughtfully converted into a very special hotel. The original estate was donated by King Athelstan in AD963 to Glastonbury Abbey. In the early 1600s it passed into the hands of the Popham family, whose home it was for 350 years. Today it is owned by the exclusive small US chain *Romantic Places* (see also Culloden House on our front cover). Set in classical English countryside on the edge of the Mendip Hills, yet only eight miles from both Bath and Bristol, many rooms have uninterrupted views over undulating fields and woodlands, and deer graze in the park beside the house. The reception rooms are beautifully furnished with antiques, paintings and a profusion of flowers from the lovely gardens. The bedrooms are all individually decorated and furnished to a high standard with the atmosphere of an exclusive country house. The Terrace dining room overlooks a delightful flower-filled courtyard. Head Chef Stewart Eddy and his six-man team, winners of three AA rosettes and other awards, offer light and interesting dishes, using the best English meat and fish as well as produce from the hotel's own immaculate kitchen garden.

Rates: *Single with breakfast from £120; double inc. breakfast from £170.* V
Bargain Breaks: *2 and 3 night-breaks available in off-peak months - details on application.*

- *23 en suite bedrooms (inc 2 family, one four-poster), all with direct-dial telephone, colour TV+satellite, hairdryer, laundry service, room service, radio, trouser press.*
- *Table d'hôte lunch from £14.95; tdh dinner from £29.95; à la carte & special diets catered for. Non-smoking restaurant. ⊛⊛⊛ & other awards. Last orders 9.30 pm.*
- *Croquet, outdoor swimming pool, tennis.*
- *Business services inc meeting room, capacity 50*
- *Children welcome. No pets.*
- *Open all year. All major cerdit cards accepted.*

Bath 8, Bristol 8, Radstock 8, Bridgwater 35, Yeovil 31, London 120.

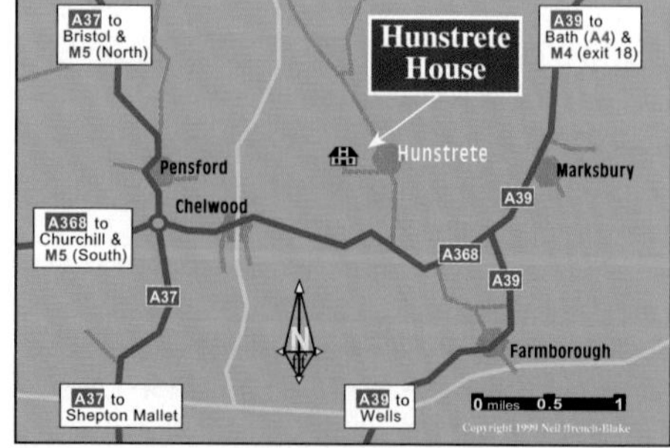

The Walnut Tree Hotel

North Petherton, Bridgwater,
Somerset TA6 6QA
Tel: (01278) 662255; Fax: (01278) 663946
E-Mail: sales.walnuttree@btinternet.com
Internet: http://www.travel-uk.net/walnuttreehotel

The Walnut Tree Hotel is a former 18th Century coaching inn, set in the heart of the pretty Somerset village of North Petherton, on the A38. Traditional values have been maintained here over the years. All the rooms are quietly located at the rear of the Inn, and every possible comfort is provided for guests. Each of the thirty two bedrooms offer superb amenities. The décor is tasteful and warming, and the four-poster bed suite is a popular choice for those seeking a special or romantic weekend break. The Walnut Tree also specialises in receptions, meetings and weddings, the public rooms having an abundance of charm and character. The popular bar and *Dukes* Restaurant & Bistro can tempt you with real ales, light bar snacks, succulent steaks and first class international cuisine, with presentation, service and excellent wines making for a memorable repast. The Walnut Tree Hotel is a hostelry of high standards with friendly staff attending to your every need. Well located for touring the South West. Do sample the charm of this hotel, and you are bound to return.

***Room** and breakfast from £40 inc. VAT;* V
***Dinner, room** and breakfast from £52 inc. VAT.*
***Bargain breaks**: Special weekend packages available.*

- *32 en suite bedrooms (inc. suites) (3 for the disabled), all with direct dial telephone and TV; room service; baby listening; night service.*
- *Last orders for dinner 10 p.m., bar meals, special diets.*
- *Children welcome; meetings/conferences to 110.*
- *Solarium; extensive parking facilities.*
- *Open all year; all major credit cards accepted.*

M5 (exit 24) 1, Bridgwater 1½, Taunton 8, Wells 12, Bristol 35, Exeter 40, London 150

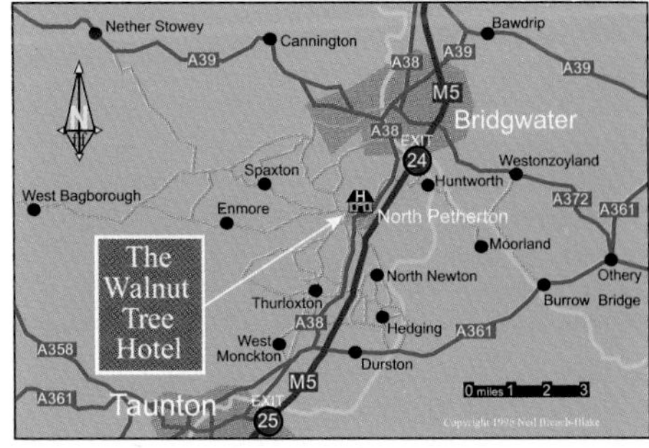

Bindon Country House Hotel & Restaurant

Langford Budville, Wellington, Somerset TA21 ORU
Tel: (01823) 400070; Fax: (01823) 400071
E-mail: Bindonhouse@msr.com

Bindon House is not just an hotel but also a home. Owned by a succession of aristocrats and distinguished families documented since 1237, it clearly has been and still is a centre of gracious living. The present buildings date from the 17th century. It became an hotel in 1997. The staircase is a delight to behold. One almost needs a map to find one's way through the labyrinth of old passages on the first floor. Furnished with beautiful antiques and nestling in seven acres of stunning woodland gardens, the house's motto is, unsurprisingly, *Je trouve bien*, (I find well). One need venture no further than the hotel grounds to find this 'well-being'. Guests can also ride a bicycle or stroll in the nearby 180-acre Langford Heath nature reserve. The 12 bedrooms are sumptuously decorated with many pampering extras in the bathrooms. The *Wellesley* Restaurant specialises in an eclectic mix of classical French style and imaginary British cuisine, with fine wines complimenting the meal. There are two private conference rooms with all modern facilities. Truly an atmospheric spot for a short leisure break or small business conference.

Rates: *Single room with breakfast from £85;* **V** *double room inc. breakfast from £95.*
Bargain Breaks: *min two-day break, dinner, b & b £90 per person per night superior room.*

Taunton 6, Tiverton 15, Honiton 20, Dunster 22, Exeter 25, London 150.

- *12 en suite bedrooms with colour TV, direct-dial telephone, hairdryer, laundry service, 24-hour room/meal service, music/radio/alarm clock, trouser press. All bedrooms non-smoking. Facilities for disabled.*
- *Table d'hôte dinner £32.50; à la carte, lunch & special diets available; last orders 9.30 pm.*
- *Croquet, outdoor swimming pool, tennis at hotel; fishing one mile, golf, riding, shooting 4 miles.*
- *Business services inc 2 meeting rooms, cap'y 50.*
- *Open all year. Visa, Amex, Mastercard, Switch, Diners accepted. Car parking for 28/rental by arr't.*

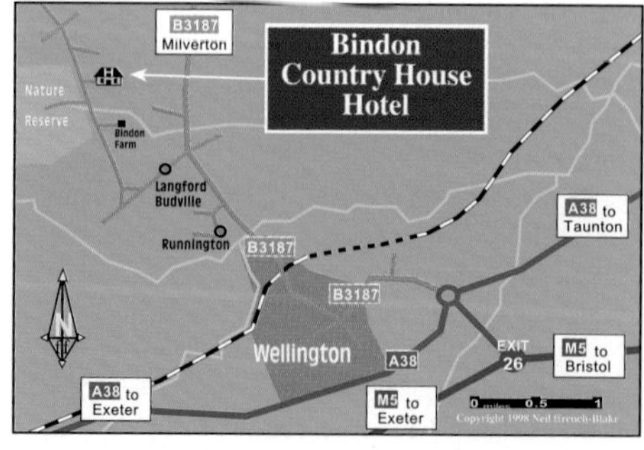

Central Southern England

Historic Houses, Gardens & Parks

Berkshire
Beale Wildlife Gdns, Lower Basildon
Cliveden, Nr. Maidenhead
Dorney Court, Nr. Windsor
Forbury Gardens, Reading
Highclere Castle, Nr. Newbury
Mapledurham House and Watermill, Nr. Reading
Stonor House, Henley-on-Thames
Stratfield Saye House, Nr. Reading

Buckinghamshire
Claydon House, Nr. Winslow
Hughenden Manor, High Wycombe
Stowe Landscape Gdns, Nr. Buckingham
Waddesdon Manor, Nr. Aylesbury
West Wycombe Park, Nr. High Wycombe

Dorset
Athelhampton House & Gardens, Puddletown, Dorchester
Forde Abbey & Gardens, Chard Hardy's Cottage Garden, Higher Bockhampton, Dorchester
Kingston Lacey House, Nr. Wimborne

Hampshire
Breamore House & Museums, Nr. Fordingbridge
Broadlands, Romsey
Exbury Gardens, Nr. Southampton
Furzey Gardens Minstead, Nr. Lyndhurst
Highclere Castle
Lymington Vineyard
Lymore Valley Herb Garden, Nr. Milford-on-Sea
Sir Harold Hillier Gardens & Arboretum, Ampfield, Nr. Romsey
Stratfield Saye House & Wellington Country Park

Oxfordshire
Basildon Park, Nr. Pangboume
Blenheim Palace, Woodstock
Peoples Park, Banbury
Rousham House & Gardens, Steeple Aston
Waterperry Gardens, Wheatley

Wiltshire
Avebury Stone Circles, Nr. Marlborough
Great Western Railway Museum, Swindon
Longleat House, Warminster
Museum & Art Gallery, Swindon
Old Wardour Castle, Tisbury
Salisbury Cathedral
Stonehenge, Nr. Amesbury

Walks & Nature Trails

Berkshire
Riverside & Country Walk to Speen Moors
Heritage Walk, Reading
Look Out Countryside & Heritage Centre Nr. Bracknell
Reading Town Trails

Dorset
Brit Valley Walk
The Dorset Coastal Path
Hardy's Dorset Walk

Hampshire
Avon Valley Path, Salisbury to Christchurch
Itchin Way, Southampton to Hinton Ampner
Solent Way, Milford on-Sea to Emsworth
Three Castles Path, Windsor to Winchester

Oxfordshire
Guided Walking Tours of Oxford
Oxford Ecology Trail

Historical Sites & Museums

Bedfordshire
Bunyan Museum, Bedford
Elstow Moot Hall, Church End
Stockwood Craft Museum & Gardens
Shuttleworth Collection, Biggleswade

Berkshire
Blake's Lock Museum, Reading
Foxhill Collection of Historic Carriages, Nr. Reading

Newbury Museum
Reading Abbey
St. George's Chapel, Windsor Castle
Windsor Castle

Buckinghamshire
Buckinghamshire County Museum,

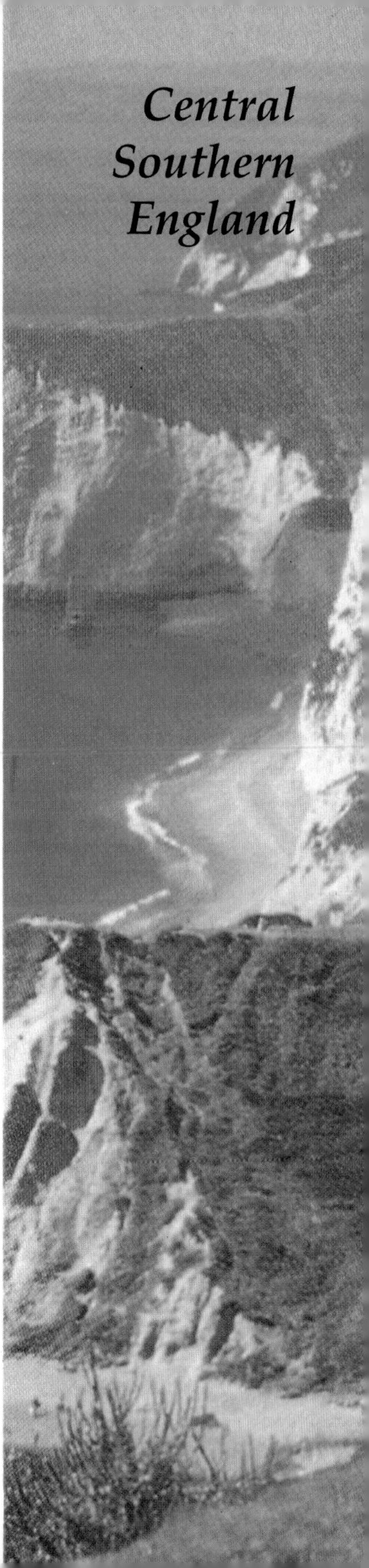

Aylesbury
Chiltern Brewery, Terrick, Aylesbury

Hampshire
D Day Museum, Portsmouth
Hurst Castle, Keyhaven
New Forest Museum & Visitor Centre, Ashurst,
Portchester Castle
The Sammy Miller Museum, New Milton

Oxfordshire
Banbury Museum & Art Gallery
Broughton Castle, Banbury
Cogges Manor Farm Museum, Witney
Didcot Railway Museum
The Oxford Story, Oxford

Entertainment Venues

Berkshire
Bucklebury Farm Park Nr. Reading
Crown Jewels of the World Exhibition, Windsor
Holme Grange Craft Centre / Art Gallery, Wokingham Trilakes
Country Park & Fishery, Sandhurst
Legoland, Windsor
Wyld Court Rainforest, Nr. Newbury

Buckinghamshire
Flamingo Gardens & Zoological Park, Olney
Glass Craft, Holtspur, Beaconsfield
Gullivers Land, Milton Keynes
West Wycombe Caves

Dorset
Brownsea Island, Poole
Lyme Regis Marine Aquarium
Lodmoor Country Park, Weymouth
Weymouth Sea Life Park

Hampshire
Lepe Country Park, Exbury
Marwell Zoological Pk, Winchester
Swimming & Diving Complex, Southampton
New Forest Buttefly Farm, Ashurst
Paultons Park, Nr. Lyndhurst
Portsmouth Sea Life Centre

Oxfordshire
Cotswold WildDife Park, Burford
CuriOXiTy (Science Gallery) Oxford
The Oxford Story, Oxford
Waterfowl Sanctuary, Hook Norton

Wiltshire
Lions of Longleat Safari Park, Warminster

For further details contact:
The Southern Tourist Board
40 Chamberlayne Road, Eastleigh, Hampshire SO5 5JH
Tel: (01703) 620006

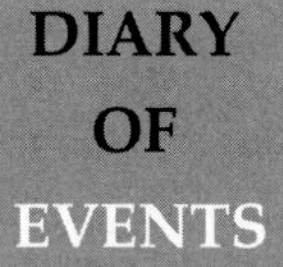

January

1-3. **New Millennium.** Didcot Railway Centre, Berks

February

15*. **Sway Pancake Race.** Village Centre, Sway, Hampshire

April

7-Oct 29. **A Century of Solent Sea & Sail Exhibition.** Shanklin, Isle of Wight
14-15. **Newbury Spring Meeting.** Newbury Racecourse, Berks.
12-16. **'Tall Ships 2000'.** Trans -atlantic race, Southampton.
24. **St George's Festival,** Salisbury, Wiltshire.
29-1 May. **Alton Heritage Festival**. Civil War Society, Alton, Hants.

May

1-3* **Newbury Steam Funtasia** Steam Rally. Newbury Showground, Chieveley, Berkshire.
6-20*. **International Newbury Spring Festival.** Various venues, Newbury, Berkshire.
11-14*. **Royal Windsor Horse Show.**Windsor Home Pk, Berks
May-June. **Salisbury Festival.** Music/arts etc. Var's venues.

June

1-30. **British Art Show** Southampton City Art Gallery
23-25. **Goodwood Festival of Speed.** Motor Sport Event, Goodwood House, W Sussex
9-11. **Wimborne Folk Festival 2000.** Wimbrone, Dorest.
4. **'Seawings 2000'** Airshow, Southampton, Hants.
20-23. **Royal Ascot Race Meeting.** Ascot Racecourse, Berks
24-July 8*. **Bournemouth Musicmakers Festival**. Various venues, Bournemouth, Dorset.
28-July 2. **Henley Royal Regatta** Henley-on-Thames, Oxfordshire.
15-24. **Millennium Festival Arena 2000**. Weymouth, Dorset
24-30. **Int'l Exhibition & Flying Display.** Farnborough, Hants.

July

24-30. **Farnborough International Air Show**, Farnborough, Hants.
28-30. **King George VI & Queen Eklizabeth Meeting.** Ascot,Berks
29-5 Aug. Skandia Life **Cowes Week** , Isle of Wight

August

6-8*. **Portsmouth & Southsea Show,** Seafront, Portsmouth.
18-28. **Millennium Youth Games** Bassett Sports Ctre, Southampton
22-31*. **Arundel Festival,** Various venues, Arundel, West Sussex.

September

1-.**BT Global Challenge**. Round the world yacht race, Southampton
8-17*. **Southampton International Boat Show 2000.** Western Esplanade, Southampton, Hants.
9*. **Romsey Show**. Broadlands Park, Romsey, Hampshire.
16-17*. **Newbury & Royal Co Berkshire Show.** Chieveley, Berks
23-24. **Ascot Festval Meeting.** Ascot, Berks.
25-26. **Queen Elizabeth II Stakes/Fillies Mile.** Ascot Racecourse, Berkshire.
25-27. **Holiday & Park Homes Exhibitions.** National Motor Museum, John Montagu Bldg, Beaulieu, Hampshire.

October/November

24-25 Nov. **Hennessy Meeting.** Newbury Racecourse, Berkshire.
*(*Denotes provisional date)*

Central Southern England

The Solent waterway between Southamp - ton and the Isle of Wight is the sailing playground of southern England.

Portsmouth Harbour is home to Nelson's *Victory*, the restored Elizabethan galleon recently brought to the surface The *Mary Rose* and *HMS Warrior*, Britain's first iron-clad warship.

Beaulieu on the west side of the Solent is the site of Lord Montagu's *National Motor Museum*. *Broadlands* at Romsey nearby was the seat of Lord Mountbatten and houses an exhibition from his life of public service.

On the way north from the south coast the visitor passes through Winchester with its 11-13th centruy cathedral and castle remains, where King Arthur's reputed Round Table can be viewed.

North of Winchester on the way to the Midlands, the visitor passes over the chalk Newbury Downs, site of some of the most famous racing stables in England, on his or her way to Oxford. The dreaming spires, echoing quads and cloistered lawns of the colleges have a timeless beauty. The *Ashmolean* Museum is Britain's oldest public museum, opened in 1683. It contains gold and jewellery beleived to have been the property of King Alfred, the lantern carried by Guy Fawkes and riches from ancient Egypt and Greece. The *Bodleian* Library, founded in 1596, is one of six University Libraries in the British Isles which receives a copy of every book published in the UK.

Wiltshire to the west of the region was the cradle of Druidic early English life and Stonehenge must be one of the seven wonders of Britain, a must-see for visitors. Neraby the Avebury stone circle is equally puzzling. Salisbury Cathedral's 404ft spire is the tallest in England.

Southwest of Wiltshire lies Dorset, Thomas Hardy's county, with the ancient cities of Dorchester (Roman remains), Hardy's *Casterbridge* and hilltop Shaftesbury (Hardy's *Shaston*). Cerne Abbas dates form the 10th centur y and has the (in)famous 180-ft Chalk Giant looking down on the village. Elsewhere there are prehistoric erathworks and white chalk horses carved into the hills of Dorset and Wiltshire.

Buckinghamshire, northeast of Oxford, contains Stowe, now a public school, with parks landsacped by Capability Brown, and Waddesdon, seat of the Rothschild Collection.

Neighbouring Berkshire's most visited monument is Windsor Castle, now fully restored after the fire of 1995.

The Swan Diplomat

Streatley-on-Thames,
Berkshire RG8 9HR
Tel: (01491) 878800; Fax: (01491) 872554
E-mail: sales@swan-diplomat.co.uk

Set on the banks of the River Thames in 23 acres of grounds, this well established hotel offers a welcoming and caring service to its guests. The spacious bedrooms, some with balconies, are individually designed and furnished and many look on to the river or have views to the Streatley hills. The comfortable lounge overlooks the river and the hotel's own island. Guests may choose to dine either in the elegant Dining Room or the Club Room, both of which offer a choice of traditional and modern English cuisine, combined wih European dishes. Other facilities include the *Reflexions* Leisure Club (free membership for hotel guests during stay) and the rebuilt 19th-century Magdalen College barge - a wonderful venue for meetings or cocktail parties. There are many short walks around the hotel, a number of National Trust properties and stately homes within easy reach and arrangements can be made for golf at local courses or the hire of a river cruiser. To sum up, this is a luxurious hotel in a marvellous setting which offers plenty to do and see - or you can even just relax by the river!

Rates: *Bed and full English breakfast Monday to Thursday from £108.50; Friday-Sunday from £73.50.*
Weekend breaks: *From £85 per person per night.*

- *46 en suite bedrooms, all with telephone, colour TV+ satellite channels, minibar, hairdryer; limited 24 hour room service.*
- *Last orders 9.30p.m; light lunches; diets.*
- *Children welcome, baby listening; dogs by arrangement; conferences up to 90.*
- *Indoor heated fit-pool, spa bath, steam room, multi-gym, sauna, solarium, bicycle hire, beauty treatments; golf, tennis and fishing 1/2 mile; shooting and riding five miles.*
- *Amex, Diners, Barclaycard and Mastercard accepted. Open all year.*

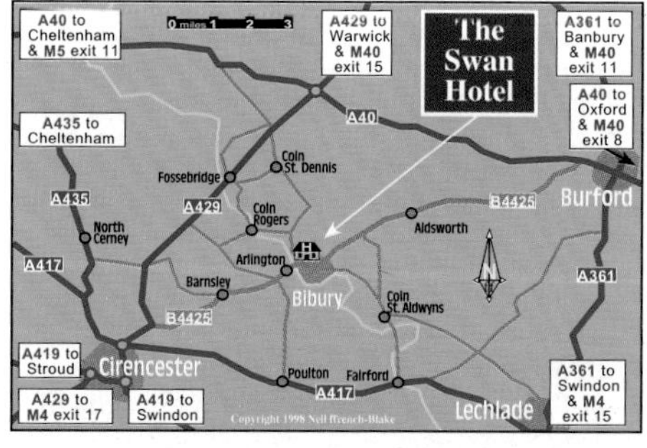

The Manor Hotel

West Bexington, Dorchester,
Dorset DT2 9DF
Tel: (01308) 897616; Fax: (01308) 897035

The Manor Hotel, located amidst some of the most dramatic scenery on the South Dorset coast, is somewhere very special just waiting to be discovered. This ancient manor house is well mellowed with age, and offers a wonderful combination of flagstone floors, panelled walls, beamed ceilings, cellar rooms, yet has been provided with en suite bedrooms including every modern comfort and facility. The décor of the en suite rooms certainly brings the vibrance of Dorset flowers and countryside through every window. Views are breathtaking. The natural gardens of the hotel are colourful and well established. Beyond is the sweeping geographical landmark of Chesil Bank with the clear seas of Lyme Bay lapping and ebbing over miles of pebbles. A more dramatic and scenic, yet quiet and relaxing situation for an hotel, one could not wish to find. The Cellar Bar provides a varied choice of bar meals through the day and in the evening, the elegant restaurant enjoys a fine reputation for well chosen culinary specialities, with fresh local produce, vegetables and especially seafood being used by the chef to present an excellent menu. A fine wine list satisfies all tastes. With the owners, Richard and Jane Childs stating that, for their guests *"nothing is too much trouble"*, please discover and pamper yourself with a visit to the Manor Hotel - a real treat!

Rates: *Room and breakfast from £46.50; dinner, b & b weekly charge from £405.* V
Bargain breaks: *Two-day stay - dinner, bed & breakfast £132 per person; five-day stay - dinner, bed & breakfast £310 per person.*

- *13 en suite bedrooms, all with direct-dial telephone, colour TV, room service, baby listening.*
- *Last orders for dinner 9.30 pm; bar meals; special diets available.*
- *Children welcome; conferences max. 60.*
- *Sea bathing; golf five miles; riding two miles.*
- *Open all year. Major credit cards accepted.*

Bridport 7, Dorchester 10, Weymouth 11, Lyme Regis 14, Bournemouth 50, Exeter 50, London 135.

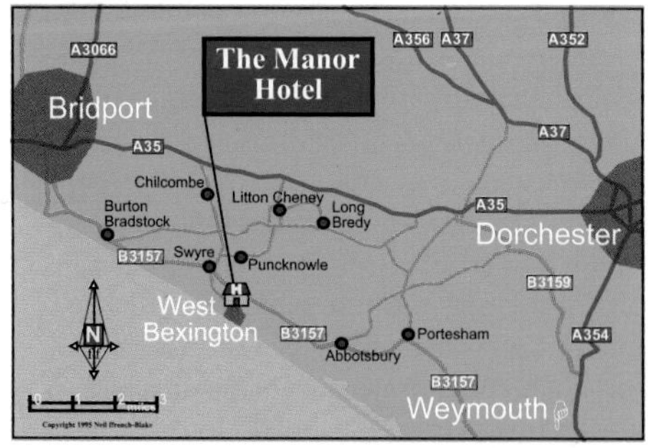

Knoll House Hotel

Studland Bay, Dorset BH19 3AH
Tel: (01929) 450450; Fax: (01929) 450423
E-mail: enquiries@knollhouse.co.uk;
Internet: http://www.knollhouse.co.uk

This delightful hotel is situated on the finest stretch of Dorset heritage coastline surrounded by some of the prettiest countryside in the West and it is well worth a visit. It is within a National Trust Reserve and overlooks three miles of golden beach with first class swimming, fishing, boating and windsurfing. Knoll House is an independent country house hotel under the personal management of its family owners and is set in pine trees with the most attractive gardens where you can relax away from the cares of everyday life. The sporting facilities are numerous - tennis courts, a nine-hole par 3 golf course and outdoor heated swimming pool. For relaxation there is a sauna, steamroom, Jacuzzi, plunge-pool, solarium and gym set in a marvellous health hydro complex with fruit juice and coffee bar. Many of the bedrooms are arranged as suites, ideal for families. Log fires and an attractive cocktail bar add to the unique atmosphere of this extremely efficiently run hotel. The quality, choice and presentation of the menus is excellent. At lunchtime a superb hors d'oeuvres selection and buffet table laden with cold meats, pies and salads is a speciality, followed by delicious puddings and a good English cheeseboard. Young children are catered for in their own dining room and there are many and varied facilities to keep them amused all day. Sandbanks and Bournemouth are easily reached via the car ferry. Dorchester, Corfe Castle and the picturesque villages of Dorset are only a short drive away.

Rates*: Half board from £70 daily or full board (weekly) from £470 (April) to £740 (August). Generous full board terms for five nights out of season.*

Special Breaks: *'Family Five' (two adults, one or two children under 13) - five nights full board in low season £897. Purbeck Five (single or twin rooms without private bathroom) five nights* *full board in low season £299 per person. September 17th-October 12th, two nights full board £139-£159 per person. Prices include VAT. There is no service charge.*

- *79 bedrooms (many ground floor), comprising 30 family suites, 29 single, 20 twin bedded rooms; 57 with private bathrooms.*
- *Five lounges; children's dining room; self-service laundry, giftshop, colour TV lounge.*
- *Three games rooms; solarium; children's disco in season; 9 acre golf course; two hard tennis courts, playground, outdoor swimming and paddling pools; full leisure centre; adjoins clean sandy beach, safe bathing; Isle of Purbeck Golf Club two miles, two courses.*
- *Open April to October.*
- *Mastercard, Visa, Eurocard accepted.*

Studland 1, Swanage 3, Corfe Castle 6, Bournemouth 8, London 113.

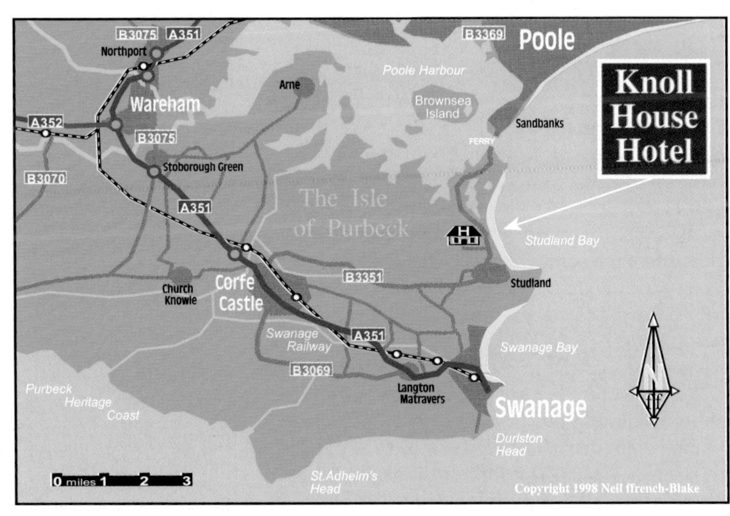

Manor House Hotel

Studland Bay, Nr. Swanage, Dorset
BH19 3AU
Tel & Fax: (01929) 450288

The site of the Manor House is mentioned in the Domesday Book and parts of the present rambling Gothic house date back to 1750. Set within 20 acres of elevated grounds, the hotel commands beautiful views overlooking the beaches and waters of Studland Bay. History and character are in abundance; the hotel's medieval carvings are said to have come from the residential quarters of Corfe Castle, home of the famous Mary Banks, who defended it so bravely against Cromwell's troops. Most of the en suite bedrooms (four with four-poster beds) have spectacular views over the bay and out to Old Harry Rocks. Wall carvings in the Westminster Bedroom are of particular interest, reputed to have come from the Old Palace of Westminster, circa 1636. A delightful conservatory has extended the dining area, where décor is sophisticated, and the atmosphere and service is most warming. The menu has an excellent choice of fresh local produce and the delicious Studland Lobster is a must! The Manor House is an ideal base from which to explore the beauty, beaches and nature trails of Studland and surrounding Dorset.

***Rates:** Dinner, room & breakfast from £56 per person. **Bargain Breaks:** Three or five night specials - 3 nights = 10% off daily rate; 5 nights = 20% off daily rate.* V

- *18 en suite bedrooms, all with colour TV, radio, tea/coffee making facilities, telephone, hairdryer.*
- *Last orders for dinner 8.30 pm; bar lunches & vegetarian diets available.*
- *Children over five welcome; dogs allowed.*
- *Sea bathing three miles with sandy beach, sailing and boating; two hard tennis courts. Riding & golf within two miles.*
- *Hotel closed Christmas to mid-January.*
- *Mastercard & Visa cards accepted.*

Swanage 3, Corfe Castle 6, Bournemouth 8, Dorchester 26, London 113.

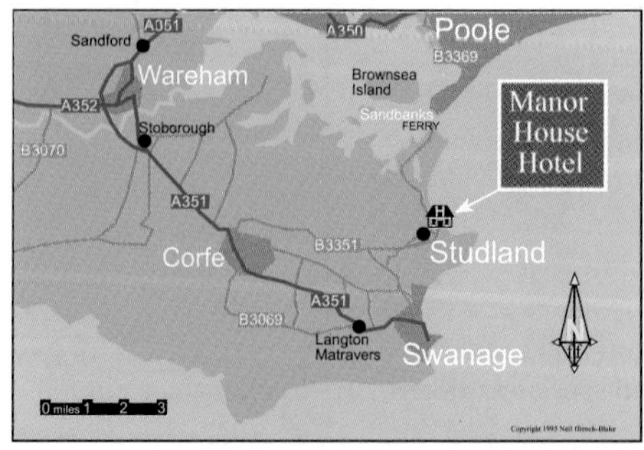

Tylney Hall

Rotherwick, Nr. Hook, Hampshire
RG27 9AZ
Tel: (01256) 764881; Fax: (01256) 768141
E-mail: sales@tylneyhall.co.uk

The approach to Tylney Hall, through avenues of chestnut and lime trees, gives a clue to the style of the hotel. The present hall dates from 1900. A fine Grade II building, it re-opened, after extensive renovation, as an hotel in 1985, owned by the *Elite* hotel group. (See also the *Grand* at Eastbourne (see page 91) and *Ashdown Park* (page 93). Honeymooners, weekenders, business executives or less hurried visitors cannot fail to appreciate the well appointed bedrooms and the views of lawns and lakes which surround the house. At different times of the year the various Gardens come into their own: The Italian, Rose and Azalea Gardens, the Water Gardens, Dutch Gardens and Water Tower. Tylney is convenient for Stratfield Saye, Broadlands, Highclere and Beaulieu. Activities from riding to hot air ballooning can be arranged. A focal point of the hotel is the glass-domed Oak Room Restaurant and there are 12 state-of-the-art conference and banqueting suites for meetings and special occasions. An exceptionally comfortable hotel for business and leisure traveller alike.

Rates: *Single room inc. breakfast from £115 ; double/twin room from £145.* V
Bargain Breaks: *Min 2-night stay inc table d'hôte dinner & breakfast from £185 per couple per night*

- *110 bedrooms (inc. 25 suites), all with colour TV + satellite, direct-dial telephone, trouser press, hairdryer, laundry/valet service, radio/alarm clock, 24-hr room/meal service, safety deposit box.*
- *Oak Room Restaurant. A la carte; lunch & special diets available; last orders 9.30 pm.*
- *Business services inc 12 meeting rooms (largest 110 cap'y). Car parking for 120.*
- *Billiards/snooker, croquet, gymnasium, indoor & outdoor swimming pools, jacuzzi, sauna, massage, jogging track, clay shooting, tennis. Golf adjacent. Sailing, squash, riding, watersports within 8 miles.*
- *Open all year. Major credit cards accepted.*

M3 (junc.5) 1, Basingstoke 6, Camberley 11, Farnham 11, Reading 13, London 41.

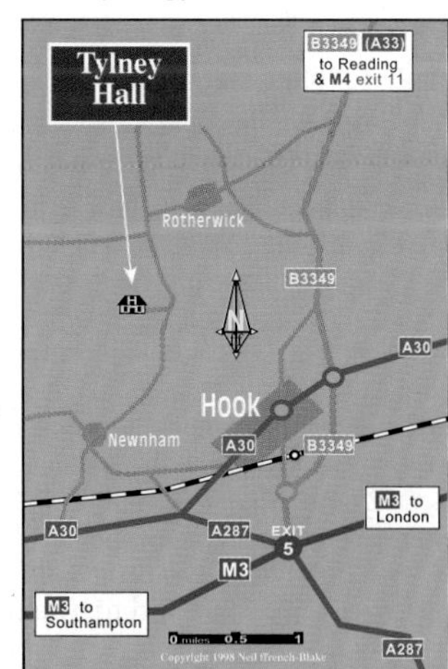

The Royal Hotel

St. Peter Street, Winchester,
Hampshire SO23 8BS
Tel: (01962) 840840; Fax: (01962) 841582
E-mail: info@the-royal.com
Internet: http://www.the-royal.com

The Royal Hotel is located in a quiet backwater just a hundred or so yards from the bustle of the pedestrian High Street, close to the famous cathedral and most of the historic attractions in Winchester, England's ancient capital. Built as a private residence in the mid 16th century, it has served as a bishop's house, a Benedictine convent and, since 1857, an hotel. In recent years the Royal has been extended and refurbished. However many of the original features have been retained and the atmosphere is one of warmth and comfort rarely found. As soon as you walk through the door, you know you are somewhere special. The AA rosetted restaurant produces daily changing menus, accompanied by a varied and sensibly priced wine list. In summer afternoon tea can be taken in the tranquillity of the garden. The Royal is owned and run by Tony and Pam Smith and their daughters. As you would expect in a family run hotel, the staff are friendly and welcoming as well as being most knowledgeable about the city and surrounding area.

Rates: *Single room with breakfast from £94 ; double room inc. breakfast from £112.50.* **V**
Getaway Breaks: *Min. two nights from £47 per person inc. dinner, b & b. 3 & 4-day breaks available Easter & Xmas; 2-day New Years Eve New Orleans Gala. Details on application or check our web-site (see address at left)*

- *75 en suite bedrooms, all with colour TV+ satellite, direct-dial telephone, hairdryer, laundry service, tea/coffee making facilities, trouser press. Non-smoker bedrooms available. Car parking for 80.*
- *Table d'hôte dinner £23.50; last orders 9.30 pm; à la carte, lunch & special diets available.*
- *Tennis 1/2 mile; golf & riding three miles.*
- *Open all year. All major credit cards accepted.*

Romsey 10, Southampton 12, Basingstoke 18, Salisbury 23, Newbury 24, London 65.

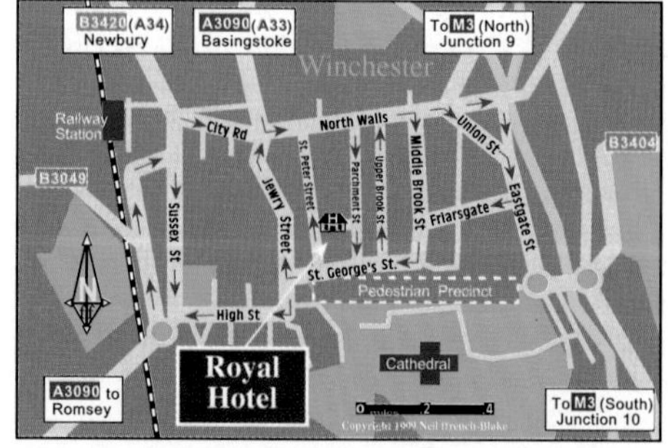

Beechfield House Hotel & Restaurant

Beanacre, Melksham,
Wiltshire SN12 7PU
Tel: (01225) 703700; Fax: (01225) 790118

Set in the pretty village of Beanacre between Chippenham and Melksham, Beechfield House is approached by a lovely, long leafy drive. This sets the scene for this delightful hotel built in Victorian times and set in a haven of eight acres of gardens and grounds. Antiques abound in this country house hotel but comfort is not lost and décor is exquisite. As you would expect, all 21 bedrooms are en suite, well appointed and include a charming four-poster room. The main dining room overlooks the heated outdoor swimming pool and a wisteria-clad walled garden. A private dining room caters for smaller functions or special occasions. Cuisine is largely modern English, offering a delicious and imaginative range of menus plus an excellent wine list. Hunting, shooting, fishing and golf can be arranged nearby. The hotel is one mile south of the National Trust village of Lacock. Beanacre is a good centre for visiting the Georgian city of Bath and the stately homes Bowood, Longleat and Corsham Court.

***Single** room inc. breakfast from £80;*
***Double** room inc. breakfast from £100.*
***Bargain Breaks.** £120 per night (minimum two night stay) to include 4-course dinner, bed & breakfast for two persons sharing twin or double.*

- *21 en suite rooms (16 double, 5 twin), all with telephone, colour TV, laundry/valet service, hairdryer, tea/coffee making, music/radio/alarm clock, trouser press; non-smoker rooms available.*
- *Table d'hôte and à la carte dinner, lunch & special diets available; last orders 9 pm.*
- *Croquet, outdoor swimming pool. Fishing, golf, riding, shooting, squash, tennis nearby.*
- *Business services inc. three meeting rooms, capacity 25. Car parking for 45.*
- *Open all year. Major credit cards accepted.*

Melksham 1, Chippenham 7, Bath 12, Bristol 25, Swindon 28, Salisbury 35, London 94.

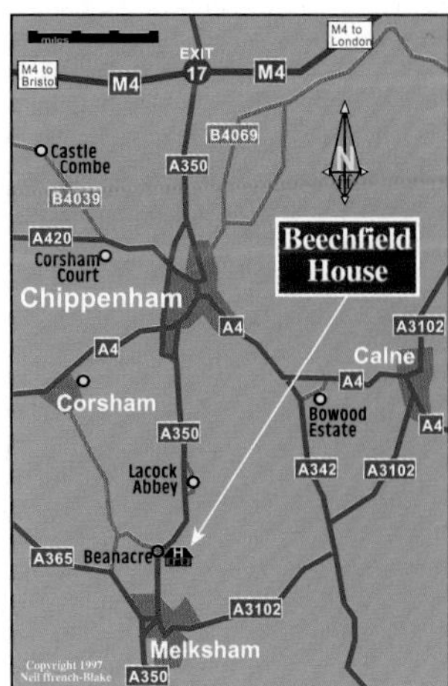

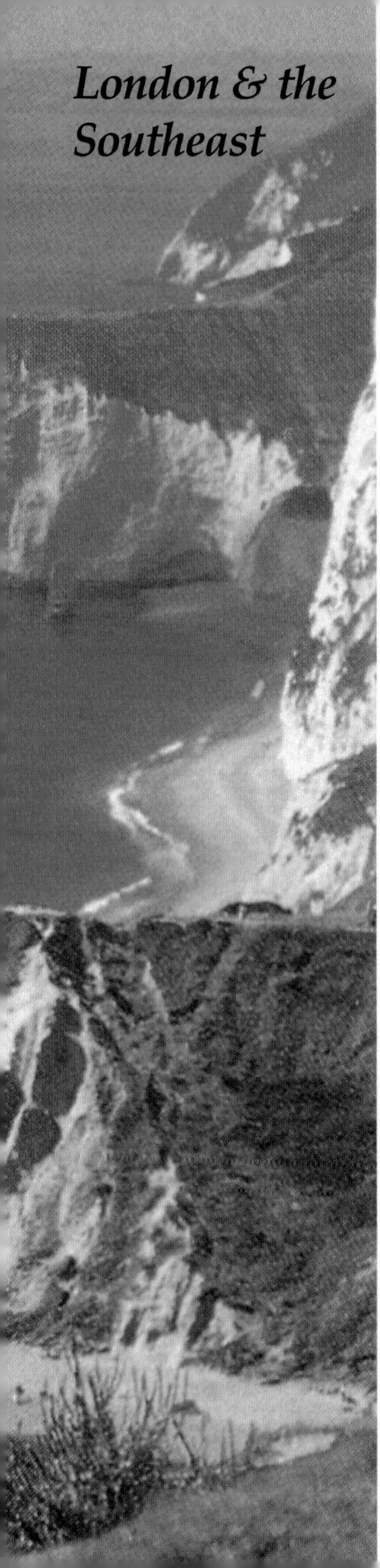

London & the Southeast

Historic Houses, Gardens & Parks

London
Carlyle's House, Chelsea
Fenton House, Hampstead
Kensington Palace, Kensington Gardens, W8
Osterley Park, Isleworth
Tower of London, Tower Hill, EC3
Westminster Abbey Chapter House, SWI

Kent
Bedgebury National Pinetum, Nr. Goudhurst
Chilham Castle Gardens, Nr Canterbury
Doddington Place Gardens, Nr Sittingboume

Godington House & Gardens, Godington Park, Ashford
Goodnestone Park, Wingham, Nr. Canterbury
Iden Croft Herbs, Staplehurst
Kent Garden Vineyard, Headcorn
Penshurst Place & Gardens, Nr. Tonbndge
Sissinghurst Garden

Surrey
Clandon Park, West Clandon
Claremont Landscape Garden, Esher
Ham House, Richmond
Hampton Court Palace, East Molesey
Hatchlands Park, East Clandon
Kew Gardens (Royal Botanic Gar dens), Richmond
Polesden Lacey, Great Bookham, Nr. Dorking
The RHS Garden, Wisley, Nr. Woking
The Savill Garden, Nr. Egham
Winkworth Arboretum, Hascombe, Nr. Godalming

East Sussex
Alfriston Clergy House, Alfriston
Battle Abbey, Battle
Brickwall House & Gardens, Northiam, Nr. Rye
Carr Taylor Vineyards, Hastings
Great Dixter House & Gardens, Northiam, Nr. Rye Michelham Priory, Upper Dicker, Nr. Hailsham
Merriments Gardens, Hurst Green
Pashley Manor Gardens Ticehurst
Preston Manor, Preston Park, Brighton
Royal Pavilion, Brighton
Sheffield Park Garden, Danehill, Nr. Uckfield

West Sussex
Denmans Garden, Fontwell, Nr. Arundel
GoodwoodHouse,Goodwood
Leonardslee Gardens, Lower Beeding, Horsham
Parham House & Gardens, Parham Park, Pulborough
Petworth House & Park
St. Mary's House,Bramber, Nr. Steyning
Standen, East Grinstead
Wakehurst Place Gardens, Ardingly, Nr.Haywards Heath

Walks & Nature Trails

Kent
Bewl Water Walks and Rides, Nr. Lamberhurst
Cobtree Manor Park Nature Trail
The Ecological Park, Elms Vale
Hastings Country Park, Hastings
Haysden Country Park Nature Trail
The Western Heights, Dover
White Cliffs Country Trail (various walks), around Kent

West Sussex
Burton Pond Nature Trail
Worth Way Walk, from Worth Way to East Grinstead

Historic Sites & Museums

London
Bntish Museum Great Russell Street, WC1
Guinness World of Records, The Trocadero Centre
The London Dungeon, 28 -34 Tooley Street, SE1
Mall Galleries The Mall, SWl
National Portrait Gallery, St. Martin's Place, WC2
Natural History Museurn, Cromwell Road, SW7
The Queen's Gallery, Buckingham Palace, SWl
Royal Mews Buckingham Palace Road, SWI
Science Museums, Exhibihon Road, SW7
The Tate Gallery, Millbank, SWl
Tower Bridge SEl
Victoria & Albert Museum,Cromwell Road, SW7

East Sussex
Anne of Cleves House Museum, Lewes
Bodlam Castle, Bodlam
Brighton Museum & Art Gallery
Filching Manor Motor Museum, Polegate
Hastings Castle & 1066 Story, West Hill, Hastings Hove Museum & Art Gallery
Quarry Farm Rural Experience, Robertsbridge

West Sussex
Arundel Castle, Arundel

Kent
Canterbury Cathedral
The Canterbury Tales, Canterbury
The Dickens Centre, Rochester
Dover Castle & Hellfire Comer
Eurotunnel Exhibition Centre, Folkestone
Guildhall Museum, Rochester
Leeds Castle, Nr. Maidstone
Lympne Castle, Nr. Hythe
Rochester Castle

Surrey
Brooklands Museum, Weybndge

Entertainment Venues

London
Madame Tussaud's & The London Planetarium, NWl
London Zoo, Regent's Park, NWl

East Sussex
The Bluebell Railway - Living Museum, Shenfield Park
Hastings Sea Life Centre

West Sussex
Butlins Southcoast World, Bognor Regis
Coombes Farm Tours, Lancing
Pulborough Brooks RSPB Nature Reserve

Kent
The Buttefly Centre, Swingfield Dover
Kent & East Sussex Steam Railway, Tenterden
Port Lympne Wild Annmal Park, Mansion & Gardens
Toy & Model Museum, Lamberhurst

Surrey
Birdworld, Nr. Farnham
Gatwick Zoo, Charlwood
Thorpe Park, Chertsey

New London Telephone numbers from April 22, 2000.
From the above date, London telephone numbers will change as follows:
Existing code 0171 becomes 020 7... (followed by the former 7-digit number).
Existing code 0181 becomes 020 8... (followed by the former 7-digit number).
Other exchanges changing are Cardiff, Coventry, Portsmouth and Southampton.

Bank & Public Holidays in the British Isles 2000

1 January. *New Year's Day*
3 January. *New Year Holiday*
1 March. *St David's Day (W)*
17 March. *St Patrick's Day (RI,NI)*
21 April. *Good Friday*
24 April. *Easter Monday (exc. Scot)*
1 May. *Early May Bank Holiday*
29 May.*Spring Bank Holiday(UK)*
5 June. *June Holiday (RI)*
12 July. *Bank Holdiay (NI)*
7 August. *Bank Holiday (RI,S)*
30 August.*Bank Holiday (E,NI,W)*
30 October. *October Holiday (RI)*
30 November. *St Andrew's Day (S)*
25 December. *Christmas Day*
26 December. *Boxing Day*

E = England; NI = Northern Ireland; RI = Republic of Ireland; S = Scotland; W = Wales.

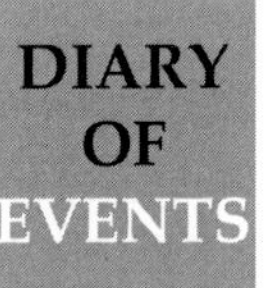

January

1-12*. **Hastings International Chess Congress**. Cinque Ports Hotel, Hastings.
14-16*. **Daily Telepgraph Travel & Sports Show.** Olympia 2, London W14.
6-16. **46th London Internat'l Boat Show**, Earls Court, London SW5

February

5. **Rugby International.** Lloyds/TSB Six Nations: England v Ireland, Twickenham
22-27. **Olympia Fine Arts & Antiques Fair,** London W14.

March

4. **Rugby International.** Wales v England, Twickenham.
16-10Apr*. **Daily Mail Ideal Home Exhibition**, Earls Court, London W5.
16-22*. **British Antiques Dealers Fair,** Chelsea Town Hall,London SW3
18. **Head of the River Race** - Mortlake to Putney, London.
27-29. **London International Book Fair**. Olympia, SW5

April

2*. **Oxford v Cambridge University Boat Race,** Putney to Mortlake, London
22-25*. **Chelsea Art Fair,** Chelsea Old Town Hall, London SW3
17*. **London Marathon**
21. **Greenwich Passion Play.** Greenwich Park, London SE10
28-29. **Whitbread Meeting.** Sandown Park, Surrey.

May

1-22*. **Brighton International Festival.** Various venues, Brighton, East Sussex
May 1-4*. **Eastbourne International Folk Festival.** Various venues, Eastbourne, E. Sussex.
13. **Tetleys Bitter Cup Final** Twickenham, SW London.
14-3 June. **BOC Covent Garden Festival.** Hyde Park W2
23-26. **Chelsea Flower Show** Royal Hospital, London SW3.
27. **European Rugby Cup Final,** Twickenham.
26-26.8. **Glyndebourne Festival Opera Season.** Glyndebourne, Lewes, E Sussex.
26-June 4. **Milliennium Maritime Festival.**Docklands, SE10

June

3-13. **Olympia Fine Arts & Antiques Fair,** Olympia, SW5.
9-10. **Vodafone Oaks/Vodafone Derby Days**. Epsom Racecourse, Surrey.
12. **Trooping the Colour.** Queen's birthday parade, Horse Guards, London SW1
8-14*. **Stella Artois Tennis Championships.** Queen's Club, London W14.
10-19. **Grosvenor House Antiques Fair.** Grosvenor Hse, London W1.
12-19*. **Eastbourne International Ladies Tennis Championship.** Int'l Lawn Tennis Centre, Eastbourne, E Sussex.
19-26. **Broadstairs Dickens Festival.** Various venues, Broadstairs, Kent.
18-25. **Covent Garden Flower Festival**, Covent Garden WC2
26-July 9. **Wimbledon Lawn Tennis Championships.** All England Lawn Tennis Club, London SW19.
27-July 12. **Chichester Festival,** Chichester, West Sussex.

July

1-31. **Greenwich & Docklands Int'l Festival.** Var. venues, Greenwich.
7-8. **Eclipse Race Meeting.** Sandown Park, Surrey.
14-16*. **Kent County Show.** Showground, Detling, Kent.
14 -Sept 9. **BBC Henry Wood Promenade Concerts.** Royal Albert Hall, LondonSW7
19-20 Aug***Royal Tournament** Earls Court, London SW5

August

1-6. **Glorious Goodwood.** Goodwood, West Sussex.
6-14*. **Broadstairs Folk Week** Var. venues, Broadstairs, Kent
19-23*. **Kensington Art Fair,** London W8.
22-Sept 1*. **Arundel Festival.** Various venues, Arundel, West Sussex.
27-28. **Notting Hill Carnival.** Ladbroke Grove, London W14

September

17. **Thames Festival**. Night-time illum. procession betwn Westminster / Southwark.
12-16. **String of Pearls** Son et Lumière. Royal Hospital,SW3
16-26. **Chelsea Antiques Fair** Town Hall, London SW3.
27-1 Oct. **Horse of the Year Show.** Wembley Arena, Wembley, Middx.

October

22-30*Nov.**London Motor Show** Earls Court, Lon'nSW5
29*. **Grand Firework Spectacular.** Leeds Castle, Kent.

November

5. **London to Brighton RAC Veteran Car Run.** London
12. **Remembrance Sunday Ceremony.** London SW1.
11. **Lord Mayor's Show**.City.
13-16. **World Travel Market.** Earls Court, London SW5
26-29.**Royal Smithfield Show**

December

15-19*. **Olympia Int'l Show-jumping Championship.** Olympia London W14.
31. **New Year Firework Display.** Battersea Park, SW11

• • • • • • • • • • • • • • •

*Denotes provisional date
For further details, contact:

The South East England Tourist Board
The Old Brew House
Warwick Park, Tunbridge Wells, Kent TN2 5TU.
Tel: (01892) 540766 *or*
London Tourist Board & Convention Bureau. 26, Grosvenor Gardens Victoria. London SWIW ODU.
Tel: 0171 730 3450

The South-East

Kent is the garden of England - and its oldest city Canterbury, with its cathedral, is the centre of the Anglican faith. The impressive Knole Park, near Sevenoaks, was built in the 15th century by an Archbishop of Canterbury. Near Maidstone is the impeccable Leeds Castle, founded in 857 and later improved by Henry VIII. In East Sussex lies the peaceful Bodlam Castle (below), surounded by its moat and never breached by an enemy,

Over the South Downs lies Brighton, Regency summer capital of Britain with the eccentric Pavilion and to the west of Brighton is the impressive Arundel Castle, Norman stronghold,

now inhabited by the Duke of Norfolk (above). Chichester, west of Arundel, has an 11th century cathedral, narrow streets of timber-clad houses and an annual drama festival.

Ashdown Forest, now more heath than forest in East Sussex covers some 6000 acres and is home to badgers and fallow deer.

On the outskirts of London, near Bromley, Kent, Chislehurst Caves have long been a favourite with children. Further East Chat-ham's 400-year old dockyard provides a history of Britain's fighting ships. Ashford in southeast Kent is the mouth of the Channel Tunnel, Gateway to Europe. Dover Castle houses the White Cliffs Experience and Churchill's War Rooms - nerve centre for the Dunkirk evacuation and the Battle of Britain of 1940.

London

London's treasures are well chronicled. Most visitors prefer to stay in the west /central Knightsbridge/Kensington areas which are handy for shopping and allow quick access into the West End for theatres and other functions. London's main museums - the Natural History, Science and Victoria and Albert are also in this area.

In the Central/West End area most visited sights are the (now) public rooms of Buckingham Palace, the National Gallery in Trafalgar Square, Westminster Abbey and the Houses of Parliament, the Cabinet War Rooms by Admiralty Arch, whence Churchill directed the second world war when bombing made the rest of the capital unsafe (the 70 rooms, of which 19 are open to the public, cover a subterranean warren of three acres), the Tate Gallery on the Embankment, containing mainly 20th century masterpieces.

Westminster Abbey, nearly a thousand years old, has tombs of many English kings queens, statesmen and writers. The British Museum in Bloomsbury houses one of the world's largest collections of antiquities, including the *Magna Carta,* the Elgin Marbles and the first edition of Alice in Wonderland.

Further east in the city of London is St Paul's Cathedral, designed by Sir Christoher Wren after the original was destroyed in the Great Fire of London (1666), whose epitaph is below the dome *"if you seek his monument, look around you".* Other notable buildings of the city are the Guildhall, the Mansion House, official residence of the Lord Mayor of London and further East, the Tower of London, a medieval fortress dominated by the White Tower and dating from 1097. The Crown Jewels are housed in the tower, which is policed by the famous Beefeaters.

In North Central London (Baker St - home of the fictitious Sherlock Holmes) are the Planetarium and Madame Tussauds, although the London Dungeon, near London Bridge Station, has recently overtaken Tussauds' *Chamber of Horrors* as childrens' favourite collection of gruesome displays.

London's parks are its 'lungs' and a pleasant place to relax on a summer's afternoon. St James, the oldest one, was founded by Henry VIII in 1532, is the most central and covers 90 acres. Hyde Park, bordering Kensington, Mayfair and Marylebone is the largest at 630 acres and includes the famous Serpentine artificial lake where the hardy still swim on Christmas Day. Regents Park, lies north of Oxford Circus, and was given to the nation by the Prince Regent. Further out are Richmond Park in the southwest, where deer still abound, and Kew Gardens, with its famous tropical greenhouses and plants.

In the south-east of the capital, land to the East of the Tower of London has been reclaimed and Canary Wharf and the Docklands area provide an interesting study of urban renewal. On the south bank opposite Docklands is Greenwich Observatory , the National Maritime Museum and the Millennium dome where many events take place in 2000.

The Cavendish St James's

81 Jermyn Street, St James's, London SW1Y 6JF
Tel: (0171) 930 2111; Fax: (0171) 839 2125

Rates: *Single room incl. breakfast & service from £165; double from £195. All prices VATexclusive.* ***Bargain Breaks:*** *Midweek and weekend leisure breaks available from £78 per person sharing twin or double, b & b; from £99 pp dinner, b & b.*

The most surprising characteristic of this stylish, modern hotel is its aura of tranquillity. It is an ideal base for shoppers - a short distance to Bond Street, theatre- and clubland - and just two minutes' walk from the bustle of Piccadilly. The calming ambience starts with the welcoming reception area and is continued in the Bar where wood panelling and leather seating make a popular meeting place for business or pleasure. An elegant staircase is dominated by a portrait of Rosa Lewis, the "Duchess of Duke Street", whose influence on an earlier Cavendish made it so much a part of the social scene that Edward VII preferred entertaining there to nearby Buckingham Palace. "The Lounge" on the first floor serves light menus; the more sophisticated *Tapas Bar* and *Leyton's Brasserie* providing superb European cuisine and pre-theatre dinners. Travellers on vacation will enjoy the traditions of the Cavendish; business travellers will appreciate the modern facilities ranging from on-site parking to air-conditioned meeting rooms. Unsurprisingly, the hotel has won many top awards for quality, comfort and service.

● *251 en suite rooms with colour TV + satellite, direct-dial telephone; hairdryer, trouser press, laundry service, minibar, 24-hour room/meal service. 75% of bedrooms non-smoking.*
● *2-cse table d'hôte dinner from £14.50. A la carte, lunch & special diets available. Last orders 10.30 pm. Ring anytime for current special offers.*
● *Business services inc. 4 meeting rooms, capacity 100. Car parking. Gymnasium and pool nearby.*
● *Open all year. Mastercard, Visa, JCB, Diners Club, Amex credit cards accepted.*

Basil Street Hotel

Basil Street, Knightsbridge,
London SW3 1AH
Tel: (020) 581 3311; Fax: (020) 581 3693
E-Mail: TheBasil@aol.com
Internet: http//www.absite.com/basil

A rare example of a major London hotel still in private ownership, the Basil Street Hotel is a reminder of a more gracious age. It is a treasure trove of fine paintings, antiques and objets d'art, now discreetly adapted to provide contemporary comforts in the heart of fashionable Knightsbridge. A country house hotel in the middle of London, each of the bedrooms is individually furnished and the longstanding staff are reminiscent of family retainers who recognise regular guests. The country house tradition is further preserved by the Afternoon Tea tradition in the lounge. In the evening piano playing adds to the pleasure of eating in *one of the loveliest dining rooms in London* where menus offer a choice from a light lunch to a sumptuous dinner. Meeting rooms can cater for up to 50 people and the Parrot Club, recently profiled on BBC television, offers lady guests a soothing retreat. The Hotel is within easy walking distance of Harrods, Harvey Nichols and Peter Jones, convenient for museums and via Knightsbridge Underground Station, has excellent connections to the West End.

Single *room incl. VAT, service & continental breakfast from £149.00.*
Double *room as above from £230.00.*
Bargain Breaks: *Weekend, Xmas/New Year, August and Long Stay rates available on request.*

- *80 en suite rooms inc. 4 family rooms all with satellite TV, radio, direct-dial telephone; hairdryer, 24-hour room/meal service, safety deposit box (at reception). Non-smoker bedrooms available.*
- *A la carte restaurant; lunch & special diets available; last orders 10 pm.*
- *Business services inc 3 meeting rooms, cap'y 50.*
- *Airport pickup and car rental can be arranged.*
- *Open all year. All major credit cards accepted.*

Harrington Hall Hotel

5-25 Harrington Gardens, Kensington,
London SW7 4JW
Tel: (0171) 396 9696; Fax (0171) 396 9090
E-mail: harringtonsales@compuserve.com
Internet: http: / / www.harringtonhall.co.uk

Harrington Hall, a hotel of elegance located in the heart of London is one of the few remaining privately owned hotels. This luxury 200 bedroom, fully air-conditioned property is situated in the exclusive Royal Borough of Kensington and Chelsea, within easy reach of Knightsbridge. Behind the splendour of the original period facade, Harrington Hall is a new hotel providing every modern convenience in a beautifully designed, classical setting. In the open plan lounge, which combines warmth and elegance with comfortable traditional furnishings and a beautiful marble fireplace, snacks and refreshments are offered. Wetherby's, the spacious and refreshingly airy restaurant, has a tempting selection of dishes available from the choice of buffet or à la carte menu. Harrington Hall's bedrooms are large and all contain an extensive array of facilities which include satellite TV, mini-bar, a state of the art message system and of course air-conditioning. A number of rooms have been allocated for non-smoking guests. Harrington Hall's nine conference and banqueting suites provide a sophisticated venue for conferences, or corporate hospitality and are ideal for luncheons, or receptions. Harrington Hall also has a Business Centre for the exclusive use of guests, which provides a range of secretarial services including word processing and facsimile. Guests can tone up in the private Fitness Centre which boasts a multi-gym as well as saunas and showers.

Room rates *from £180.00 incl. VAT and service. Continental breakfast £9.95; Full English breakfast £13.95.*

- *200 en suite air-conditioned bedrooms with radio, satellite TV, direct dial telephones with personal numbers; hairdryer, trouser press, laundry service; tea/coffee making facilities, mini-bar, safety deposit box; 24-hour room service; non-smoker bedrooms available.*
- *Last orders for dinner 22.30 hrs. Special diets available.*
- *Fitness Centre/gym, sauna.*
- *Full business services inc. nine meeting rooms , capacity up to 250. Car parking off site. Car rental can be arranged.*
- *Open all year. Credit cards accepted.*

Kingsway Hall

Great Queen Street, London WC2B 5BZ
Tel: (0207) 309 0909; Fax: (0207) 309 9696
E-mail:kingswayhall@compuserve.com
Internet: http: / /www.kingswayhall.co.uk

Kingsway Hall is located in2 the heart of fashionable Covent Garden. Situated just minutes away from Holborn and Covent Garden Underground Station and with close proximity to the City and the Eurostar terminal at Waterloo. This superior four star hotel is adjacent to the New Connaught Rooms, close to the Royal Opera House, Theatreland, The British Museum and Oxford Street. Its 170 bedrooms are decorated to the highest international standards. Each guestroom offers an extensive array of facilities including satellite and interactive television, minibar, in-room safe, a state of the art message system including a personal telephone number. Harlequin, the hotel's spacious and refreshingly different restaurant combines daring decoration with superb cuisine and service. The 9 conference rooms feature the most up-to-date equipment to provide a sophisticated venue for a business or social event. A fully equipped fitness studio, complete with whirlpool, is also available for the exclusive use of guests.

***Single** room inc breakfast from £199.00;*
***Double** room inc breakfast from £226.00*
***Bargain breaks:** Weekend theatre rates: Executive Double Room £200 per night inc full b'fast. (Min 2-night stay inc Saturday).*

- *170 en suite bedrooms (inc 2 suites) with air-conditioning, colour TV + satellite, radio, direct-dial telephone, hairdryer, laundry service, minibar, tea/coffee making facilities, 24 hour room/meal service, safety deposit box, trouser press, iron + board. Non-smoker & disabled bedrooms available.*
- *Table d'hôte dinner 3-courses £21; last orders 10.30 pm; lunch & special diets available.*
- *Fitness Centre/gym. Car rental.*
- *Nine meeting rooms, capacity up to 150.*
- *Open all year. All major credit cards accepted.*

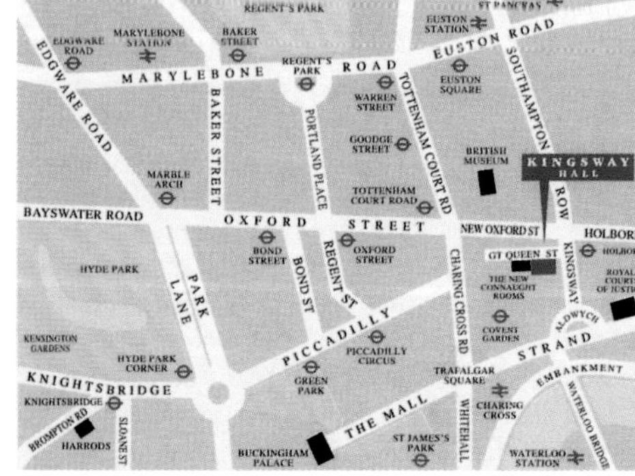

The Montcalm

Great Cumberland Place,
London W1A 2LF
Tel: (0171) 402 4288; Fax: (0171) 724 9180

Located on a delightful, tree-lined street behind Marble Arch, this sometime Georgian town house lives up to the dignity and style of the 18th century general, the Marquis de Montcalm. A recent winner of the *AA Courtesy and Care Award*, the emphasis is on discreet service to each guest. This begins with the welcome at the imposing entrance, continues in the club-like atmosphere of the foyer and extends to the cosy bar and adjoining area where a relaxing pianola plays classical music. The ✿✿ AA *Crescent* restaurant is dominated by an idyllic country garden mural and offers a variety of good value menus as well as private dining and conference facilities and a special supper service for theatre-goers. The 120 air-conditioned bedrooms (including 12 duplex suites) exude comfort, reinforced by luxury furnishings and marble tiled bathrooms. If you would like to turn the clock back to Georgian style and forward to flawless comfort, The Montcalm is your connection.

***Single** room from £205.00 + VAT; **Double** room from £225.00 + VAT; breakfast extra.*
***Bargain breaks:** Montcalm Interlude - Fri to Mon and Bank Holidays from £176.25 for two people per night (min. two nights) inc. traditional English breakfast and VAT.* [V]

- *120 en suite bedrooms (15 double, 46 twin, 45 single, 14 suites) with airconditioning, satellite TV, radio, direct-dial telephone, hairdryer, laundry service, voice mail & fax machines, 24 hour room/meal service, safety deposit box, trouser press*
- *Table d'hôte dinner or lunch 3-courses £24 inc. half bottle of house wine, coffee, petit fours & VAT; last orders 10.30 pm; lunch & special diets available*
- *Three meeting rooms - capacity to 80.*
- *Open all year. Access, Visa, Amex, Diners & JCB credit cards accepted.*

Pembridge Court

34 Pembridge Gardens, London W2 4DX
Tel: (0171) 229 9977; Fax: (0171) 727 4982
E-mail: Reservations@pemct.co.uk

This privately owned Victorian town house hotel is situated in quiet tree-lined gardens close to the Portobello Road Antiques Market. The location is very appropriate, for the Pembridge Court has been beautifully restored and reflects the character of its distinctive environs. As you step up through a colourful array of shrubs and flowers you may be greeted by the two handsome, TV personality ginger cats Spencer and Churchill. A fine display of Victorian artefacts and prints jostle for space on the walls. An unusual collection of framed fans decorates the bedrooms. The cosy cellar bar, with its own unique display of headgear, is a popular place for our guests to unwind and enjoy a drink or snack after a busy dau in the metropolis. Several of the twenty comfortable rooms are spacious and de luxe and all are tastefully decorated with nicely coordinated fabrics and furnishings. The tone of this stylish hotel is set by the book-lined drawing room - with its deep sofas, open fire and fresh flowers is ideal for relaxation or for working in peace and quiet. The Pembridge Court has won many prestigious awards for its sheer quality, but its greatest accolade is represented by the number of guests who return again and again to savour the welcome and charm of this hotel with a difference.

Single *room inc. Eng. breakfast & VAT £120-155;*
Double *room inc. breakfast & VAT £150-190.*

- *20 en suite rooms all with radio, satellite TV, direct-dial telephone, hairdryer, trouser press, laundry service, tea/coffee making facilities, air-conditioning.*
- *Room service menu available until 12 midnight (hot & cold snacks); soup/snack lunch available.*
- *Business services; airport pick-up; car rental; car parking (2 cars).*
- *Temporary membership to nearby health club*
- *Open all year. Amex, Visa, Diners, Access credit cards accepted.*

Uptown Reservations

41 Paradise Walk, Chelsea,
London SW3 4JL
Tel: 0171 351 3445; Fax: 0171 351 9383
E-mail: uptown@dial.pipex.com
Internet: http://fenet.co.uk/uptown

Uptown is a new concept for Signpost. It was founded in 1992 to provide upmarket bed & breakfast accommodation for those visiting London. Uptown's portfolio comprises some 80 properties in the most fashionable parts of London: Knightsbridge, Belgravia, Kensington and Chelsea. All homes have private bathrooms (usually en suite) and guests take breakfast with their hosts. Dinner is not provided but most homes are near to a wide selection of restaurants. Advantages of Uptown's selection of accommodation include the provision of a safer environment, in particular for the single female traveller, and the benefit of advice from your hosts on shopping, shows, how to get around, local eating places etc. Also the homes provide a unique insight into the English way of life for overseas leisure or business travellers. Most homes have been selected bearing in mind their convenience for local public transport. We recommend that you book at least 7 days in advance. A deposit of 28% of the booking will be required by Uptown, who will arrange your accommodation for you, with the balance being paid to the home owner.
Signpost also recommends *Elegant Ireland* for private accommodation on the Emerald Isle. See beginning of Irish section of this guide.

Rates: *Single room, with private bath or shower and continental breakfast £70 per night; double £90 per night; family room £115 per night. £5 supplement for single night's stay. The agency operates all year. Mastercard, Amex, Eurocard and Visa accepted.*

The Westbury Hotel

Bond Street, Mayfair, London W1A 4UH
Tel: (0171) 629 7755; Fax: (0171) 495 1163

E-mail: westburyhotel@compuserve.com
Internet: http://www.westbury-London.co.uk

Named after the famous polo ground on Long Island, the Westbury was the first American-owned hotel in Britain 45 years ago. Subsequent owners have maintained the character of discreet luxury and service which are the hallmarks of the hotel today. It is situated on Bond Street, Mayfair, 'possibly the best address in town', at the centre of London's prestigious shopping area and is ideal for both business and pleasure. London's theatreland, parks and gardens are but a short walk away. A spacious, welcoming reception area leads into the hotel's first class restaurant. Here cuisine is English in style and served in a light, airy room which overlooks the flower garden. It also leads towards the Polo Bar and Lounge, where one of London's favourite rendezvous provides light refreshments all day and entertainment in the evening. Air-conditioned bedrooms and sizeable de luxe suites put the emphasis on home comforts and also offer complete technical facilities for the business traveller. In addition there are fully equipped meeting rooms and guests may use a health & fitness club and pool nearby.

Rates: *single room inc. breakfast from £221.95; Double inc. breakfast from £248.90.*
Bargain breaks: *A 'Majestic Weekend' rate, valid any Fri/Sat/Sun. Superior room for two inc. break fast & morning paper - prices from £250 per night inc.*

- *244 en suite bedrooms (inc. 19 suites) with colour TV + satellite, radio, direct-dial telephone, hairdryer, laundry service, tea/coffee making facilities, 24 hr light snack service, safety deposit box, trouser press. Non smoker rooms available.*
- *Restaurant, polo bar, polo lounge. Lunch & special diets catered for. Last orders 2230.*
- *Complimentary use of leisure centre & pool nearby*
- *Full businsss services inc. 4 meeting rooms to 150*
- *Open all year. All major credit cards accepted.*

The Clarendon Hotel

Montpelier Row, Blackheath,
London SE3 ORW
Tel: (0208) 318 4321;
Fax: (0208) 318 4378

The location of the Clarendon, on the edge of the beautiful Blackheath common and close to the many attractions of historic Greenwich makes it an alternative to staying in the centre when visiting London. It is a short walk to the railway station and a 20-minute journey to Central London. Stone from the old London Bridge is reputed to have been used in the construction of the hotel, which was later home to rich Georgian merchants and shipbuilders. The nautical background is reflected in the bar which has many maritime artefacts including sea charts. Home comfort is a feature of the bedrooms and the Meridian Restaurant, overlooking the gardens, serves a good choice of cuisine. Otherwise modest in appearance and price , the Clarendon also caters for wedding receptions and has conference facilities for 150 in 5 well-equipped suites.

***Rates**: Single inc. breakfast from £60; double/twin inc. breakfast from £79.* V

- *185 bedrooms, 3 suites, all en suite, all with cable TV, radio, direct-dial telephone, hairdryer, tea/coffee making facilities.*
- *Table d'hôte £15; à la carte, lunch & special diets available; last orders 9.45 pm.*
- *Conference room, capacity 150. Car parking 80.*
- *Open all year. All major credit cards accepted.*

Greenwich 1, Central London 6, Rochester 30, Canterbury 55, Dover 72.

The Langorf Hotel

20 Frognal, Hampstead, London
NW3 6AG. Tel: (0171) 794 4483;
Fax: (0171) 435 9055.
Toll-free from USA: 1-800-925 4731.

This delightful town house hotel is discreetly situated in a quiet residential street just ten minutes by public transport from the West End, and south of fashionable Hampstead Village with its quality shops, fine restaurants and historic Kenwood House, renowned for open air concerts. The first impression is of friendly, attentive staff for whom nothing is too much trouble, and the second of a welcoming ambience throughout the hotel. The bright reception area adjoins the restaurant-bar, which overlooks a leafy walled garden and is open for breakfast and snacks throughout the day. Accommodation includes a number of serviced apartments.
A deserved holder of "Commended" and "Highly Acclaimed" awards, the Langorf guarantees a comfortable stay, offering its guests amongst the best value in town.

***Rates:** Single room with breakfast from £73; double inc. breakfast from £90. **Apartments** (4 pers) from £115 nightly. Leisure Breaks: rates on application* V

- *31 en suite bedrooms (+ 5 apartments) with colour TV + satellite, radio, direct-dial telephone, hairdryer, laundry service, tea/coffee making facilities, 24-hour light snack service, safety deposit box.*
- *Horse riding nearby; leisure centre 15 minutes.*
- *Open all year. All major credit cards accepted.*

Grand Hotel, Eastbourne

King Edward's Parade, Eastbourne,
East Sussex BN21 4EQ
Tel: (01323) 412345; Fax: (01323) 412233
E-mail: reservations@grandeastbourne.co.uk
Internet: http://www.grandeastbourne.co.uk

The commanding presence of the Grand Hotel overlooks the Western promenade at Eastbourne. Affectionately known as the 'White Palace', it was built in 1875 and epitomises the grandeur of Victorian and Edwardian eras. The *Grand* is part of the *Elite* group of hotels which also owns *Ashdown Park Hotel* (page 70) *Tylney Hall* (page 51), and which acquired Luton Hoo in 1999. The hotel's exterior is magnificently elaborate, whilst the lavishly appointed interior provides spacious reception rooms. During the summer months, the terrace beside the outdoor swimming pool is an alluring spot. Impressive banqueting and conference rooms are available.A short stroll from the Grand are the famous grass tennis courts of Devonshire Park where the long-established pre-Wimbledon Ladies' Tournament takes place. In addition to tennis stars, the Grand continues to play host to political and business leaders. Communications are good, with Gatwick less than an hour away. Brighton, Beachy Head and the battlefield site at Hastings are also close by, as is Newhaven sea ferry terminal. Glyndebourne and the glorious South Downs countryside are on the hotel's doorstep.

Rates: *Single room with breakfast from £120; Double room with breakfast from £152.* **V**
Short Breaks: *Min 2-night stay inc tdh dinner & breakfast from £195 per couple per night.*

● *152 en suite bedrooms (inc 48 suites), all with colour TV + satellite, direct-dial telephone, hairdryer, laundry/valet service, tea/coffee-making facilities (on request), 24 hour room service, music/radio/alarm clock, trouser press; safety deposit boxes, non-smoker & disabled bedrooms available.*
● *Garden Restaurant 4-course table d'hôte £32.50; last orders 9.30 pm; à la carte, lunch &diets available.* ◎◎ *Mirabelle restaurant.*
● *Business centre inc. 17 meeting rooms, max. 350.*
● *Billiards/snooker, gymnasium, spa bath, 8 beauty treatment rooms, hairdressing salon, saunas, steam rooms, outdoor and indoor swimming pools. Tennis, fishing, watersports, sailing nearby; squash, golf 1 m; riding, shooting 3-5 m.*
● *Open all year. All major credit cards accepted.*
Newhaven 12, Hastings 20, Brighton 25, Tunbridge Wells 29, Dover 61, London 63.

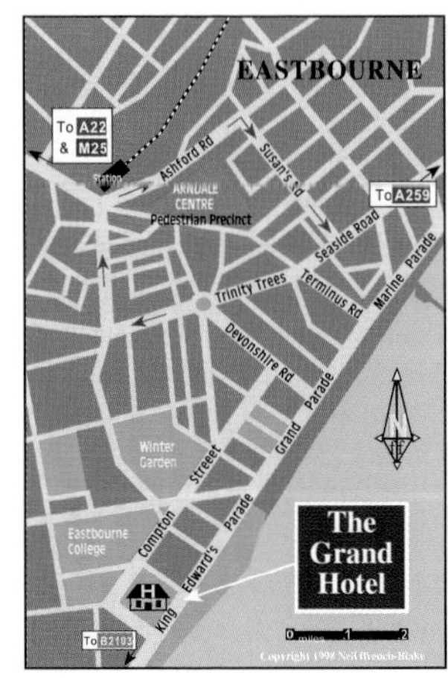

Lansdowne Hotel

King Edward's Parade, Eastbourne,
East Sussex BN21 4EE
Tel: (01323) 725174; Fax: (01323) 739721
E-mail: the.lansdowne@btinternet.com
Internet: http://www.btinternet.com/-thelansdowne

AA 'Courtesy & Care' Award 1992.
RAC Merit Awards for Hospitality, Service & Comfort 1995/6/7/8/9.

RAC ★★★ AA

The Lansdowne Hotel commands a fine view over Eastbourne's beach to the sea beyond. Owned by the same family since 1912, this hotel has the true hallmark of hospitality and comfort. Bedrooms are gracefully furnished with many rooms overlooking the sea-front. There is a choice of elegant lounges all of which benefit from a view across the Western Lawns as well as several refreshment places from the attractive Regency Bar to the stylish Devonshire Restaurant serving fixed price menus of traditional English cuisine. A comprehensive bar and lounge menu is available daily at lunchtime. Traditional Sunday lunch and 4-course dinner is served every evening in the restaurant. Conferences and seminars are well provided for in a selection of rooms. Two snooker rooms, table tennis, darts and a pool table provide every opportunity for relaxation. Eastbourne is an active resort offering a world famous tennis centre, a first class yachting marina, 200 acres of parks and gardens and the Lansdowne hotel is the ideal base from which to explore all that is offered in the area.

Single *room rate including breakfast from £52.00.*
Double *room with breakfast from £84.00.* V
Bargain Breaks *weekend/weekday from 14th January -14th May (exc. Easter) & 22 October- 22nd December. Prices from £41 pppn d,b&b. Social bridge weekends once a month exc. June, July, Sept. & Oct; prices pp from £93 (2 nights) or £127 (3 nights). Duplicate bridge weekends (3 nights only) from £137 Jan, March, May, July, Sept & Nov'br. Golf Breaks all year from £135 per golfer for 2 days.*

● *121 en suite bedrooms with colour/satellite TV, radio, direct-dial telephone, hairdryer, laundry service, tea/coffee making facilities, 24-hour room service, trouser press.* ● *Last dinner orders 20.30.*
● *Snooker, indoor games room. Special arrangements for golf with seven local clubs. Sky Sports TV in the Berwick Room.*
● *Complete business service. Five fully equipped conference rooms with capacity of 330.*
● *Car parking: 22 lock-ups.* ● *Hotel closed 1-13 January.* ● *All major credit cards accepted.*

Newhaven 12, Hastings 20, Brighton 25, Tunbridge Wells 29, Dover 61, London 63.

Ashdown Park Hotel

Wych Cross, Forest Row RH18 5JR
Tel: (01342) 824988; Fax: (01342) 826206
E-mail: sales@ashdownpark.co.uk
Internet: http://www.ashdownpark.com

Not much more than an hour's drive from Central London, yet in the heart of Ashdown Forest - home of Pooh Bear - lies Ashdown Park Hotel & Country Club, sympathetically restored in the 1990s and now part of the *Elite* Group (see also *Tylney Hall* on page 51 and *The Grand Hotel, Eastbourne* on page 68). Convenient for the summer delights of Glyndebourne, Hickstead, Hever Castle and the stunning gardens and country houses of Sussex, the hotel gives a marvellous sensation of comfort and space. There are some 186 acres of parkland in which to roam, with gardens, lakes and woodland trails - and no shortage of activities on site. The charms of Tunbridge Wells and Brighton and the international connections at Gatwick and the Channel Tunnel terminal at Ashford are nearby. Gourmet evenings are held monthly throughout the year in the award winning Anderida Restaurant. The Country Club now boasts a beautiful swimming pool and some of the latest cardiovascular equipment, together with a wide range of hair and beauty treatments. Ashdown Park offers a selection of short breaks and celebration packages for honeymooners and romantics. A second 9 holes have been added, now making a testing 18-hole par 3 golf course in the grounds. There are also superb conference facilities.

Rates: *single room rate inc. breakfast from £120; double room with breakfast from £152 .* V
Short Breaks: *min 2-night stay inc table d'hôte dinner & breakfast from £195 per couple per night.*

● *95 en suite bedrooms with colour/satellite TV, radio, direct-dial telephone, hairdryer, laundry service, trouser press, safety deposit boxes available.*
● *Last dinner orders 21.30. Lunch & special diets available. Car parking for 120.*
● *Billiards/snooker, croquet, fitness centre/ gym, jacuzzi/whirlpool, jogging track, massage, sauna/solarium, indoor swimming pool, tennis, barber shop/hairdresser, beauty salon, 18-hole par 3 golf course. Fishing 7m. Riding 3 miles. Sporting equipment avilable for hire.*
● *Business services inc. 16 meeting rooms, capacity 150.* ● *Open all year. Major credit cards accepted*

East Grinstead 6, Haywards Heath 10, Tunbridge Wells 12, Lewes 15, London 39.

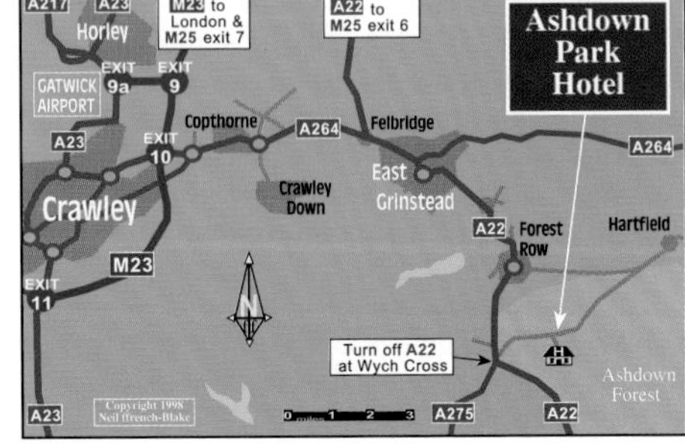

Beauport Park Hotel

Battle Road, Hastings, East Sussex
TN38 8EA
Tel: (01424) 851222; Fax: (01424) 852465

This fine house was built in 1719 and remodelled by a former Governor of Quebec who named it Beauport after his summer home in Canada. It is unspoiled by its transition from residence to first class hotel and guests will particularly enjoy the three most attractive features - seclusion, the stylish elegance of the interior and the extensive range of leisure facilities. Set at the end of a winding drive in 33 acres of tranquil parkland, you are welcomed by a perfect example of a Georgian country house. The tastefully modernised lounge and bar areas are warmed by open log fires, and the candlelit restaurant, renowned for its cuisine, overlooks the formal Italian and sunken gardens. This year a Victorian conservatory has been added. The bedrooms too are furnished to a high standard and leave nothing to chance in terms of additional luxuries. Beauport is close to the Channel ports and the many attractions of this beautiful part of Britain. Yet in these historic surroundings anyone seeking either peace and quiet or a more active holiday need look no further than this lovely hotel, whose rating of Highly Commended and awards for comfort we found to be fully justified.

Rates: *Single room inc. breakfast from £85. Double room inc. breakfast from £110.* V
Bargain Breaks*: Minimum two night short breaks available all year. A four poster room, dinner & breakfast starts at £77 per night.*

- *25 bedrooms (7 four-poster rms, 7 double, 7 twin, 3 single, 1 suite), all with colour TV + satellite, direct-dial telephone, hairdryer, laundry/valet service, tea/coffee making facilities, trouser press. Non-smoker bedrooms available.*
- *Table d'hôte dinner £24. A la carte, lunch & special diets available. Last orders 9.30 pm*

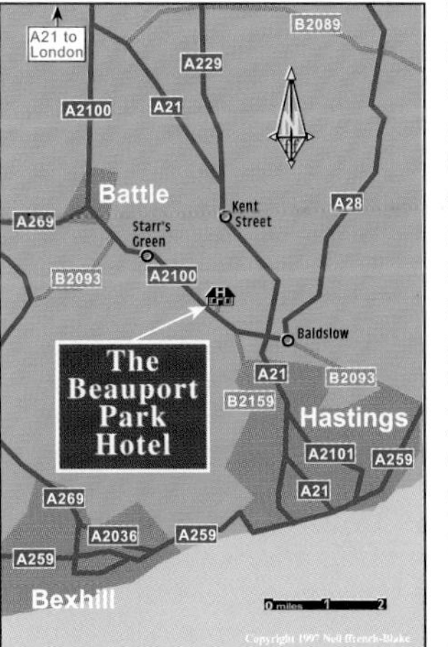

- *Golf, riding, outdoor swimming pool, tennis.*
- *Full business services inc, 3 meeting rooms - capacity 70. Car parking for 60.*
- *Open all year. Major credit cards accepted.*

Rye 11, Lewes 29, Brighton 37, Folkestone 37, London 65

Flackley Ash Hotel

Peasmarsh, Near Rye,
East Sussex TN31 6YH
Tel: (01797) 230651; Fax: (01797) 230510

This is one of Sussex' most charming small country house hotels. Rye is only a few miles away with its many historic buildings including the 15th century church, the Ypres Tower, the famous Landgate and Henry James' Georgian residence, Lamb House. Local activities are many and varied, with antique shops, potteries, local crafts and boutiques and a market on Thursdays. Camber Sands, with its beautiful beaches and safe bathing, is only a few miles further on; and of course there are castles, abbeys, a cathedral and many gardens in the locality to be visited.

The hotel has an indoor swimming pool and leisure complex, with whirlpool spa, mini gymnasium, steam room, sun bed, aromatherapy and beautician, sun terrace and croquet lawn. This Georgian house offers its visitors a warm and friendly atmosphere and comfortable en suite bedrooms. The dining room has an AA Rosette for its food. Dishes are interesting and well presented by friendly and willing staff. Most vegetables are locally grown and emphasis is on fresh local fish and seafood.

***Rates**: Room and breakfast from £57.50 sharing twin/double per person per night.* V
***Getaway Breaks** from £72-£87 pppn - min. 2 nights. Winter price buster £130 pp for 3 nights. Summer price buster £198 pp for 3 nights or £310 pp 5 nights; weekly £325-£395.*

- *42 en suite bedrooms, all with direct dial telephone and TV.*
- *Last orders 9.30 p.m.; bar meals available.*
- *Children welcome; dogs accepted; conferences/receptions to 100 max.*
- *Indoor heated swimming pool; leisure centre; sauna; solarium; spa pool; steam room; gymnasium;*
- *Open all year; all major credit cards accepted.*

Rye 3, Hastings 11, Folkestone 29, Dover 36, London 60.

Rye Lodge Hotel

Hilder's Cliff, Rye, East Sussex TN31 7LD
Tel: (01797) 223838; Fax: (01797) 223585
E-mail: info@ryelodge.co.uk
Internet: http://www.ryelodge.co.uk

Rye - Ancient Town of the Cinque Ports. No town in England evokes the atmosphere of medieval times better than Rye with the charm and character of its cobbled streets, picturesque period houses, historic buildings and ancient fortifications. Situated on the East Cliff overlooking the estuary and Romney Marshes, yet within yards of the High Street of this beautifully preserved ancient town, stands Rye Lodge, acclaimed and acknowledged as one of the finest small luxury hotels in Southeast England. Much thought has gone into the décor, furnishing and equipping of the bedrooms and public rooms, creating an oasis of tranquillity and comfort for guests. The Terrace Restaurant is elegant, candlelit and its fine cellar houses some rare vintages. The hotel is centrally located, so that all antique shops, art galleries etc are within walking distance. This delightful privately owned hotel is run by the de Courcy family. It offers a degree of comfort and personal service rarely found in hotels these days and only achieved by experienced hoteliers through hard work and dedication to their art.

***Rates**: Single room with breakfast from £49.50-75; double room with breakfast £65-110.* V
***Short Breaks**: Midweek Short Breaks - any 2 nights dinner room & breakfast from £55-85 pppn. Mini Holidays - 3 nights+ from £52.50-82.50 pppn dinner b&b.*

● *20 en suite bedrooms with radio, colour TV, direct-dial telephone; hairdryer, laundry service, tea/coffee making facilities; de luxe rooms with video films, trouser press & room safe.*
● *A la carte and table d'hôte (£22.50) dinner - last orders 21.00. Special diets available. Ω 20.*
● *Swimming pool, sauna, jacuzzi & spa bath.*
● *Open all year. Amex, Diners, Mastercard, Visa, Switch & Delta cards accepted.*

Hastings 11, Folkestone 25, Maidstone 33, Dover 32, Brighton 49, London 63.

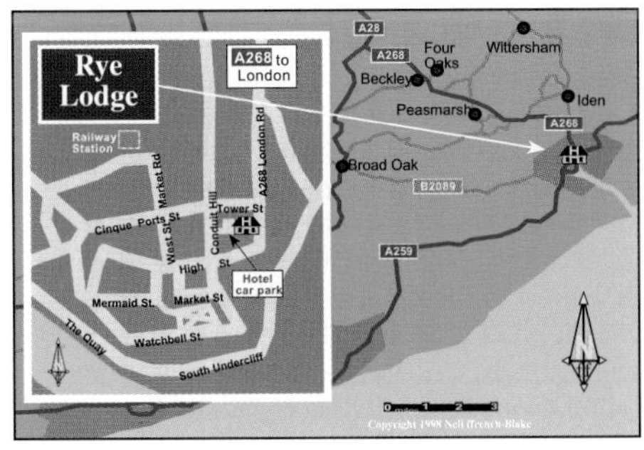

Little Hemingfold Hotel

Telham, Battle, East Sussex
TN33 0TT
Tel: (01424) 774338; Fax: (01424) 775351

This enchanting place answers perfectly to the description of a farmhouse hotel. The home of Allison and Paul Slater, this part 17th century and part Victorian building is situated well away from a busy road down a half mile track in a world of its own, comprising 40 acres of farm and woodland with a two-acre spring-fed trout lake. The warmth of the welcome is matched by the comfortable furnishings of the lounges and a cosy bar area. The beamed candlelit dining-room serves an ample farmhouse breakfast as well as a freshly prepared 4-course dinner using home grown fruits and vegetables in a daily changing menu. The personal touch and the charm extend to the individually designed bedrooms. In these magical surroundings, you could remain happily undisturbed and quietly spoiled for many weeks.

Rates: *Single room inc breakfast from £38;double from £76.Weekly terms from £52 pppn, dinner b&b*
Bargain Breaks: *2 nights dinner, b&b £56-58 pppn*

- *12 en suite bedrooms, all with radio, colour TV,* V *direct dial telephone, hairdryer, laundry/valet service, tea/coffee making facilities, radio/alarm clock.*
- *Table d'hôte 4 courses £22.50; last orders 7.00 pm.*
- *Fishing, boating, swimming in the lake, grass tennis court, boules. Squash, riding & golf nearby.*
- *Closed Jan 2nd-Feb 10th* ● *Dogs welcome.*
- *Access, Visa, Amex & Mastercard accepted.*

Hastings 6½, Maidstone 30, Brighton 34, Folkestone 43, London 56.

Thanington Hotel

140 Wincheap, Canterbury, Kent
CT1 3RY. Tel: (01227) 453227;
Fax: (01227) 453225;
E-mail: Thanington_hotel@compuserve.com
Internet: http://www.thanington-hotel.co.uk

Originally a Georgian farmhouse listed Grade II for its architectural interest, Thanington became an hotel in 1987. Guests can enjoy a quiet drink in the bar or drawing room or sample the delightful walled garden - a real suntrap in the summer months. The indoor heated swimming pool is open all year round and, for the less energetic, there is the snooker room, darts board and various board games. The hotel is just a ten-minute stroll to Canterbury city centre and its host of cosmopolitan restaurants, shops and magnificent cathedral. It is close to the seaside towns and famous castles and houses of Kent and gives convenient access to the Channel terminals. Accommodation is modern and attractive with superior double rooms having queen size four posters or antique Victorian bedsteads.

Rates: *Standard double or twin room with breakfast £69-89.*
Bargain Breaks: *2 persons for 2 nights Jan-Mar £130-£150, Apr-Dec £135-160.*

- *15 en suite bedrooms with radio, colour TV, direct dial telephone, hairdryer, tea/coffee making facilities, trouser press, personal safe. Non-smoker rooms avail.*
- *Snooker room, indoor swimming pool.*
- *Open all year. Access, Diners, Visa & Amex credit cards accepted.*

Ashford 14, Dover 15, Margate 15, Folkestone 16, Maidstone 27, London 58.

Walletts' Court Country House Hotel

Westcliffe, St Margaret's Bay, Dover,
Kent CT15 6EW
Tel: (01304) 852424; Fax: (01304) 853430
E-mail: WallettsCourt@compuserve.com
Internet: http://www.WallettsCourt.com

This lovely old country manor house set in beautiful grounds is located just outside St. Margaret's and dates back to the Domesday Book but is essentially a celebration of a former Elizabethan era. The earlier part is explained on a frieze and the rest is evident in the atmosphere of the house. Built in 1627, it has many unusual features: carved wooden porch, ancient staircase, original wall-painting, even a priesthole, and historical associations with such eminent figures as Queen Eleanor of Castille, Gibbon and Pitt. Today Walletts'Court testifies to the Oakley Family philosophy of making a home of the place they discovered 22 years ago. The Conservatory is a breakfast room with views across the North Downs. The beamed, candlelit restaurant is an award-winning gourmets' paradise, which offers deliciously robust and hearty cuisine with menus changing regularly to incorporate fresh seasonal ingredients. The bedrooms are divided between the main house and converted barns whose comfortably furnished rooms are named according to original usage such as *Dairy* or *Stable*. There are four luxury bedrooms: the *William Pitt*, the *Sir Edward de Burgh*, the *Lord Aylmer* rooms and *Crèvecoeur's* Tower. Guests will also enjoy the Romanesque indoor pool and spa. The Elizabethans built to last; happily enjoyment of all good things from that era lives on in Walletts' Court.

***Single** room, inc. breakfast from £70;* V
***double** room inc. breakfast from £80;*
***Bargain breaks**: 2 nights inc. dinner for two £240*

● *15 en suite bedrooms with colour TV, direct-dial telephone, hairdryer, laundry/valet service, tea/coffee making facilities, radio alarm clock.*
● *Table d'hôte & à la carte dinner in AA restaurant; last orders 2030 hrs; special diets avail.*
● *Croquet, fishing, tennis, indoor swimming pool, jacuzzi, sauna & steam rooms. Golf 6 m, sea 1 mile*
● *Open all year. Visa, Amex, Mastercard, Switch accepted.*

Folkestone 7, Canterbury 15, Margate 20, London 74

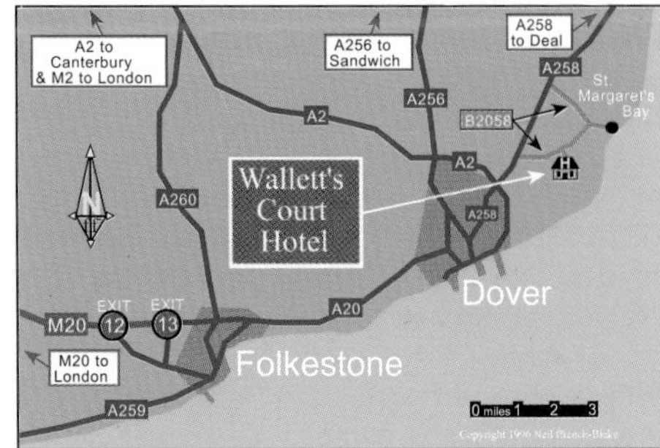

Stade Court Hotel

West Parade, Hythe, Kent CT21 6DT
Tel: (01303) 268263; Fax: (01303) 261803
E-mail: stadecourt@marstonhotels.co.uk
Internet: http://www.marstonhotels.co.uk

Standing proudly on the seafront of the picturesque Cinque Port of Hythe stands Stade Court, which has been welcoming both business and leisure guests to this historic corner of Kent since 1938 and is thus nearly as old as *Signpost* itself! It provides a quieter and pleasing alternative to its big sister, the Hythe Imperial, just 600 yards away, for those who prefer smaller hotels and the personal service they provide. Many of the 42 beautifully furnished en suite bedrooms, including five family rooms, have lounges with views directly overlooking the Channel. Stade Court's charming location features a promenade along the beach and is a popular fisherman's haunt. Fresh local seafood is regularly featured on the menu in the award-winning Lukin Restaurant where a wide selection of quality wines at favourable prices are also available. Complimentary access is allowed to the excellent leisure facilities at the nearby Hythe Imperial, including a 9-hole golf course and a beauty parlour. The hotel is well situated for visits to Dover Castle and the White Cliffs Experience, the Romney, Hythe and Dymchurch Light Railway; also Howletts and Port Lympne wild animal parks.

Rates: *Single room and breakfast from £75.00; double room inc. breakfast from £105.00.* V
Bargain breaks: *Marston breaks - 2 nights dinner, b&b per person sharing from £62 per night; Romantic Breaks from £71.00; Golfing Breaks from £69.50.*

● *42 en suite bedrooms with colour TV + satellite, direct-dial telephone, hairdryer, laundry service, minibar, tea/coffee making facilities, 24 hr room/meal service, music/radio/alarm clock, trouser press, safety deposit box.*

● *Table d'hôte dinner £20.00; à la carte, lunch & special diets available; last orders 9.30 pm.*

● *Business services inc 4 meeting rooms, capacity 40*

● *Billiards, croquet, gymnasium, golf, indoor games, jacuzzi, massage, sauna, squash, indoor swimming pool & tennis all available 600 metres at Hythe Imperial Hotel. Car rental and parking for 12.*

● *Open all year; Visa, Mastercard, Diners and Amex accepted.*

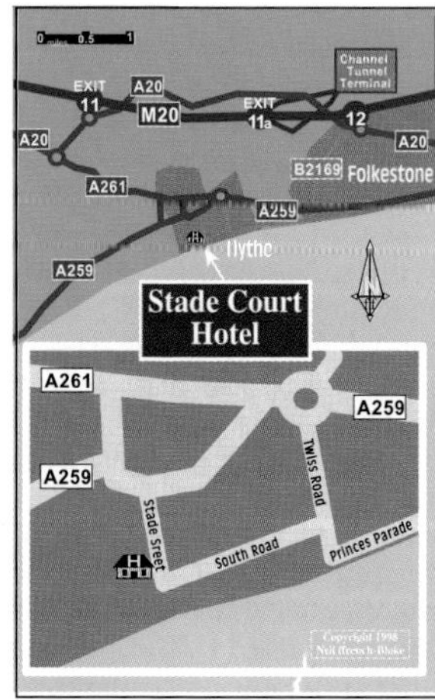

Folkestone 5, Ashford 11, Canterbury 17, Rye 21, London 66.

Coulsdon Manor

Coulsdon Court Road, Old Coulsdon.
Nr. Croydon, Surrey CR5 2LL
Tel: (020) 8668 0414; Fax: (020) 8668 3118
E-mail: coulsdonmanor@marstonhotels.co.uk
Internet: http://www.marstonhotels.co.uk

Set in 140 acres of beautiful Surrey parkland, a large part of it laid down as a challenging 18-hole golf course, yet just 15 miles from both central London and Gatwick and easily accessible to the motorway network. Built for Thomas Byron in the 1850s and sympathetically restored, inside you will discover a country house flavour reflected in beautiful woodwork and chandeliers. Relax in the lounge or bars and soak up the atmosphere as it is now and imagine how life was at Coulsdon Manor over 100 years ago. Dine in the award winning Manor House restaurant or choose lighter fare in the popular Terrace Bar. Many of the 35 bedrooms have views over the golf course. Coulsdon Manor is an ideal base from which to explore many places of interest. Children of all ages will enjoy Thorpe Park and Chessington World of Adventures. Croydon Palace, Wisley RHS Gardens, Wakehurst Place and Hever Castle are also near at hand. As well as golf, many other activities are available at Coulsdon and there are five conference rooms which can cater for up to 180 delegates.

Single *room with breakfast from £108;* **V**
Double *room including breakfast from £137.*
Leisure Breaks*: 2-night Marston Breaks, dinner, b&b £77.50 per head; Romantic Break £96.50 per head; Golfing Break inc 2 rounds per person £97. Special Xmas/New Year/Bank Holiday breaks avail. 5 nights d,b&b £362.50; 7 nts £465.*

● *35 en suite bedrooms with colour TV+ satellite, direct-dial telephone, hairdryer, laundry service, tea/coffee making facilities, minibar, 24-hr room/meal service, radio, safety deposit box, trouser press. Non-smoker bedrooms available.*

● *Table d'hote dinner £26. A la carte, lunch & special diets available. Last orders 21.30.*

● *Fitness centre, golf, sauna/solarium, squash, tennis. Riding, dry ski slope, water park nearby.*

● *Business services inc 9 meeting rooms - cap. 175.*

● *Open all year. All major credit cards accepted.*

Croydon 6, M25 Motorway 6, Gatwick Airport 15, Central London 15

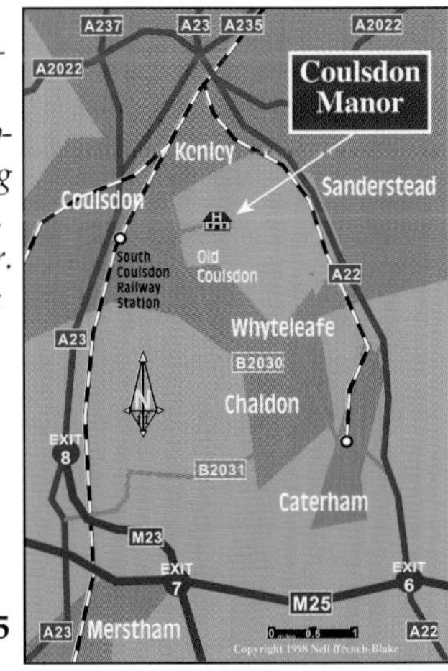

Chase Lodge Hotel

10 Park Road, Hampton Wick, Kingston-upon-Thames, Surrey KTl 4AS
Tel: (0181) 943 1862;
Fax:(0181) 943 9363

The Stafford Haworths own and personally run this extremely popular little gem of an hotel, situated just 20 minutes from the heart of London and the same distance from Heathrow. Chase Lodge has been cleverly amalgamated from two old cottages dating from 1870 and is situated in a quiet street adjacent to Bushy Park and very near Hampton Court Palace. Each bedroom is different (one has a four-poster) and decorated with charm and homely colours, which puts the guest immediately at ease. La Cigale restaurant offers imaginative English and French dishes - avocado with crab, langoustine and pernod to start, followed by roast barbary duck or venison casserole in a port and redcurrant sauce being just some examples. Meals are served in the conservatory, which is bordered by the prettiest little floodlit courtyard garden. Light bar snacks can be enjoyed in the adjoining sitting room. Chase Lodge is becoming increasingly popular with business people and overseas visitors who do not wish to be in Central London. I too can thoroughly recommend it to anyone who is looking for good food and the comfort and personal service of a small family-run hotel.

***Single** room and breakfast from £65 inc.VAT.* V
***Double** room with breakfast from £71 (inc VAT).*
***Bargain breaks:** Discounts available for stays of 3 nights or more. Also Xmas/New Year programmes.*

● *12 en suite bedrooms, all with direct dial telephone and TV + satellite; tea/coffee making facilities; room service; baby listening; night service.*

● *Dinner from £16 per head (inc VAT); last orders 10.00 p.m; bar meals; special diets.*

● *Children welcome; dogs accepted.*

● *Gymnasium 500 yds; tennis $\frac{1}{2}$ mile; indoor heated swimming pool, leisure centre, squash, golf and riding 1 $\frac{1}{2}$ miles; ample parking.*

● *Open all year. All major credit cards accepted.*

AA ★ ★ ★

Hampton Court $1\frac{1}{2}$, Kew Gardens 4, London 7, Wimbledon 7, Heathrow 8.

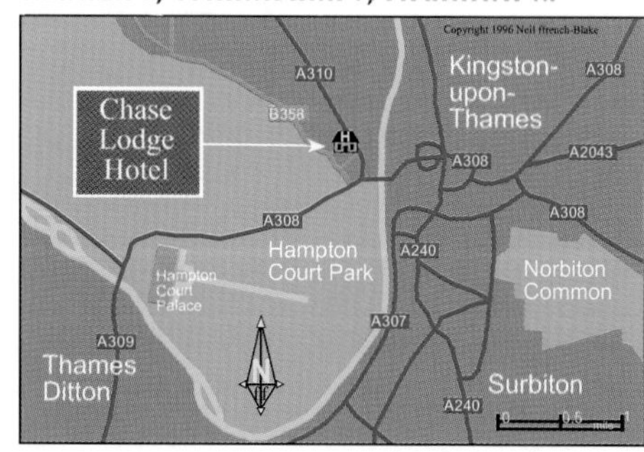

SIGNPOST'S RECOMMENDED AGENT FOR HOTEL SALES & VALUATIONS

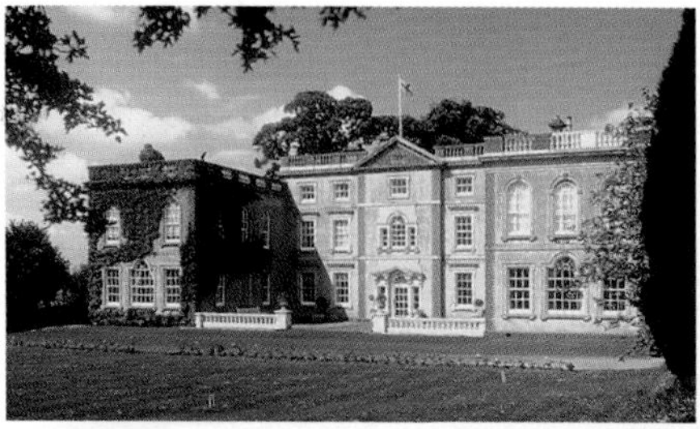

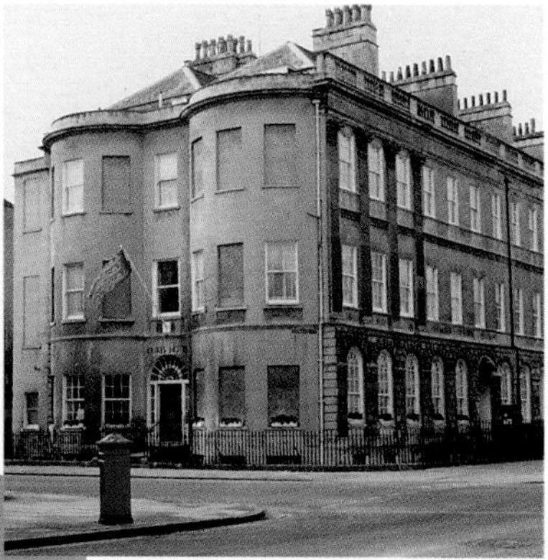

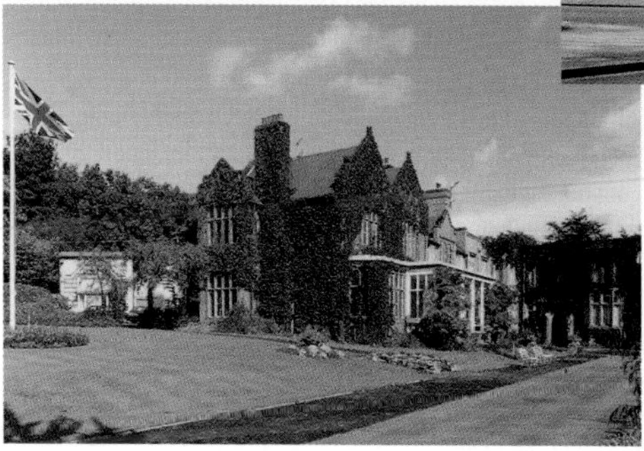

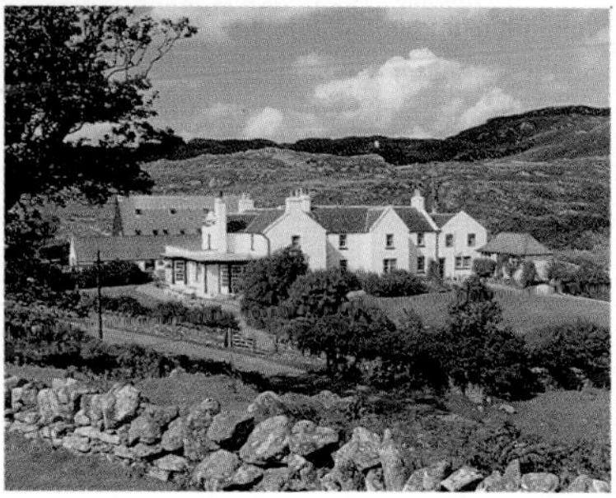

ROBERT BARRY & Co

HOTEL, LEISURE & LICENSED PROPERTY SPECIALISTS

LONDON	CIRENCESTER	PLYMOUTH	HARROGATE	EDINBURGH
020 7 344 6666	01285 641642	01752 664499	01423 566362	0131 225 2944
l@robertbarry.co.uk	c@robertbarry.co.uk	p@robertbarry.co.uk	h@robertbarry.co.uk	e@robertbarry.co.uk

www.robertbarry.co.uk

Associated Offices: HONG KONG • SINGAPORE

Oatlands Park Hotel

Oatlands Drive, Weybridge, KT13 9HB
Tel: (01932) 847242; Fax: (01932) 842252
E-mail: oatlandspark@btinternet.com

This majestic hotel is set in acres of parkland overlooking Broadwater Lake in the heart of the Surrey countryside, yet is only a 25-minute train journey to central London. Records show that Henry VIII had his hunting lodge on the estate; it was used by many subsequent monarchs and rebuilt as a country residence for the Duke and Duchess of York until 1820. It became an hotel in 1856, patronised by many famous writers such as Zola, Lear and Trollope, and today the historic character remains very apparent. You pass through the porticoed entrance into the splendid galleried lounge, with marble columns and tapestries under a large glass dome, where refreshments and light meals are served throughout the day. The lounge bar and Broadwater Restaurant are equally stylish offering table d'hôte and à la carte menus, and a particularly popular traditional Sunday lunch. The bedrooms are designed to high standards of comfort. The hotel has everything for the leisure guest but also excels as a conference venue with an expert staff and a variety of rooms equipped for every need. The awards won for customer care, whether corporate or leisure, are much in evidence and Oatlands Park's standards remain second to none.

***Single** room with breakfast from £117.50;* V
***Double** room with breakfast from £165;*
***Bargain Breaks:** Weekend rates available from £45 per person per night, bed & full Eng. b'fast*

● *136 en suite bedrooms (59 double, 48 twin, 26 single, 3 suites, all with colour TV + satellite, direct-dial telephone, hairdryer, laundry/valet service, tea/coffee-making facilities, 24 hour room/meal service, music/radio/alarm clock, safety deposit box, trouser press; non-smoker bedrooms available.*

● *Broadwater Restaurant table d'hôte £26; last orders 9.30 pm; à la carte, lunch & special diets available.*

● *Business centre inc. meeting rooms for 300.*

● *Croquet, gym, 9-hole golf course. Car parking for 100.*

● *Open all year. All major credit cards accepted.*

Woking 7, Kingston-upon Thames 8, Bagshot 11, Epsom 12, London 18.

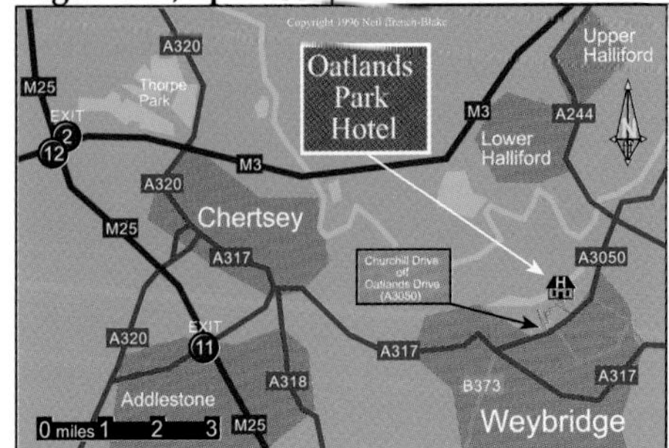

Historic Houses, Gardens & Parks

Bedfordshire
Luton Hoo, Luton
The Swiss Garden, Old Warden
Woburn Abbey, Woburn
Wrest Park House & Garden, Silsoe

Cambridgeshire
Anglesey Abbey Nr. Cambndge
Chilford Hundred Vineyard, Linton
Docwra's Manor Garden, Shepreth
Elton Hall, Elton, Peterborough
Hinchingbrooke House, Huntingdon
Kimbolton Castle
Peckover House, Wisbech
University of Cambridge Botanic Garden

Essex
Audley End House & Park, Saffron Walden
BBC Essex Garden, Abridge
Bridge End Gardens, Saffron Walden
Felsted Vineyard
New Hall Vineyards, Purleigh
Ingatestone Hall
Layer Marney Tower
Priory Vineyards, Little Dunmow
RHS Garden, Rettendon, Chelmsford

Hertfordshire
Ashridge Estate, Nr. Berkhampstead
Cedars Park Waltham Cross
The Gardens of the Rose, Chiswell Green, St Albans
Hatfield House

Knebworth House
The National Trust Wimpole Hall, Arrington, Nr. Royston
Priory Gardens, Royston
Verulamium Park, St Albans

Norfolk
Beeston Hall, Beeston St Lawrence
Bickling Hall
Fairhaven Garden Trust, South Walsham
Felbrigg HallFritton Lake Countryworld
Holkham Hall, Wells-next-the-Sea
Sandringham
Hoveton Hall Gardens, Wroxham
Mannington Gardens, Norwich
Norfolk Lavender Ltd, Heacham
Rainham Hall and Gardens, Tasburgh

Suffolk
Blakenham Woodland Garden, Nr Ipswich
Bruisyard Vineyard and Herb Centre
Euston Hall, Thetford
Haughley Park
Helmingham Hall Gardens
Kentwell Hall, Long Melford
Melford Hall, Long Melford
Somerleyton Hall & Gardens

Walks & Nature Trails

Bedfordshire
Greensand Ridge Walk from Leighton Buzzard to Gamlingay
Upper Lea Valley Walk, from Leagrave Common to E Hyde

Cambridgeshire
Bishops Way, north of Ely
Devil's Dyke, from north of Feach to south of Stechworth
Grafham Water Circular

Hertfordshire
The Lea Valley Walk, from Ware to Stanborough Lakes
Tring Reservoirs

Lincolnshire
Chambers Farm Wood Forest Nature Reserve, Aply, Lincoln
Hartwholme Country Park, Lincoln
Tattershall Park Country Club, Tattershall, Lincoln

Norfolk
Peddars Way & Norfolk Coast Path with Weavers Way
Marriott's Way, between Norwich & Aylsham

Suffolk
Constable Trail
Painters Way from Sudbury to Manningtree
Suffolk Coastal Path, from Bawdsey to Kessingland

East of England

Suffolk Way, from Flatford to Lavenham

Historical Sites & Museums

Bedfordshire
Bunyan Museum, Bedford
Elstow Moot Hall, Church End
Stockwood Craft Museum & Gardens
Shuttleworth Collection, Biggleswade

Cambridgeshire
Ely Cathedral
Imperial War Museum, Duxford
Fitzwilliam Museum, Cambridge
Oliver Cromwell's House, Ely
Cromwell Museum, Huntingdon

Essex
Central Museum and Planetarium, Southend-on-Sea
Colchester Castle
Hedingham Castle, Castle Hedingham
Maritime Museum, Harwich
National Motorboat Museum, Pitsea
Working Silk Museum, Braintree

Hertfordshire
Berkhamsted Castle
Hertford Castle
Roman Baths, Welwyn Garden City
Roman Theatre, St Albans
Verulamium Museum, St Albans

Lincolnshire
Bishop's Palace, Lincoln
Bolingbroke Castle, Spilsby
Lincoln Castle
Lincoln Guildhall
Woolsthorpe Manor, Nr. Grantham
The Incredibly Fantastic Old Toy Show, Lincoln

Norfolk
100th Bomb Group Memorial Mu seum, Dickleburgh
Alby Lace Museum and Study Centre
Ancient House Museum, Thetford
Bygones Collection, Holkham Hall,
Wells-next-the-Sea Bygone Heritage
Villa, Burgh St Margaret
Charles Burrell Museum, Thetford
City of Norwich Aviation Museum, Horsham St Faith
Maritime Museum, Great Yarmouth
Muckleburgh Collection, Weybourne
Shrine of our Lady of Walsingham, Walsingham
Wolverton Station Museum
Tales of the Old Gaol House, King's Lynn

Suffolk
Bridge Cottage, Flatford
Dunwich Underwater Exploration Exhibition, Orford
Framlingham Castle
Gainshorough's House, Sudbury
Guildhall of Corpus Christi, Lavenham
Moot Hall & Museum, Aldeburgh
National Horse Racing Museum, Newmarket
Sizewell Visitors Centre, Sizewell B Power Station
Sue Ryder Foundation Museum, Cavendish
Tolly Cobbold Brewery, Ipswich
Woodbndge Museum

Entertainment Venues

Bedfordshire
Stagsden Bird Gardens
Whipsnade Wild Animal Park, Dunstable
Woburn Safari Park, Woburn

Cambridgeshire
Grays Honey Farm, Warboys
Hamerton Wildlife Centre
Linton Zoo
Peakirk Waterfowl Gardens Trust, Peterborough
Sacrewell Farm & Country Centre, Thornhaugh

Essex
Colchester Zoo
Dedham Rare Breed Farm
Layer Marney Tower
Mole Hall Wildlife Park, Widdington
Southend Sea Life Centre

Hertfordshire
Maltings Centre, St Albans
Paradise Wildlife Farm, Broxbourne
Water Hall Farm & Craft Centre, Nr. Hitchin

Lincolnshire
Brandy Wharf Cider Centre, Gainsborough
Battle of Britain Memorial Flight, RAF Coningsby, Lincoln
The Butterfly & Falconry Park, Long Sutton
Skegness Natureland Sea Sanctuary, Skegness
Cobb Hall Craft Centre, Lincoln

Norfolk
Banham Zoo
Kingdom of the Sea, Great Yar mouth
Norfolk Wildlife Centre & Country Park, Great Witchingham
Otter Trust, Earsham
Park Farm & Norfolk Farmyard Crafts Centre, Snettisham
Pensthorpe Waterfowl Park
Thrigby Hall Wildlife Gardens, Filby

Suffolk
East of England Birds of Prey and
Conservation Centre, Laxfield
Suffolk Wildlife Park, Kessingland

DIARY OF EVENTS

February

3-6*. **Springfields Horticultural Exhibition,** Spalding, Lincs. Indoor spring flowers.
18-20*. **Motorbike 2000.** Springfields, Spalding, Lincs. 2-wheeled show for the road.
26-5 Mar*. **Bedfordshire Festival of Music, Speech & Drama.** Corn Exchange, St Paul's Sq, Bedford

March

5-2 April. **Lambing Sunday and Spring Bulb Days.** Kentwell Hall, Long Melford, Suffolk
13-7 May. **World of Flowers.** Springfields Show Gardens, Camelgate, Spalding, Lincs.
20-21*. **National Shire Horse Show.** East of England Showground, Alwalton, Nr. Peterborough, Cambs.

April

8-9. **Thriplow Daffodil Weekend.** Thriplow, Cambs.
15. **Easter Fayre.** Southend High Street, Southend-on-Sea
29-May 1. **Spalding Flower Festival and Springfields Country Fair.** Springfields, Camelgate, Spalding, Lincs.

May

5-7. **2000 Guineas/1000 Guineas Classic Race Meeting**. The Racecourse, Newmarket, Suffolk.
1*.**Stilton Cheese Rolling/May Day**. North St, Stilton,Cambs
1-2*. **Knebworth County Show.** Knebworth House, Hertfordshire.
2-4*. **Horse Racing: The Guineas Meeting.** Racecourse, Newmarket, Suffolk.
12-28. **Bury St Edmunds Festival.** Various venues in Bury St. Edmunds, Suffolk.
14. **The Colchester Classic Vehicle Show**. Colchester Institute, Sheepen Road.
18-22*. **Tallington Beer Festival/Steam & Country Festival,**Tallington, Lincs.
28-30*. **Fellbrigg Coast & Country Craft Fair.** Fellbrigg Hall, Norfolk.
29. **Luton International Carnival.** Luton, Beds.
27-28*. **Air Fete 2000.** RAF Mildenhall, Suffolk.
27-28*.**Herts County Show.** Redbourn, Herts.
31-1 June. **Suffolk Show**. Suffolk Showgr'd, Ipswich.

June

1-Aug 30*.**Stamford Shakespeare Co 2000 Summer Open Air Season.** Rutland Open Air Theatre, Tolethorpe, Casterton, Leics.
9-11. **Maritime Ipswich.** Ipswich Wet Dock, Town Centre, Ipswich, Suffolk.
9-24*. **53rd Aldeburgh Festival of Music & Arts.** Snape Maltings (and various venues), Aldeburgh, Suffolk. World renowned festival including operas, concerts, recitals etc.
16-18. **East of England Show.** East of England Showground, Alwalton, Cambs.
28-29. **Royal Norfolk Show 2000.** (agricultural) The Showground, Dereham Road, New Costessey, Norwich.
28-July 2*. **Wisbech Rose Fair.** St Peters Church, Wisbech, Cambs.

East of England

East of England Tourist Board area encompasses the predominantly agricultural counties of Bedfordshire, Hertfordshire, Norfolk, Suffolk, Cambridgeshire and Essex. Norfolk is thickly afforested in the west around Thetford, whereas the east is crisscrossed by waterways and Lakes known as *The Broads* - the remains of medieval man's peat diggings.

The county town of Norfolk and informal capital of East Anglia is the university city of Norwich, whose fine cathedral with walls decorated with biblical scenes dates from 1046. There are 30 medieval churches in central Norwich dominated by Norwich Castle Museum. Brideswell Museum and Church Museum should also not be missed.

Near King's Lynn in the northwest of the county is Sandringham, royal palace bought for King Edward VII while prince of Wales by Queen Victoria in 1862. Rising above the fens south of Kings Lynn is the magnificent 11th century Ely Cathedral, built on the site of a 7th century Benedictine Abbey.

East Suffolk's coast with its inlets and estuaries is popular with yachtsmen. Framlingham Castle, near Aldeburgh, stands intact since the 13th century. The hills and river valleys surrounding the Suffolk-Essex border open up to magnificent skies, captured in paintings by Constable and Gainsborough. Heart of Constable country is Nayland and Dedham Vale. Fine woollen towns are exemplified by Lavenham, Long Melford and Sudbury, among others.

Cultural capital of East Anglia is the tranquil city of Cambridge whose colleges, dating from the 13th century, were mostly founded as acts of piety. Most are open during daylight hours. Evensong at Kings College Chapel on Sundays is memorable. Rubens' *Adoration of the Magi* hangs there. The Fitzwilliam Museum is one of Europe's treasure houses, housing antiquities from Egypt, Greece and Rome as well as English and Chinese porcelain. Also worth a visit is the University Museum of Archaeology and Anthropology, with emphasis on prehistoric artefacts from the Cambridge area. Cambridge is also a centre for shopping and theatre.

Bedfordshire has the palace and theme park of Woburn to visit and Luton Hoo. Whipsnade open air zoo will appeal particuarly to children.

St Albans in Hertfordshire has Verulamium Roman remains and Hatfield House was the home of Elisabeth I. Tewin Hoo is an example of a small Elizabethan Manor.

July

2. **Ipswich Music Day**. Christchurch Park, Ipswich, Suffolk.
11-13. **Newmarkety July Meeting.** Newmarket Racecourse, Newmarket, Suffolk
14-16. **Weeting Steam Engine Rally**. Fengate Farm, Weeting, Brandon, Suffolk.
20-29*. **Kings Lynn Festival 1999**. Various venues, Kings Lynn, Norfolk.
24*. **Sandringham Flower Show**, Sandringham, Norfolk
29-30. **Basildon Zoo Festival** Wat Tyler Cntry Pk, Pitsea,Esx

August

1-31*. **Snape Proms.** Maltings, Aldeburgh, Suffolk
17-18*. **Thorpeness Regatta & Fireworks**Thorpeness, Sfk
28. **Aylsham Agricultural Show**.Blickling Hall, Norfolk

September

1-4*. **Burghley Horse Trials.** Burghley Park, Stamford, Lincolnshire
22-24*. **Woodhall Spa Festival of Flowers.** Var. venues, Woodhall Spa, Lincs.

October/November

1-16 Oct*. **Norfolk & Norwich Festival 2000.** Various venues, Norwich, Norfolk
12-14 Oct. **Newmarket Champions Meeting.** Suffolk.

** = Provisional Date. For further information contact:*

TOURIST BOARD

East of England Tourist Board. Toppesfield Road, Hadleigh, Suffolk, Suffolk IP7 5DN. Tel: 01473 822922

The Bedford Arms

George Street, Woburn MK17 9PX
Tel: (01525) 290441; Fax: (01525) 290432

The Bedford Arms is part of the Woburn Estate, an area of great historical interest, at the heart of which lies Woburn Abbey and its magnificent 3000-acre deer park and safari park, both open to the public. This Georgian former coaching inn has been superbly modernised, yet retains its old world charm. The timber beamed Tavistock Bar, with its horse brasses and racing memorabilia from the estate's Bloomsbury Stud, specialises in conditioned ale and serves excellent bar meals and snacks. Hollands Restaurant, named after the architect of the hotel and much of Woburn Abbey, has a local reputation for its high standards of cuisine and service. All the bedrooms have been beautifully refurbished. There are a number of executive rooms (one with a four-poster) and a luxurious suite. The hotel is superbly run with quiet efficiency by an excellent team. The village of Woburn has retained most of its quiet Georgian character, yet is convenient for Milton Keynes, Bedford, Luton and London. I strongly recommend the Bedford Arms, especially for a Weekend Break. Woburn Abbey is on the doorstep and there are three major golf courses nearby.

Rates: *Single room with breakfast from £120.* V
Double room inc. breakfast from £138.
Weekend Breaks: *Dinner, b & b from £65 per person per night, two people sharing*

- *53 en suite bedrooms, all with colour TV+ satellite, direct-dial telephone, hairdryer, laundry/valet service, minibar, tea-coffee making facilities, 24-hour room/meal service, radio/alarm clock, safety deposit box, trouser press. Non-smoker bedrooms available. Car parking for 80.*
- *Table d'hôte £19.95. A la carte, lunch & special diets available. Last orders 10 pm.*
- *Golf one mile; riding, squash, swimming, leisure centre within 5 miles; sailing, shooting 10 miles.*
- *Business services inc 2 meeting rooms, cap'y 50*
- *Open all year. All major credit cards accepted.*

M1 (junc 13) 4, Milton Keynes 6, Dunstable 9, Bedford 13, London 43.

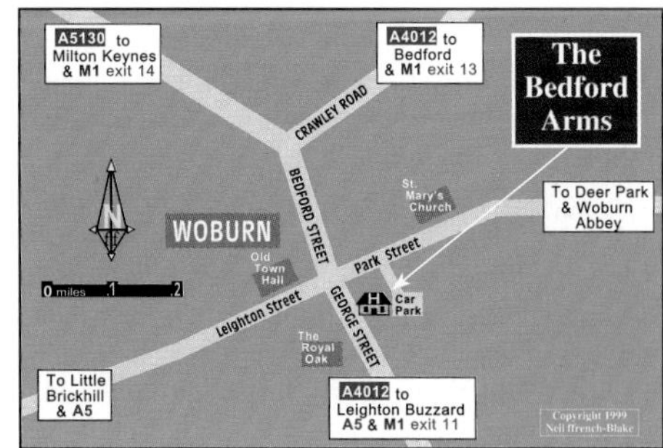

Arundel House Hotel

Chesterton Road, Cambridge CB4 3AN
Tel: (01223) 367701; Fax: (01223 367721)

The Arundel House Hotel occupies one of the finest sites in the City of Cambridge, overlooking the River Cam and open parkland. It is only a short walk across the park known as Jesus Green to the city centre with its wealth of historic buildings. The hotel is well known for its bar and restaurant. The bright, cheerful colours in the bar, coupled with beautiful chintz curtains, comfortable sofas and armchairs, sumptuous carpeting and leather bound books create a warm and refreshing atmosphere. With its magnificent Victorian-style bar, carved out of solid American red oak, and two beautiful fireplaces, it is a comfortable setting for a pre-dinner drink.
The restaurant has a reputation for providing some of the best food in the area. All tastes are catered for, thanks to the several different menus on offer, all featuring a wide range of imaginative dishes, freshly prepared in the hotel's award winning kitchen. As an alternative to the restaurant, there is a Victorian style conservatory, providing a luscious green environment. The Conservatory is open all day and offers a wide range of different options from cooked meals to cream teas, all of which can also be served in the hotel's secluded garden (weather permitting).

Single room *with breakfast from £47.* V
Bargain Breaks*: £110 per person sharing for two nights dinner, bed & breakfast. Singles £100 2 nts*

● *105 bedrooms, 102 en suite with colour TV, direct-dial telephone, hairdryer, tea-coffee making facilities, radio/alarm clock. Non-smoker bedrooms available.* ● *Car parking for 70.* ● *Open all year.*
● *Table d'hôte £15.95. Table d'hôte lunch, à la carte, special vegetarian and children's menu also available. Last orders 9.30 pm restaurant, 10 pm conservatory.*
● *Three meeting rooms, maximum capacity 50.*
● *Visa, Mastercard, Amex, Diners accepted.*

Newmarket 13, Ely 16, Stansted 26, Ipswich 54. Norwich 61. London 55.

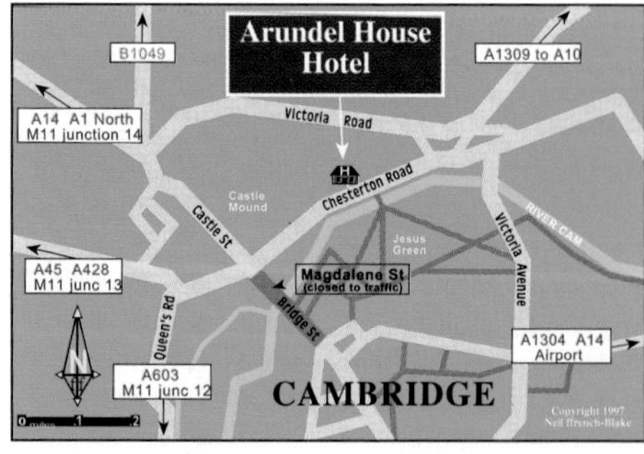

Redcoats Farmhouse Hotel

Redcoats Green, Nr. Hitchin,
Hertfordshire SG4 7JR
Tel: (01438) 729500; Fax: (01438) 723322
E-mail:priory@redcoats.co.uk
Internet: http://www.redcoats.co.uk

Near Little Wymondley village, set amidst rolling Hertfordshire countryside, yet only a few minutes from the A1, lies the 15th century Redcoats Farmhouse. It has been in the Butterfield family for generations and in 1971 Peter and his sister Jackie Gainsford converted the building into an hotel. Today it retains its relaxed and easy going country atmosphere. The bedrooms, where pictures abound, are in the main house or in the adjacent converted stables, some having exposed beams. One room is particularly suitable for a long stay, opening onto the very pretty country garden, where marquees can be erected for weddings. Three intimate dining rooms and the new conservatory serve outstanding cuisine. Menus are changed every two weeks and include a good choice of delicious dishes such as Danish herring with dill sauce and new potatoes, half a Gressingham duckling with peach and ginger sauce or a Fillet Steak Carpetbagger. Redcoats is ideal for visiting Knebworth or Woburn, Hatfield House or the Shuttleworth Aircraft Collection.

Rates: *Single room with breakfast from £75.* V
Double room inc breakfast from £90.
Bargain Weekend Breaks *from £105 per person for two nights, b & b.*

- *13 en suite bedrooms, 9 ground floor; all with colour TV, direct-dial telephone.*
- *Last dinner orders 9-9.30 pm; children welcome; conferences max. 40; garden suitable for wedding & other marquee receptions.*
- *Tennis one mile; golf $1^1/_2$ miles.*
- *Visa, Mastercard, Amex, Switch accepted.*
- *Closed Dec 24-Jan 3 except Christmas lunch & New Year's Eve dinner.*

A1(M) 1 mile, Hitchin 3, Hatfield 10, Woburn 15, Cambridge 25, London 35.

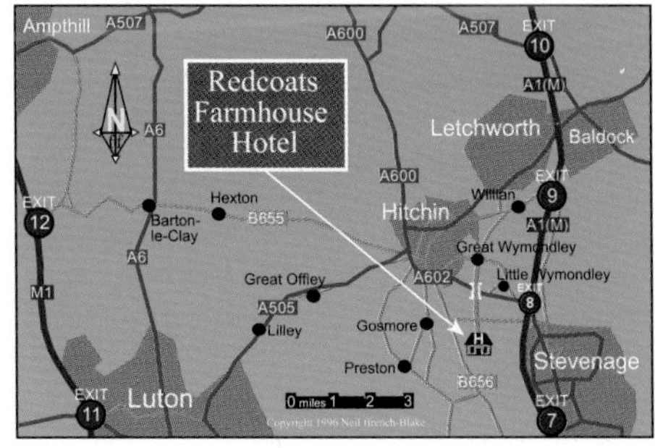

Kenwick Park Hotel

Kenwick Park, Louth LN11 8NR
Tel: (01507) 608806; Fax: (01507) 608027

E-mail: enquiries@kenwick-park-co.uk
Website: www.kenwick-park.co.uk

The Kenwick Park Hotel stands within the grounds of the 350-acre Kenwick Park Estate, itself set in area of outstanding natural beauty. The hotel is approached through a magnificent avenue of majestic broadleaf trees, overlooking the superb and exclusive Kenwick Park Golf Course. For the business user, for golfers or for those who enjoy a health and leisure break, the Kenwick Park is ideal. I was pleased to stay here in early Summer. Rooms are large with spacious bathrooms and you need a session in the leisure club after one of chef Paul Harvey's gourmet meals. I had duck and a *banoffie* (banana and toffee dessert) to follow, which was memorable. The restaurant has two AA rosettes. Paul has twice been placed in the top 10, Northern Region, in the *Potters 500 Chef of the Year* competition. At lunchtime, guests can enjoy a lighter meal in the Keepers Bar, which overlooks the golf course. Louth is a fascinating Georgian market town. The 16th-century Church of St James has the county's tallest spire at 295 ft and the neighbouring Lincolnshire Wolds are host to rare birds and inspired the poetry of Alfred, Lord Tennyson, among others.

***Rates**: Single inc. breakfast from £79.50; double room inc. breakfast £98. Without breakfast - subtract £7.95 per person.*
***Bargain Breaks:** Weekends Oct-April £44 per person per night b &b or £59 per person, dinner, b & b. Summer short breaks £47 pppn b & b; £62 pppn d, b & b. All breaks include full use of the Health & Leisure Club*

- *24 en suite bedrooms (3 suites), all with colour TV + satellite, direct-dial telephone, hairdryer, laundry/valet service, tea/coffee making facilities, 24-hour room/meal service, radio/alarm clock, trouser press. Non smoker bedrooms and rooms for disabled available.*
- *Table d'hôte 3-course dinner £19.50; à la carte, lunch & special diets available; last orders 2115.*
- *Billiards, fitness centre/gym, own 18-hole golf course, indoor games, jacuzzi/whirlpool, massage, sauna/solarium, squash, indoor swimming pool, tennis.*
- *All business services including four meeting rooms with capacity up to 70 and audio-visual facilities. Licensed for civil weddings.*
- *Open all year. All major credit cards accepted.*

Kenwick Woods

The Kenwick Woods development is set amongst glorious mixed mature woodland immediately adjacent to the golf course with 19 acres dedicated to high specification Norwegian log houses. Each unit consists of three bedrooms, open plan lounge, dining and kitchen area, bathroom, utility room and covered verandah. Material is Norwegian spruce, kiln dried and treated and cabins come with a 10-year construction warranty. Kenwick Woods is a 'Second Home' scheme whereby 25 plots are for sale on a 125-year leasehold basis. The purchase of a Kenwick Woods log cabin is seen as an opportunity for investment. Purchasers will then be eligible for Golf Club membership and will be able to use the hotel with its quality health and leisure facilities (see below). As an alternative to purchase, the cabins are available for Timeshare occupation or for short lets.

The Kenwick Park Health & Leisure Club

This club provides some of the best facilities in Lincolnshire. These include an indoor heated swimming pool, sauna, steam room and jacuzzi; also a fully equipped gymnasium and aerobic studio offering a comprehensive range of classes including circuit, step, aerobics, yoga and line dancing. A fitness assessment is available and an individual gym programme suggested before the equipment is used. Additionally there are squash and tennis courts, a games room, sunbed and crèche facilities and a Clarins Health & Beauty Centre (also open to non-members). Here a wide range of beauty treatments are available including aromatherapy, reflexology and sports massage. There is a poolside bar where members and their guests can relax after sessions. Use of the Health and Leisure Club is complementary to guests in the hotel.

Horncastle 13, Grimsby 16, Boston 30, Hull 32, Lincoln 26, London 148.

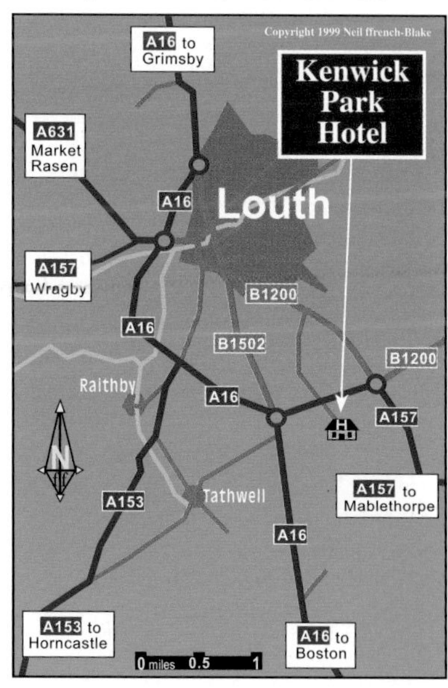

The Links Country Park Hotel & Golf Club

West Runton, Cromer NR27 9QH
Tel: (01263) 838383; Fax: (01263) 838264
E-mail: sales@links-hotel.co.uk

West Runton is an unspoiled hamlet with a sandy beach on the north Norfolk coast, dominated by the Links Hotel and its golf course. The Links is set in 35 acres of lightly wooded coastal parkland in an area of Outstanding Natural Beauty. It makes a first class venue for a family holiday and facilities include an indoor heated swimming pool, sauna, sunbed and solarium. The Links is also popular for wedding receptions and conferences. The dining room has a reputation for excellent cuisine, serving local dishes such as Cromer crabs and lobsters in season, all graced by fine table settings of silver, cut glass and best linen. The Fairways Bar, near the ninth tee of the golf course, offers a cold buffet, grills and snacks. Nearby attractions include bird sanctuaries, Sandringham Royal Estate, the shrines to Our Lady of Walsingham and the North Norfolk Steam Railway. The fine shopping and cultural city of Norwich and the Norfolk Broads, ideal for sailing and walking, are within easy day trip distance.

Rates: *Single room with breakfast from £42.50.* V
Double room inc breakfast from £85.
Bargain Summer Breaks *2 nights b & b from £55 per person per night; Xmas, New Year, Bank Holiday, Halloween breaks also available. Weekly rates from £320 b & b/£410 dinner, b & b.*

- *43 en suite bedrooms, inc suites, all with air conditioning, colour TV+ satellite, direct-dial telephone, hairdryer, laundry service, baby listening, tea/coffee making, radio/alarm clock. Facilities for the disabled. Car parking for 100.*
- *3 bars, grill room & restaurant; tdh £19.95; à la carte, snack lunch (Sunday full lunch) & special diets available; Last orders 9.30 pm.*
- *Full business services inc 3 meeting rms for 150*
- *9-hole golf, tennis, indoor pool, sauna/solarium at hotel; bathing and riding 500/200 yds.*
- *Open all year. Visa, M'card, Amex, Switch accepted*

Cromer 2, Sheringham 2, Norwich 25, Kings Lynn 43, Leicester 118, London 136.

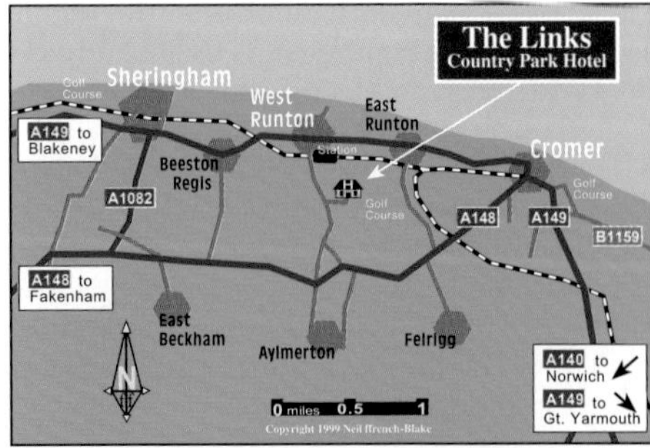

The Hoste Arms

The Green, Burnham Market,
PE31 8HD
Tel: (01328) 738777;
Fax: (01328) 730103
E-mail: thehostearms@compuserve.com
Internet: http://www.hostearms.co.uk

The Hoste Arms has had a chequered past, having been variously a court assizes, an auction house and a brothel. When Paul Whittome bought it in 1989, his aim was to restore it to be the finest inn in England. Combining his love of people, good food and drink, music and art, he has succeeded admirably. The Inn was awarded a *Golden Pillow Award* by The Times and its readers in June 1999, having in February been named by the same newspaper as its *2nd Favourite Hotel in England*. Food and wine are central to the Hoste Arms experience. The delicious menu has Oriental and European influences and uses fresh local produce. The conservatory serves light lunches and breakfasts. All restaurants are air-conditioned. A pianist plays every Friday night in the winter (October to March). An excellent port of call.

Rates: *Single room with breakfast £52-60.* V
Double room inc. breakfast £64-76.
Bargain Breaks: *Dinner, b&b Mon-Thurs two nights from £70 per person.*

- *29 en suite bedrooms (inc 7 suites) all with AC, TV, direct-dial telephone, hairdryer, tea/coffee making, radio/alarm clock, safe, trouser press.* ♿
- *A la carte dinner fm £25; lunch & special diets available; last orders 9.15 pm. Car parking for 50.*
- *Business services inc 3 meeting rooms for 45.*
- *Tennis, bathing, riding, watersports, shooting, sailing all within 6 miles.*
- *Open all year. Mastercard & Visa accepted.*

Fakenham 8, Kings Lynn 20, Norwich 33, London 119.

Elderton Lodge

Gunton Park, Thorpe Market,
North Walsham NR11 8TZ
Tel: (01263) 833547;
Fax: (01263) 834673

Set in the heart of beautiful unspoiled North Norfolk countryside, Elderton Lodge was once the shooting lodge and Dower House to adjacent Gunton Park estate. Pheasant and deer still roam in the neighbouring parkland. According to legend, Lily Langtry entertained Edward VII at Gunton Hall when he was Prince of Wales. There are eleven comfortable individually decorated bedrooms, each with its own character. Public rooms include the Lounge Bar with views across the park, the conservatory and the elegant, candle-lit Restaurant, recognised for fine food. The emphasis is on fresh local produce with fish, lobster and crab from the nearby coast and game in season. Martine and Christine Worby do their utmost to make your stay comfortable, with genuine concern for every guest.

Rates: *Single room with breakfast £57.50* V
Double room inc. breakfast from £90.
Bargain Breaks: *On application.*

- *11 en suite bedrooms all with colour TV, direct-dial telephone, hairdryer, tea/coffee making, radio/alarm clock, trouser press. Non-smoking rooms.*
- *Table d'hôte dinner £25; lunch & special diets available; last orders 9.15 pm. Car parking for 50.*
- *Business services inc 2 meeting rooms for 30.*
- *Fishing, golf, riding, shooting nearby. Dogs welcome*
- *Open all year. Major credit cards accepted.*

North Walsham 3, Cromer 10, Norwich 12, London 123

Wentworth Hotel

Wentworth Road, Aldeburgh IP15 5BD
Tel: (01728) 452312; Fax: (01728) 454343
E-mail: wentworth.hotel@anglianet.co.uk

The Pritt family have been the owners of this charming Victorian hotel for over 75 years and they are continually upgrading and refurbishing it. The Wentworth Hotel is ideally situated on the sea front in the historic town of Aldeburgh, a centre for music lovers worldwide. The atmosphere is very much of a country house. The lounge is beautifully furnished with antiques and decorated in restful yellows and russets, picking out the colours of the elegant Crown Derby china. The walls are hung with a large collection of Russell Flint prints. The cuisine is excellent, offering local produce such as shellfish (the famous Aldeburgh sprats), fresh fish and asparagus. Bedrooms are individually decorated, many overlooking the sea. Each contains a copy of *Orlando the Marmalade Cat*, the childrens' story set in Owlbarrow (Aldeburgh). Superior rooms have king size beds and there is one lovely pine-panelled suite on the ground floor. This is a truly special hotel, with Michael Pritt always on hand to ensure the well-being of guests, many of whom return year after year.

Rates: *Single room with breakfast from £65.*
Double room inc. breakfast from £105.
Bargain Breaks *available throughout the year with specuial value breaks Jan-March and Nov/Dec*

- *37 bedrooms, 35 en suite. all colour TV, direct-dial telephone, tea/coffee making facilities. Non-smoker and disabled bedrooms available.*
- *Restaurant, bar & 2 lounges; table d'hôte from £13.50; lunch and special diets available; last orders 9 pm. Car parking for 30. Meeting room for 14.*
- *Sea adjacent; golf, sailing, tennis nearby. Squash 4m, riding 15m, shooting 10 miles.*
- *All major credit cards accepted.*
- *Closed Dec 28-Jan 7.*

Saxmundham 7, Ipswich 25, Lowestoft 27, Norwich 41, London 103.

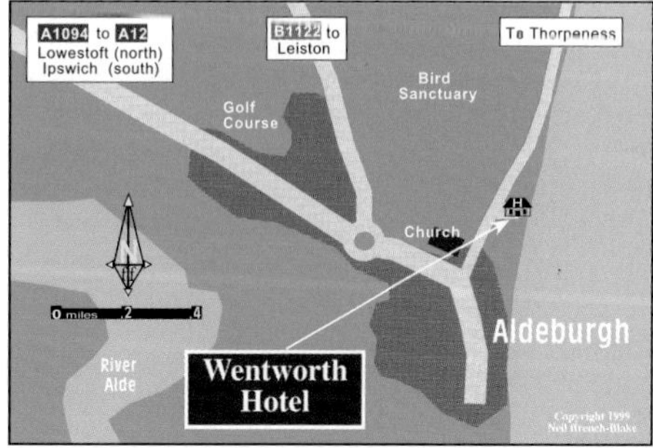

The Angel Hotel

Angel Hill, Bury St Edmunds, IP33 1LT
Tel: (01284) 753926; Fax: (01284) 750092

The Angel, originally a Coaching Inn dating back to 1452, stands in a commanding position overlooking the ancient abbey. For over 400 years, members of the Royal family, artists and renowned writers have stayed here. Charles Dickens wrote part of the Pickwick Papers here, his room still being intact. The advantage of a period hotel like the Angel is that each room is different, very comfortable and beautifully furnished. In the public rooms, the relaxed atmosphere is enhanced by an interesting collection of antiques, art and photographs chronicling the hotel's rich heritage. There is a choice of two restaurants - the Vaults, situated in the 12th century undercroft and reputed to be part of the old Abbey. This provides a unique medieval ambience in which to enjoy moderately priced informal Brasserie-style dishes and special events, such as jazz evenings are held here. The elegant AA two rosette Abbeygate Restaurant offers a more sophisticated type of menu using local produce wherever possible and offering an excellent selection of wines. The Angel is also popular as a meeting and banqueting venue.

Rates: *Single room inc. breakfast from £53; double from £106.* V
Bargain Breaks*: Special Sunday night rate from £25 per person b&b. Fri/Sat nights from £49 pp b&b; dinner, b&b from £69 per person per night.*

- *42 en suite bedrooms (one suite), all with colour TV+satellite, radio/alarm clock, direct-dial telephone, hairdryer, laundry service, tea/coffee making facilities, safety deposit box, 24-hour room/meal service, trouser press.*
- *Table d'hôte dinner £22.95; last orders 9.30 pm. A la carte, lunch and special diets available.*
- *Business centre inc. 4 meeting rooms, capacity 60. Car parking for 60. Car Hire can be arranged.*
- *Fishing, golf, watersports, riding all within 4 m*
- *Open all year. All major credit cards accepted.*

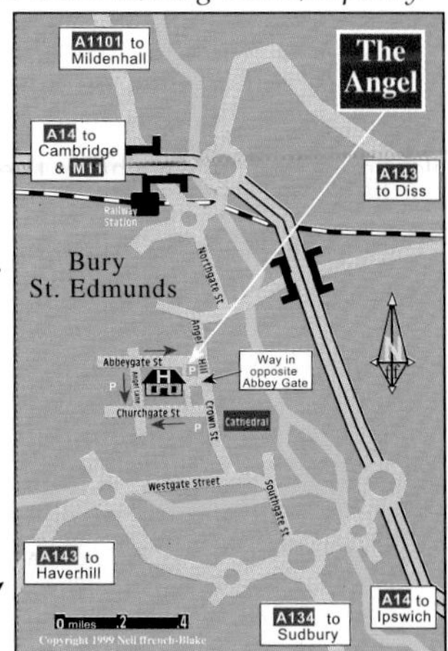

Sudbury 16, Ely 24, Ipswich 26, Harwich 41, Newmarket 14, Cambridge 27, London 79.

Hintlesham Hall

Hintlesham, Nr. Ipswich IP8 3NS
Tel: (01473) 652268; Fax: (01473) 652463
E-mail: reservations@hintlesham-hall.co.uk

I always enjoying visiting Hintlesham Hall - it is like the Jewel in the Crown - one of the loveliest hotels in England, superbly situated in over 175 acres of unspoiled Suffolk countryside - a beautiful building steeped in history. The hotel's magnificent Georgian façade, Elizabethan red brick chimney stacks, splendid carved oak staircase built in the Stuart period and wonderful plasterwork on the ceiling of the Carolean Room, are just some of its architectural delights. The bedrooms vary from Georgian to timbered Tudor, all different and enhanced by elegant fabrics, antiques and works of art and some with four-posters. Dining at Hintlesham is always a treat. Cuisine in the three dining rooms is under the supervision of Head Chef Alan Ford, and the 300-bin wine list includes a good range of New World vintages. Hintlesham has an integrated 18-hole golf course and Leisure Club which makes it popular for corporate events. Guests can wander in the attractive gardens or attend cookery demonstrations which are arranged throughout the year. Constable Country is on the doorstep, and Cambridge and Newmarket are nearby. An excellent spot for a relaxing break, whether travelling on business or pleasure.

Rates: *Single room with breakfast from £89; double room inc. breakfast from £115.*
Short Breaks: *Sun-Thurs from £160 per couple per night, dinner,b&b. Fri/Sat from £190 per couple, min. two nights.*

- *33 en suite bedrooms inc 4 suites, all with TV, direct-dial telephone, hairdryer, laundry service, minibar, 24-hour room service, radio/alarm clock.*
- *Table d'hôte £26.50. A la carte, lunch & special diets available. Last orders 9.30 pm.*
- *4 meeting rooms, capacity 80. Car parking 100.*
- *Billiards/snooker, croquet, fitness centre, golf, whirlpool/sauna/massage, clay shooting, outdoor swimming pool, tennis, beauty salon. Fishing and Riding five miles. Airport pickup by arrangement.*
- *Open all year. All major credit cards accepted.*

Ipswich 5, Hadleigh 5, Colchester 18, Cambridge 45, Norwich 48, London 60.

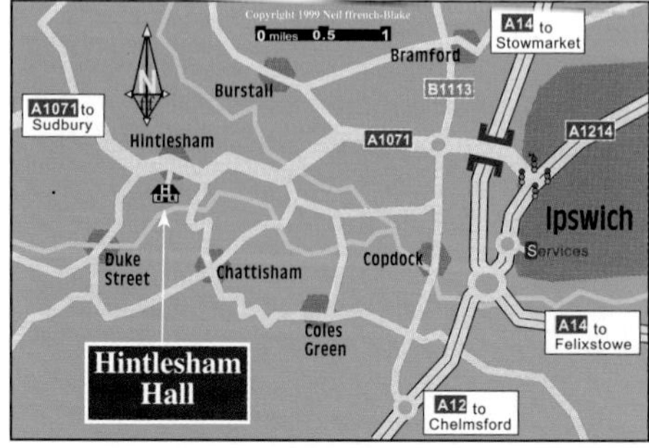

Bedford Lodge Hotel

Bury Road, Newmarket CB8 7BX
Tel: (01638) 663175; Fax: (01638) 667391

Set in three acres of secluded gardens in the heart of Newmarket, the Bedford Lodge Hotel, Conference and Leisure Centre is a striking combination of the classic and the modern. The Georgian hunting lodge was built for the Duke of Bedford in the 18th century. Recent developments, made in keeping with the existing style, have provided more excellent accommodation with all rooms individually decorated to a high standard, making the hotel one of the best appointed in East Anglia. Each bedroom is named after one of the country's racecourses. The Roxana bar provides real ale and an extensive selection of bar meals throughout the day whilst the Restaurant serves excellent menus with an extensive wine list. Throughout the hotel, there are references to the Sport of Kings and Newmarket's unique racing heritage. The extensive leisure and meeting facilities make the Bedford Lodge an ideal location for business and leisure traveller alike.

Rates: *Single room with breakfast from £84 ; double room inc. breakfast from £109.* V
Weekend Breaks: *Based on 2 people sharing min two nights £65 per person per night, dinner,b&b.*

- *56 en suite bedrooms inc 7 suites, all with TV, direct-dial telephone, hairdryer, laundry service, tea-coffee making facilities, minibar, safe, trouser press. Non-smoker bedrooms available.*
- *Table d'hôte £16.95. A la carte, lunch & special diets available. Last orders 9.30 pm.*
- *6 meeting rooms, capacity 200. Car parking 100*
- *Fitness centre, whirlpool/sauna/solarium, indoor swimming pool, beauty salon.*
- *Visa, Mastercard, Amex, Diners, JCB accepted.*

Bury St Edmunds 14, Ely 13, Cambridge 13, Thetford 18, Norwich 48, London 63.

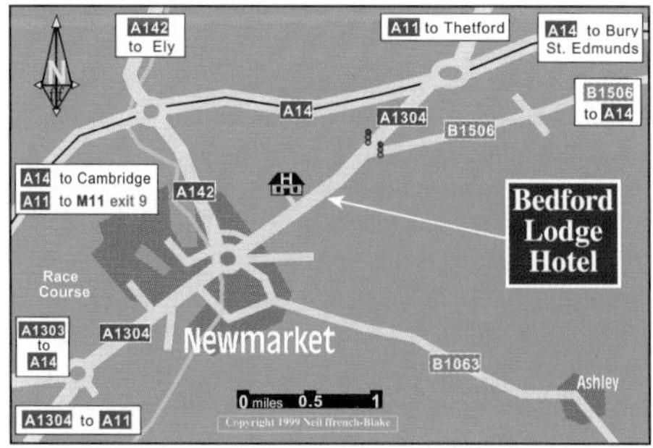

The Swan

Market Place, Southwold, Suffolk IP18 6EG
Tel: (01502) 722186; Fax: (01502) 724800

The Swan has occupied its present site since the 14th century. Following the Great Fire of 1659, it was rebuilt in time to provide refreshments for bell-ringers pealing out the restoration of Charles II in 1660. In 1880 the owner at the time substantially remodelled the hotel and built himself a fine house next door, now the Town Hall. Subsequent alterations of great character were made in 1938 and in more recent times the Swan has been fully restored and refurbished in a most comfortable and attractive style. There are 26 bedrooms in the main building and a further 17 clustered round the old bowling green in the garden - a quiet place to enjoy a game of croquet. The public rooms have the traditional character of an English country house, enhanced by fine furniture, carved 18thC doorframes and mantelpieces, prints, paintings and photographs connected with the history of Southwold. The menu in the dining room changes daily and is complemented by a fine wine list. The relaxed and homely atmosphere at The Swan, backed up by friendly and attentive staff, will ensure that your stay will be a memorable one.

***Single** room with breakfast from £62; **double** from £99. **Midweek breaks** (Sun-Fri inc.) available annually Oct-April £60 pppn inc. breakfast, 3-course dinner, newspaper, early morning tea, VAT.*

- *43 en suite bedrooms with colour TV, direct-dial telephone, hairdryer, music/radio/alarm clock.*
- *Table d'hôte dinner £25. Last orders 2130. Lunch available April-November. Special diets.*
- *Business services inc meeting room for 20.*
- *Croquet. Fishing, golf, riding, sailing/boating, tennis nearby. Car parking for 30.*
- *Open all year. Amex, Diners, Switch, Visa, Mastercard accepted.*

Darsham Station 9, Lowestoft 12, Norwich 34, Ipswich 34, Gt Yarmouth 24, London 108.

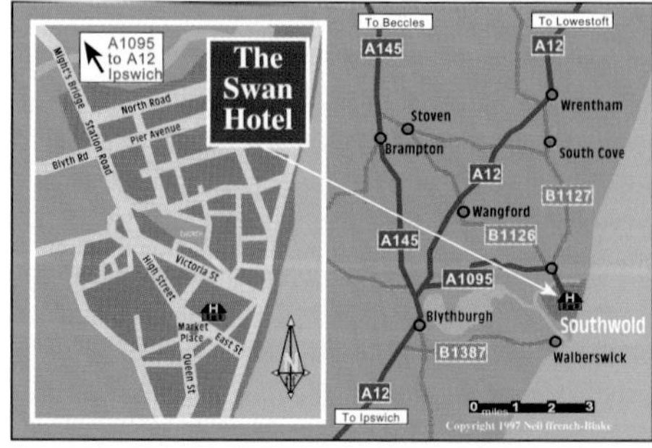

Historic Houses, Gardens & Parks

Derbyshire
Calke Abbey Park & Gardens, Ticknall
Chatsworth House & Gardens, Bakewell
Eyam Hall, Eyam
Haddon Hall, Bakewell
Kedleston Hall, Derby
Lea Gardens, Matlock
Melbourne Hall, Gardens & Craft Centre
Sudbury Hall & Museum of Child Care, Sudbury

Gloucestershire
Berkeley Castle
Barnsley House Garden
Buscot House, Nr. Lechlade
Hidcote Manor Garden, Hidcote Bartrim
Painswick Rococo Garden
Snowshill Manor, Nr. Broadway
Stanway House, Nr. Winchcombe
Sudeley Castle & Gardens

Herefordshire
Abbey Dore Court Gardens
Berrington Hall, Nr. Leominster
Burford House Gardens, Burford
Eastnor Castle, Nr. Ledbury
Eastgrove Cottage Garden Nursery, Nr. Shrawley
Hergest Cloft Gardens, Kington
Hill Court Gardens, Nr. Ross-on-Wye
How Caple Court Gardens
Moccas Court, Moccas
Queenswood Country Park, Nr. Leominster

Leicestershire
Belgrave Hall, Belgrave
Stanford Hall, Lutterworth
Whatton Gardens, Loughborough

Northamptonshire
Althorp, Nr Northampton
Castle Ashby House & Gardens
Canons Ashby House, Nr Daventry
Coton Manor, Nr Guilsborough
Cottesbroke Hall, Cottesbroke
Elton Park, Peterborough
Deene Park, Nr Corby
Holdenby House Gardens, Nr Northampton
Lamport Hall, Lamport
Rockingham Castle, Market Harborough

Nottinghamshire
Naturescape Wildflower Farm, Langar
Newstead Abbey, Linby
Wollaton Hall Natural History Museum

Shropshire
Attingham Park, Nr. Shrewsbury
Benthall Hall, Broseley
Boscobel House, Nr. Albrighton
Goldstone Hall Garden, Market Drayton
Hawkstone Hall, Weston
Weston Park

Staffordshire
Biddulph Grange Garden & Coun try Park,Biddulph
Chillington Hall, Codsall Wood
Greanway Bank Country Park, Nr. Biddulph
Hanch Hall, Lichfield
Shugborough, Milton
Trentham Gardens

Warwickshire
Arbusy Hall, Nr. Nuneaton
Baddesley Clinton House
Charlecote Park, Nr. Wellesboume
Coughton Court
Harthill Hayes Country Park, Nr. Nuneaton
Jephson Gardens, Leamington Spa
Kingsbury Water Park
Middleston Hall
Packwood House, Nr. Hockley Heath
Ragley Hall, Nr. Alcester
Ryton Organic Gardens, Coventry

West Midlands
Aston Hall, Birmingham
Birmingharn Botanical Gardans
Clent Hills Country Park, Nr. Stourbridge
Coombe Abbey Country Park, Nr. Coventry
Moseley Old Hall, Fordhouses
Selly Manor & Minworth Greaves, Bourneville
Sutton Park, Sutton Coldfield
Wightwick Manor, Wolverhampton

Worcestershire
Hagley Hall, Nr. Stourbridge,Worcs
H anbury Hall, Nr.Droitwich,Worcs
Spetchley Park, Nr. Worcester
The Picton Gardens at Old Coust Nurseries, Colwall Village

Walks & Nature Trails

Derbyshire
Carsington Water, Ashbourne
Gulliver's Kingdom, Matlock Edge
Longshaw Estate, Hathersage

Gloucestershire
Cotswold Water Park, South of Cirencester
Crickley Hill Country Park. Nr. Great Witcombe
Dean Heritage Centre, Nr. Cinderford
Great Western Railway Museum, Coleford
Forest of Dean Trails, starts at Cannop Ponds
Gloucester Guided Walks

Herefordfshire
City of Hereford Guided Walks
Croft Garden Centre, Nr. Leominster

The Heart of England

Kingsford Country Park, Wolverley
Symonds Yat Forest Trail, SW of Ross-on-Wye

Leicestershire
Beacon Hill Country Park, Woodhouse Eaves
Bradgate Park, Newtown Linford
Burbage Common Visitors Centre
Melton Mowbray Country Park
Watermead Country Park, Syston
Rutland Water, Oakham

Northamptonshire
Barnwell Country Park, Oundle
Brigstock Country Park, Kettering
Daventry Country Park, Daventry
Pitsford Water, Brixworth
Sywell Country Park, Northampton

Nottinghamshire
Burnstump Country Park, Arnold
C lumber Park, Worksop
Colwick Park, Colwick
Portland Park & Visitor Centre, Kirkby-in-Ashfield
Rufford Country Park & Craft Centre
Rushcliffe Country Park, Ruddington
S herwood Pines Country Park, Edmonstowe

Shropshire
Broadway Tower Country Park
Cardingmill Valley, Long Mynd
Clee Hills, Cleobury Mortimer
Offa's Dyke, Clun Forest
Historic Hawkstone Park & Follies, Weston-under-Redcastle

Staffordshire
Cannock Chase Country Park
Codsall Nature Trail
Deep Hayes Country Park, Nr. Longsdon
Manifold Valley, Nr. Waterhouses
The Wildlife Sanctuary, Nr. Cheadle

Warwickshire
Crackley Wood , Kenilworth
Edge Hill, Nr. Kineton
Hatton Locks, Nr. Warwick
Ufton Fields Nature Reserve

West Midlands
Birmingham City Centre Canal Walk
Longmore Nature Trail
Wren's Nest National Nature Reserve, Dudley

Worcestershire
Malvern Hills Walks & Trails
The North Worcestershire Path
The Worcestershire Way

Historical Sites & Museums

Derbyshire
Arkwrights's Cromford Mill, Matlock
Bolsover Castle, Bolsover
Blue John Museum, Ollernshaw Collection, Castleton
Hardwick Old Hall, Doe Lea
Natiuonal Trust Museum of Child hood, Sudbury Hall
National Tramway Museum, Crick
Peveril Castle, Castleton

Gloucestershire
Chedworth Roman Villa, Nr. Cheltenham
Clearwell Caves, Nr. Coleford
Corinium Museum, Cirencester
Cotswold Motor Museum & Toy Collection, Bourton-on-the-Water
Gloucester Cathedral
Gloucester City Museum & Art Gall.
Gloucester Folk Museum
Holst Birthplace Museum, Cheltenham
Tewkesbury Abbey

Herefordshire
Goodrich Castle, Nr. Ross-on-Wye
Hereford Cathedral

Leicestershire
Ashby-de-la-Zouche Castle
Bradgate House, Newtown Linford
Stanford Hall, Lutterworth
Bosworth Battlefield Visitor Centre & Country Park
Donington Collection of Grand Prix Racing Cars, Castle Donington

Northamptonshire
Althorp House, Nr Northampton
Boughton House, Nr Kettering
The Canal Museum, Stoke Bruerne
Chichele College, Higham Ferrers
Lyveden New Bield, Oundle
Rushton Triangular Lodge, Rushton

Nottinghamshire
Holme Pierrepoint Hall, Nottingham
Newark Castle
Newstead Abbey, Linby
Brewhouse Yard Museum of Social History, Nottingham
DH Lawrence Birthplace Museum, Eastwood, Nottingham
N ottingham Castle Museum & Art Gallery

Shropshire
Acton Scott Historic Working Farm
Aerospace Museum, Cosford
Blists Hill Open Air Museum, Ironbridge
The Childhood & Costume Museum, Bridgnorth
Coalbrookdale Furnace & Mu seum of Iron
Ludlow Castle
Midland Motor Museum, Nr. Bridgnorth
Wroxeter Roman City, Nr. Shrewsbury

Staffordshire
Bass Museum, Visitor Centre & Shire Horse Stables, Burton-on-Trent
The Brindley Mill & Museum, Leek
Gladstone Pottery Museum, Longton
Lichfield Cathedral
Samuel Johnson Birthplace Mu seum, Lichfield
Stafford Castle
Wall (Letocetum) Roman Site, Nr. Lichfield

Warwickshire
Anne Hathaway's Cottage, Shottery
James Gilbert's Rugby Football Museum, Rugby
Kenilworth Castle
Shakespeare's Birthplace, Stratford-upon-Avon
The Shakespeare Countryside Museum & Mary Arden's House, Wilmcote
Warwick Castle

West Midlands
Bantock House Museum, Wolver hampton
Birmingham Cathedral
Birmingham Museum & Art Gallery
Birmingham Museum of Science & Industry
Black Country Museum, Dudley
Broadfield House Glass Museum, Kingswinford
Coventry Cathedral
Jerome K Jerome's Birthplace Mu seum, Nr Walsall
The Lock Museum, Willenhall
Midland Air Museum, Coventry
Museum of British Road Transport, Coventry
National Motor Cycle Museum, Bickenhill
Walsall Leather Museum

Worcestershire
Avoncroft Museum of Buildings, Nr. Bromsgrove
Cotswold Teddy Bear Museum, Broadway
Elgar's Birthplace, Lower Broadheath
Hartlebury Castle State Rooms, Nr. Kidderminster
The Droitwich Spa Brine Baths
Worcester Cathedral
Worcester Royal Porcelain Dyson Perrins Museum

Entertainment Venues

Derbyshire
American Adventure, Ilkeston
Cauldwell's Mill & Craft Centre, Rowsley
Bentley Fields Open Farm, Longford
Denby Pottery Visitors Centre, Denby
Lathkill Dale Craft Centre, Bakewell
Royal Crown Derby Museum & Factory, Derby

Gloucestershire
Bibury Trout Farm
Birdland, Bourton-on-the Water
Cheltenham Hall of Fame, Race-course
Cotswold Woollen Weavers, Nr. Lechlade
Gloucester Docks
House of Tailor of Gloucester
Model Village, Bourton-on-the-Water
National Birds of Prey Centre, Newent
The Wildfowl & Wetland Trust Centre, Slimbridge

Herefordfshire
Cider Museum & King Offa Distillery
The Hop Pocket Farm, Bishop's Frome
The Jubilee Park, Symonds Yat West

Northamptonshire
Billing Aquadrome, Northampton
Wickstead Park, Kettering

Nottinghamshire
The Lace Centre, Nottingham
The Tales of Robin Hood, Nottingham
Newark Air Museum
Nottingham Industrial Museum
Patchings Farm Art Centre, Calverton
Sherwood Forest Visitor Centre & Country Park, Edwinstowe

Shropshire
Dinham House Exhibition Centre
The Domestic Fowl Tr't,Honeybourne
Lickey Hill Country Park
The Shrewsbury Quest, Shrewsbury
Twyford Country Centre, Nr. Evesham

Staffordshire
Alton Towers, Alton
Drayton Manor Family Theme Park & Zoo, Nr. Tamworth
Stoke-on-Trent - china factory tours

Warwickshire
Ashorne Hall Nicklodeon, Ashorne Hill
Heritage Motor Centre, Gaydon
Royal Shakespeare Theatre, Strat ford
Stratford open-top Bus Tours
Swan Theatre, Stratford
Twycross Zoo, Atherstone

West Midlands
Birmingham Jewellery Quarter Discovery Centre
Cadbury World, Bourneville, Bir-mingham
Cannon Hill Park, Edgbaston, Birmingham
Royal Doulton Crystal, Amblecote

Worcestershire
Severn Valley Railway, Bewdley to Bridgnorth
West Midlands Safari Park, Nr. Bewdley

The Heart of England

February

5-7. **Cheltenham Folk Festival.** Folk Concerts & events. Town Hall Cheltenham, Glos
20-28 **National Boat, Caravan & Leisure Show.** National Exhibition Centre, Birmingham
16. **Ashbourne Shrovetide Football,** Ashbourne, Derbs

March

11-14. **Crufts Dog Show.** National Exhibition Centre, Birmingham
10-14 .**Yonex All England Open Badminton Championships.** National Indoor Arena, Birmingham.
14-16. **Gold Cup National Hunt Week.** Cheltenham Racecourse, Cheltenham, Glos
16-17. **Careers Live.** Careers Exhib'n. NEC, Birmingham, West Midlands
20. **Midlands Grand National.** Uttoxeter Racecourse, Staffs

April

2-5. **Civil War Encampment** The Commandery, Worcester
9-11. **Cheltenham Jazz Festival,** Gloucestershire.
24-25. **Victor ian Extravaganza.** Riverside Meadow, Stourport-on-Severn,Worcs.
30-May 3. **Upton Folk Festival.** Various venues, Upton-upon-Severn, Worcs.

May

1-2. **National Classic Motor Show.** NEC, Birmingham.
2. **Cheese Rolling** Parish Chch Randwick, Stroud, Glos.
6-9. **Mitsubishi Motors Horse Trials.** Badminton House Grounds, Badminton, Gloucestershire.
7-9. **Malvern Spring Gardening Show.** 3 Counties Showground, Malvern, Worcestershire.
8-15. **35th Buxton Antiques Fair**, Buxton, Derbyshire.
8-9. **Chatsworth Angling Fair.** Chatsworth House & Gardens, Bakewell, Derbs.
9. **National Vintage Communications Fair.** NEC Birmingham.
10. **Warwickshire v West Indies.** One Day Match. Edgbaston Cricket Ground, Birmingham, West Midlands
13-16. **National Dog Show.** Perry Park Showground, Parry Barr, Birmingham.
21-22.. **Shropshire & West Midland Agriculture Show.** Shrewsbury Showground.
23-25. **Leicester Early Music Festival.** Castle Park, Leicester
29. **Cricket World Cup**. 12 teams compete. Edgbaston CG

June

6. **Midland Counties Show.** Uttoxeter Racecourse, Staffs
11-20. **Leicester Int'l Chamber Music Festival.** Various venues, Leicester, Leics.
15-17. **Three Counties Show.** 3 Counties Showground, Malvern, Worcs.
16. **RAF Cosford Open Day.** Aerospace Museum, Cosford, Shropshire
17. **Cricket World Cup.** Semi-final. Edgbaston Cricket Club, Birmingham.
29-July 7. **Ludlow Festival.** Ludlow Castle, Shropshire.
30-July 11. **Warwick & Leamington Festival.** Various venues,Warwicks.

July

2-11. **HMV Birmingham Int'l Jazz Festival.** Various

venues Birmingham,W Mids
3-18. **Cheltenham International Festival of Music.** Cheltenham Town Hall, Cheltenham, Glos.
5-8. **The Royal Show.** National Agricultural Centre, Stoneleigh, Warwicks.
9-11. **British Grand Prix.** Silverstone Racing Circuit, Northamptonshire
17-27. **Buxton International Festival,** Buxton, Derbyshire.

August

1-31. **Malvern Festival.** Malvern Theatres, Worcs
4-5. **169th Bakewell Show.** Bakewell, Derbyshire.
13-15*. **Balloon Festval,** Northampton.
14-24. **Ross-on-Wye Int'l Festival,** Ross-on-Wye, Herefordshire
13-15*. **British Open Horse Trials Championship.** Gatcombe Park, Minchin-Hampton, Glos.
15-20*. **Three Choirs Festival.** Worcester Cathedral, Worcestershire.
21-22. **Game Fair**. Ragley Hall, Alcester, Warwicks.

September

11-12. **15th Buxton Country Music Festival.** Octagon Pavilion Gardens, Buxton, Derbs
12. **Heart of England Judo Association Championships.** National Indoor Arena, Birmingham.
18-Oct.30. **Walsall Illuminations.** Walsall Arboretum, Walsall, West Midlands
23-25. **Burton-on-Trent Beer Festival.** Town Hall, Burton-on-Trent, Staffs.

October

7. **Nottingham Goose Fair.** Forest Recreation Ground, Nottingham.
8-24. **Cheltenham Festival of Literature**. Cheltenham Town Hall, Gloucestershire.
10*. **Pearl World Conker Championships,** The Village Green, Ashton, Northants
20-1 Nov. **International British Motor Show.** National Exhibition Centre, Birmingham

November

4-14. **Int'l Motor Cycle Show,** NEC Birmingham.
10. Worcester Novices Chase, Worcester Racec'se.
10-12. **Murphy's Gold Cup Chase/Murphy's Draughtflow Hurdle.** Cheltenham Racecourse, Glos.
13-14. **National Classic Motor Show,** NEC Birmingham

December

8-9. **December Race Meeting.** Cheltenham Racecourse
11-12. **Christmas Craft Fair.** Pavilion Gardens, Buxton, Derbyshire

**Denotes provisional date*
For further information contact

TOURIST BOARD

The Heart of England Tourist Board, Larkhill Road, Worcester WR5 2EF. Tel: (01905) 763436.

Fotheringhay Church, Northants

The Heart of England

The Heart of England

The Heart of England: a name that defines this lovely part of the world so much better than its geographical name: *The Midlands*. It is certainly at the very centre of England, with the advantage of fast motorway access from all parts of the UK, but, once off the major roads - whether you strike out north, south, east or west - you will quickly be deep into countryside of huge variety, from stark and dramatic moorlands in the north, to the gentler landscapes of the Cotswolds, dotted with dozens of picturesque tiny villages with "twinned" names such as Lower and Upper Slaughter, Little and Great Rissington, Temple Guiting and Guiting Power; the magnificent churches at Fairford, Cirencester and Chipping Campden, built by prosperous wool merchants of earlier days; and the relics of Roman settlements of even earlier days - all slumber in a timeless beauty. Some of Britain's best country house hotels are in this area and it is was the birthplace of SIGNPOST.

Boscobel House, Shropshire

If you really want to escape to unknown places, head west to Herefordshire and the lovely Wye Valley, or to Shropshire - both counties are bordered by the Welsh Marches where England meets Wales - the scene of many past conflicts. But today all is peaceful - you can drive for miles without meeting another car, though undoubtedly the best way to experience the lovely views and fresh air is at a more leisurely pace, by cycle. You will pass through countryside that changes quickly from rich pastureland and small villages to wild hill land dotted with ancient castles and fortified manor houses. Here you will find few large hotels but any amount of country inns - often old black and white timbered buildings that have provided simple accommodation and food for centuries.

The Welsh border lands are perfect for walkers whether you want to tramp along Offa's Dyke, climb the mountains of Long

Bibury

Mynd or wander the wooded lanes of the Wrekin; Staffordshire too, in the northern part of the region, offers superb walking and cycling in the moorlands of the southern Peak district.

In Warwickshire Stratford-upon-Avon attracts huge numbers of visitors but retains the charm of a riverside market town. Experience a performance by the Royal Shakespeare Company at one of the three theatres in season (April-November) and visit the old timbered houses of Shakespeare's time.

The Heart of England has always played an important part in England's history: from the early border conflicts with the Welsh to the series of battles in the Civil War. This has left a heritage of great fortifications: the castles at Warwick, Kenilworth, Goodrich and Berkeley are especially worth a visit - and inevitably many homes of the aristocracy which display art and architecture of special interest.

The Wye Valley

Ragley Hall

Ragley, near Stratford, and the home of the Marquess of Hertford, has a magnificent Great Hall decorated with some of the finest baroque plasterwork in England. Weston Park, the home of the Earls of Bradford, on the Staffordshire/Shropshire borders, is a superb Restoration house with a noted art collection; Hagley Hall, home of Lord Cobham, is another beautiful Palladian house with fine Italian plasterwork; and Sudeley Castle was the last home and burial place of Katherine Parr, the only one of Henry VIII's queens to outlive him.

These houses are all surrounded by acres of landscaped parkland and beautifully kept gardens. Garden enthusiasts should visit Hidcote and Kiftsgate in the Cotswolds, both of which are famous for their rose gardens; and also Hodnet Hall and Hergest Croft high up on the Hergest ridge looking towards Wales. Many of these gardens provide wonderfully atmospheric settings for out-of-doors performances of plays and music, notably at Sudeley and Ludlow, but also at several National Trust properties. There is also a great variety of festivals throughout the summer months (*see previous pages*), many of international repute: The Malvern Festival, the Cheltenham International Festivals of Music and Literature, the Ludlow Festival, the Buxton Festival, the Stratford Festival, the Lichfield Festival and the oldest musical festival of them all: the Three Choirs, held in 1998 in Gloucester, but rotating on a 3-year cycle to the cathedral cities of Hereford and Worcester.

The area holds many reminders of England's industrial history. In Staffordshire, the manufacturers of Stoke on Trent, centre of the world's ceramic industry, demonstrate the traditional skills still used in china making, and the Gladstone Pottery Museum in Longton tells the story of British ceramics. At the Chatterley Whitfield Mining Museum, visitors can tour the coalface 700 feet underground. Shropshire's Ironbridge Gorge holds a complex of fascinating museums centred around the iron bridge over the river Severn, and the whole area at the Heart of England is criss-crossed by waterways. The canal system in Birmingham's city centre can be explored on a trip by long boat.

Birmingham also offers important museum collections of fine and applied arts, historic buildings to study and explore, Botanical Gardens covering 10 acres as well as theatres, the new Indoor Arena and Symphony Hall with its resident symphony orchestra, and nearby the National Exhibition Centre. In the northeast of the area the most touristic county is Derbyshire, with its celebrated Peak District, recently portrayed to good advantage in the BBC's *Pride and Prejudice* serialisation. The 17th-century palladian Chatsworth, home of the Duke & Duchess of Devonshire, is one of the country's finest palaces. Nottingham is famous for its Museum of Costume and Castle Museum, whereas our home county of Northamptonshire boasts several stately homes and castles including Fotheringhay and Althorp, where there is now an exhibition, open July & August only, dedicated to the late Diana, Princess of Wales.

So the contrasts in the Heart of England are many, the choice is wide. Whatever your interest, there will be something to entertain and inspire you: walks in the Cotswolds, Malvern Hills or Derbyshire Dales, Shakespeare Country, Shropshire's Uplands, gardens, music or theatre and some of England's grandest stately homes and castles. All within one hour's drive of an area which was the powerhouse of the Industrial Revolution.

Riverside House Hotel

Ashford-in-the Water, Nr. Bakewell,
Derbyshire DE45 1QE
Tel: (01629) 814275; Fax: (01629) 812873

The new owners of the Riverside, the Thornton family (whose excellent chocolates are in each bedroom), are busy refurbishing bedrooms and public areas to make this gem even more attractive. It nestles by the river Wye in a quiet cul-de-sac with the beauties of the Peak District National Park on all sides and several classic stately homes: Chatsworth, Haddon Hall and Hardwick Hall near at hand. The country house, Georgian in origin, stands in mature gardens in this quaint unspoiled village of stone houses between Bakewell and Buxton, a wonderful spot for those seeking peace and quiet. Oak panelling and crackling log fires in cooler weather welcome the visitor who is then shown to one of the individually decorated and named bedrooms, some of which have four-posters. The restaurant has two AA rosettes and an excellent local reputation for seasonally available game and fish from the neighbouring river. There is a separate meeting/dining room for that important private party and the hotel has a civil wedding licence. An excellent centre for touring the Peak District or for relaxing in 'home-from-home' comfort.

***Rates**: Single room and breakfast from £95.00; double room inc. breakfast from £115.00.* V
***Bargain breaks** - 2-day inclusive break (dinner, b & b) from £195 per person.*

- *15 en suite bedrooms (10 double, 5 twin) all with direct-dial telephone, hairdryer, laundry service, colour TV, tea/coffee making facilities, music/radio/alarm clock, trouser press. All bedrooms non-smoking.*
- *4-course dinner £39.95; lunch & special diets available. Last orders 9.30 pm.*
- *Facilities for the disabled. Car parking for 30.*
- *Business services inc meeting room for 15.*
- *Fishing, riding, walking, shooting in the area.*
- *Open all year. All major credit cards accepted.*

Matlock 9, Buxton 10, Chesterfield 12, Ashbourne 17, Sheffield 18, London 186.

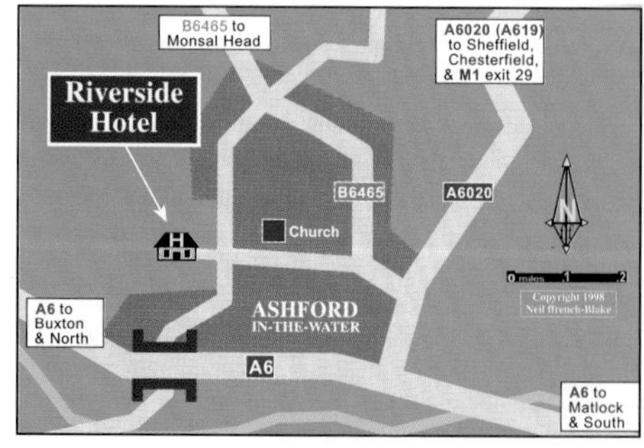

Biggin Hall

Biggin-by-Hartington,
Buxton, Derbyshire SK17 0DH
Tel: (01298) 84451;
Fax: (01298) 84681

Biggin Hall is an historic manor house of 17th century origin, situated 1000 ft above sea level in the Peak District National Park. The Hall is Grade II listed and stands in its own grounds of some eight acres. There are eight bedrooms furnished with antiques in the main house (inc. one suite) and a further nine studio apartments in a bothy and barn in the grounds. Dinner is a daily changing menu of traditional home cooking with the emphasis on local ingredients and free range wholefoods. Guests will feel very much at home in this exceptionally welcoming, comfortable house. A superb centre for walking or touring in Derbyshire, with many historic houses within a 20 mile radius. Packed lunches can be arranged. There is even stabling for those who wish to bring their own horse or pony.

***Rates**: Double/twin room and breakfast from £49 (apartments); £59 (main house & bothy). Dinner, bed & breakfast from £35 pppn midweek (low) to £65 pppn weekend (high). **Bargain breaks:** Ice-breaker specials - 2 nights midweek, dinner b & b from £70 pp to inc b&b,dinner, packed lunch, Glühwein.* V

● *17 en suite bedrooms all with colour TV, hairdryer, telephone, tea/coffee making. Dogs allowed in bothy/annex.* ● *Table d'hôte dinner £14.50 @ 7 pm.*
● *Car parking for 20. 2 meeting rooms - cap 10/20*
● *Open all year. Visa, Mastercard, Switch accepted*

Ashbourne 9, Buxton 10, Leek 15, Derby 22, London 153

Dannah Farm Country Guest House

Bowmans Lane, Shottle, Nr.
Belper, Derbyshire DE56 2DR
Tel: (01773) 550273;
Fax: (01773) 550590
E-mail: reservations@demon.co.uk

Dannah Farm was a great find, an 18th century farmhouse situated high within the Chatsworth estates between Belper and Wirkworth. Bedrooms are very appealing, furnished with antiques and old pine. Unusual touches include first aid kits and communal umbrellas in the hall. Hopefully neither will be needed! One unit is The Cottage with separate entrance and consisting of two double rooms. The *Mixing Place* Restaurant has just been awarded the coveted Derbyshire Life *Golden Goblet* and has an enviable local reputation for good food and wine. Breakfast is also a special treat, with free range eggs, Dannah's own organic sausages and home made bread. An outstanding spot for a short break and a great centre for touring Derbyshire's Peak District and many stately homes.

***Rates**: Single room and breakfast from £45; double from £70. Major credit cards accepted* V

● *8 en suite bedrooms (3 suites) all with colour TV, direct-dial telephone, hairdryer, tea/coffee making facilities, radio/alarm clock. All bedrooms non-smoking. Parking for 12.*
● *3-course tdh dinner £18; special diets available. Last orders 6.30 pm.* ● *Open all year exc. Xmas.*
● *Meeting room for 15. Riding next door.*
● *Directions: Take turning for Shottle off A517 Ashbourne-Belper road, straight on through village northbound, branch right down Bowmans Lane.*

Belper 2½, Derby 10, Ashbourne 10, Matlock 9, London 144.

The Peacock Hotel

Rowsley, Nr Matlock, Derbyshire DE4 2EB
Tel: (01629) 733518; Fax: (01629) 732671

At the Peacock, part of the Jarvis Hotel Group, the welcome is warm and the unwinding process begins as soon as you walk in. This 17th-century house, set on the banks of the river Derwent, is furnished with antiques and many original features are preserved. The Peacock Bar with its oak beams and rough stone walls is a fine example and an excellent place to enjoy a pre-dinner drink after a busy day visiting the sights of Derbyshire. The restaurants provide a perfect setting for a delicious dinner or lunch, where the menus focus on modern British cooking using a variety of fresh, local ingredients. Some of the individual bedrooms have four-posters or half-testers and most are grouped around central landings, lending a country house atmosphere. Bathrooms were refurbished in 1999. A nice touch for families is board games and books/videos placed at strategic points. The many attractions in the neighbourhood include historic houses such as Chatsworth, Haddon Hall and the Heights of Abraham; yet understandably the hotel's speciality is fishing and packages are available which include tuition. The hotel has 12 rods on the river Wye (for trout) and two on the river Derwent. Roger Hudson took over as manager in 1998, bringing his 35 years of Jarvis expertise to the hotel.

Rates: *Single room inc. breakfast from £80; double room with breakfast from £100.*
Leisure breaks: *Min 2-night stay to include room, breakfast & dinner £140 per room per night; VIP Break - 2 nights £300 for two persons.*

- *16 en suite bedrooms all with direct dial telephone, colour TV, hairdryer, laundry/valet service, tea/coffee making facilities, room service.*
- *Table d'hôte 3-course dinner £20.50/lunch £13.50; special diets available. Last orders 9.30 pm*
- *Two meeting rooms, capacity 30 theatre-style or 12 & 8 board meeting. Car parking for 35 cars.*
- *Walking. Fishing. Golf, shooting available nearby.*
- *Open all year. All major credit cards accepted.*

Chesterfield 11, Sheffield 16, Derby 23, Nottingham 30, M1 (exit 28 south, 29 north) 20 minutes, London 148.

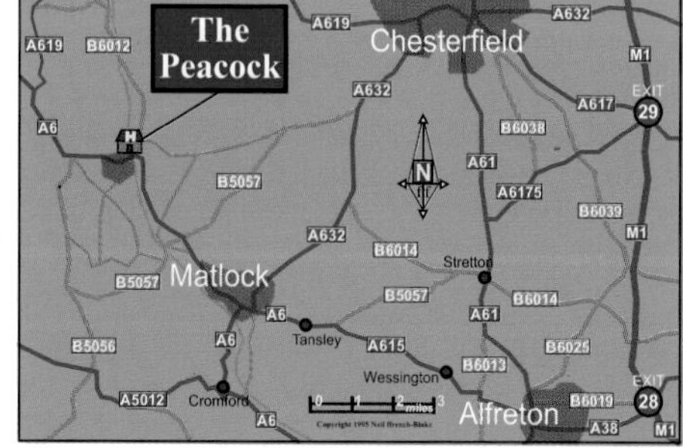

The Swan Hotel

Bibury, Gloucestershire GL7 5NW
Tel: (01285) 740695; Fax: (01285) 740473
E-mail: swanhot1@swanhotel-cotswolds.co.uk
Internet: http://www.swanhotel.co.uk

William Morris called Bibury the prettiest village in England. The Swan hotel is proud to be at its heart. Summer or Winter the village has so much charm with the river Coln running past the front of the hotel and through the village. Indeed the hotel has its own beat on the river. The Swan Hotel is enchanting - privately owned, efficiently run and managed by very friendly staff. It has elegance yet the feeling of being welcomed into a private home. A choice of formal or informal dining is on offer - I actually sat outside in glorious sunshine on the terrace full of flowers and sampled the Bibury-reared trout which is to be heartily recommended. The bedrooms are wonderful - all individually decorated in luxurious style with good sized bathrooms. The Swan is a marvellous retreat for relaxation and perfectly placed for visiting all the interesting towns and villages of the Cotswolds - Rosemary Verey's garden at Barnsley is three miles away; the Roman Villa at Chedworth ten. I very much look forward to returning here myself.

***Rates:** Double/twin room inc. breakfast from £165; family room from £250.*
***Cotswold Breaks:** Min 2-night stay, 4-course dinner, b & b, VAT from £195 per room per night*

- *18 en suite bedrooms, all with direct dial telephone, colour TV, hairdryer, laundry/valet service, room service, trouser press. Non-smoker bedrooms available.*
- *A la carte dinner £28.50; lunch, special diets available. Last orders 9.30 pm.*
- *Two Conference rooms. Car parking for 20.*
- *Fishing. Cirencester Leisure Centre 7 miles. Golf, shooting, riding nearby.*
- *Open all year. Amex, Visa, Mastercard, JCB, Delta, Switch credit cards accepted.*

Cirencester 7, Burford 10, Kemble 10, Stow-on-the-Wold 14, Cheltenham 17, London 96.

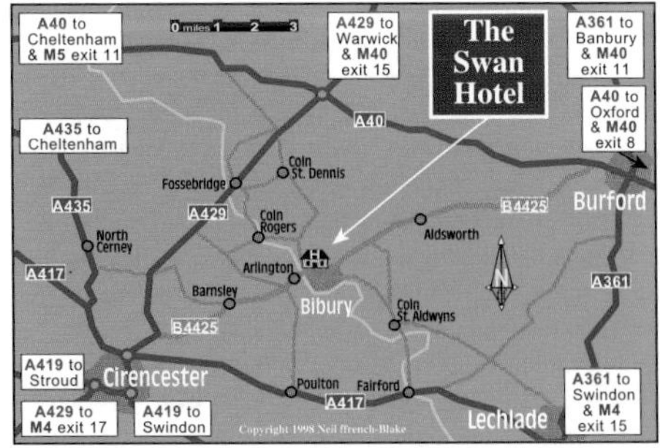

Tudor Farmhouse Hotel & Restaurant

Clearwell, Nr. Coleford, Gloucestershire GL16 8JS
Tel: (01594) 833046; Fax: (01594) 837093
E-mail: reservations@tudorfarmhouse.u-net.com
Internet: http://www.tudorfarmhousehotel.co.uk

What a wonderful find! Nestling in the small village of Clearwell, almost touching the border with Wales, this is a haven of warmth and charm. You can be sure to find a friendly welcome from new owners Colin and Linda Gray, whether you are looking to relax for a few days, are on business or simply want to tour this wonderful area. The cuisine is outstanding, with two menus to choose from, both with a good accompanying wine list. On the night I stayed, I enjoyed an excellent dinner of local salmon and scallops, with an abundance of fresh vegetables. You will ceratinly not leave the table hungry! The actual house was built in the 13th century and features oak beams and original wall panelling. A large roughstone fireplace roars in the lounge in winter months. Some of the bedrooms are reached via an original oak spiral staircase, two have four-posters and others are located in cider makers' cottages and barns. Clearwell Caves are nearby where Midsummer and Halloween Balls are held. Make sure to book early so as not to miss out!

Rates: *Single room inc. breakfast from £48.50; double from £60.00; Corporate Business Rate from £62.50 to include dinner,bed & b'fast &VAT* V
Bargain Breaks: *2 days inc dinner, b & b from £80 (standard room) to £89 (luxury) per room per night.*

- *21 bedrooms (inc 2 four-posters), all en suite with colour TV, direct-dial telephone, hairdryer, laundry/valet service, tea/coffee making facilities. Separate Cottage Suite for up to 6 persons, self-catering if required.*
- *Table d'hôte dinner £21.95; traditional bar lunch & special diets available. Last orders 9.30 pm*
- *Golf three miles. Fishing nearby.*
- *Closed 23-30 Dec; all major credit cards accepted*

Monmouth 6, Chepstow 9, Ross-on-Wye 14, Gloucester 22, Birmingham 55, London 125.

Burleigh Court Hotel

Burleigh, Minchinhampton, Stroud,
Gloucestershire GL5 2PF
Tel: (01453) 883804; Fax: (01453) 886870

Try as I might to avoid hotel brochure hyperbole, the phrase *hidden gem* could not be more appropriate for Burleigh Court. It lies off the beaten track near the pretty village of Minchinhampton and set in 3½ acres of beautiful gardens with the most outstanding views of the South Cotswolds. It is a privately owned hotel under the personal supervision of Ian Hall, the proprietor, who believes that happy and friendly staff are the key to running a successful hotel. Burleigh Court is impressive and sophisticated and yet has the feeling and welcome of a family home. The dining room is elegant and offers a delicious menu with an extensive wine list. Fresh, local produce is used, complemented by herbs from the hotel's private herb garden. The bar is friendly and relaxing with panelled walls and scattered sofas and chairs. Bedrooms are individually decorated and the coach house has some wonderful family rooms leading onto the garden and the Victorian plunge pool. With its log fires in winter and fresh flowers in summer, this is certainly a hotel for all seasons.

Rates: *Single room with breakfast from £72.50; double £100.* V
Bargain breaks: *Double room two people dinner, b&b £140 per night, weekends included.*

● *18 en suite bedrooms (inc. 2 suites), all with colour TV+video, direct-dial telephone, laundry/valet service, tea/coffee making facilities, radio/alarm clock. Non smoker and disabled bedrooms available.*
● *Table d'hôte dinner £22.50. Lunch £17.50. Special diets available. Last orders 9 pm.*
● *Outdoor swimming pool, putting lawn. Golf, riding, tennis nearby.*
● *Business services inc. meeting room for 16*
● *Open all year. Diners, Mastercard & Visa accepted.*

Stroud 5, Gloucester 11, Cheltenham 13, Bristol 26, Oxford 27, London 116

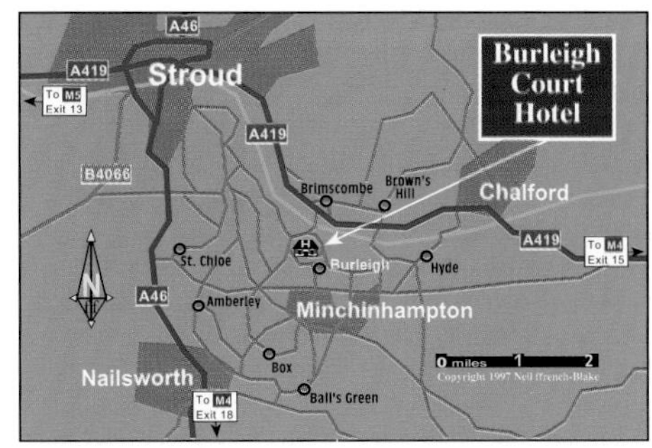

Hare and Hounds

Westonbirt, Nr. Tetbury,
Gloucestershire GL8 8QL
Tel: (01666) 880233; Fax: (01666) 880241

This most attractive Cotswold stone Country House has been owned by the Price family for over forty years, and the two brothers, Martin and Jeremy, now run the hotel. The house, set in many acres of garden and woodland, stands well back from the A433 between Tetbury and Bath with the M4 and M5 both within 12 or 13 miles. There are always plenty of fresh flowers around the hotel and the spacious, comfortable lounges have views of the garden, and a log fire in winter. Many of the bedrooms have recently been refurbished to the highest of standards. The extremely pleasant Coach House rooms are located on ground floor level at the side of the hotel with one of these particularly suitable for disabled visitors. You can dine either in the elegant Westonbirt Restaurant overlooking the garden or informally in Jack Hare's bar where there are also outdoor tables in the warmer months. Both offer a high standard of modern and traditional cooking. Westonbirt is of course also the site of the famous Arboretum and the well known girls' school.

Rates: *Single room from £65.00, doubles from £75.00. Dinner from £19.50* V
Bargain breaks: *2 nights inc dinner, b & b January-December 2000 - from £124.00.*

- *31 en suite bedrooms, all with colour TV, radio, hairdryer and direct dial telephone.*
- *Restaurant and informal bar dining; diets available.*
- *Tennis, squash, half-size snooker, croquet in summer, table tennis. Golf one mile.*
- *Children welcome; dogs welcome; conference rooms; large garden.*
- *Open All Year. Member of Best Western Hotels.*
- *Major Credit Cards accepted.*

Cirencester 13, Castle Combe 10, Wildfowl & Wetlands Trust 15, Bath 20, Gloucester 22, Bristol 25, Cheltenham 26, Birmingham 78, London 105.

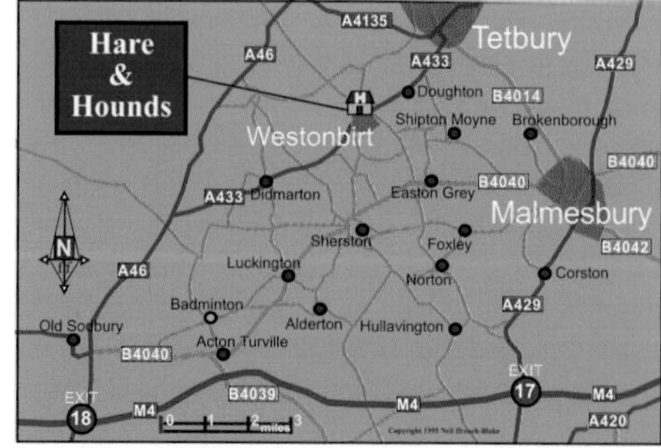

Stapleford Park

Nr. Melton Mowbray, Leicestershire
LE14 2EF
Tel: (01572) 787522; Fax: (01572) 787651

Casual luxury at its very best is how Stapleford has been described and, with its character and sumptuous comforts, it is one of the finest country house hotels in the world. Across acres of parkland, a tree lined avenue, through the arched stable block you reach the mellow facade of this Stately Home with every architectural style since the 16th Century. The public rooms reflect the majesty of the house: high ceilings, mahogany panelling, open fires and unique features such as a *trompe d'oeil* and a 450 year old vaulted kitchen. Meals are taken here and in the ornately carved Grinling Gibbons dining room which serves an outstanding cuisine conveying traditional but unpretentious British country cooking. The bedrooms have been individually created by famous designers and more unexpectedly by names such as Tiffany and Wedgwood, and they are unashamedly luxurious, offering simply everything including splendid marble bathrooms. A four bedroom cottage is also available nearby. All conventional leisure activities are possible here, and of course more exotic pursuits such as carriage driving and falconry. Stapleford is ideally situated for exploring England's finest heritage from York or Lincoln to Stratford. A stay here is unforgettable, combining as it does the grand style of bygone centuries with present day luxury, whilst the attentive service instils the feeling of home without any of the worries.

Room rate from £194.

- *51 en suite bedrooms with radio,CD player & colour TV; direct-dial telephone; hairdryer, trouser press, laundry service.*
- *Last orders for dinner 21.30 hrs weekdays, 22.00 hrs weekends. Special diets available.*
- *Swimming pool and full Health Spa facilities, billiards, croquet, jogging track, riding, shooting, tennis, falconry, golf academy.*
- *All business services including nine meeting rooms with capacity up to 260 in largest room.*
- *Airport pick-up. Car rental can be arranged. Facilities for the disabled. Ample car parking.*
- *Open all year. All major credit cards accepted.*

Leicester 15, Loughborough 15, Grantham 16, Kettering 29, London 104.

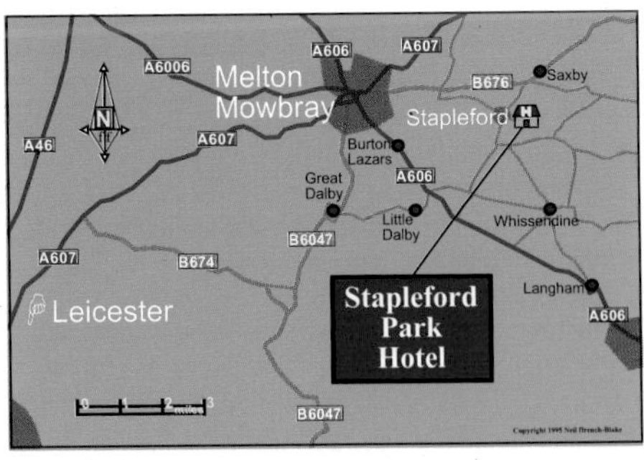

The Windmill at Badby

Main Street, Badby, Nr. Daventry, Northamptonshire NN11 6AN.Tel: (01327) 702363; Fax: (01327) 311521

We were pleased to find The Windmill in our home county of Northamptonshire - an area not over-endowed with Signpost-profile hotels. It is a homely village inn with a popular and imaginative restaurant. Specialities include *Barbarie Duck Breast* and *Chargrilled Cajun Chicken* and there is always a selection of 'Fresh Specials', Grills and a sensible childrens' menu. The bar serves cask-conditioned ales. Décor is bright; bedrooms are economically laid out with individual names like the *Fawsley Room* and there is one family or honeymoon room - *The Windmill Room*. Badby is in excellent walking and cycling country (both The Knightley Way and The Nene Way start here) and local places to visit include Althorp, Sulgrave Manor, Silverstone Circuit, Warwick and Stratford-upon-Avon.

Rates: *Single inc. breakfast from £49; double from £65.* ***Bargain Breaks****: Summer Weekend Breaks from £109 per room for two nights/£163.50 for three nights. Dinner to be taken in hotel.* V

- *8 rooms, all with colour TV + satellite, direct-dial telephone, hairdryer, laundry service, tea/coffee making, trouser press, music/radio/alarm clock.*
- *A la carte restaurant open lunch & dinner. Special diets avail. Last orders 9.30 pm. Parking 25.*
- *Meeting room to 40. Airport pickup on demand.*
- *Open all year. Visa, M-card, Amex,Diners accepted.*

Daventry 3, Northampton 10, Banbury 13, Stratford 30, London 86

The Falcon Hotel

Castle Ashby, Northampton NN7 1LF.Tel: (01604) 696200; Fax: (01604) 696673

This traditional 16th century country cottage is made for relaxation. The Falcon is cosy, warm and comfortable. The pretty restaurant , serving modern English cuisine, overlooks the lawns, and is divisible into three. In season there is a special 'asparagus' menu. The oak-beamed cellar bar offers a fine selection of real ales to accompany the excellent value bar meals. Michael and Jennifer Eastick are 'hands-on' hosts who will make you feel very much at home. Each of the 16 bedrooms, 5 in the main old house and 11 in a cottage across the car park, is individually decorated, with scrubbed or painted pine wardrobes and restful lighting. Bathrooms have power showers, complimentary toiletries and bathrobes. The hotel can also cater for business meetings and wedding receptions. The Falcon is minutes from Castle Ashby House and well placed for Silverstone, Stratford, Woburn and Althorp.

Rates: *Single inc. breakfast from £79.50; double/twin from £95.50.* V
Bargain Breaks: *Min 2 nts d,b&b£67.50 pppn.*

- *16 en suite bedrooms, all with colour TV+ satellite, direct-dial telephone, radio, tea/coffee making, hairdryer, bathrobe, trouser press.*
- *Table d'hôte 3 cse £23.50; à la carte, lunch & bar meals available. Last dinner orders 10 pm.*
- *Two meeting rooms to 40. Car parking for 50.*
- *Golf, riding, clay pigeon shooting, fishing nearby*
- *Open all year. All major credit cards accepted.*

Directions: Off A428 Northampton-Bedford road.

Olney 5, Northampton 8, Wellingboro' 10 , Bedford 16, London 76.

Langar Hall

Langar, Nottinghamshire
NG13 9HG
Tel: (01949) 860559;
Fax: (01949) 861045
E-mail: langarhall-hotel@ndirect.co.uk
Internet: www.langarhall.com

I always love my visits to Langar Hall. Although close to Nottingham, it is beautifully situated overlooking the Vale of Belvoir - a lovely country house, built in 1837, standing beside an early English church, with glorious views over the gardens, moat and parkland. The Hall is the family home of Imogen Skirving, where her father used to entertain famous cricketers of the 1930's. Nowadays the Test Match Special team stay here during Trent Bridge test matches! The public rooms are delightful. The charming proprietor and her excellent team make every effort for their guests' happiness. Together with her chef Toby Garratt, Imogen works to produce excellent, reasonably priced à la carte menus of French and English food which include such dishes as local lamb, turbot, steak and chips with bernaise sauce or lobster. One room has recently been extended to accommodate small conferences and private dinner parties. All the bedrooms are charming and uniquely furnished, and one has a four-poster bed. New for 1999 is a timber-built 'den' suite in the garden. This is a truly lovely place to stay, with a peaceful and relaxing atmosphere.

***Rates**: Single room and breakfast from £75; double room and breakfast from £100; suite from £150. **Weekend breaks** - room and breakfast 2-night stay for 2 people from £150.* V

- *10 en suite bedrooms, all with direct dial telephones, TV; room service; baby listening.*
- *Weekday table d'hôte dinner menu £17,50; à la carte menus from £20; lunch from £10; last orders 9.30 p.m.*
- *Children welcome; dogs by arrangement. (£10)*
- *Own coarse fishing - bring your own rod; golf four miles. Hunting and shooting can be arranged.*
- *Open All year. Mastercard, Visa and Amex Credit Cards accepted.*
- *Licensed to hold marriages; exclusive house party booking; conferences 20 max.*

Nottingham 12, London 120, York 90.

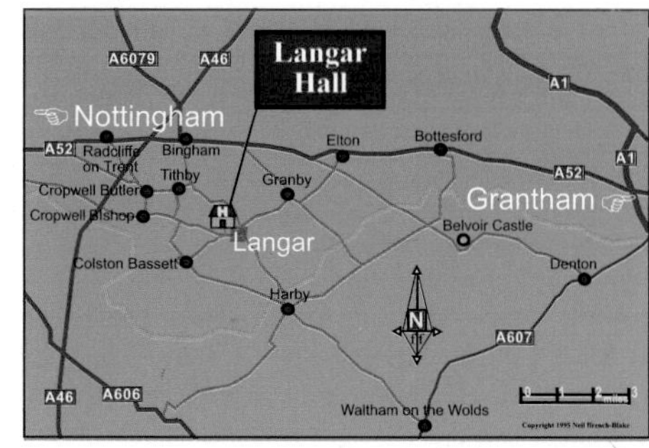

The Old England

Sutton-on-Trent, Nr. Newark, Nottinghamshire NG23 6QA
Tel: (01636) 821216; Fax: (01636) 822347

The Old England is a real home from home. The Pike family have run the hotel since we first published Signpost and, more than 60 years later, we are still pleased to recommend it. This most attractive country house is situated in a large very well kept garden, which must be a haven of peace on a fine day. The house is continually being updated by its owners. All bedrooms have their own private bathrooms and are cheerful, cosy and well furnished. Those of you who appreciate good furniture, will be delighted with the beautifully polished antique tables and chairs in the dining room, and the many other interesting pieces and lovely old china throughout the hotel. The food, supervised by the Pike family, is really good British fare, such as steak, roasts and poached Scotch salmon, and always plenty of it. Later, I was assured by regular diners at the hotel that their high standard of food never varies. If you are travelling north or south, you can be assured of a very warm welcome at this lovely hotel.

Rates: *Single room and breakfast from £52.50; double from £75.00 including VAT.* V
Midweek breaks: *£42.00 per person per night (min. stay two nights), including dinner, bed, breakfast & VAT.*

- *10 en suite bedrooms (1 ground floor), all with TV; room service.*
- *Last orders for dinner 9. 00p.m.; special diets.*
- *Children welcome; dogs accepted; conferences max. 45.*
- *Grass tennis court; shooting/fishing four miles; golf eight miles.*
- *Open all year; Amex, Mastercard and Visa credit cards accepted.*

Newark 8, East Retford 12, Lincoln 24, Leicester 41, London 128.

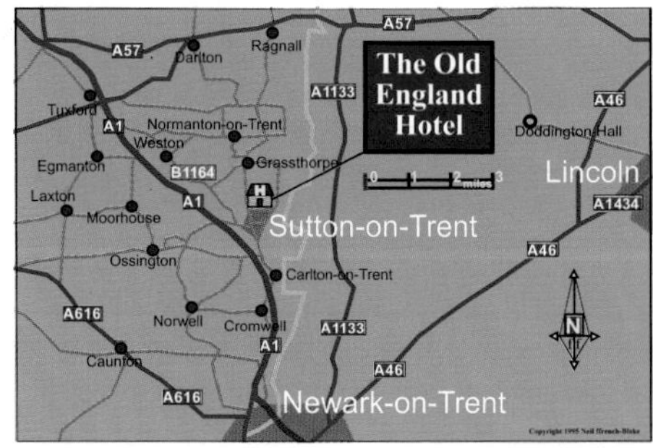

Stratford Victoria

Arden Street, Stratford-upon-Avon,
Warwickshire CV37 6QQ
Tel: (01789) 271000; Fax: (01789) 271001

I highly recommend this luxurious new hotel in the centre of Stratford. Opened in 1996, it is a welcome addition to the room stock in the town and gives excellent value for money.
It is privately owned and the attitude of such a highly motivated and loyal staff, I have always found, rubs off to give the visitor a warm and personal welcome. The Victoria Restaurant and Bar will tempt you with snacks throughout the day or main meals from the carvery and grill menus. Purpose-built conference suites and board rooms seating up to 140 have all modern facilities and full back-up from the hotel's conference office. There is a well-equipped gym to work off those extra calories gained in the restaurants! Bedrooms are generously proportioned and for special occasions there are Premier Rooms, a four-poster room or the luxury suite. There are also family rooms, interconnecting rooms and rooms for the disabled. The hotel is very well run and a great centre for visiting the heart of Shakespeare country. It is within walking distance of the Royal Shakespeare Theatre and the Town Centre and adjacent to the Railway Station.

Rates: *Single room and breakfast from £87.50; double inc. breakfast from £107.50.* V
Bargain Breaks: *Two nights, dinner b & b from £67.50 per person per night, based on 2 people sharing. 4-poster rooms/suites avail. at a suppl't.*

● *102 en suite bedrooms, all with colour TV + satellite, direct-dial telephone, hairdryer, laundry service, tea/coffee making facilities, trouser press. Non-smoking and rooms for disabled available. Car parking for 104 cars.*
● *Table d'hote £19.50; à la carte, lunch & special diets available. Last orders for dinner 10.00 p.m.*
● *Business services inc 6 meeting rooms to 140*
● *Fitness centre/gym, jacuzzi/whirlpool, beauty salon.*
● *Open all year. All major credit cards accepted*

Warwick 8, Banbury 20, Birmingham 23, Oxford 39, London 93.

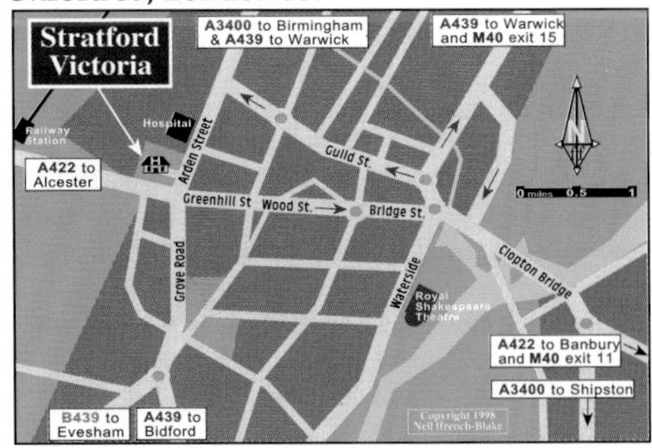

Dormy House Hotel

Willersey Hill, Broadway,
Worcestershire WR12 7LF
Tel: (01386) 852711; Fax: (01386) 858636

It has always been a great joy for me to visit the Dormy House Hotel. The standards are high, yet the hotel is so welcoming and friendly. The hotel is under the personal management of Ingrid Philip-Sorensen, whose style and taste are impeccable and who cares for her staff as much as for her guests. All 48 bedrooms are beautifully and individually decorated with all modern luxuries and the public lounges are comfortable and inviting - one has a large inglenook with a roaring log fire. Flowers are arranged beautifully throughout the hotel. In *Tapestries* restaurant you can enjoy Chef Cutler's wonderfully varied menus and in the *Barn Owl* Bar less formal lunches and evening meals are available throughout the week. The building is a beautifully converted 17th century farmhouse with spectacular views over the Cotswold escarpment and is adjacent to Broadway golf course. Guests who stay at Dormy House receive the hotel's newsletter *Dormy Days* which details special events throughout the year: New Year's Eve, Opera Evening, Jazz Brunch, Easter, Summer Ball, Special August Breaks and Tapestries Champagne Dinners.

Rates: *Single room with breakfast from £73. Double room including breakfast from £146.* ***Champagne Weekend breaks*** *Fri/Sat incl. room, table d'hôte dinner, full English breakfast, fresh flowers and champagne.* ***Carefree Break*** *- any 2 nights Sun-Thurs as above less flowers/ champagne. Please enquire for prices.* V

- *48 en suite bedrooms with radio & TV, direct-dial telephone, hairdryer, trouser press, laundry service; tea/coffee making facilities, safety deposit box.*
- *Last orders for dinner 21.30 hrs. Special diets.*
- *8 meeting rooms - capacity 170. Car parking 80.*
- *Billiards, croquet, putting, gym, sauna/steam, indoor games on site. Jogging trail, riding, boating, shooting, tennis & fishing by arrangement.*
- *Open all year exc. Xmas/Boxing Day. All major credit cards accepted.*

Broadway 2, Cheltenham, Stratford-upon-Avon 15, Birmingham Airport 40, London 95.

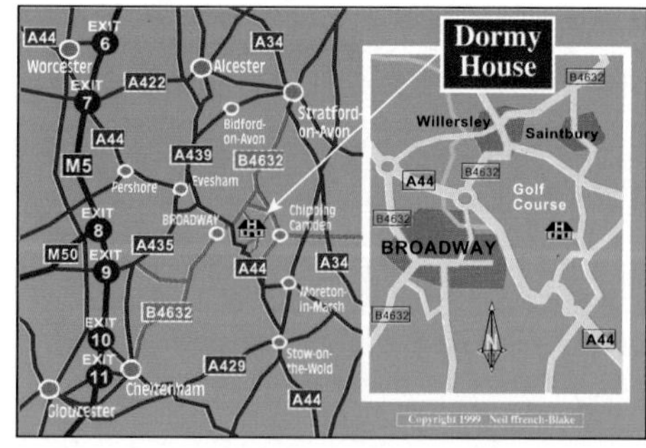

The Cottage in the Wood Hotel

Holywell Road, Malvern Wells
Worcestershire WR14 4LG
Tel: (01684) 575859; Fax: (01684) 560662

__Rates:__ Single room with breakfast from £74. V
Double room including breakfast from £89.50.
__Bargain Breaks:__ 2 day breaks available any time. Prices range fm £58 pppn Nov-March to £95 pppn in peak season in the largest four-poster.

High above the village of Malvern Wells, half hidden amongst hillside trees, you will find the Cottage in the Wood. Formerly a Georgian dower house, it is now an hotel of charm and character owned and run by John and Sue Pattin and family. Within the 7-acre grounds are the Coach House and Beech Cottage. Secluded and peaceful, they have been converted to provide 12 further delightful, if smaller, bedrooms. They share with the main house those things which make the Cottage in the Wood so special - the wonderful view and the friendliness of the Pattin family and their team. In the Dower House, the spacious partially book-lined sitting room can be enjoyed in every season of the year. There are log fires in Winter and, in the summer months, the windows are thrown open onto the terrace and garden. The elegant dining room serves a menu essentially modern English in style, with a first class wine list completing a superb dining experience. If you can be persuaded to leave the seductive comfort of the house, you can walk directly from the grounds onto the Malvern Hills. By car the area from the Welsh Marches to Shakespeare's Stratford awaits you, whilst all around is Elgar country, from where the great composer drew much of his inspiration.

- *20 en suite bedrooms with radio & TV+video, direct dial telephone, hairdryer, trouser press (some), laundry service; tea/coffee making facilities.*
- *A la carte from £27.50; lunch & special diets available; last orders 21.00 hrs (20.30 Sundays)*
- *Meeting rooms - capacity 14. Car parking for 40*
- *Golf one mile, clay shooting 3 miles, squash 1/2 mile, riding 2 miles.*
- *Open all year. Mastercard, Visa Amex accepted*

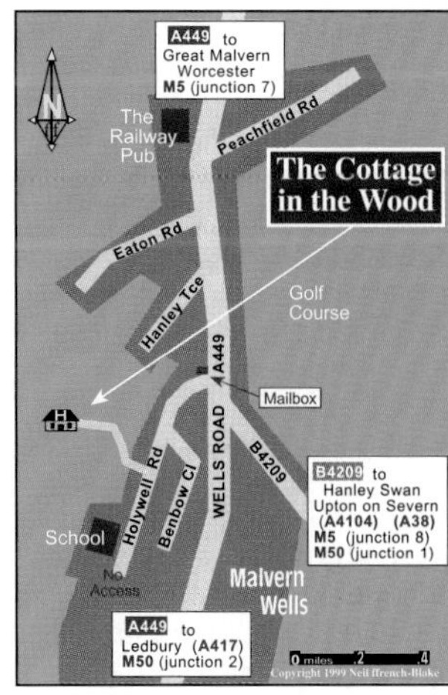

Gt Malvern 3, Worcester 11, Cheltenham 24, Stratford-upon-Avon 35, London 120.

Cumbria - English Lakeland

In this beautiful corner of England, there is beauty in breathtaking variety - in the famous Lake District, loved by so many who come back again and again to its inspirational magic, brilliant blue lakes and craggy mountain tops.

There are other kinds of beauty to be enjoyed too. The central Lake District with its mountains, lakes and woods is so well known and loved that there is a tendency to forget that the rest of Cumbria contains some of the most varied and attractive landscape in Britain. In the east of the county, the lovely peaceful Eden Valley is sheltered by the towering hills of the Pennines, and everywhere are dotted charming little red sandstone villages. Further north, the border lands are flatter, with forests and lush green fields patterned by the typically English hedges and lanes. Cumbria's long coastline is itself full of variety. There are rocky cliffs with myriad sea birds, sandy estuaries, miles of sun-trapping sand dunes and friendly harbours, and everywhere something interesting to see, from reminders of our Roman occupation to the Flookburgh shrimp fishermen who go fishing, not in boats, but on tractors!

Wherever you choose to stay in Cumbria, you will not be far away from beautiful scenery: and whatever kind of accommodation you would like, Cumbria has it, from gracious country house hotels to country inns and bed-and-breakfasts. Don't think that summer is the only time when Cumbria is beautiful. In autumn the deciduous woodlands and bracken-covered hillsides glow with colour. In winter, the mountain tops stand in dazzling magnificence against blue skies. In spring, you can discover the delights of the magical, constantly changing light and joy of finding carpets of wild flowers. This is really the best time of the year to go walking or climbing - spending each day in the crisp fresh air to return in the evening with a healthy appetite to enjoy a delicious Cumbrian meal by the fireside in a cosy pub or friendly hotel.

There are many holidays in Lakeland which offer both activity and instruction in a range of sports - walking, climbing, orienteering, potholing, cycling, riding, golf, sailing, sailboarding, water-ski-ing, canoeing and fishing. A good way to absorb the beauty of this unique area is to plan your own personal route on foot or on cycle. *The Cumbria Cycle Way*, designed to avoid all the cyclist's problems like main roads and precipitate hills takes a circular route 250 miles (400 kms) long around this beautiful county. There are also good, cheap public transport services, and, where the big coaches cannot go, *Mountain Goat* minibuses run, even over the steepest mountain passes.

Above: Coniston Water. **Below:** Chester town centre

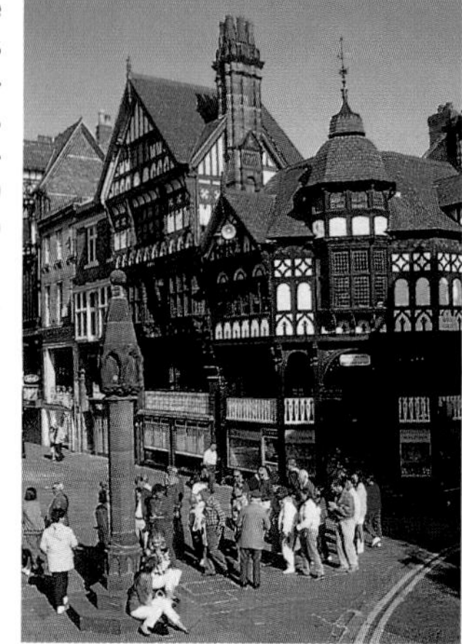

For a change from the great outdoors, there is a wealth of historic houses to visit, including a uniquely constructed thatched farmhouse, stately homes that have seen centuries of gracious living and the small cottages where famous writers have lived. Other houses are important because of their architecture, like the round house on Belle Isle, or majestic Hutton-in-the-Forest, which has a central tower dating from the 14th century, surrounded by later additions. The Cumbrian climate is ideal for gardens and the area is famous for the rhododendrons and azaleas which grow in abundance.

You will find out more about the secrets of this ancient kingdom by watching, or even joining in, some of its old customs, some of which are unique to Cumbria. There are many traditional agricultural shows displaying the essence of the English countryside - spiced in Cumbria with local specialities like *hound trailing*, which is like hunting but without the fox, and *fell races* - crazy lung-bursting ascents of the nearest hill, followed by a bone-bruising descent! For further information, contact the Cumbria Tourist Board, address on page 135.

The North West

Historic Houses, Gardens & Parks

Cheshire
Arley Hall & Gardens, Nr. Great Budworth
Bridgemere Garden World, Nr. Nantwich
Brookside Garden Centre, Poynton
Cholmondeley Castle Gardens
Dunham Massey, Nr. Altrincham
Gawsworth Hall Nr. Macclesfield
Little Moreton Hall, Nr. Nantwich
Ness Gardens Neston
Stapeley Water Gardens, Nantwich
Tatton Park, Knutsford

Cumbria
Acorn Bank Garden, Nr. Temple Sowerby
Brantwood House, Coniston
Dalemain Histonc House & Gar dens, Nr. Pooley Bridge
Graythwaite Hall Gardens, Newby Bridge
Holker Hall & Gardens, Cark-in-Cartmel
Hutton-in-the-Forest, 6 miles from Penrith
Larch Cottage Nurseries, Melkinthorpe
Levens Hall & Topiary Garden, Nr. Kendal
Lingholme Gardens, Linghholme, Keswick
Mirehouse, Underskiddaw
Sizergh Castle, Nr. Kendal

Lancashire
All in One Garden Centre, Middleston
Astley Hall & Park, Nr. Chorley
Catforth Gardens & Nursery, Nr Preston
Gawthorpe Hall, Burley
Leighton Hall, Carnforth
Rufford Old Hall, Ormskirk
Williamson Park, Lancaster

Merseyside
Croxteth Hall & Country Park, Nr. Liverpool
Speke Hall, Liverpool

Walks & Nature Trails

Cheshire
Jodrell Bank Science Ctre & Arboretum, Nr. Holmes Chapel
Styal Country Park
Walk the Walls, Chester
Wirral Peninsula

Cumbria
Cark to Cartmel Village
Dodd Wood
Dunnerdale Forest Nature Trail
Grange-over-Sands to Hampsfell
Grizedale Forest Park Visitor Centre Hawkshead
Numerous fell walks and trails throughout Cumbria
Ulverston Town Trail

Tatton Park

Lancashire
Carnforth Canal Circuit, from Camforth Railwayto Bolton-le-Sands
Pendle Way Walk at Pendle Heritage Centre, Nelson
The Weaver's Shuttle, around Pendle

Historical Sites & Museums

Cheshire
The Boat Museum, Ellesmere Port
Chester Cathedral
Experience Catalyst, Widnes
Macclesfield Silk Museum
Peckforton Castle, Nr. Tarporley
Quarry Bank Mill, Styal

Cumbria
Abbot Hall Art Gallery, Kendal
Appleby Castle, Appleby-in-Westmoreland
Birdoswald Roman Fort, Brampton
Brough Castle, Kirkby Stephen
Brougham Castle, Nr. Penrith
Carlisle Castle
Cartmel Priory
The Cumberland Pencil Museum & Exhibition Centre, Keswick
Dove Cottage, Grasmere
Furness Abbey, Barrow-in-Furness
Heron Corn Mill & Museum of Papermaking,
Milnthorpe Laurel & Hardy Museum, Ulverston
Museum of Natural History, Kendal
Penrith Museum
Rydal Mount, Nr. Ambleside
Stott Park Bobbin Mill, Newby Lake
Wordsworth Museum, Grasmere

Greater Manchester
Castlefield Urban Heritage Park, Manchester
Manchester Cathedral
Manchester United Football Museum

Newton, Forest of Bowland

The North West

Museum of Science & Industry, Manchester

Lancashire
Lancaster Castle, Lancaster

Merseyside
Liverpool Museum
Merseyside Maritime Museum, Albert Dock, Liverpool Museum of Liverpool Life, Pier Head
Pilkington Glass Museum, St Helens

Entertainment Venues

Cheshire
Cheshire Candle Workshops, Burwardsley
Chester Zoo, Upton-by-Chester
Gulliver's World, Warrington
Port Sunlight Visitor Centre, Wirral
Wetlands & Wildfowl Trust Centre, Martin Mere

Cumbria
Cumbria Crystal, Ulverston
Fell Foot Park, Newby Bridge
Lake District National Park Visitor Centre, Windermere Lakeland Bird of Prey Centre, Lowther
Ravenglass & Eskdale Railway, Ravenglass
Sellafield Visitors' Centre
South Lakes Wild Animal Park, Dalton-in-Furness
Ullswater Cruises
Webb's Garden Centre, Kendal
Windermere Lake Cruises
World of Beatrix Potter, Bowness-on-Windermere

Greater Manchester/Lancashire
Alexandra Craft Centre, Saddleworth
Blackpool Tower & Pleasure Beach
Butterfly World, Bolton
Camelot Theme Park, Chorley
Frontierland, Morecambe Bay
Granada Studio Tours, Manchster
Lakeland Wildlife Oasis, Nr. Camforth
Life Centre, Blackpool
Noel Edmonds' World of Crinkley Bottom, Morecambe Sea

Merseyside
The Beatles Story, Albert Dock, Liverpool
Knowsley Safari Park, Prescot
Pleasureland Amusement Park, Southport
The Tate Gallery at the Albert Dock, Liverpool

DIARY OF EVENTS

February

1-31.12 00. **Wordsworth Museum Exhibition.** The Wordsworth Museum, Grasmere, Cumbria.
18* **Chinese New Year Celebrations**.In and around Chinatown, Liverpool.
26*. **Horse Racing: The Greenall Grand National Trial Chase**. Haydock Park Racecourse, Newton-le-Willows, Merseyside.

March

18-19*. **Ambleside Daffodil & Spring Flower Show.** Old Junior Sch, Ambleside.
24-26. **Naworth Castle Spring Antiques Fair.** Naworth Castle, Brampton, Ca

April

6-8. **Martell Grand National Race,** Aintree Racecourse, Merseyside.
21-23. **Forum 28.** Furness Model Railway & Transport Exhib'n, Barrow-in-Furness.
30-1 May. **Carlisle & Borders Spring Flower Show.** Bitts Park, Carlisle.

May

9-11. **Chester May Meeting**. Chester Racecourse, Chester
5-28.8. **Collection 2000.** Year 2000 products. Saddleworth Museum, Oldham, Lancs.
19-21. **Jennings Keswick Jazz Fest.** Keswick,Cumbria
15. **Lancashire Clog Dancing** Festival. Accrington Town Centre, Lancashire.
20-23*.**Chester Folk Festival.** The Morris Dancer, Chester

Rd, Tarporley, Cheshire.
21-29*. **Coniston Water Festival,** Cumbria
29. **Cartmel Steeplechases.** Cartmel, Cumbria.
26-27. **Tote Credit Silver Bowl.** Haydock Park, Merseyside.
29*. **Kendal Medieval Market.** Market Place, Kendal.

June

1-12*.**Isle of Man TT Motor Festival**. Motorcycle Racing. Various venues, Isle of Man.
2-3. **Keswick Beer Festival.** Keswick Rugby Club, Cu'a.
2-4. **Holker Garden Festival,** Holker Hall & Gardens, Cark in Cartmel, Cumbria.
8-10. **John of Gaunt Stakes.** Haydock Park Racecourse, Merseyside.
11. **Carlisle Festival**. Bitts Park, Carlisle.
20-21*. **Cheshire County Show 2000.**The Showground, Tabley, Cheshire.

July

1*.**Whitehaven Carnival & Gala Fair.** Whitehaven, Cumbria
6 8.**Letherby & Christopher Lancashire Oaks.** Haydock Park, Merseyside.
8-15*. **Wigan Jazz Festival.** Various venues, Wigan, Lancs
15. **Cumberland County Show.** Rickerby Park, Carlisle, Cumbria.
16. **Race Meeting.** Haydock Park, Merseyside.
21-23*. **Cumbria Steam Gathering.** Cark Airfield, Flookburgh, Cumbria.
23-31*. **Lake Windermere Music Festival**. Bowness-on-Windermere, Cumbria
28-29*. **Royal Lancashire Show.** Astley Park, Chorley.
28-29*. **St Helens Show,** Sherdley Park, St Helens, Lancs.
30-11 July*. **Lake District Summer Music Int'l Festival & Summer School**. Concerts/ Classes Var. venues, Cumbria.

August

1-15*. **Wordsworth Summer Conference**. Dove Cottage, Grasmere, Cumbria.
1*.**Cockermouth Agricultural Show**, Cockermouth, Cumbria
3-4*. **Lake District Sheepdog Trials.** Hill Fm, Kendal, Cumbria
4-6*. **Lowther Horse Driving Trials & Country Fair.** Lowther Castle, Lowther, Cumbria
11-13. **Ambleside Garden Festival & Craft Fair.** Ambleside, Cumbria.
17-19***Southport Flower Show** Victoria Park, Southport,Lancs
21. **Race Meeting**. Carlisle
21-22*. **Crewe Carnival.** Queens Park, Crewe, Cheshire
27. **Grasmere Lakeland Sports & Show.** Grasmere, Cumbria.
26*. **Isle of Man Int'l Jazz Festival.** Various venues, Isle of Man.
28. **Keswick A griculturakl Show**. Keswick Showground, Cumbria.

September

1-2. **Haydock Sprint Cup Meeting.** Haydock Park, Merseyside
1-Nov 6*. **Blackpool Illuminations.** Talbot Square, Blackpool Lancashire. Illuminations from 7 p.m. nightly.
2***Kirkby Lonsdale Victorian Fair.** Kirkby Lonsdale, Cumbria
2*. **Stanley Leisure Sprint Cup.** Haydock Park Racecourse, St Helens, Lancashire.
3-5*. **Crewe & Nantwich Folk Festival**. Various venues, Nantwich, Cheshire
7*.**Westmoreland County Show.** Westmoreland Showfield, Crooklands, Cumbria.
9. **Kendal Gathering & Torchlight Procession.** Kendal, Cumbria.
12. **Doll's House & Miniature Fair.** Marine Hall, Fleetwood, Lancs.
17. **Borrowdale Shepherds Meet & Show**. Rosthwaite.
23*. **Eskdale Show.** Brotherilkeld Farm, Boot, Cumbria

October

15-17*.**Kendal Mountain Film Festival**. Highgate, Kendal.
16-22*. **Windermere Power Boat Record Attempts** Lake Windermere, Cumbria.
29*. **Cumbria Brass Band Association** (open contest).Lowther St, Whitehaven, Cumbria

November

5*.**Cumbria Brass BandAssoc Annual Open Contest.**Whitehaven Civic Hall, Cumbria.
6. **Carlisle Fireshow**. Bitts Park, Carlisle, Cumbria.
16*. **Biggest Liar in the World Competition.** Bridge Inn, Santon Bridge, Cumbria.
16-18***British National Dance Championships**. Empress Ballroom, Blackpool, Lancs.

**Denotes provisional date .*

For further information, contact:

TOURIST BOARDS

The Cumbria Tourist Board
Ashleigh, Holly Road, Windermere, Cumbria LA23 2AQ.
Tel: (015394) 44444

The North West Tourist Board
Swan House, Swan Meadow Road, Wigan Pier, Wigan, Lancashire WN3 5BB.
Tel: (01942) 821222

Sutton Hall

Bullocks Lane, Sutton, Nr.
Macclesfield, Cheshire SKll OHE
Tel: (01260) 253211; Fax: (01260) 252538

If, like I do, you enjoy staying at an hotel of character, then Sutton Hall is one of the finest in which to indulge yourself. A wealth of beams, log fires and four poster beds are all in evidence, and the ales, conditioned in cask, are matched by the choice of food from an excellent menu. As with the inns of old, there is an atmosphere of warmth, hospitality and good cheer. This, married to such modern conveniences as en suite bathrooms and colour TV, makes a very happy amalgam of past and present. To travel, even from afar, is well worth while and this is made easy by the fact that the M6 and Manchester Airport are less than half an hour away. Also in the area are many other famous old houses as well as the scenic beauty of the Peak District. The hotel is personally run by Mr. and Mrs. Bradshaw.

Rates: *Room and breakfast from £75.00 single, £45.00 double, per person, inclusive of VAT and full English breakfast.*

- *10 en suite bedrooms, all with four poster beds, colour TV, direct dial telephones, tea/ coffee maker; trouser press; full central heating.*
- *Late meals to 10 p.m.; diets available.*
- *Dogs welcome; conferences up to 20.*
- *Golf, tennis, riding nearby; Peak National Park adjacent. Civil wedding licence.*
- *Open all year. Most credit cards accepted.*

Macclesfield 1, M6 (J18/19) 1/2 hour, Manchester Airport 1/2 hour, London 240.

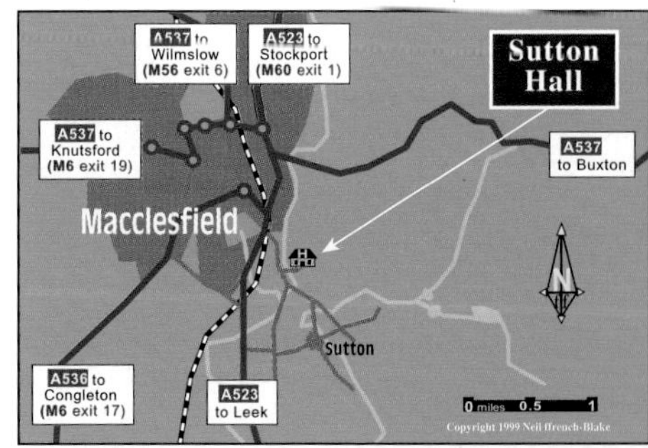

Rothay Manor Hotel

Rothay Bridge, Ambleside, Cumbria
LA22 OEH
Tel: (015394) 33605; Fax: (015394) 33607
E-mail: hotel@rothaymanor.co.uk
Internet: http://www.rothaymanor.co.uk

If you believe, as I do, that one of the main ingredients of civilised life is good food and wines taken in comfortable surroundings, then Rothay Manor is, without a doubt, one of the finest venues in which to enjoy that life. The hotel has been voted top of the list by a publication on hotel breakfasts, and the excellence of the lunches and dinners complements the sumptuous surroundings. Antiques and fresh flowers are abundant, and the feeling of warmth and well-being are everywhere. The whole ambience is orchestrated by Nigel and Stephen Nixon and their wives, and the reputation that they have gained for all round excellence is more than justifiably deserved. These impressions were echoed by many of the other guests to whom I spoke, and even from the elegant brochure, you too will begin to feel the atmosphere of Rothay Manor. It seems unnecessary to add that the surrounding mountains, lakes and the air of the Lake District, make a superb backdrop and atmosphere in which to indulge these pleasures.

Rates: *Double room and breakfast from £120.00 for 2 people; dinner, room and breakfast from £155.00 for 2 people.*
Bargain breaks *November-March, midweek, dinner, room & breakfast from £150 per night for 2 people; weekend break from £160 per night.*

- *18 en suite bedrooms (2 for the disabled) all with direct dial telephone and TV, room service; baby listening.*
- *Last orders for dinner 9.00 p.m.; special diets.*
- *Children welcome; conferences max. 20.*
- *Free use of nearby leisure centre; tennis and fishing 1/4 mile; sailing/boating 1/2 mile.*
- *Open all year; all major credit cards accepted.*

Kendal 13, Manchester 80, London 280.

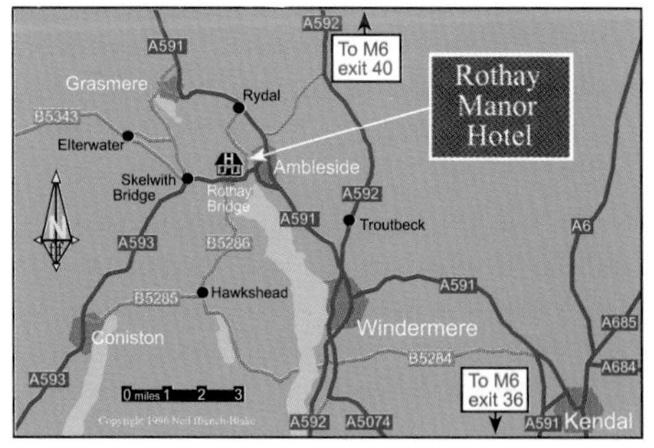

Wateredge Hotel

Borrans Road, Ambleside,
Cumbria LA22 OEP
Tel: (015394) 32332; Fax: (015394) 31878
E-mail: Reception@wateredgehotel.co.uk
Internet: http://www.wateredgehotel.co.uk

It is not often that one comes across a hotel that has excellent food, is immaculately and comfortably furnished and decorated, and yet is perfectly situated, but the Wateredge Hotel is exactly that. There are beautiful views from the public rooms, delightful bedrooms and delicious meals, making the Wateredge an idyllic venue for a holiday in the Lake District. In 1999 the hotel extended its lake frontage with garden swings for its guests. Not only is there the peace and quiet of the hotel itself, but there is the tranquillity of a stroll on the nearby fells to be enjoyed. For those seeking a more active time, there is boating and fishing on the doorstep; there are sporting facilities of all kinds, both indoor and out, in the immediate vicinity. In addition,Ambleside is a lively and bustling town with everything that a holiday maker or tourist could need. The Wateredge is an unpretentious, "honest to goodness" hotel which makes any visit to the Lake District well worthwhile.

Rates: *Dinner, room and breakfast from £68.00 single, £114.00 double/twin.*
Bargain breaks*: 3 day midweek & weekend breaks from £162 per person including dinner, room and breakfast.*

- *23 en suite bedrooms (5 ground floor), all with radio, TV and telephone, complimentary morning tea and coffee tray.*
- *TV lounge; full central heating; diets, children over 7 welcome, dogs not allowed in public rooms or suites; small conferences.*
- *Lake bathing; boat launching & mooring on private jetty; complimentary use of nearby leisure club*
- *Mastercard, Amex and Visa credit cards accepted. Closed mid-December to early January.*

Kendal 13, Keswick 17, Penrith 30, London 300.

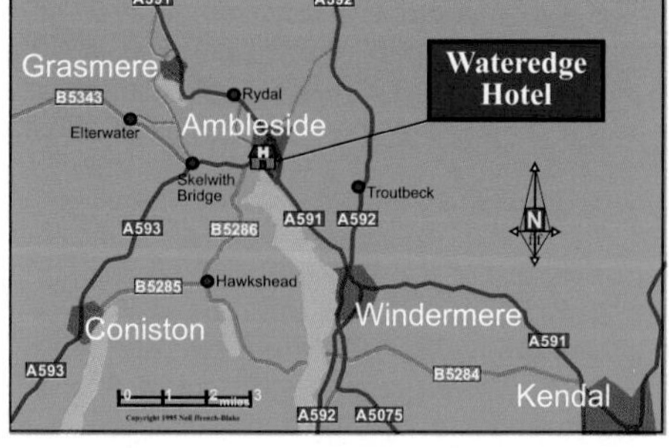

Appleby Manor Country House Hotel & Leisure Club

Roman Road, Appleby-in-Westmorland, Cumbria CA16 6JB
Tel: (017683) 51571; Fax: (017683) 52888
E-mail: reception@applebymanor.co.uk
Internet: http://www.applebymanor.co.uk

Appleby Manor stands high, commanding views of the historic little town, its romantic castle and the sweeping countryside and fells beyond. Within you will find relaxing and friendly courtesy, and most attractive and spacious public rooms. Facing south, the house gives shelter to its sunny gardens onto which some of the delightful rooms in the new wing have direct access. The spotlessly clean bedrooms are comfortable and furnished in keeping with the period of the house. The popular award-winning restaurant offers an international and imaginative selection of tasty dishes. The wine list offers a selection of wines from 20 countries and the bar stocks over seventy single-malt whiskies. There is plenty to see and do locally, with walks to suit all abilities. Appleby is ideally situated for touring the scenic Lake District, and the Borders Hadrian's Wall, the Roman Camps, the high Pennines and the Yorkshire Dales are all within easy motoring distance.

***Rates** per person start at £52 for bed and breakfast, £62 for dinner, bed and breakfast; weekly rates from £372, including dinner, bed and breakfast.*
***Bargain breaks:** min. 2 nights from £62 pppn; also "Flying Falcon" breaks, 2 nights from £189 and the "Cloud Nine Experience" from £155 and "Hangover Breaks" from £151 - all inc. dinner, b & b & VAT.*

- *30 en suite bedrooms (10 ground floor; 5 four-posters), all with telephone, hairdryer, colour TV, satellite and video film channels.*
- *Last orders 9. 00 p.m; diets available.*
- *Children welcome; baby listening; dogs in coachhouse bedrooms only; conferences 30 max.*
- *Games room; snooker and pool; indoor heated swimming pool; jacuzzi; sauna, solarium, leisure centre, squash 1/2 mile, fishing locally; riding 13 miles; golf 2 miles.*
- *Hotel closed 3 days at Christmas only. All major credit cards accepted.*

M6 (junctions 38 & 40) 13, Penrith 13, Ullswater 15, Kendal 25, Keswick 31, Scotch Corner 37, London 272.

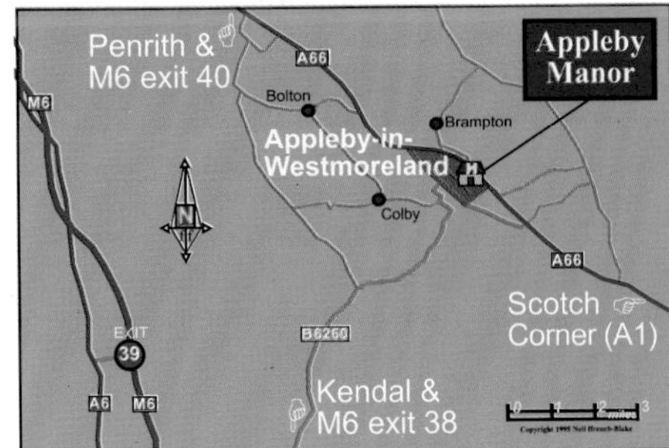

Armathwaite Hall Hotel

Bassenthwaite Lake, Keswick,
Cumbria CA12 4RE
Tel: (017687) 76551; Fax: (017687) 76220
E-mail: reservations@armathwaite-hall.com
Internet: htp://www.armathwaite-hall.com

Few hotels are as beautifully situated as Armathwaite Hall - one of the original stately homes of England, set magnificently in 400 acres of deerpark and woodland, bordered by the beauty of Bassenthwaite Lake and framed by the dramatic vista of Skiddaw Mountain and the surrounding fells. The Graves family, who have owned and run Armathwaite Hall for twenty years, know exactly how to pamper their guests. Cuisine is under the supervision of Masterchef Kevin Dowling. Style is traditional English, with Cumbrian specialities and using local produce, and classical French, but with a light touch. This is just a prelude to all the activities available. Discreetly hidden is the magnificent 'Spa' Leisure Club with indoor pool, gymnasium, beauty salon etc. and in the grounds is a farm with rare breeds and a BHS-approved Riding Centre. Fishing and boating are on the doorstep. Armathwaite Hall is the perfect base from which to enjoy the Northern lakes area.

Rates: *single with breakfast £65; double with breakfast £116.* ***Breaks:*** *Easter, Christmas/New Year, Bank Holiday and other packages available. Details on request.* V

- *43 en suite bedrooms with colour TV + satellite, telephone, hairdryer, laundry/valet service, tea/ coffee making facilities, 24-hr room/meal service, radio/alarm clock, safety deposit box at reception, trouser press.*
- *6-course table d'hôte dinner £34.95. Last orders 9.30 p.m. à la carte, lunch & special diets available*
- *Business services inc. 3 conference rooms to 100*
- *Billiards/snooker, croquet, fishing, indoor heated swimming pool; jacuzzi; sauna, solarium, fitness centre, equestrian centre, clay shooting, beauty therapy, tennis, falconry on premises; golf $1^1/_2$ miles.*
- *Open all year. Amex, Diners, Visa, Mastercard.*

Cockermouth 5, Keswick 5, Carlisle 25, London 295

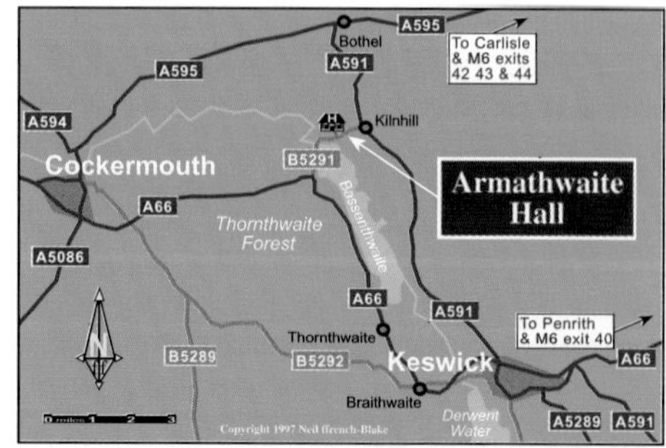

Graythwaite Manor Hotel

Grange-over-Sands, Cumbria LAll 7JE
Tel: (015395) 32001 / 33755;
Fax: (015395) 35549

What first impressed me here was the courtesy and thoroughness with which one of the owners showed me round. As a result of what I saw and felt, I returned a few days later for a night's lodging and this is what I found. A largish and substantial house, beautifully appointed and with every indication that the detailed comfort of visitors had been most conscientiously achieved. The armchairs were cosy enough to go to sleep in. The dining room, an imposing affair, displays cut glass chandeliers and some fine oil paintings. There was a choice from the à la carte or table d'hôte menus at dinner, both excellently cooked and served. I made a special note, too, of how pleasant and attentive the staff were, obviously taking their cue from the owners. Bedrooms, all with private baths fulfilled the expectation of the downstairs comfort and elegance. Faithful guests return year after year for Graythwaite and Grange are within easy reach of the Lake District.

Rates: *Dinner, room and breakfast from £57.50 single, £115.00 twin.* V
Special breaks *of two days or more available November to March; prices on request.*

- *22 bedrooms (some ground floor), 20 with private bathrooms and all with telephone, TV, tea/coffee making facilities, electric blankets.*
- *Drying room; small conferences.*
- *billiards; attractive gardens; golf locally, putting green; hard tennis court; riding nearby.*
- *Open all year. All major credit cards accepted.*

Lake District (Windermere) 15, Carlisle 58, Liverpool 76, London 261.

Netherwood Hotel

Grange-over-Sands, Cumbria LAll 6ET
Tel: (015395) 32552; Fax: (015395) 34121

Rates: *Room and breakfast from £50 single, £100 double.* ***Winter breaks*** *from 1st Nov. 1999-31st March 2000 (exc. Fridays & Saturdays): 2 nights £130; 3 nights £180. Prices per person include dinner, bed & breakfast and VAT.*

This imposing hotel, set in its own topiary gardens on a woodland slope, dominates the main road into Grange-over-Sands. The house dates back to 1893, and it retains all the original panelling, wood-carvings and fireplaces. However, modern conveniences also have their place here, and you will find a lift servicing the first floor bedrooms, and all the dining areas are air conditioned. There is a honeymoon suite with all its original furniture, to help you re-live the romance of days gone by, and there are ten new bedrooms, all non-smoking, furnished in harmony with the rest of the hotel. The food at the Netherwood is excellent, being prepared from the freshest ingredients with imagination and flair. It is easy to over-indulge in the dining room, but downstairs there is a heated swimming pool, spa bath, steam room and beauty salon where you can work off those extra inches gained, or simply relax after perhaps a tiring day touring this lovely area. The southern Lake District offers much for the nature lover and tourist alike, and the delights of Morecambe Bay and the Lune Valley are on the doorstep.

- *28 en suite bedrooms (1 for disabled); two pairs of intercommunicating bedrooms; all have radio, telephone, TV; night service; lift to 1st floor.*
- *Late meals, special diets; children welcome; baby listening; dogs allowed, conferences.*
- *Indoor heated swimming pool, spa bath, steam room, gymnasium, beauty area, parking for 160 cars, dancing, 11 acres of gardens; tennis 1/2 mile; squash, badminton, riding, shooting and fishing all five miles.*
- *Open all year. Major credit cards accepted.*

Lake District (Windermere) 5, Kendal 12, Keswick 41, Carlisle 58, Liverpool 82, London 262.

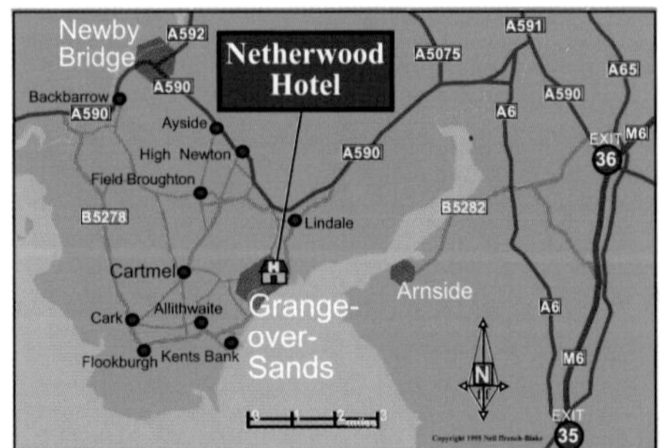

Dale Head Hall Lakeside Hotel

Thirlmere, Keswick, Cumbria CA12 4TN
Tel: (017687) 72478; Fax: (017687) 71070
E-Mail: enquiry@dale-head-hall. co.uk
Internet: http: / / www.dale-head-hall.co.uk

At the northern end of Thirlmere, you will find an hotel situated in one of the most idyllic positions in the Lake District. Set in a clearing on the shores of the lake, with Helvellyn rising majestically behind, you cannot help falling in love with Dale Head Hall. A small, yet luxurious hotel, this 16th century Hall is beautifully decorated in keeping with the age of the building. It exudes that intimate atmosphere of a true family home. The untiring enthusiasm, skill and innate sense of hospitality of the resident proprietors, Alan and Shirley Lowe, combine to make it a very special place. Three red squirrels play on the lawn. The sun sets over the lake and fell, as I join fellow guests in the lounge for an aperitif, all in eager anticipation of yet another wonderful meal. The award-winning cuisine is truly superb. They even grow their own vegetables, fruit, herbs and flowers in the Victorian kitchen garden. Dale Head Hall is in an ideal position for exploring the Lake District, with all the major attractions not far away. It comes highly recommended and represents some of the best value in Cumbria.

Rates: *Room and breakfast from £35; dinner, room & breakfast from £62.50. Cumbria Tourist Board 3 Star Silver Award.* V
Bargain Breaks: *Logfire Winter Breaks available from 1.11.99-27.04.00 any 2 nights from £57.50. Spring Breaks available from 2.5.00-1.8.00 any two nights from £67.50. All are based upon dinner,b&b per person per night.*

- *9 en suite bedrooms, all with direct dial telephone, room service.*
- *Last orders for dinner 8.00 p.m.; special diets*
- *Sailing, boating, shooting, fishing, tennis, spa pool, gymnasium, squash courts nearby. Golf five miles, riding seven miles.*
- *Open all year. All major credit cards accepted.*

Keswick 4, Grasmere 5, Penrith 16, London 285.

Hilton Keswick Lodore Hotel

Keswick, Cumbria
CA12 5UX
Tel: (017687) 77285;
Fax: (017687) 77343

The Hilton Keswick Lodore Hotel, situated overlooking Derwent Water and at the foot of the famous Lodore Falls, is an hotel of international class and reputation. It caters superbly for all manner of guests and their families. One of the most impressive aspects is the way in which children are looked after by N.N.E.B. nurses, with their own playroom and kitchen, providing parents with a welcome rest. The public rooms are all bright and airy, the bedrooms are spacious and well appointed, and the whole hotel is beautifully decorated and cheerful. Many of the excellent dishes served are from original Swiss recipes, and the staff are all courteous and friendly. The gardens are a delight, and the immediate environs have the most imposing views, yet there is also a gentler beauty in the landscape. All the Lake District, with its sporting facilities, as well as its natural and historical features is easily accessible, so whether you are holidaying as a family or alone, there is something here to suit you. The hotel also has its own many and varied facilities for guests to enjoy.

- *75 bedrooms all with en suite bathroom, satellite TV and telephone; room and night service; baby listening; lift.*
- *Last orders 9.15 p.m.; bar lunches; special diets.*
- *Children welcome; registered nursery with NNEB trained nannies; conferences up to 120.*
- *Games room; outdoor/indoor heated swimming pool; leisure centre; sauna; beautician; gymnasium; sunbed; squash and tennis; sailing, boating and riding nearby; fishing by arrangement; free golf Mon-Fri (18 hole course), Sat-Sun £20 per person.* ● *New air-conditioned function rooms.*
- *Open all year. All major credit cards accepted.*

***Rates**: Dinner, bed & breakfast from £67.00;* V *weekly rates (including dinner) from £416.00.*
***Bargain Breaks** - for a minimum of 2 nights, holiday rate from £41.00 per person per night applies, to include dinner, bed & breakfast.*

Keswick 3½, Penrith 21, Carlisle 38, London 300.

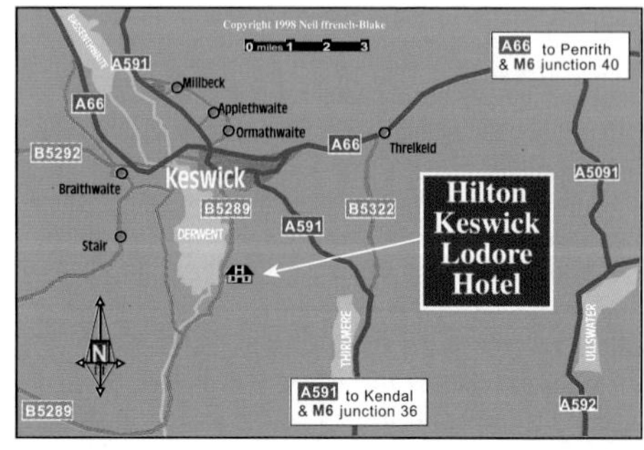

Scafell Hotel

Borrowdale, Nr. Keswick, Cumbria
CAl2 5XB
Tel: (017687) 77208; Fax: (017687) 77280

It is not surprising that the Scafell is becoming one of Lakeland's leading hotels following its recent improvements and the consistent efforts of its management. Situated almost at the head of the beautiful Borrowdale Valley, its position is as outstanding as the service and comfort which it provides for all its guests. There is an excellent table d'hôte menu and for those wishing to dine later, a comprehensive à la carte supper menu. Both menus are accompanied by a well balanced wine list. Year after year guests return to walk and climb for they know that they are going to be comfortable and well looked after. For the less energetic, there are cosy and homely lounges. The bedrooms are comfortable and attractively furnished, all of them having their own private bathroom. Pleasant views are to be had of the sheltered garden ringed by mighty mountains on which internationally famous climbers have learned their craft. Yes, this is a home for the visitor seeking peace or exercise and wishing to 'get away from it all'.

Rates: *Dinner, bed and breakfast from £48.00 to £60.00.*
Midweek breaks *available : any two consecutive nights Sunday-Thursday inclusive £79.00 per person, dinner, bed and breakfast. Fell Break Week-ends are available: Friday evening to Sunday lunch and include all dinners, packed lunches, breakfasts, afternoon tea and Sunday lunch - £118.00.*

- *24 en suite bedrooms (8 ground floor), all with direct-dial telephone, tea/coffee making facilities, TV; full central heating.*
- *Children welcome and dogs accepted; bar meals.*
- *Drying room; river bathing; boating; fishing; pony trekking; tennis six miles; golf ten miles.*
- *Hotel open all year.*

Keswick 6, Penrith 24, Carlisle 36, Kendal 36, London 291.

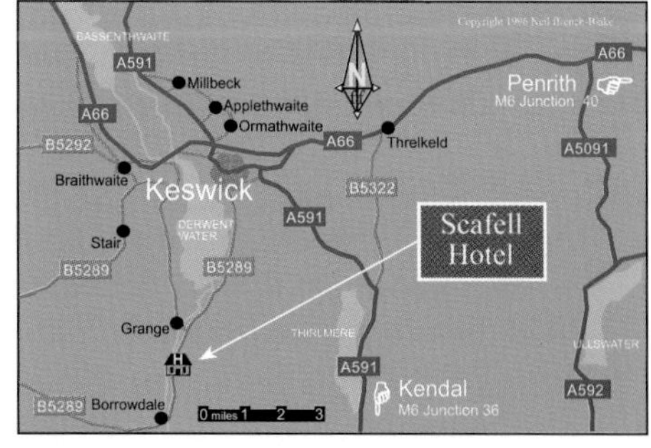

Our 52nd season

In 1948 Francis' father, James Coulson, threw a copy of the Manchester Guardian *on to his bed, and suggested that he looked to see if there were any properties on the market in the Lake District. There, to his amazement, he saw a small advertisement:* "Family mansion on the edge of Lake Ullswater, with half a mile of lake edge and twelve acres of woodlands. Offers".

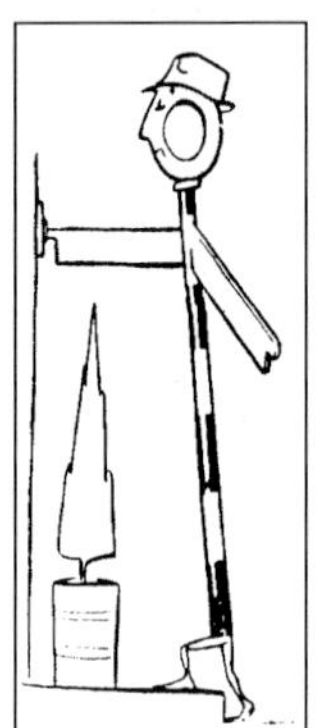

To cut a long story short, Francis came up to see this idyllic sounding place! Remember that just after the war there were no motorways, petrol was rationed, food was rationed, furniture required dockets and the Lake District was very unfashionable.

However, in October 1948 he arrived with very little capital, but the full support of his father and family. With the help of friends he was able to open Sharrow for guests at Easter 1949, with just a few rooms and a lot of faith!

Progress was slow but in a very short time Francis' baking became renowned and people were queuing up for the home made teas at two shillings and sixpence (12 1/2 pence) each!!

In 1952 fate stepped in and Brian Sack met Francis and likewise fell in love with Sharrow. They complemented one another perfectly with Francis producing his superb food and Brian running the dining room and the office. They both have a love of people and their interests were identical.

In 1958 Sharrow was accepted into the Signpost Hotel Guide, *created by Mr Mc Minnies (*"weekly terms from nine and a half guineas - reduced in winter"). *Gradually rooms were developed, twelve in the main house, four in the Lodge annexe, three in the cottage in the grounds, two in Thwaite cottage four miles away, and finally seven in Bank House, a converted 17th century farmhouse one mile away with a magnificent panoramic view of Ullswater.*

And so, having reached our 52nd season, nothing could have been achieved without the help and loyalty of so many people. Now we are trying to maintain the standards that are expected of us, as we are told that we have become a living legend!

Sharrow Bay Country House Hotel

Ullswater, Howtown, Nr. Penrith,
Cumbria CA10 2LZ
Tel: (017684) 86301 / 86483;
Fax: (017684) 86349
E-mail:enquiries@sharrow-bay.com

Away from the bustle of the holiday rush, in one of the most envied positions in the Lake District lies Sharrow Bay. The late Francis Coulson M.B.E. and Brian Sack M.B.E. must be congratulated on their 52nd year of service to the gourmets of the world, providing the most exquisite food and wines in the most comfortable of atmospheres. The reputation of being the first Country House Hotel in this country and being the oldest British member of *Relais et Chateaux* collection is surely recommendation enough, but people who have stayed here will still describe in nothing but superlatives the home from home atmosphere that the owners have worked so hard to create and maintain. The décor is superb, the service impeccable and the overall effect is a tribute to these two brilliant hoteliers. Add to all this the beauty of the Lake and mountains and you have total perfection. I should add that there is now a beautiful converted farmhouse called Bank House, about a mile from Sharrow, which has seven superbly furnished bedrooms, all with private bathrooms and lake views . Breakfast is served in the magnificent Refectory dining room, which was converted from the seventeenth century barn. It has a striking Portland stone fireplace and over-mantle, which came from Warwick Castle. It also has incredible English silk damask curtains, old English furniture and a specially made carpet - a copy of one in the Royal Opera House. Some of the staff have been with the hotel for over 30 years, and Brian Sack with Nigel Lightburn, who is now managing director, will carry on Sharrow Bay's renowned traditions. Tariff on application.

- *26 bedrooms; 24 with private bath and/or shower, including 6 cottage suites, TV, radio, antiques, peace. Small conference facilities.*
- *Golf locally, lake bathing, boating, riding, fishing*
- *Closed end-November to end-February.*

Penrith 7, Keswick 20, Kendal 33, London 289

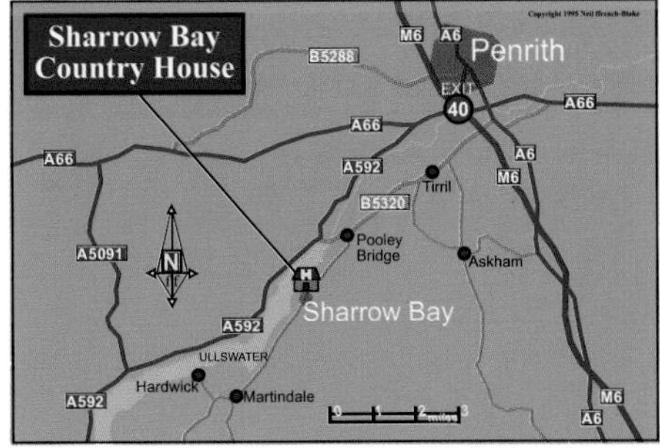

The Old Church Hotel

Old Church Bay, Watermillock,
Cumbria CA11 OJN
Tel: (017684) 86204; Fax: (017684) 86368
E-mail: info@oldchurch.co.uk
Website: http://www.oldchurch.co.uk

A long drive through meadowland to the shores of Lake Ullswater (one of the less touristy areas of the Lake District) brings you to this delightful hotel. Its extensive lawns run down to the lake and the surroundings are of great beauty with magnificent views of lake and mountain scenery. On entering the gracious hall, the visitor has his first impression of the pleasures and comforts to come. The bedrooms and public rooms are all beautifully and decorated to create the ambience of a country house of bygone days - the building dates from 1734 and is on the site of a 12th century church. The owners, Kevin and Maureen Whitemore, ensure that the service is discreetly impeccable, that the food is delicious and that the well-being of their guests remains of primary concern. All the Lake District's attractions are close by: climbing and walking from the hotel and sailing and boating on the doorstep. The less energetic can just savour the air, good food and comfort.

Rates: *single room inc. breakfast from £65.00 double/twin inc. breakfast from £90.00*
Bargain Breaks: *Rates on application.*

- *10 en suite bedrooms, all with colour TV, direct-dial telephone, hairdryer tea/coffee making facilities*
- *A la carte dinner from £20. Last order 8.00p.m. (Closed Sunday evenings). Car parking for 20 cars*
- *Airport pick up and car rental by arrangement.*
- *Fishing. Sailing/boating, riding, watersports four miles.*
- *Closed beginning of November to end-March.*
- *Mastercard, Amex, Visa credit cards accepted*

M6 (Junction 40) 7, Penrith 7½, Ambleside 15, Keswick 17, Kendal 26, London 281.

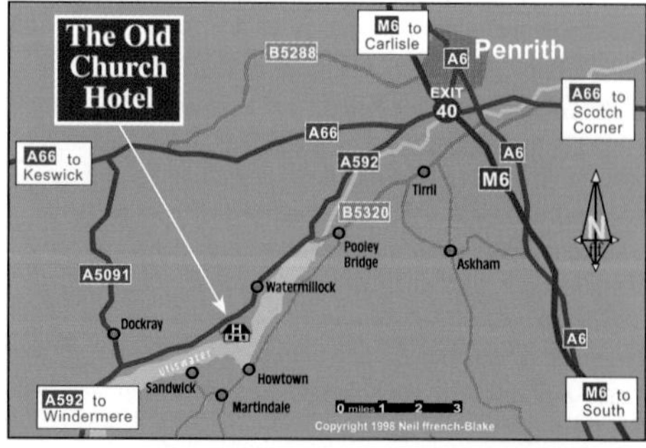

Cedar Manor Hotel

Ambleside Road, Windermere,
Cumbria LA23 1AX
Tel: (015394) 43192; Fax (015394) 45970
E-mail: cedarmanor@fsbdial.co.uk
Internet: http://www.cedarmanor.co.uk

True lovers of the Lake District wishing to immerse themselves in everything that the beautiful area has to offer will naturally seek out a smaller, more intimate hotel. They need look no further than the Cedar Manor which is a traditional and very genuine Lakeland house, with some interesting architectural features, in a country garden setting. Moreover all that is within the hotel is a reflection of its peaceful and secluded location for it exudes an air of comfort, friendliness and quiet efficiency with the added bonus of immaculate decoration and elegant furnishings in the public rooms. The bedrooms too are very comfortable and some have lovely views towards Lake Windermere. The reputation of the restaurant had preceded it and is reflected in the many awards and accolades it has received from connoisseurs. The food was indeed excellent with fresh local produce and I enjoyed a roast leg of lamb Westmoreland style with Cumberland sausage stuffing and other trimmings. This homely country hotel, so close to Cumbria's beauties and not far from its many other attractions, is a place for the lover of good things in life. The Cedar Manor puts it another way: "Often sought, seldom found".

***Rates:** Single room including breakfast from £40.00. Double room with breakfast from £60.00.*
***Leisure Breaks**: Christmas & New Year Pro grammes; Golf Breaks - throughout the year. Honeymoon Package. Details of all these are available upon request.*

- *12 en suite bedrooms with radio & colour TV, direct-dial telephone, hairdryer, laundry service; tea/coffee making facilities.*
- *4-course table d'hôte £18.50; last orders 20.30 hrs. A la carte and special diets available.*
- *Fishing, watersports, riding, tennis & golf - all nearby. Hotel offers free use of local leisure facilities. Car parking for 16 cars.*
- *Open all year. All credit cards accepted (except Amex and Diners).*

Kendal 8, Penrith 26, Lancaster 28, London 246.

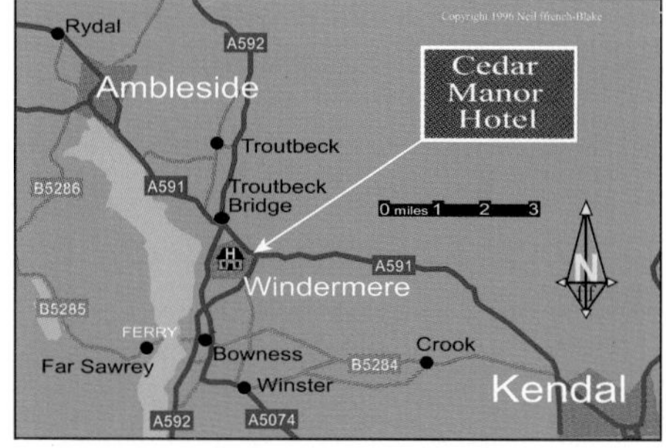

Linthwaite House Hotel

Crook Road, Windermere, The Lake District, Cumbria LA23 3JA
Tel: (015394) 88600; Fax: (015394) 88601
E-mail: admin@linthwaite.com

This hotel, situated on the B5284 Bowness to Kendal road, only a mile or so from Bowness, is surely the epitome of what every Signposter would like to find. It is set in 14 acres of superbly kept grounds with magnificent views of Lake Windermere and of every major peak in the Lake District. There is a well stocked tarn (in which 5 lb trout have been caught) and where one can while away the day with a picnic. The golf practice area is surrounded by lovely woodland walks. Naturally, within a very short distance are all the other amenities that one expects in the area, such as swimming, yachting and tennis. But enough of outside activities! Inside the hotel is immaculate, tastefully interior designed. A feature is the use of old trunks and suitcases. The food is superb and many of the guests return to Linthwaite again and again. Surely this speaks more eloquently than any words? Any Signposter who visits here for the first time will, like others, keep coming back to the atmosphere of peace and tranquillity.

Rates: *Room and breakfast £75-£250.* V
Romantic breaks *(minimum 2 nights) - including champagne in room on arrival, box of hand made chocolates, canopied king size double bed with lake view, breakfast and candlelit dinner.*

● *26 en suite bedrooms (7 ground floor), all with direct dial telephone and satellite TV; room service* ● *Last orders for dinner 8.45 p.m., light lounge lunches; special diets. No under 7s in restaurant for dinner.* ● *Children welcome. Conferences to 30* ● *Sauna, solarium, spa pool, gymnasium and golf one mile; mountain walking and riding three miles; sailing/boating and water-skiing one mile; golf practice hole par 3; own tarn brown trout. Mountain bikes to hire at hotel.*
● *Open all year; all major credit cards accepted.*

Bowness 1, Kendal 7, Manchester 76, London 280.

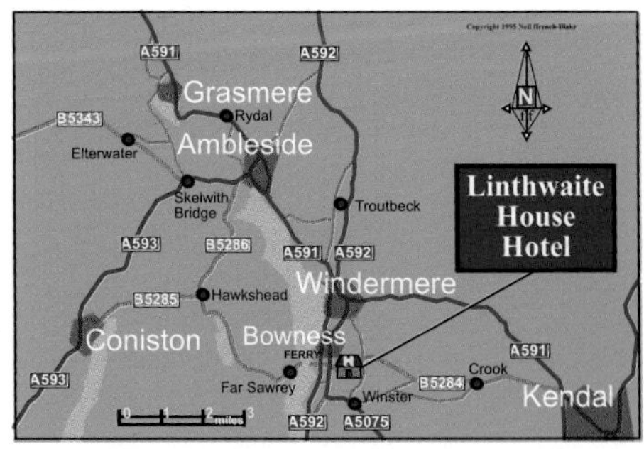

The Old Vicarage Country House Hotel

Witherslack, Cumbria LAll 6RS
Tel: (015395) 52381; Fax: (015395) 52373
E-Mail: hotel@old-vic.demon.co.uk
Internet: http://www.oldvicarage.com

The Old Vicarage was recommended to me by one of the country's top hoteliers - and how right he was. For those wishing to visit the Lake District, to remain in perfect peace and seclusion and yet to sample the art of cooking and service at their best, then here is the venue in which to do so to perfection. The hotel is set in a particularly beautiful valley and it offers the finest of food prepared only from the freshest of ingredients. It is indeed a haven. The atmosphere is of unhurried simplicity but the thought and energy expended to achieve this ambience is, I am sure, immeasurable. The Browns and the Reeves, joint owners, have set a standard that many hotels will strive to match but which few will attain. I look forward to visiting this unique hotel again, and especially to staying in the "Celebration Suite", one of the new bedrooms in the Orchard House, with its terraces overlooking unspoilt woodland.

Rates: *Dinner, room and breakfast £70-95 per person, inc VAT & service. Celebration suite £100.* V
Bargain breaks *- near to the lakes, far from the crowds. Any two nights, midweek or weekends, fully inclusive from £60 per person, dinner, bed and breakfast per night.*

- *14 en suite bedrooms including five in the Orchard House, all with telephone, colour TV.*
- *Dinner 7.00 p.m. until 9.00 p.m; diets available. Non-residents 3-course à la carte from £20.*
- *Children by arrangement; dogs by arrangement.*
- *All weather tennis court for guests' use; sailing, golf, squash, badminton, riding, shooting, fishing all nearby.*
- *Open all year. Major credit cards accepted.*

M6 Junction 36 10 mins., Sea 4, Lake Windermere 6, Kendal 8, Lancaster 19, London 263.

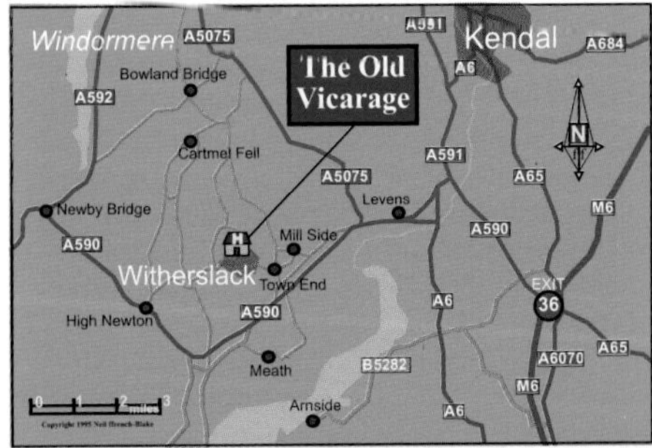

Chadwick Hotel

TOURISM AWARDS 1999

Best Small Hotel *of the* Year Award

South Promenade, Lytham St Annes, Lancashire FY8 1NP

Tel: (01253) 720061; Fax: (01253) 714455

E-mail: sales@chadwickhotel.com

Internet: http://www.chadwickhotel.com

I was most impressed with this award winning hotel. It is owned and run by the Corbett family and every detail has been carefully thought out and provided. The staff are particularly charming and helpful and they immediately make you feel at home. The décor is bright and airy and all the rooms are well decorated and comfortable. Here are all the facilities of a large international hotel, but without the pomposity sometimes associated with them. There are rooms for the disabled; there is a health club with an indoor heated swimming pool, spa bath, solarium & gymnasium and the bedrooms have every convenience including in-house movies and satellite TV. The Chadwick Hotel's newly refurbished restaurant serves excellent food and has an extensive wine list. The Bugatti Bar features over 100 malt whiskies. The Chadwick is situated right on the sea front of this pretty town and there are particularly good rates for families with children and also for the keen golfer with many superb courses within a very short distance.

Rates: *Double/twin room and breakfast from £30 per person, including VAT.* **V**

Bargain breaks. *Midwinter breaks with two persons sharing £39.50 for dinner, bed & breakfast. Alternatively our popular dinner dance and speciality weekends include entertainment on Friday and 7-course banquet with dancing on Saturday for £85.50 per person for the complete weekend.*

● *75 en suite bedrooms (2 for the disabled), some with 4-poster beds, some with spa baths, all with direct dial telephone and TV; room service; baby listening; night service; 24-hour food service; lift.* ● *Last orders for dinner 8.30 p.m., bar meals; diets.* ● *Children welcome. Conferences max. 50.* ● *Childrens' soft adventure playroom; indoor heated swimming pool; leisure centre/gym; sauna; solarium; spa pool; sea fishing; golf ½ mile; sailing, boating, tennis & squash courts 1 mile; riding 3 m.* ● *Open all year; all major credit cards accepted.*

Blackpool 7, Preston 14, Lancaster 30, London 224.

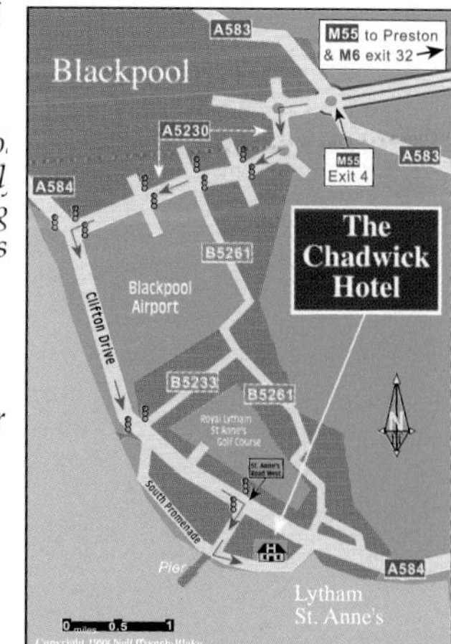

Yorkshire & The North East

Historic Houses, Gardens & Parks

Cleveland
Burn Valley Gardens, Hartlepool
Fairy Dell, Middlesbrough
Ormesby Hall, Ormesby, Middles brough
Ward Jackson Park, Hartlepool

County Durham
Eggleston Hall Gardens, Eggleston
Hardwick Hall Country Park, Stockton-on-Tees
Houghall Gardens, Durham

East Riding of Yorkshire
Burton Agnes Hall, Driffield
Burton Constable Hall & Country Park, Nr. Hull
Sledmere House, Driffield

Northumberland
Alnwick Castle
Belsay Hall, Castle & Gardens, Belsay
Cragside House & Country Park, Rothbury
Hexham Herbs, Chollerford
Howick Hall Gardens, Alnwick
Hulne Park, Alnwick
Lady Waterford Hall, Berwick on-Tweed
Meldon Park, Morpeth
Otterburn Hall
Paxton House, Berwick on-Tweed
Seaton Delaval Hall, Blyth
Shaw Garden Centre Cramlington
Wallington House Walled Garden & Grounds, Morpeth

Tyne & Wear
Bessie Surtees House, Newcastle-upon-Tyne
Bolam Lake Country Park, Newcastle-upon-Tyne
Kirkley Hall Gardens, Ponteland
Rising Sun Country Park & Countryside Centre, Benton
Saltwell Park, Gateshead

Yorkshire - North, West & South
Allerton Park, Knaresborough
Beningbrough Hall, York
Bramham Park, Wetherby
Burnby Hall Gardens, Pocklington
Castle Howard, Coneysthorpe
Constable Burton Hall Gardens, Leyburn
Duncombe Park, Helmsley
East Riddlesden Hall, Keighley
Epworth Old Rectory, Doncaster
Fairfax House ,York
Golden Acre Park, Bramhope
Harewood House, Leeds
Harlow Carr Botanical Gardens, Harrogate
Japanese Garden, Horsforth
Kiplin Hall Richmond
Land Farm Garden, Hebden Bridge
Lotherton Hall, Leeds
Margaret Waudby Oriental Garden, Upper Poppleton Newburgh Priory, York
Newby Hall Gardens, Ripon
Normanby Hall, Scunthorpe
Nostell Priory, Wakefield
Nunnington Hall, York
Parceval Hall Gardens, Skipton
Ripley Castle, Harrogate
St Nicholas Gardens, Richmond
Sheffield Botanical Gardens
Sheriff Hutton Park, Nr. York
Stockfield Park, Wetherby
Sutton Park, Nr. York
Temple Newsam House, Leeds
Thorp Perrow Arboretum, Bedale

Walks & Nature Trails

Cleveland
Bilingham Beck Valley Country Park

County Durham
Allensford Park, Consett
Blackton Nature Reserve, Teesdale
Derwent Walk, Consett
Durham Coast, Peterlee
Hamsterley Forest, Bishop Auckland

East Riding of Yorkshire
Elsham Hall Country & Wildlife Park, Brigg
Humber Bridge Country Park, Hessle
Normanby Hall Country Park, Scunthorpe

Northumberland
Allen Banks Woods, Hexham
Bedlington Country Park
Carlisle Park & Castle Wood, Morpeth
Fontburn Nature Reserve
Hareshaw Dene, Bellingham, Hexham
Ingram National Park Visitor Centre
Northumberland Coast, Newton-by-the-Sea, Alnwick
Plessey Woods Country Park
Scotch Gill Wood Local Nature Reserve, Morpeth

Tyne & Wear
Derwent Walk Country Park, Rowlands Gill
The Leas & Marsden Rock, S.Shields
Thornley Woodlands Centre, Rowlands Gill

Yorkshire - North, West & South
Anglers Country Park, Wintersett
Barlow Common Nature Reserve, Selby
Bretton Country Park, Wakefield
Bridestones Moor, Pickering
Brimham Rocks, Harrogate
Cannon Hall Country Park, Barnsley
Chevin Forest Park, Otley
Dalby Forest Drive & Visitor Centre, Pickering
Hardcastle Crags, Hebden Bridge
Howstean Gorge, Pateley Bridge
Malham Tarn, Settle
Millington Wood Local Nature Reserve

Marston Moor, Huddersfield
Newmillerdam Country Park, Wakefield
Ogden Water, Halifax
Ravenscar Coastline, Scarborough
Rother Valley Country Park, Sheffield
Sutton Bank Nature Trail - between Helmsley & Thirsk
Ulley Country Park, Sheffield
Worsbrough Country Park, Barnsley

Historical Sites & Museums

Cleveland
Guisborough Priory, Guisborough
Gray Art Gallery & Museum, Hartlepool
Guisborough Museum, York
Saltburn Smugglers Heritage Centre
PSS Wingfield Castle, Hartlepool

County Durham
Barnard Castle
Beamish - The North of England Open Air Museum
Durham Cathedral
Durham Castle
Raby Castle, Staindrop

East Riding of Yorkshire
Burton Agnes Manor House, Driffield
Maister House, Hull
Wilberforce House, Hull

Northumberland
Aydon Castle
Bamburgh Castle
Berwick Castle, Berwick on-Tweed
Brinkburn Priory, Longframlington
Chesters Roman Fort, Hexham
Chillingham Castle
Dunstanburgh Castle
Edlingham Castle
Etal Castle, Etal, Cornhill-on-Tweed
Grace Darling's Museum, Bamburgh
Hadrian's Wall
Hexham Abbey
House of Hardy Museum & Country Store, Alnwick
Lindisfarne Castle, Holy Island, Berwick-on-Tweed
Marine Life Centre & Fishing Museum, Seahouses
Norham Castle, Berwick-on-Tweed
Prudhoe Castle
Warkworth Castle
Wine & Spirit Museum & Victorian Chemist Shop, Berwick-on-Tweed

Tyne & Wear
Castle Keep, Newcastle-upon-Tyne
Hatton Gallery, Newcastle-u-Tyne
The Laing Art Gallery, Newcastle-upon-Tyne
Newbum Hall Motor Museum, Newcastle-upon-Tyne
The Shipley Art Gallery, Gateshead
South Shields Museum, South Shields

Yorkshire North, West & South
Aldborough Roman Town, Nr. Borougbridge
Assembly Rooms, York
BardenTower, Bolton Abhey
Barley Hall, York
Beverley Minster, Beverley
Bishops House, Sheffield
Bolling Hall, Bradford
Bolton Castle, Leyburn
Borthwick Institute of Historical Research, York
Bronte Parsonage Museum, Haworth
Captain Cook Memorial Museum, Whitby
Clifford's Tower, York
Dales Countryside Museum, Hawes
Eureka! The Museum for Children, Halifax
Fountains Abbey a Studley Royal, Ripon
Fulneck Moravian Settlement & Museum, Nr. Pudsey
Gainsthorpe Deserted Medieval Village
Georgian Theatre Royal & Museum, Richmond
Jervaulx Abbey, Ripon
Jorvik Viking Centre & Brass Rubbing Centre, York
Kirstall Abbey, Leeds
King's Manor, York
Marmion Tower, Ripon
Mount Grace Priory, Northallerton
National Museum of Photography, Film & Television, Bradford
National Railway Museum, York
Red House, Gomerad
Rievalulx Abbey, Rievaulx
Sion Hill Hall & Birds of Prey Centre, Kirkby Wiske
Skipton Castle, Skipton
The Old Smithy & Heritage Centre, Owston Ferry
Tetleys Brewery Wharf, Leeds
Treasurer's House, York
York Castle Museum, York
York Story, York
York Minster, York

Entertainment Venues

Cleveland
Botanic Centre, Middlesbrough
Cleveland Craft Centre, Middlesbrough
Margrove South Cleveland Heritage Centre, Boosbeck, Saltburn-by-Sea
Stewart Park, Middlesbrough

County Durham
Bowlees Visitor Centre, Middleton-in-Teesdale

East Riding of Yorkshire
Bondville Miniature Village, Sewerby
Fosse Hill Jet Ski Centre, Driffield
Humberside Ice Arena, Hull
Sewerby Hall, Park & Zoo, Bridlington

Northumberland
Belford Craft Gallery
Tower Knowe Visitor Centre, Kielder Water, Hexham

Tyne & Wear
Bowes Railway Centre, Gateshead
Predator Paintball, Newcastle-upon-Tyne

Yorkshire North, South & West
Catterick Indoor Ski Centre, Catterick Garrison
Flamingo Land Family Funpark & Zoo, Malton
Harrogate Ski Centre, Yorkshire Showground
Hemsworth Water Park & Playworld
Hornsea Pottery Leisure Park & Freeport Shopping Village
Kinderland, Scarborough
Lighwater Valley Theme Park, North Stainley
North of England Clay Target Centre, Rufforth
Piece Hall, Halifax
Sheffield Ski Village, Sheffield
The Alan Ayckbourn Theatre in the Round,Scarborough
Tockwith (Multi-Drive)Activity Centre, Tockwith Thybergh Country Park
Turkish Baths, Harrogate
Watersplash World, Scarborough
The World of Holograms, Scarborough

DIARY OF EVENTS

January

5*. **Sainsbury's Classic Cola National Basketball Cup Finals.** Sheffield Arena.
16. **Epiphany Procession.** Sheffield Cathedral.

February

19.* **Jorvik Viking Festival.** Various venues, York. Viking themed - combat, feasts, fireworks, music etc.
25*.**Greenalls Grand National Trial Chase**, Haydock Park
26*. **Northern Classic Restoration Show.** Flower Hall, Gt Yorks Showgr'd, Harrogate

March

3-19* **Bradford Film Festival** National Museum of Photography, Pictureville, Bradford.
10-31 Dec.**Science City York Festival**. Var venues in York
13-18*. **Skipton Music Festival.** Town Hall, Skipton, North Yorkshire,
29. **Leeds Doll & Teddy Fair.** Civic Hall, Pudsey, West Yorkshire.

April

1-2. **Complementary Medicine Festival.** Ilkley
1-2. **Exhibition: Eat, Drink & Be Merry.** Fairfax House, York.
15. **Open Dog Show.** Hull Indoor Bowls Centre, Hull
21-28. **Harrogate International Youth Music Festival.** Var. venues, Harrogate.
22-25. **York Model Railway Show.**York Racecourse, The Knavesmire,York, N Yorks
27-30. **Harrogate Antique & Fine Art Fair.** Harrogate Conference Centre, N Yorks.
27-30. **Harrogate Spring Flower Show.** Great Yorkshire Showground, Harrogate
15*. **Thirsk Classic Trail**. Race meeting, Thirsk, N York
28-May 7*. **Bridlington Arts Festival.** Var. venues, Bridlington, ex-Humberside.

May

May*.**Railway Festival.** National Railway Museum, York
4-7. **Great Northern Needlework Fair.** Gt Yorkshire Showground, Harrogate.
6-1st Oct. **Summer in the City.** Var venues in/ardYork
7-21*. **Sheffield Chamber Music Festival - Music of the Millenium.** Crucible Studio Theatre, Sheffield.
7. **41st Annual Brass Band**

Contest. Grand Hall, Scarboro'
27-June 5*. **Scarborough Fayre.** Worldwide Morris & Folk Festival. Var. venues, Scarborough, North Yorks.
14-21. **Wharfdale Festival**. Rural Arts. Ilkley, West Yorks
16-18. **Race Meeting**.York RC
27-29. **Window on the World Int'l Music Festival.** Nth. Shields Fishquay & Town Centre,Tyne & Wear.
29. **Northumberland County Show.** (agricultural) Tynedale Park, Corbridge, Northumberland.

June

1-31 July. **Hull International Festival.** Var venues, Hull.
3-4. **Archery Weekend.** Yorkshire Archery Assoc'n, Clifton Park, Clifton.
10. **Halifax Charity Gala & Procession.** Halifax.
16-18. **Beverley & E. Riding Folk Festival**. Beverley.
20-21. **Durham Regatta.** River Wear, Durham.
22-22 July. **York Millennium Mystery Play.** York Minster.
29-1 July. **Newcastle Plate Meeting.** Ncastle Race C'se

July

1-9. **Thirsk Festival.** Bewerley Park, Pateley Brdg
8. **Durham Miners Gala.** Racecourse / streets.Durham
7-14.**York Early Music Festival.** Various venues, York, North Yorkshire.
7-8. **Music by Moonlight.** Magic, Fountains Abbey, Ripon.
8-9. **Riverside Music Festival.** Calder Homes Pk, Hebden Br.
11-13. **Great Yorkshire Show.** Gt Yorks Showground, Harrogate.
ships. Gateshead Stadium, Neilson Rd,Gateshead
21-22. **Open Air Opera.** Fountains Abbey, Ripon, North Yorkshire.

August

5-6. **Sunderland Int'l Air Show.** Promenade, Sea Front, Seaburn, Sunderland
2-6. **Jazz on the Waterfront.** Hull Jazz Festival, various venues, Hull, E Yorkshire.
8. **Halifax Agricultural Show.** Savile Park, Halifax, W Yorks
8-15*. **Leeds International Piano Competition.** Theatre Royal, Leeds, West Yorks.
12-13. **Driffield Steam & Vintage Rally.** The Showground, Driffield.
22-24. **York Races.** York Racecourse.

September

31 Aug-3 Sept. **International Sea Shanty Festival**.The Marina & var. venues, Hull.
7-23. **Leeds Int'l Pianoforte Competition.** Leeds,W York
15-17. **Autumn Flower Show.** Gt Yorks Showgrd, Harrogate.
22-23 **York Book Fair**, Barbican

October

6-14. **Hull Fair.** Walton St Fairground, Hull, E. Riding.
21. **Leeds Doll & Teddy Fair.** Civic Hall, Pudsey, West Yorks.
23. **National Classic Motorcycle Rest'n Show,** Gt Yorks Showground, Harrogate.

November

8-19. **Hull Literature Festival,** various venues, Hull.
15-26. Huddersfield Contemporary Music Festival.

December

1-9. **Christmas Concert Series**, Fountains Abbey, Ripon
2-3. **City of Durham Christmas Festival.** Var. Durham
15-21. **York Early Music Christmas Festival.**Var.York.

Yorkshire Tourist Board
312 Tadcaster Road
York YO2 2HF.
Tel: (01904) 707961

Northumbria Tourist Board
Aykley Heads, Durham DH1 5UX
Tel: (0191) 375 3000

Northumbria

Northumbria is an undiscovered holiday para dise, where the scenery is wild and beautiful, the beaches golden and unspoiled, and the natives friendly. The region is edged by the North Sea, four national parks and the vast Border Forest Park. Its eastern boundary with the sea is a stunning coastline - stretching 100 miles from Staithes on the border of Cleveland and North Yorkshire to Berwick-on-Tweed, England's most northerly town. In between you'll find as many holiday opportunities here as changes of scenery. There's a wonderful variety of seascapes, from Cleveland's towering cliffs to the shimmering white sands of Northumberland, where you can lose yourself in the dunes. Inland you will find the remarkable Hadrian's Wall, the National Park, hills, forests, waterfalls, castles, splendid churches and quaint towns and villages. Northumbria combines the fun of a seaside holiday with the relaxation of a break in the country.

History books come alive in Northumberland and exploring its heritage could take a lifetime. In the far north, Berwick-on-Tweed (fought over by the English and Scots for centuries) is steeped in history and has the finest preserved example of Elizabethan town walls in the country. The town is an ideal gateway to the Borders. Visitors can trace man's occupation of the region from prehistoric times to the Victorian age of invention. Prehistoric rock carvings, ancient hill forts, Roman remains, Saxon churches, Norman priories, medieval castles and a wealth of industrial archaeology can all be discovered here.

The region has a rich maritime heritage too. Imposing ruins, such as the gaunt remains of Dunstanburgh or fairy-tale Lindisfarne, are relics of a turbulent era when hordes of invaders landed on Northumberland's shores. Of course you don't have to explore castles and museums to capture the maritime flavour. Instead laze on a beach, fish from the end of the pier or take a trip from the fishing village of Seahouses, Northumberland, to the Fame Islands - a marvellous bird sanctuary and breeding ground of the Atlantic Grey Seal.

Lovers of the great outdoors will find Northumbria a paradise. In the National Park, where sheep outnumber people, the views will take your breath away. It is possible to enjoy the splendours of this area by car, but the remote hills are for the walker. Some of the wildest, highest and most beautiful scenery in England can be seen in the North Pennines. The noisiest thing in this peaceful refuge is the dramatic waterfall High Force! You'll pass through pretty villages such as Cotherstone in Teesdale, St John's Chapel in Weardale and Blanchland in Northumberland.

Holy Island. Photo - Northumbria Tourist Board

Searchers for activity will find the perfect base here also. Hike it, bike it, watch it - whatever your sport, you can do it in Northumbria. The countryside is ideal for pony trekking, walking, climbing, ballooning, orienteering, cycling, fishing, watersports and golf. Some hotels offer activity packages, such as golf or fishing weekends. More traditional local sports such as *hound trailing* and *Cumberland Wrestling* can be found at agricultural shows.

Naturally with so much countryside, agriculture is one of the region's most important industries. A super place to take children is Heatherslaw Mill, near Ford (a delightful model village), a restored water-driven corn mill and agricultural museum. If you were a fan of the television series *One Man and His Dog*, then the skill of shepherd and dog can be seen at sheepdog trials and country shows.

The ancient crafts and customs of Northumbria provide a fascinating insight into the character of this lovely region. It is said that fact can be stranger than fiction, and you'll have fun exploring some of the local myths, from the tiny island of Lindisfarne to the church in the pretty village of Kirknewton, close to the Cheviots, where the sculptured *Adoration of the Magi* depicts the Wise Men wearing kilts!

A less well known feature of the region is that is has one of the liveliest arts scenes outside London. The Theatre Royal, Newcastle, is the third home of the Royal Shakespeare Company and a venue for other major touring companies. Throughout the region you can enjoy first class entertainment from open air Shakespeare to costumed pageants; from the Royal Ballet to Rock N Roll, from Mozart to music hall.

Warkworth Castle. Photo - Northumbria Tourist Board

Wherever you go, from the traditional pub in a tiny village to a top class hotel, you'll always find a warm welcome. The region is well served by trunk roads, high speed trains and airports. Please contact the Northumbria Tourist Board, address on previous page, for details.

Yorkshire

Yorkshire, so rich in history and tradition, boasts some of the country's most splendid scenery. For wide open spaces, visit the North York Moors with their 500 square miles of hills, dales, forest and open moorland, neatly edged by a spectacular coastline. Walking, cycling and pony trekking are ideal ways to savour the scenery; alternatively take the steam train from Pickering to Grosmont on the famous North Yorkshire Moors Railway.

Numerous greystone towns and villages dotted throughout the Moor2s are ideal bases from which to explore the countryside. From Helmsley, visit the ruins of Reivaulx Abbey, founded by Cistercian monks in the 12th century. In Hutton-le-Hole, the fascinating story of moorland life is told in the award-winning Ryedale Folk Museum. Likewise the Beck Isle Museum in Pickering provides a remarkable insight into the life of a country market town. A few miles down the road, you'll find Malton, once a Roman fortress, and a little further on, Castle Howard, (*see right*) the setting for *Brideshead Revisited.*

From the Moors to the Dales and a total change of scene. Wherever you go in the Dales, you'll come across visible reminders of the rich and changing past. In medieval days, solid fortresses were built to protect the area from marauding Scots, like Richmond, guarding on one side the Northern Dales and Middleham the other. Knaresborough, the home of the prophetess Mother Shipton, Ripley and Skipton all had their massive strongholds while Bolton Castle in Wensleydale once imprisoned Mary, Queen of Scots. The pattern of history is also enshrined in the great abbeys like Jervaulx Abbey, near Masham, where the monks first made Wensleydale cheese, Eastby Abbey on the banks of the river Swale, and the majestic ruins of Fountains Abbey (*below*) in the grounds of Studley Royal.

When exploring the Pennines, you will find history written across the landscape. For centuries sheep have grazed the uplands and cloth has been spun from their wool. The industrial revolution began here and, with the introduction of machinery, the mills sprang up. The fascinating story of England's Industrial Heritage can now be seen in the numerous craft centres and folk museums throughout West Yorkshire. To enjoy the countryside, take a trip on the steam hauled Keighley and Worth Valley Railway. Step off at Haworth, home of the Brontë sisters, a nd experience the rugged atmosphere of Wuthering Heights. Nor far from Haworth is Bingley, where the Leeds and Liverpool canal takes its famous uphill journey. In the past coal barges came this way, but nowadays holiday-makers in gaily painted boats have taken their place.

Moving into the East Riding, the scenery changes again. From the dramatic 400ft cliffs at Flamborough Head, sweeps south a forty-mile stretch of perfect sandy beach. Along this magnificent coastline, you will find the day and night entertainments of Cleethorpes and Bridlington, contrasting with the less boisterous attractions of Hornsea and Withernsea. From any of the seaside resorts it is an easy drive into the peaceful countryside of the Wolds, where you will find delightful old villages like Skidby, Thorngumbald , Fridaythorpe and Wetwang. The town of Beverley is a jewel of architectural heritage with its magnificent 13th-century minster and beautiful St Mary's Church, both set in a delightful lattice work of medieval streets and Georgian houses.

Back to the sea and to the city of Hull, you will find a lot has been happening: the Humber Bridge - the world's longest single span bridge at 1452 yards, and the colourful yacht haven, created from two abandoned city centre docks, to name but two. Hull's maritime history is recorded in the Museum.

No visit to the Northeast would be complete without savouring the delights of York. Wherever you turn within the city's medieval walls, you will find fascinating glimpses of the past. It can be seen in the splendours of the 600-year old Minster, the grim stronghold of Clifford's Tower, The National Railway Museum, the medieval timbers of the Merchant Adventurers Hall and the Jorvik Viking Centre which illustrates life in a 10th century Viking township. Throughout the city, statues and monuments remind you that this was where Constantine was proclaimed Emperor, Guy Fawkes was born and Dick Turpin met his end.

Headlam Hall Hotel & Restaurant

Headlam, Nr. Gainford, Darlington, Co Durham DL2 3HA
Tel: (01325) 730238; Fax: (01325) 730790
E-mail: admin@headlamhall. co.uk
Internet: http://www.headlamhall.co.uk

This magnificent Jacobean manor house offers all that is best in country house accommodation. The Hall, built in the 17th century, has a rich history, having been the home of the Brockett family and more recently of Lord & Lady Gainford. The present owners, the Robinson family, took ownership in 1977 and have developed a super hotel, blending ancient and modern. It has 36 en suite individually furnished bedrooms, many with period furniture and some with four-posters. The restaurant is divided into four rooms, ranging from the elegance of the Victorian Room to the more modern warmth of the Patio Room. The Main Hall features an original carved oak fireplace and open staircase, and the Georgian drawing-room overlooks four acres of walled gardens featuring ancient beech hedges, colourful borders and a fishing lake. For the active guest, there is a tennis court and indoor pool among other leisure facilities. A good centre for touring Teesdale, Barnard Castle and Durham, Headlam Hall is a wonderful place for a superb leisure break.

Rates: *Single room and breakfast from £65; double room inc. breakfast from £80.* V
Short Breaks: *Min. 2 nights shared room, d, b & b pp per night Summer (May-Sept) £58; Winter (Oct-April) £53. Lord Gainford suite supp + £20; single room supplement +£15.*

- *36 en suite bedrooms (inc 2 suites), all with direct dial telephone, colour TV+ satellite; hairdryer, laundry/valet service, tea/coffee making facilities, trouser press, radio alarm clock. Disabled & non-smoker bedrooms available.*
- *A la carte dinner; lunch & special diets available. Last orders 9.45 pm.*
- *Business services inc 4 meeting rooms to 100.*
- *Snooker, croquet, fishing, fitness centre, sauna, clay shooting, indoor swimming pool. Riding and golf 7 miles. Car parking for 80+.*
- *Open all year exc. Xmas Day; major credit cards accepted.*

Barnard Cas. 8, Darlington 8, Bishop Auckland 9, Scotch Cnr 10, Durham 19, London 246

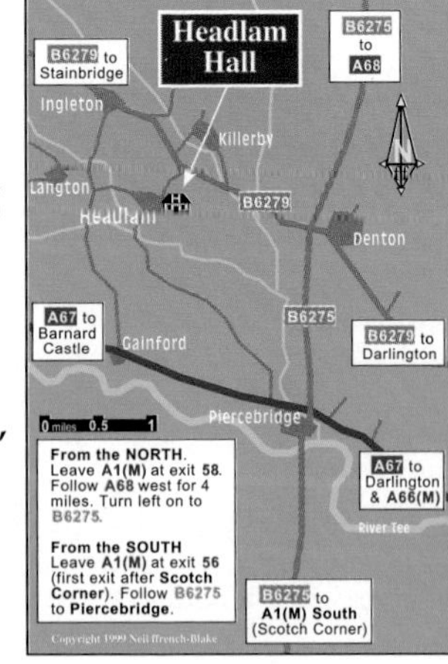

Waren House Hotel

Waren Mill, Belford, Northumberland
NE70 7EE
Tel: (01668) 214581; Fax: (01668) 214484
E-mail: enquiries@warenhousehotel. co.uk
Internet: http: / / warenhousehotel.co.uk

Waren House is quite simply one of the best Country House hotels in the north-east. Set in six acres of gardens and woodland, it is a peaceful and tranquil centre from which to visit one of this country's most naturally beautiful and historic areas, largely unspoiled by tourism and commercialism. The castles of Bamburgh, Dunstanburgh, Alnwick and Warkworth are all easily accessible; there is a wealth of birdlife along miles of magnificent coastline, particularly at Bundle Bay and Farn Islands and there is the Holy Island of Lindisfarne, the Cheviot s and Scottish Borders near at hand. After a day out sightseeing, you can return to the quiet luxury of Waren House where owners Peter and Anita Laverack and their staff will pamper you. Bedrooms are decorated in either Edwardian, Victorian, Oriental or French style and the public areas of the hotel are full of beautiful antiques and coll-ectibles. Then enjoy a gastronomic treat in the dining room and reflect on your good fortune. How many people speed by on the A1 without knowing the splendours that lie just off it both in this historic region in general and at Waren House in particular?

Rates: *Single room and breakfast from £57.50; double room inc. breakfast from £115.* V
Bargain Breaks: *2 nights - 4-course dinner, room & breakfast from £149 per person standard room. For stay of 7+ nights, free upgrade standard→ superior/superior→suite.*

● *10 en suite bedrooms (inc 2 suites), all with direct dial telephone, colour TV; hairdryer, tea/ coffee making facilities, trouser press. Non-smoker bedrooms available. Car parking for 15.*
● *Table d'hôte dinner £25; special diets available. Last orders 2030.*
● *Business services inc meeting room to 20. Children over 14 welcome; dogs welcome by arrangement; conferences (boardroom) 20 max*
● *Sea/river bathing, watersports. Tennis and golf 2 miles; riding 1/2 mile.*
● *Open all year; major credit cards accepted.*

Berwick 14, Alnwick 14, Newcastle 45, London 350.

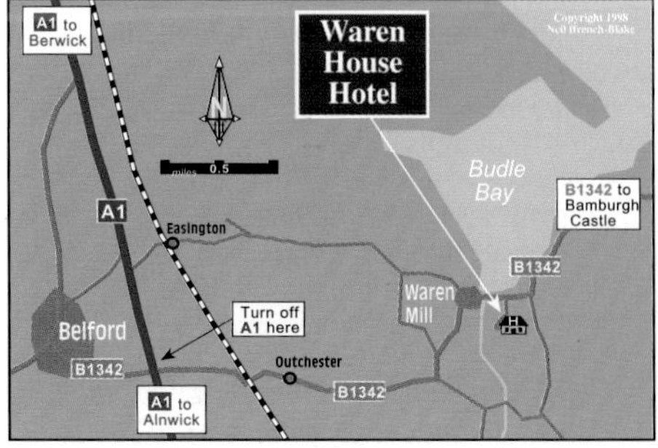

Aldwark Manor Hotel, Golf & Country Club

Aldwark, Nr. Alne, York YO6 2NF
Tel: (01347) 838146; Fax: (01347) 838867

The 15p toll paid at the old bridge in Aldwark is a very small price to pay to enter the peace and tranquillity of this lovely area of Yorkshire. The hotel - originally commissioned by Lord Walsingham in 1865 and steeped in history - continues to develop its facilities in order to provide every convenience for its guests. Retaining much of the opulence of the Victorian era, the hotel boasts 27 comfortable en suite bedrooms, spacious and elegant public rooms and two restaurants providing contrasting but equally delicious cuisine. The Rendlesham presents imaginative table d'hôte and à la carte menus and fine wines, whilst the delightful alfresco Brasserie offers a lighter menu. Both are superb venues for relaxation after a day enjoying the hotel and its environs - York, Harrogate, Castle Howard, the North Yorkshire moors or any of the six racecourses nearby. The hotel's own 6171 (par 71) 18-hole golf course is challenging, with every hole bordered by trees, a lake, a fountain or the meandering river Ure. No wonder the hotel is developing a reputation as one of the premier golfing & leisure centres in the north. Come on - spoil yourself !

Rates: *Single room with breakfast from £55; double room with breakfast from £110.*
Leisure Breaks: *Golf Break mid-week £130 pp, weekend £150 2 nights+. Yorkshire Break midweek £95 pp/weekend £110 pp 2 nights+.*

- *28 en suite bedrooms (inc one suite), all with direct-dial telephone, colour TV; hairdryer, laundry service, tea/coffee making facilities, 24-hour room service. Non-smoker bedrooms available.*
- *Last dinner orders 2130; lunch, bar meals, special diets available.*
- *Airport pickup by arrangement. Conferences to 80.*
- *Own 18-hole golf course. Fishing, riding by arrangement. Hair salon. Car parking for 80 cars.*
- *Open all year. All major credit cards accepted.*

Easingwold 3, Boroughbridge 7, Thirsk 12, York 14. London 212.

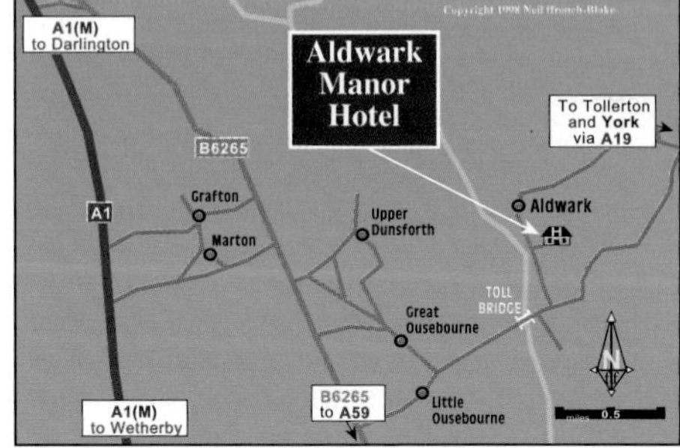

The Devonshire Arms Country House Hotel

Bolton Abbey, Skipton, North Yorkshire BD23 6AJ
Tel: (01756) 710441; Fax: (01756) 710564

The Devonshire Arms at Bolton Abbey continues to develop its reputation as one of Yorkshire's finest hotels. The superb furnishings and décor have been most tastefully chosen by the Duchess of Devonshire herself, using many paintings and antiques from her home at Chatsworth. One reason for the hotel's continued popularity is its ability to combine the warmth and comfort of the original coaching inn with the light and space of the more modern additions. These include the Devonshire Club, which offers an extensive range of leisure facilities. The two restaurants offer contrasting first class cuisine: Head Chef Andrew Nicholson has won for the Burlington two AA rosettes, and is aiming for a third. The restaurant now extends into a conservatory looking onto the Italian garden towards the moors and fells of Lower Wharfedale. A Brasserie and Bar, designed by Lady Hartington, opened in 1998 and serves lighter meals. The award-winning Devonshire Arms has it all - whether you are in this part of Yorkshire for business or pleasure, you will not tire of its character, luxury and beautiful Wharfedale location.

Rates: *Single room with breakfast from £110; Double room including breakfast from £155.*
Bargain Breaks*: 2-night breaks, dinner, b & b at £90 per person per night, based on 2 sharing.*

- *34 en suite bedrooms (inc. 7 4-posters), all with colour TV, direct-dial telephone, tea/coffee making facilities, hairdryer, laundry service, safety deposit box, trouser press. Disabled & non-smoker bedrooms available. Car parking for 150.*
- *Table d'hôte dinner £37; lunch & special diets available; last orders 10 pm.*
- *Croquet, fishing, fitness centre, jacuzzi/massage/sauna, indoor pool, tennis. Golf & riding 6 m.*
- *Busines sservices inc 4 meeting rooms to 100.*
- *Open all year. All major credit cards accepted.*

Airport 15, Harrogate 17, Leeds 23, York 37, Manchester 51, London 223.

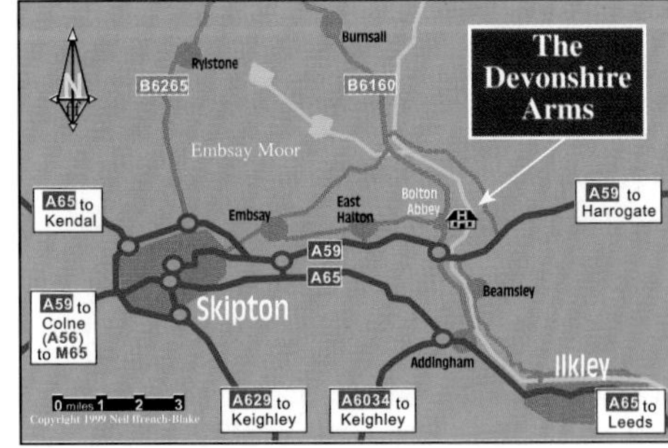

The Balmoral Hotel

Franklin Mount, Harrogate,
North Yorkshire HGl 5EJ
Tel: (01423) 508208; Fax: (01423) 530652
E-mail: info@balmoralhotel.co.uk
Internet: http: / / www.balmoralhotel.co.uk

What a delightful surprise it was to discover this superb hotel! It is situated in its own award winning gardens, away from the centre of town and yet within walking distance of all the amenities that Harrogate provides - conference centre, shops and wonderful surrounding countryside. The Balmoral is unique - beautifully furnished, mostly with antiques and tastefully decorated to create a warm, luxurious and welcoming atmosphere. The bedrooms are all individual, many having four poster beds and again are extremely comfortable with thoughtfully chosen décor. Everything that you could possibly need is provided and to stay in one of these rooms is an experience in luxury. The food in Villu Toots Restaurant is not only imaginative but is prepared from the finest ingredients, cooked to perfection and served by friendly and attentive staff. E.T.B. ♛♛♛♛ Highly Commended.

Rates: *Room and breakfast from £70.00 single, £85.00 double and weekly rates on application.* V
Short breaks *from £40 b&b per person are available throughout the year.*

- *20 en suite bedrooms (10 four poster rooms), all with direct dial telephone and TV; room service; baby listening; night porter.*
- *Last orders for dinner 10 p.m.; lunch 12-2; special diets available.* ● *Children welcome; dogs acc'd*
- *Solarium; indoor heated swimming pool and leisure facilities 100 yards away; 4 golf courses and riding stables nearby; tennis by arrangement.*
- *Open all year; major credit cards accepted.*

Yorkshire Dales 15, Leeds/Bradford Airport 18, York 20, London 200.

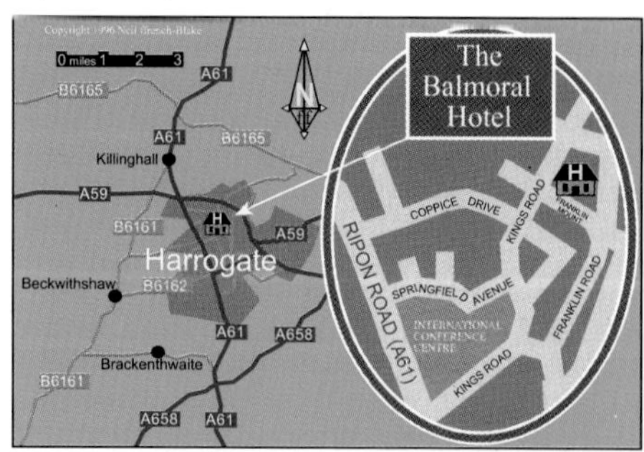

Simonstone Hall Country House Hotel

Hawes, North Yorkshire DL8 3LY
Tel: (01969) 667255; Fax: (01969) 667441
E-mail: simonstonehall@demon.co.uk

This former hunting lodge of the Earls of Wharncliffe, where many leading political and social figures were entertained, has been beautifully restored to offer elegant accommodation, superb food, friendly service and hospitality. Set in magnificent countryside near the market town of Hawes in upper Wensleydale, it has spectacular views over the dale and surrounding fells. Seven of the individually designed bedrooms enjoy this panoramic view, whilst six have four poster beds. The elegant restaurant boasts a full à la carte menu with a wide range of wines, whilst the Game Tavern offers a varied choice of wholesome dishes. The comfortably furnished lounge, with its fine carved timber fireplace and great log fires in winter, is a peaceful haven for relaxation. The hotel is an excellent base from which to explore the beautiful scenery and many attractions of the Yorkshire Dales with their charming market towns, craft centres, castles and abbeys.

***Rates:** Single room with breakfast from £55.* V
Double room including breakfast from £110.
***Midweek Breaks**: Prices on application.*

- *18 en suite bedrooms, all colour TV, direct-dial telephone, hairdryer, tea/coffee making facilities; non-smoker bedrooms; dogs welcome some rooms.*
- *Two dining rooms; lunch & special diets available; last orders 8.30 pm. Car parking for 30.*
- *Licensed for civil weddings. Meeting room for 20*
- *Fishing, shooting, paragliding from hotel.*
- *Open all year. All major credit cards accepted.*

Leyburn 16, Brough 21, Kendal 26, Skipton 36, London 250.

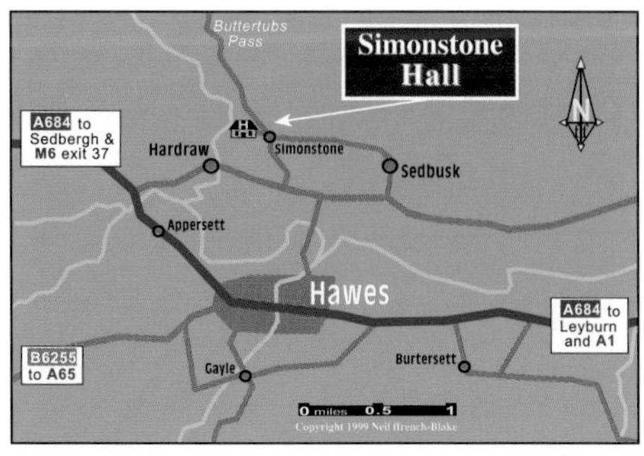

Wrangham House Hotel

10 Stonegate, Hunmanby, North Yorkshire YO14 ONS
Tel: (01723) 891333; Fax: (01723) 892973

Nestling near the church in the centre of the village of Hunmanby, this 200-year old former Georgian vicarage has recently been taken over by Mervyn and Margaret Poulter and Diane Norvick. They are justly proud of their acquisition and their plans should ensure that Wrangham continues to develop its reputation as an ideal retreat for traditional and comfortable country house hospitality.
You are assured of a warm welcome and personal service by your genial hosts, and they will do all they can to ensure your stay is to your satisfaction. This may involve your simply relaxing within the hotel or its mature garden or exploring the nearby attractions: the walking and birdatching on the Cleveland Way, the coastal resorts of Scarborough and Flamborough Head, the stately hones of Castle Howard and Burton Constable, the Yorkshire Moors or the several golf courses in the area, on which the hotel can arrange for you to play. A table d'hôte menu provides good contemporary cuisine and an affordable wine list completes the pleasures of this fine country hotel.

***Rates:** Room & breakfast inc breakfast £43.50 single, £77 twin/double.* V

- *12 en suite bedrooms (1 suite) all with colour TV, direct-dial telephone, hairdryer, laundry/valet service, tea/coffee making facilities, radio/alarm clock. Diasabled & non-smoking rooms available. Car parking for 20.*
- *Table d'hôte £19.50; special diets available; last orders 9.30 p.m.*
- *Business services inc meeting room for 40 thtr.*
- *Golf, walking and birdwatching nearby.*
- *Open all year. Visa, Amex, Mastercard, Switch accepted.*

Filey 3, Bridlington 10, Scarborough 10, Gt Driffield 14, York 35, London 206.

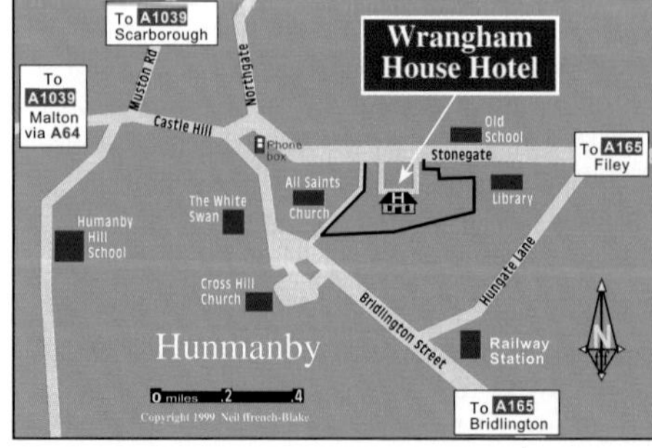

The Pheasant

Harome, Helmsley, N. Yorkshire YO62 5JG
Tel: (01439 771241; Fax: (01439) 771744
AA★★★RAC

The Pheasant was recommended to me by another hotelier of note in Yorkshire and how right he was. Set in a pretty village, overlooking the village pond, it has been imaginatively created from a group of buildings on two sides of a courtyard. Inside, the log fires, the antiques and the numerous beams lend an air of warmth and comfort to the tastefully decorated rooms. Old fashioned in atmosphere the hotel might be, but the best of all modern amenities are also there. Mrs 'Tricia Binks provides the most delicious food and many of the ingredients come from the hotel's own large garden and paddock. Holly Cottage is also available - a charming, thatched 16th century cottage just 350 yards from the hotel, with two double bedrooms and two sitting rooms, all attractively furnished to the same high standard as the hotel. It is serviced by the hotel staff and meals are taken in the hotel. A quiet and peaceful haven with a delightful atmosphere. Having said all this, The Pheasant makes an ideal base from which to explore this most beautiful part of England, where there is so much to see and do.

***Rates:** Dinner, room and breakfast from £59.50 (1st Nov-mid-May); £65-£68 (high season) per person per day including VAT.*

- *14 en suite bedrooms (1 ground floor), all with telephone, colour TV, tea/coffee making facilities; full central heating.*
- *Last orders 8.00 p.m; bar meals (lunch); diets.*
- *Children over 14 welcome; dogs by arrangement; conferences max. 12.*
- *Own heated indoor swimming pool; golf, tennis, riding, fishing all nearby.*
- *Closed January and February. Major credit cards accepted.*

Helmsley 3, York 22, Scarborough 28, Leeds 48, Edinburgh 160, London 220.

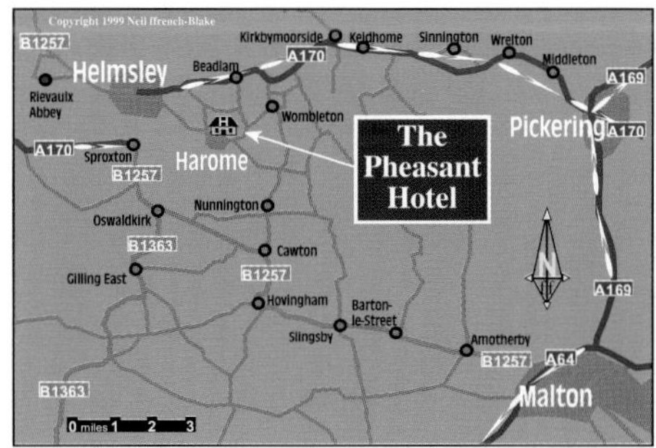

Lastingham Grange

Lastingham, Nr. Kirkbymoorside,
York YO62 6TH
Tel: (01751) 417345/417402;
Fax: (01751) 417358

You can discover this delightfully situated, elegant country house by leaving the A170 at Kirkbymoorside and making for Hutton-le-Hole. The Grange is stone-walled and built round a courtyard. It is set within 10 acres of well-kept gardens and fields, on the edge of the moors, in the historic village of Lastingham, a peaceful backwater in the heart of the National Park. Lastingham Grange is owned and personally run by Mr. and Mrs. Dennis Wood. The atmosphere, even during the height of the season, is unhurried and peaceful, the south-facing terrace providing a pleasant setting in which to relax and enjoy the beautiful rose garden, noted for the variety and rarity of its many flowering shrubs and trees. The spacious and homely lounge, with its open fire, and the comfortable bedrooms with their impressive views, are all tastefully furnished. The food is excellent - speedily and cheerfully served.

Rates: *Room and breakfast from £82.00 single; £155.00 double. Short breaks available.* V
Bargain breaks: *Dinner, bed & breakfast from £97.50 for 2 days or more; £92.50 one week or more, per person per night.*

- *12 en suite bedrooms, all with bath and shower; direct-dial telephone, trouser press, hairdryer.*
- *Table d'hôte dinner £30.75; lunch & special diets available; last orders 8.30 pm.*
- *Children welcome; baby listening in all rooms; drying room.*
- *Golf five miles; riding four miles.*
- *Open March to the beginning of December.*
- *Credit cards not accepted.*

Malton 15, Scarborough 24, Thirsk 24, Whitby 26, York 33, London 232.

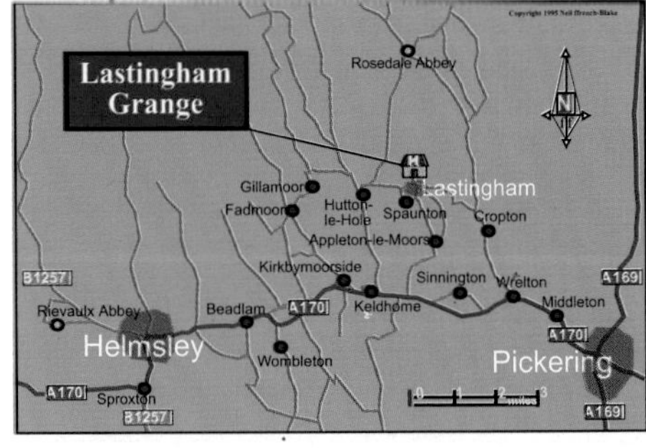

Millers House Hotel

Market Place, Middleham, Wensleydale, North Yorkshire DL8 4NR
Tel: (01969) 622630; Fax: (01969) 623570
E-Mail: hotel@millershouse.demon.co.uk

This elegant Georgian Country House nestles in the heart of the attractive Yorkshire Dales village of Middleham, once called the 'Jewel of the Dales' by James Herriot. Set between Coverdale and Wensleydale and close to Middleham Castle, northern seat of King Richard III, the Millers House is an ideal base for exploring some of the most beautiful scenery in Yorkshire and the many places associated with the Yorkshire Vet stories. Middleham itself is famous for its racehorse training and watching the moorland gallops is a favourite pastime. The area further afield abounds with ancient castles, abbeys and historic houses; local craftsman be seen working at their pottery, sculpture, brewing, violin and candle making. The hotel has recently been taken over by Ann and James Lundie, and their warmth and friendliness assures you of every comfort. One of the 7 bedrooms has a superb canopied four-poster and a free-standing Victorian roll-top bath! The elegant restaurant with its conservatory offers an imaginative menu. The Miller's House offers a range of special interest breaks and is ideal for that value-for-money holiday.

Rates: *Single room with breakfast from £52; double inc. breakfast from £84 inc. VAT.*
Bargain Breaks: *October and March Mon-Thurs inc rate is £50 per person per night, dinner, b & b.*

- *7 en suite bedrooms all with TV, direct-dial telephone, hairdryer, laundry service, radio/alarm clock, tea/coffee making, non-smoker rms available*
- *Table d'hôte £24.50. AA Restaurant. Special diets available; last orders 8.30 pm.*
- *Squash, river bathing within 2 miles; riding 5 miles; sailing 7m, fishing 10 miles.*
- *Open March-end October, Xmas, New Year & Special Winter Weekends. Visa, Mastercard, Switch accepted. Car parking for 8.*

Leyburn 2, Masham $7\frac{1}{2}$, Richmond 12, A1 15, Harrogate 30, York 40, London 230.

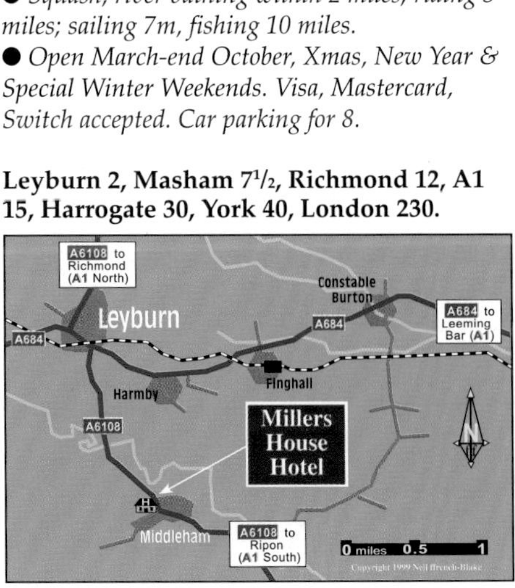

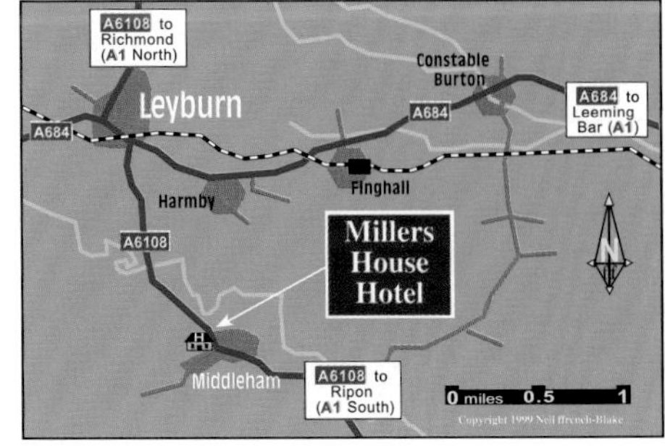

Solberge Hall Hotel

Newby Wiske, Northallerton,
North Yorkshire DL7 9ER
Tel: (01609) 779191; Fax: (01609) 780472
E-Mail: hotel@solberge.freeserve.com

A hall at Solberge was mentioned in the Domesday Book - and valued at eight shillings! The present building originated in 1824 and since then has been tastefully modernised and developed into the luxury country house it is today. As you drive up to the impressive Georgian façade, your anticipation of something special will be aroused. As you enter the Hall and reception rooms, you will not be disappointed. A warm welcome awaits you from John Hollins and his friendly and efficient staff. An open fire greets guests during the winter months, period fireplaces and panelled walls in the bar, lounge and other reception rooms create an atmosphere of elegance and Victorian splendour. All the en suite bedrooms, ranging from singles to family rooms and four posters, are individually designed with modern amenities and have been decorated to a high standard. Set in 16 acres of its own grounds, Solberge Hall lies in the midst of glorious 'James Heriot' Yorkshire countryside and is ideally placed for exploring the Dales to the West and the Moors and coast to the East.

Rates: *Single room with breakfast from £68; double inc. breakfast from £100 inc. VAT.* V
Bargain Breaks: *Reductions of up to 40% avail able for guests staying more than one night, dinner, b & b. Details on application.*

- *24 en suite bedrooms all with TV + video & satellite, direct-dial telephone, hairdryer, laundry service, radio/alarm clock, tea/coffee making, trouser press; rooms for disabled available.*
- *Table d'hôte £22.50. A la carte, lunch & special diets available; last orders 9.30 pm.*
- *Fishing, golf, clay shooting, tennis & riding 2 m.*
- *Full business services inc. 2 meeting rooms to 80.*
- *Open all year. All major credit cards accepted.*

A1 6m, Thirsk 9½, Darlington 16, Boroughbridge 19, York 32, London 227.

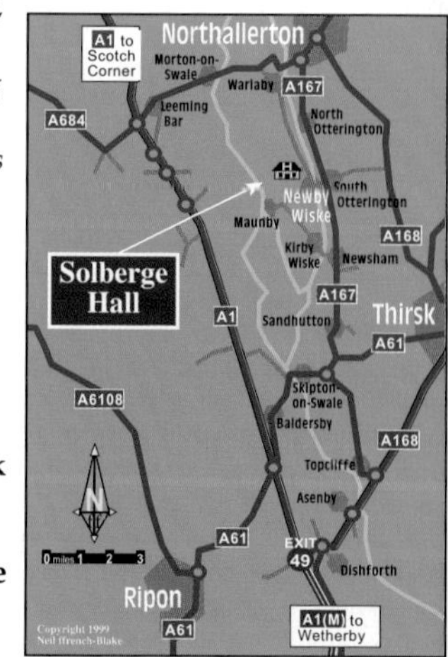

Dunsley Hall Country House Hotel

Dunsley, Whitby, North Yorkshire
YO21 3TL
Tel: (01947) 893437; Fax: (01947) 893505

This fine country house was converted into an hotel in 1987 and has evolved into a haven for visitors from all over the world. It offers traditional comfort and excellent food along with period charm and peaceful serenity, blended with modern elegance and leisure facilities. There are 18 en-suite bedrooms, all individually furnished, two with four-poster beds and two with private sitting rooms. The public rooms contain a wealth of historic features, with original oak panelling, stained glass windows, fascinating fireplaces and other period gems. The hotel is within brisk walking distance of the Heritage Coast and is well located for exploring the North Yorkshire National Park, the seafaring towns of Whitby and Scarborough, historic York, Castle Howard and TV's *Heartbeat* country. After a day's exploration, relax in one of the elegant restaurants. In the Visitors's Book when I stayed, I noticed the following comment: *"Value, class, satisfaction, excellence, consideration - I could go on...of the 50 hotels this year, this was by far the best!"*

Rates: *Single room with breakfast from £65.00; double inc. breakfast from £104.50 inc. VAT.* V
Bargain Breaks: *Weekend breaks from £120 pp, dinner b & b.*

- *18 en suite bedrooms all with TV, direct-dial telephone, hairdryer, laundry service, radio/alarm clock, tea/coffee making facilities, safety deposit box, trouser press.*
- *Table d'hôte £24.95. A la carte, lunch & special diets available; last orders 9.30 pm.*
- *2 meeting rooms for up to 60. Car parking for 40*
- *Croquet, fitness centre, sauna/solarium, indoor pool, tennis at hotel. Fishing, golf, bathing, sailing, riding all within 3 miles*
- *Open all year. M-card, Amex, Visa Switch acc'd*

Whitby 3, Scarborough 22, Middlesbrough 27, Pickering 23, York 49, London 235.

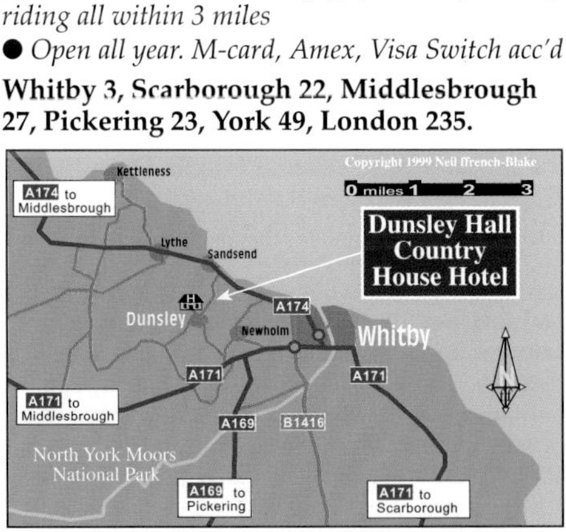

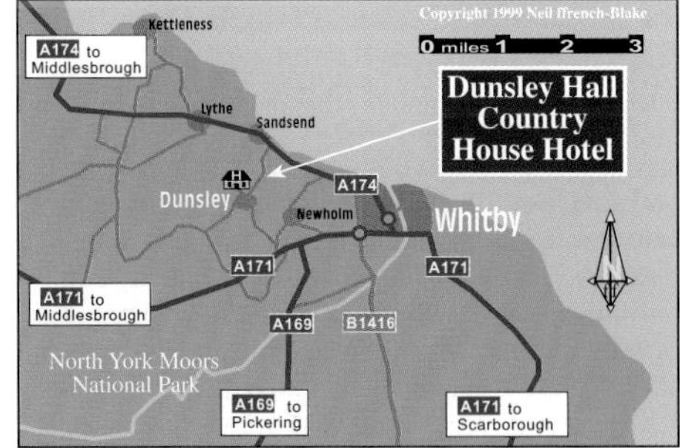

The Judges Lodging Hotel

9 Lendal, York, North Yorkshire
YO1 8AQ
Tel: (01904) 638733; Fax: (01904) 679947

Imagine yourself in York in the early 18th century. You are arriving at your grand house in the city centre. There is a glow from the windows and the servants await you. Now, retaining that ambience in your mind, transport yourself to the present day; add the comforts that we have all come to expect, and you will begin to sense the flavour of a stay at The Judges Lodging. The house has retained its original plan and atmosphere, and yet has been cleverly transformed into a small, warm and intimate hotel. The furnishings and décor are beautifully in keeping with the building. There is a new brasserie and rooftop terrace, serving delicious food with a wine list to suit all palates and also a new residents' bar and lounge. Now, when you visit York, you can not only see all the historical sites, such as the Minster, the Jorvik Viking Centre and the National Railway Museum, but also stay in one of the most historic houses in the city. A good base for exploring the many houses and abbeys in which Yorkshire abounds and the wild, exciting Yorkshire Moors.

Rates: *Single room with breakfast from £75.00; double from £100 inc. VAT.* V
Bargain Breaks: *Stay for 3 consecutive nights (inc. a Sunday) and receive 3rd night's accomm. at half price from November-February inclusive.*

- *15 en suite bedrooms with satellite TV, direct-dial telephone, hairdryer, laundry service, radio/alarm clock, tea/coffee making facilities.*
- *Extensive table d'hôte menu available in our restaurant (discounted rates for residents). Also Public Bar, Residents' Bar & Residents' Lounge*
- *Car parking. Children over 10 welcome.*
- *Open all year. All major credit cards + Switch.*
- *Boating 200 yds; 4 golf courses within 5 miles.*

Leeds 24, Manchester 72, Edinburgh 192, London 209.

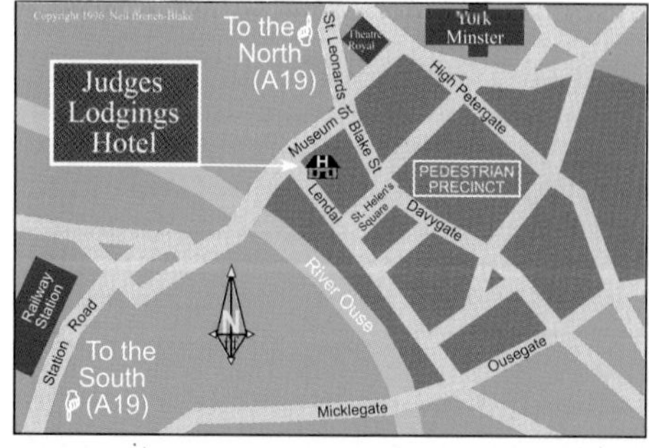

Wales

Mid Wales is a land of dramatic contrasts in which youcan enjoy the considerable pleasures of both coast and countryside. It is an area of immense natural beauty with a wide variety of scenery, each season bringing its own particular enhancement. With well over half the Snowdonia National Park lying in Mid Wales, some of the beauty is unsurpassed.The region has high mountains with breathtaking views, large attractive lakes and rambling green hills.

There is no more relaxing way of enjoying nature's wonders than on horseback. Both the regular rider and novice will find superb pony trekking country. An alternative means of seeing the countryside is by taking a ride on one of the Great Little Trains. When various industries began to develop in Mid Wales, a need for transport arose. This demand was met by a network of small railways. There are five such narrow gauge railways, most of them dating back to the last century, operating in the region - now making Mid Wales a must for all steam enthusiasts. Throughout Mid Wales a network of well surfaced roads lead towards remote uplands, winding along the contours of the slopes. These are the Cambrian 'mountains, Wales' magnificent backbone, the upland region where hamlets and farms nestle into the folds of seemingly endless hills. In this area farming life is centred around a series of small towns which often stand at an important crossroads or a ford in the river. They are linked by splendidly scenic mountain roads or old drovers' ways along which cattle were once driven to market. Llanidoes, with its 16th century market hall built of stout timber, stands almost at the centre of Wales, and at the confluence of the Severn and Clywedog Rivers.

In Mid Wales life inland revolves around the historic market towns and the old spa centres, while the coastline is punctuated by small fishing villages and popular seaside resorts. The western districts are strongholds of Welsh culture where the language is in everyday use.

The west of the region has over a hundred miles of coastline. Expansive, sandy beaches, spectacular estuaries and rugged cliffs leading down to secluded coves make this an ideal area for a holiday. It is not surprising to discover that Mid Wales has always had a seafaring tradition. In bygone days schooners sailed all over the world from the little ports of Aberaeron, Aberdyfi, Aberystwyth, Barmouth and New Quay.

Llynnau Cregennen

The harbours are still bustling and active but with a different type of craft.

To the East are the Welsh Marches with their traditional half-timbered black and white buildings. Despite being so close to England, the borderlands of Powys maintain much of their Welsh character and tradition. Many centuries ago this area was governed by the Marcher Lords on behalf of the king. Further back in time, Offa, an 8th century Saxon king, built a massive dyke to keep marauding Welsh forces out of his kingdom. Traces of these large earthworks can be seen along the border, forming the basis of the Offa's Dyke Trail, a long distance walkway of 168 miles. At Knighton a special Heritage Centre illustrates the significance of the Dyke.

The whole of Mid Wales has a colourful and exciting history and this is reflected in the many ancient buildings and other monuments which are to be seen. The struggle to keep Wales independent from the influence of numerous invaders has been a constant theme throughout history. This is evident in ruined castles such as Harlech Castle and Castell-y-Bere. Powys Castle, the home of "Clive of India" is on the other hand beautifully maintained, together with its outstanding gardens. Other popular attractions are the industries which reflect the Welsh rural life. These small industries such as woollen weaving in traditional patterns, pottery, and craft work, reflect a harmonious bond between people and environment which is typical of Mid Wales.

Ffestiniog Railway

For those wishing to learn more of the area's history there are a number of museums and interpretative centres in the region. Historical artifacts can be seen at displays in Llandrindod Wells, Llanidoes, Machynlleth, Aberystwyth, Tre'r Ddol, Newtown and Welshpool. At Llandrindod Wells a display on the *Spas of Wales* has been opened. There is also an opportunity to "take the water" in the original Pump Room, refurbished in the Edwardian style.

North Wales has been attracting holiday visitors for over two hundred years, - Wordsworth,Samuel Johnson, Turner, Nelson, George Burrows, Bismarck and Wellington have all come to the area. Nowadays we still attract artists, poets, politicians and sailors but the range of accommodation and attractions make North Wales a perfect venue, whatever your choice of holiday.

Our hotels, restaurants and inns are continually improving their standards and now compare with the best in Britain; added to this we have the unfair advantage of some of the most impressive scenery in the world. Snowdonia is justly famous for its magnificent mountains, lakes and forests, but the Hiraethog Mountains in the North East, the Berwyns, south of Llangollen and the beautiful river valleys of the Conwy, Clwyd, Dee and Glaslyn have a magic of their own. The variety of the scenery is what impresses first time visitors. Within six miles of Llandudno - our largest resort - you can find the peace of the Carneddau, one hundred square miles of beautiful mountain moorland, dotted with Neolithic trackways, standing stones, bronze age sites and beautiful lakes, without a single road crossing it (except the old Roman road from Caerhun to Carnarfon).

The past surrounds you in North Wales. You can trace the history of man in these parts from the Neolithic tombs of 6,000 years ago, to the Iron Age hill forts that were inhabited when the Roman legions came, then through the cells and abbeys of the early Celtic church to the Nonconformist chapels of the 19th century so admired by Sir John Betjeman.

The 12th century Welsh castles and 13th century castles of the Plantagenets reflect a more turbulent time, but what masterpieces of military architecture they left us - Conwy, Carnarfon, Rhuddlan, and Beaumaris are breathtaking in their size and splendour, while the Welsh keeps of Dolwyddelan, Dinas Bran and Dolbadarn will appeal to more romantic souls. Medieval towns such as Conwy and Ruthin, the splendid Elizabethan and Jacobean farmhouses and the tiny country cottages show the ordinary side of life in the 16th, 17th and 18th centuries. The Industrial Revolution brought changes to North Wales, most of which are now featured in our tourist trade. Slate was the major industry; now you can explore the slate caverns at Blaenau Ffestiniog or Glyn Ceiriog or see the Quarry Museum at Llanberis. Most of the Great Little Trains of Wales were first used to carry slate from the mines to the harbours, the one notable exception being the Snowdon Mountain Railway.

As soon as you cross the border into Wales, the look of the countryside changes, the road signs seem unpronounceable and you are met by warm hospitable people. The language, music and heritage of Wales add a special dimension to a holiday in our wonderful country. *Croeso* is the word for Welcome - you will hear it often.

Cardiff, Wales' capital is essentially a young city, even 'though its history dates back many centuries. The development of its docks during the Industrial Revolution for the export of Welsh iron and coal was the basis of its prosperity. Cardiff Castle is part Roman fort, part medieval castle and part 19th-century mansion. Its Chaucer Room has stained glass windows depicting The Canterbury Tales. Its Summer Smoking Room has a copper, brass and silver inlaid floor. The castle is the present home of the Welsh Assembly. The National Museum of Wales houses a wealth of exhibits, from impressionist paintings to examples of Swansea porcelain. To the East, near Newport is Caerleon. which was the site of the Roman fortress of Isca, built in AD75. Further East, on the Monmouth-Chepstow road is Tintern Abbey, one of the finest relics of Britain's monastic age. It was founded in the 12th century by Cistercian monks, rebuilt in the 13th-century and sacked by Henry VIII during the Dissolution of the Monasteries. Offa's Dyke, part of an 168-mile rampart built by King Offa of Mercia in the 8th century to keep the Welsh out, and now a noted walk, runs past Tintern's portals. To the northwest of Cardiff is the late 19th-century Castell Coch (Red Castle), a mixture of Victorian Gothic and fairytale styles. Well preserved is 13th-century Caerphilly Castle, with its famous leaning tower.

Further West, outside Port Talbot, the visitor comes to Margam Country Park, 850 acres including an Iron Age hill fort, a restored abbey church with windows by William Morris, Margram Stones Museum with stones and crosses dating from the 5th-11th centuries and the main house with its 327-ft long orangery.

Threecliff Bay

The Gower Peninsula, west of Swansea is a secluded world of its own, with limestone cliffs, remote bays and miles of golden sands. It is the 'Riviera' of South Wales. Sites not to miss here include the late 13th-century Weobley Castle, the ruins of Threecliff Bay and Gower Farm Museum with its 100-yr old farm memorabilia. Near Carmarthen is Dylan Thomas' village of Laugharne, in whose churchyard he is buried. The rugged Pembroke coast is guarded on its Western rim by Britain's smallest city - St David's, whose cathedral was founded by the eponymous saint in the 8th century, although the present building is believed to date from the 12th century.

Historic Houses, Gardens & Parks

Aberconwy & Colwyn
Chirk Castle, Bodelwyddan
Bodrhyddan Hall, Rhuddlan
Bodnant Garden, Tal-y-Cafn
Colwyn Leisure Centre

Anglesey
Plas Newydd, Llanfairpwll

Glamorgan
Castell Cochi, Tongwynlais, Cardiff
Cosmeston Lakes Country Park & Medieval Village
Dyffryn House & Gardens, St. Nicholas, Nr. Cardiff Llanerch Vineyard, Pendoylan

Gwynedd
Bryn Bras Castle, Llanrug, Nr. Llanberis
Parc Glynllifon, Nr. Caernarfon
'Y Stablau', Gwydyr Forest Park, Llanrwst

Monmouthshire
Bryn Bach Park, Tredegar
Caldicot Castle & Country Park, Nr. Newport
Llandegfedd Reservolr, Pontypool
Tredegar House, Newport

Neath & Port Talbot
Margam Park, Port Talbot

Pembrokeshire
Manor House Wildlife & Leisure Park, Tenby
Tudor Merchant's House, Quay Hill, Tenby

Wrexham
Erddig Hall, Wrexham

Walks & Nature Trails

Aberconwy & Colwyn
Llyn Brenig Visitor Centre, Corwen

Anglesey
Bryntirion Open Farm, Dwyran
South Stack Cliffs Reserve & Elfins Tower Information Centre,Holyhead

Blaenau Gwent
Festival Park, Ebbw Vale

Carmarthenshire
Gelli Aur Countly Park, Llandeilo

Flintshire
Greenfield Valley Heritage Park, Holywell
Logger Heads Country Park, Nr Mold

Gwynedd
Coed-y-Brenin Forest Park & Visitor Centre, Ganllwyd, Dolgellau
The Greenwood Centre, Port Dinorwic
Parc Padarn, Llanberis
Tyn Llan Crafts & Farm Museum, Nr. Porthmadog

Merthyr Tydfil
Garwnant Visitor Centre, Cwm Taf

Neath & Port Talbot
Alan Forest Park & Countryside Centre, Port Talbot
Gnoll Country Park, Neath

Pembrokeshire
Bwlch Nant Yr Arian Forest Visitor Centre, Ponterwyd
Llysyfran Reservoir & Country Park, Nr. Haverfordwest
Pembrey Country Park, Pembrey

Powys
Brecon Beacons Mountain Centre, Nr. Libanus
Gigrin Farm & Nature Trail, Rhyader
Lake Vyrnwy RSPB Reserve & Information Centre
Ynys-Hir Reserve & Visitor Cenne, Machynlleth

Vale of Glamorgan
Bryngarw Country Park, Nr. Bridgend

Wrexham
Ty Mawr Country Park, Cefn Mawr

Historical Sites & Museums

Aberconwy & Colwyn
Bodelwyddan Castle
Carreg Cennen Castle, Trapp, Llangollen
Denbigh Castle
Valle Crucis Abbey, Llangollen

Cardiganshire
Museum of the Welsh Woollen Industry, Llandysul

Carmarthenshire
Castell Henllys Iron Age Hillfort, Crymych

Flintshire
Flint Castle & Twon Walls
Rhuddlan Castle, Nr. Rhyl

Glamorgan
Aberdulair Falls, Vale of Neath, Neath
Caerphilly Castle
Cardiff Castle
Castell Coch, Cardiff
Cefn Coed Colliery Museum, Crynant, Neath
National Museum of Wales
Welsh Folk Museum,Cardiff

Gwynedd
Beaumaris Castle
Caernarfon Castle
Conwy Castle

Cymer Abbey, Dolgellau
Dolbadarn Castle, Llanberis
Dolwyddelan Castle
Harlech Castle
Llanfair Slate Caverns, Nr. Harlech
The Lloyd George Museum, Llanystumdwy, Criccieth
Penrhyn Castle, Bangor

Monmouthshire
Chepstow Castle, Chepstow
The Nelson Museum & Local History Centre
Penhow Castle, Nr. Newport
Raglan Castle
Tintern Abbey, Tintern

Pembrokeshire
Castle Museum & Art Gallery, Haverfordwest
Kidwelly Castle
Manorbier Castle, Nr. Tenby
Milford Haven Museum, The Docks, Milford Haven
Picton Castle, Haverfordwest
Pembroke Castle
St Davids Bishop's Palace

Powys
Powys Castle & Museum, Welshpool
Tretower Court & Castle, Crickhowell

Entertainment Venues

Aberconwy & Colwyn
Felin Isaf Water Mill, Glan Conwy
Llyn Brenig Visitor Centre, Cerrigydrudion

Anglesey
Anglesey Bird World, Dwyran/Sea Zoo, Brynsiencyn

Cardiganshire
James Pringle Weavers of Llanfair P.G.
The Llywenog Silver-Lead Mines, Nr Aberystwyth

Flintshire
Afonwen Craft & Antique Centre, Nr. Mold

Gwynedd
Alice in Wonderland Visitor Centre, Llandudno
Butlins Starcoast World, Pwllheli
Ffestiniog Railway, Porthmadog
Maes Artro Tourist Village Llanbedr
Penmachno Woollen Mill, Nr. Betws-y-Coed
Portmeirion Village, Nr. Porthmadog
Sygun Copper Mine, Beddgelert
Snowdon Mountain Railway, Llamberis
Trefriw Woollen Mills, Trefriw
Welsh Gold, Dolgellau
Welsh Highland Railway, Porthmadog

Neath & Port Talbot
Margam Park, Port Talbot
Penscynor Wildlife Park, Cilfrew, Nr. Neath

Pembrokeshire
Oakwood Park Theme Park, Narberth

Powys
Dan-yr-Ogof Showcaves, Abercraf
Welshpool & Llanfair Light Railway
Welsh Whisky Visitor Centre, Brecon

Rhondda Cynnon Taf
Rhondda Heritage Park

Dolbadarn Castle

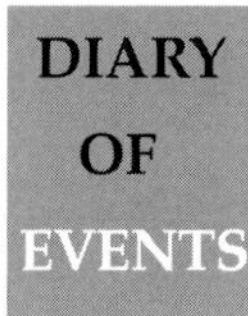

**Denotes provisional date.*

January

8. **Millennium Concert.** Brangwyn Hall, Swansea.
23-26. **Wales Spring Fair.** Llandudno, Gwynedd

February

5-6. **Swansea Antiques Fair,** Brangwyn Hall, Swansea.
5. **Rugby World Cup.** Wales v France. Millennium Stadium.
19. **Rugby World Cup.** Wales v Italy. Millennium Stadium.

March

18. **Rugby World Cup.** Wales v Scotland. Millennium Stadium
25. **Wales Beekeepers Convention.** Llanelwedd, Powys.

April

8-9. **Model Boat Festival.** Maritime & Ind Museum, Swansea
22-24. **Welsh Camping & Caravanning Show,** Llanelwedd.

May

1-3. **Llantilio Crossenny Festival of Music & Drama,** Llantilio Crossenny, Gwent.
27-June 4. **St David's Cathedral Festival,** St David's, Pembrokeshire.

June

1*. **Llangollen Choral Festival.** Royal Intl Pavilion, Llangollen. N Wales largest massed male voice festival.
4-10*. **Cardiff Singer of the World Competition**. St David's Hall, Cardiff
24-30. **Three Peaks Yacht Race: Barmouth to Fort William.** The Quay, Barmouth, Gwynedd.
23-25. **Gwyl Ifan Welsh Folk & Dancing Festival.** Various locations in Cardiff and surrounding areas

July

2. **Caerleon 10k Fun Run**, Caerleon, Gwent
4-9*. **Llangollen International Music Eisteddfod.** The Pavilion, Llangollen, Denbighshire. 54th festival.
20-29. **Welsh Proms 2000.** Cardiff.
22-23. **Swansea Antiques Fr** Brangwyn Fair, Swansea.
24-27. **Royal Welsh Show.** Showground, Llenelwedd, Builth Wells. Wales' Premier Agricultural Show.
19-26*. **Ian Rush International Soccer Tournament.** Playing Fields, Llanbadarn Fawr, Aberystwyth, Cardigans
22-29*. **Fishguard Music Festival.** Various venues.
29-Aug 5***National Eisteddfod of Wales.** Sir Ffon, Anglesey.

August

1*.**Gower Agricultural Show.** Fairwood Airport, Swansea
1*. **Brecon County Show.** The Showground, Brecon.
4-6*. **Brecon Jazz Festival.** Var's venues, Brecon, Powys.
5*. **Chepstow Agricultural Show.** Howick, Nr Chepstow, Monmouthshire.
10-11*. **United Counties Show,** Carmarthen.
12-20*. **Llandrindod Wells Victoria Festival.** Various venues in and around Llandrindod Wells, Powys
15-17*. **Pembrokeshire County Show.** Showground, Haverfordwest.

For further information contact:
Wales Tourist Board
Brunel House, 2 Fitzalan Road, Cardiff CF2 1UY. Tel: 01222 499909

September

1-10* **Barmouth Arts Festival** Dragon Theatre, Barm'th 25th annual arts festival.

October

1. **50th South Wales Miners' Eistedfodd**. Grand Pavilion, Porthcawl, S Glam
2. **Free Hurdle Race Meeting.** Chepstow, Monmouths
21-22. **Swansea Antiques Fair.** Brangwyn Hall, The Guildhall, Swansea

November

1-23 Dec*. **Rugby World Cup Festival.** In & around Cardiff City Centre.
2*. **Rugby Union World Cup Final**. New National Stadium, Cardiff, S Glamorgan.
4. **Tote Silver Trophy Hurdle.** Chepstow, Monmouths
10-19. **Welsh International Film Festival.** Various venues in Aberystwyth,Cards.

December

5. Royal Welsh Agricultural Winter Fair. Llanelwedd, Powys
26*. **Coral Welsh National Chase.**Chepstow,Monmouths.

The St Mellons Hotel

Old St Mellons, Cardiff CF3 8XR
Tel: (01633) 680355; Fax: (01633) 680399

Formerly an Edwardian gentlemen's club set in beautiful gardens, The St Mellons Hotel is a blend of many of the best things in life. There is a splendid leisure complex and all bedrooms and suites are thoughtfully presented, and tastefully decorated. Equally attractive bedrooms known as the Garden Rooms are immediately adjacent to the hotel. The Llanarthen Restaurant offers interesting and sensibly priced menus, featuring English, Welsh and International cuisine. Lighter meals may be enjoyed on the terrace or in the cocktail lounge. Functions of all types can be accommodated in the Ballroom, St Mellons Room, the Adam Room and the self-contained Terrace Suite. Conferences are extremely well catered for. I was delighted to find that Cardiff's allure as a shopping centre had not dimmed since my last visit and that parking was still cheap and easy. The Cardiff area is rich in treasures including Tredegar House, Caerphilly Castle, the Rhondda Heritage Park and the Big Pit Mine. St Mellons is away from the city's bustle yet near enough for business and leisure visitors to enjoy the city's many amenities and attractions.

Rates: *Single room and breakfast from £90; double room inc. breakfast from £100.* V
Weekend breaks: *Two nights inc. a Saturday £170 per couple including 3-course tdh dinner, b&b, VAT and use of adjoining Leisure Complex.*

● *41 en suite bedrooms, all with telephone, colour TV, radio, hairdryer, laundry/valet service, tea/coffee making facilities, trouser press. Disabled facilities.*
● *Table d'hôte & à la carte dining room; lunch & special diets available; last orders 21.30.*
● *Business services inc 7 meeting rooms, capacity 10-150. Car parking for 150.*
● *Fitness centre/gym, whirlpool, steam room, sauna, solarium, squash, indoor swimming pool, tennis.*
● *Open all year. Major credit cards accepted.*

Cardiff 5, Newport 8, Caerphilly 8, Swansea 45 , Bristol 41, London 150.

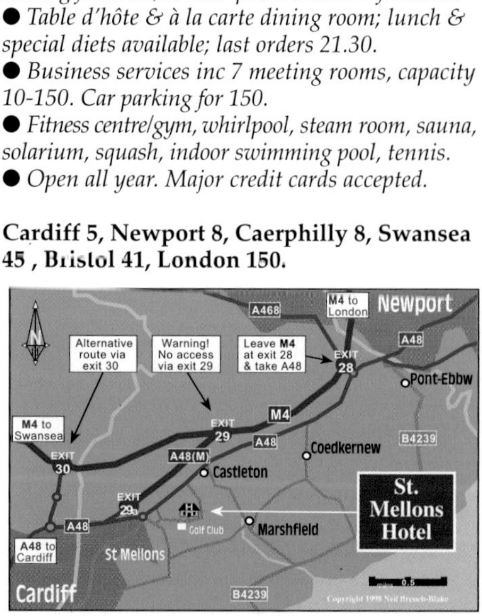

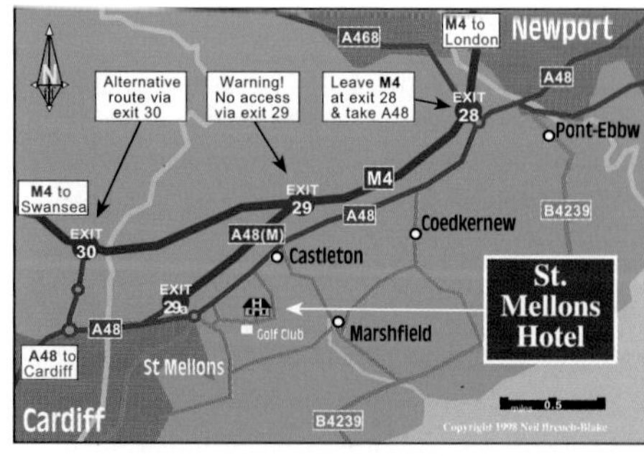

Trefeddian Hotel

Aberdovey (Aberdyfi), LL35 OSB
Tel: (01654) 767213; Fax: (01654) 767777
E-mail: tref@saqnet.co.uk

The Trefeddian Hotel stands in its own grounds, away from the main road, and is one mile from the middle of Aberdovey, a village with many attractions and which is becoming a centre where everyone, particularly the young, can pursue many outdoor activities. For example, supervision and special instruction can be arranged for sailing. The directors, Mr & Mrs John Cave and Mr Peter Cave, are responsible for the running of this first class family hotel, which has all the amenities to make a splendid holiday. The lounges are spacious, relaxing and peaceful and have recently been beautifully refurbished. The bedrooms, with views of Cardigan Bay, are comfortable and elegantly decorated. The menus offer a good choice of interesting and nicely presented dishes, complemented by a well chosen wine list. The Trefeddian is in the immediate vicinity of a four-mile stretch of sandy beach and overlooks the golf course with the ever changing view of the sea beyond. The courtesy and efficiency of the staff create a happy atmosphere.

Rates: *Bed, breakfast and dinner from £58 per person.* ***Bargain breaks:*** *Spring and Autumn breaks from late February to end-April & all November = quoted tariff less 5%. Also no single room surcharge at these times.* V

- *48 en suite bedrooms, all with telephone, colour TV, radio, hairdryer, laundry/valet service, tea/coffee making facilities. Lift to all floors. Hotel suitable for movement of wheelchair. Car parking for 50.*
- *3 self-catering properties (to 8 pers). Garaging.*
- *5-course table d'hôte dinner £17.20; children's menu, lunch & special diets avail; last orders 8.30.*
- *Billiards/snooker, indoor games, pitch & putt, watersports, solarium, indoor swimming pool, tennis, children's play area. Fishing, riding, sailing/boating, clay shooting nearby.*
- *Open March- Jan. Major credit cards accepted.*

Machynlleth 11, Talylynn & Cader Idris 14, Barmouth 34, Dolgellau 24, London 215.

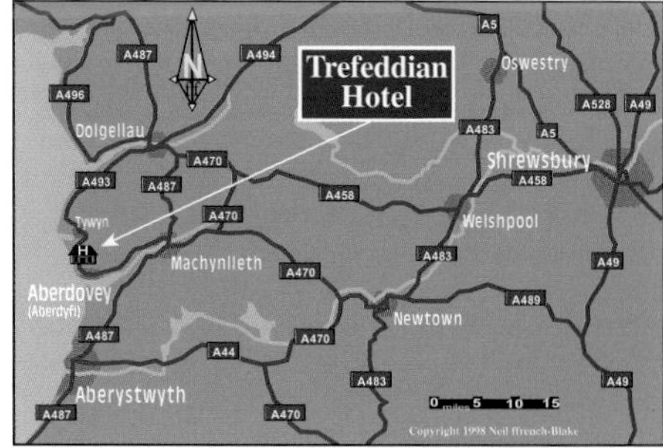

Bontddu Hall Hotel

Bontddu, Nr. Dolgellau, Gwynedd
LL40 2SU
Tel: (01341) 430661; Fax: (01341) 430284

Bontddu Hall, wonderfully situated in 14 acres of landscaped grounds, overlooks fine views of the Mawddach Estuary and famous Cader Idris range of mountains. The unspoilt charm of this attractive Victorian mansion has always made it a favourite of mine, and the owners Margaretta and Michael Ball know what is good. You will enjoy excellent food from an interesting country house evening dinner menu, dishes are varied and nicely served. Salmon and lobster are a speciality when available. A special carvery lunch is served on Sundays and an appetizing brasserie menu on other days. The furniture, pictures, colour schemes and flowers are all reminiscent of a country house and the hotel has been completely refurbished. All rooms are very comfortable and the Princess Bar extends a warm welcome. Nearly all bedrooms are with estuary and mountain views. In the Lodge, above the main drive are some additional rooms with balconies and exceptional views. I can only recommend a visit and you will want to come again and again.

Rates: *Room and breakfast from £62.50 (single), £100-£115 (double/twin), inclusive of VAT. Weekly demi-pension £450 per person; four-poster suites for romantics £160.* V
Bargain breaks: *Any two consecutive nights half board from £140-£160 per person inc. service & VAT. Extra nights pro rata.*

● *20 en suite bedrooms, all with telephone, colour TV, clock radio, hairdryer, tea/coffee making facilities; central heating; night service to midnight.*
● *Late meals to 9.30p.m.; diets; children welcome; dogs welcome.*
● *Sea bathing, golf and riding all five miles; gold mine nearby.*
● *Access, Amex, Diners & Visa credit cards accepted. Open March to December.*

Barmouth 5, Dolgellau 5, Aberystwyth 35, Caernarfon 50, Birmingham 110, London 235.

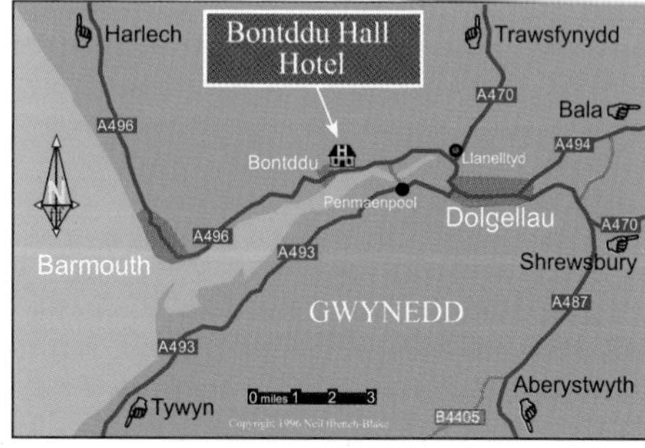

Glen-Yr-Afon House

Pontypool Road, Usk, Monmouthshire NP15 1SY. Tel: (01291) 672302/673202; Fax: (01291) 672597

Internet: http://www.glen-yr-afon.co.uk

One of the first things that the visitor will notice about the Glen-Yr-Afon is the friendliness and efficiency of owners Jan and Peter Clarke who believe in a "hands on" approach. This is reflected in their staff who cheerfully anticipate the guests' every need. Only five minutes' walk from the pleasant market town of Usk, the hotel is situated on the Pontypool road with an agreeable river walk opposite. An excellent base from which to explore South Wales and only half an hour from the motorway. Glen-Yr-Afon is an imposing and elegant Victorian house retaining many original features, yet sympathetically updated by Jan and Peter. 26 elegantly decorated bedrooms boast bathrooms with wonderfully large baths. The newly refurbished bridal suite again reflects the impeccable taste of the owners who are celebrating 25 years at the hotel this year. The oak-panelled restaurant offers an excellent choice of à la carte or table d'hôte menus, imaginatively presented with generous helpings and a well-chosen wine list. Business people and wedding parties are well cared for with a function suite seating 140, whilst the charming library is the venue for anniversaries, dinner parties and smaller functions for up to 20 people.

Rates: *Single room including breakfast from £57 + VAT. Double room with breakfast from £72+VAT.* ***Leisure Breaks:*** *Any two days sharing room, dinner, bed & breakfast per person £95.*

- *28 en suite bedrooms with satellite TV, radio, direct-dial telephone, laundry service, non-smoker bedrooms, tea/coffee making facilities.*
- *Last orders for dinner 21.00. Special diets available.*
- *Croquet, fishing, golf, gliding, grass skiing - nearby.*
- *Full business services and 2 conference rooms for total of 120 guests. AV equipment available.*
- *Car parking for 100 cars. Facilities for disabled.*
- *Open all year. Most credit cards accepted.*

Newport 10, Monmouth 13, Cardiff 22, Bristol 30, Gloucester 39, London 136 .

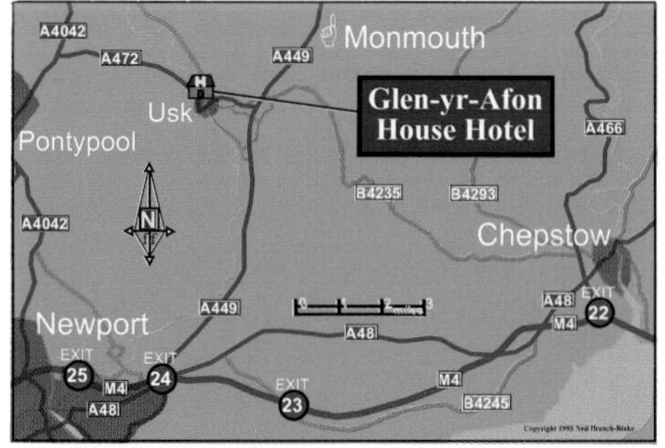

St Brides Hotel

St Brides Hill, Saundersfoot,
Pembrokeshire SA69 9NH
Tel: (01834) 812304; Fax: (01834) 813303
e-mail: ianbell@cipality.u-net.com

What a lovely surprise on my first visit to Pembrokeshire to discover St Brides Hotel! It is impressively situated in its own grounds overlooking Carmarthen Bay and the harbour and sandy beach of Saundersfoot. It is a privately owned and family run hotel offering personal and friendly service. The bedrooms are all individually designed. The Commodore Restaurant, with lovely views overlooking the bay, serves varied and interesting menus, according to season, with locally caught fish, Angle Bay lobsters and Saundersfoot crabs being a speciality. Dinner dances are held most Saturday evenings. History surrounds the hotel and there is plenty to see in the area - ancient castles which defended Pembrokeshire, the nearby medieval walled town of Tenby, elegant and majestic churches and cathedrals and notorious inlets where Vikings landed and smugglers plied their trade. I look forward to returning to St Brides.

Rates: *Single room with breakfast from £65; double room with breakfast from £94.*
Bargain breaks: *Weekends away to include dinner, bed & breakfast Fri & Sat nights £75-£99 per person. Midweek 'Shuttle' Breaks £95-£105 per person*

● *43 en suite bedrooms with colour TV + Satellite, direct-dial telephone, hairdryer, minibar, tea/coffee making facilities, radio.*
● *Non-smoker bedrooms; car parking (70) & rental.*
● *Table d'hôte dinner £18.50; lunch, à la carte and diets available; last orders 21.15.*
● *Full business & conference facilities to 150.*
● *Outdoor heated swimming pool. Fishing, watersports, boating/sailing within 1/2 mile; squash 2 miles; golf 3 miles.*
● *Open all year. All major credit cards accepted.*

Pembroke 11, Carmarthen 24, Fishguard 30, Cardigan 30, London 235.

PRINCIPALITY *International*

ROUP HANDLING-TOUR OPERATORS....

ur experts in England, Wales, Scotland and
eland for individual travel and tailor-made
oups. We shall be pleased to send you
ur brochures for:

COUNTESS WELCOME HOLIDAYS
Our voucher programme in all four countries – staying only at first class hotels.

WALKING HOLIDAYS in the National Parks of Wales

CYCLING TOURS in Wales and Ireland

GOLFING HOLIDAYS

CULTURAL and HERITAGE TOURS

GARDEN TOURS in England, Wales and Ireland, including the National Botanic Gardens of Wales.

PRINCIPALITY INTERNATIONAL
ST BRIDES HILL, SAUNDERSFOOT,
PEMBROKESHIRE, WALES SA69 9NH
Tel: +44 (0) 1834 812304
Fax: +44 (0) 1834 813303
Internet: http://www.principalityholidays.co.uk

TOLL FREE FAX from USA & CANADA
800 646 1620

Warpool Court Hotel

St. Davids, Pembrokeshire SA62 6BN
Tel: (01437) 720300; Fax: (01437) 720676
E-mail: warpool@enterprise.net

The Warpool Court is in a wonderful position overlooking the wild Atlantic and within a few minutes' walk of the famous St. David's Cathedral. This splendid country house hotel, with its unique collection of antique tiles, has been recommended by Signpost for a long time. It is owned by Peter Trier and through his expertise you can be assured of good food, gracious living and a warm welcome. The colour schemes are soft and restful and the staff cheerful and efficient. The hotel has a high reputation for good food and a fine selection of well chosen wines. Four course table d'hôte menus are excellent and, whenever possible, local produce is used. Salmon is smoked on the premises, crab and lobster are caught at the nearby village of Solva. A vegetarian menu is also available. The lounge bar provides a relaxed atmosphere for diners, and the residents' lounge ensures peace and comfort. There are numerous outdoor activities available, the most popular being walking, bird watching and surfing.

Rates: *Room and breakfast from £80 (single), £116 (twin/double) inclusive of VAT.* V
'Country House Breaks' *(2 -5 nights out of season d,b&b from £73; 6+ nights from £67 pppn). Full Christmas and New Year packages.*

- *25 en suite bedrooms all with telephone, colour TV, baby listening, tea/coffee making facilities; family rooms; full central heating.*
- *Meals to 9.15 p.m.; diets; children welcome; dogs accepted.*
- *Table tennis, gymnasium and sauna, pool table, heated covered swimming pool (Apr-Oct), all weather tennis court, 9 hole golf course nearby (2 miles); sea bathing; sandy beaches; lovely walks.*
- *Major credit cards accepted. Open Feb-December inc*

Fishguard 16, Haverfordwest 16, Carmarthen 46, Severn Bridge 130, Birmingham 177, London 264

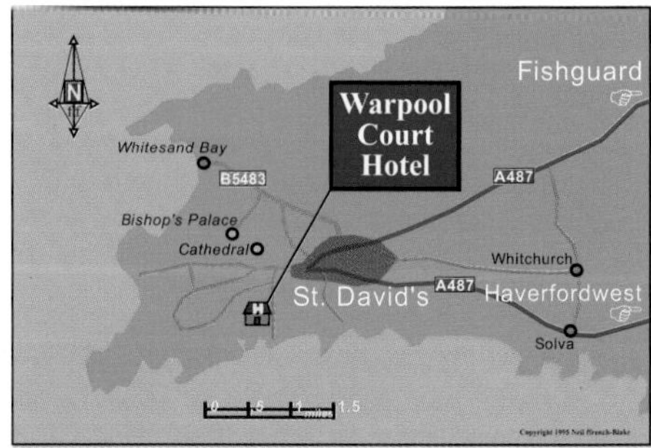

Gliffaes Country House Hotel

Crickhowell, Powys NP8 1RH
Tel: 0800 146719; Fax: (01874) 730463

Romantically situated in the lovely valley of the River Usk, Gliffaes is midway between the Black Mountains and the Brecon Beacons. 33 acres of grounds are planted with rare trees and shrubs, some dating from the nineteenth century. There is plenty to see and do in the area and the hotel has many leisure facilities. Over two miles of the river are reserved primarily for guests to fish for salmon and trout in the beautifully tranquil setting. The sitting room and the drawing room are most relaxing and French windows lead into an attractive and spacious sun room, which opens onto the terrace. The food at Gliffaes is excellent. Light lunch dishes may be ordered from the bar and home made afternoon tea is best described as a trencherman's dream! An extensive dinner menu includes plenty for vegetarians, using only the freshest ingredients and supported by a sensibly priced wine list. The bedrooms are priced according to size and views, all being comfortable and full of character. Having owned the hotel for over 50 years, the Brabner family are experienced, charming and informal hosts, as a result of which many guests return year after year. Nick and Peta Brabner have now been joined by their daughter and son-in-law, making a third generation of the family at Gliffaes.

Rates: *Single room with breakfast from £52; double/twin with breakfast from £62.85.* ***Bargain breaks:*** *Short stay and weekly rates on application.* V

- *22 en suite bedrooms all with direct-dial telephone, colour TV, tea/coffee making facilities and baby listening.*
- *Children welcome; dogs (but not in hotel).*
- *Late meals by arrangement; diets.*
- *TV room; meeting rooms for small conferences (16) available.*
- *Salmon & trout fishing; tennis; putting & practice net; croquet; billiards. Golf, riding, shooting, sailing & boating all nearby.*
- *Open all year. Amex, Diners, Access & Visa accepted.*

Crickhowell $3^1/_2$ miles, Abergavenny 10, London 160.

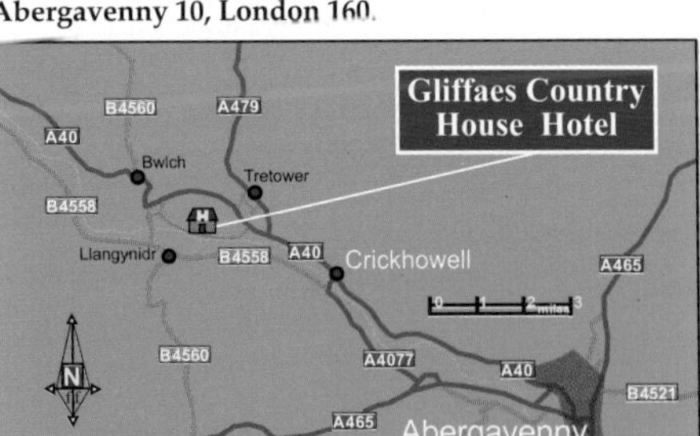

Scotland

Historic Houses, Gardens & Parks

Aberdeenshire
Castle Fraser & Garden, 4m N of Dunecht
Crathes Castle & Garden, Nr Banchory
Cruickshank Botanic Gardens, Aberdeen University
Darnside Herb Garden, Benholm by Johnshaven
DrumCastle & Garden, by Banchory
Duff House, Banff
Duthie Park & Winter Gardens, Aberdeen
Fasque, Fettercain
Fyvie Castle
Haddo House, Tarves
James Cocker & Sons, Rosegrowers, Aberdeen
Leith Hall & Garden, Kennethmont, Huntly
Pitmedden Garden & Museum of Farming by Ellon

Angus
Duntrune Demonstration Garden, Dundee
House of Dun, 3m W of Montrose

Argyll & Bute
Ardnaiseig Gardens, 22m E of Oban
Arduaine Garden, 20m S of Oban
Barguillean Garden, 3m W of Taynuilt
Brodick Castle, Garden & Country Park, Isle of Arran
Torosay Castle & Gardens, $1\frac{1}{2}$m SSE of Craignure, Isle of Mull

City of Edinburgh
Dalmeny House, By South Queensferry
The Georgian House, Charlotte Sq., Edinburgh
Gladstone's Land, Royal Mile, Edinburgh
House of the Binns, 15m W of Edinburgh
Hopetoun House, W of South Queensferry
Inveresk Lodge Garden, 6m E of Edinburgh
Malleny Garden, Balerno, W of Edinburgh
Royal Botanic Gardens, Edinburgh

City of Glasgow
Greenbank Garden, Clarkston, Glasgow

Dumfries & Galloway
Drumlanrig Castle & Country Park, 3m N of Thornhill Galloway House Gardens, Garlieston
Maxwelton House, 13m NE of Dumfries
Meadowsweet Herb Garden, Castle Kennedy, Stranraer
Threave Garden, Castle Douglas

East Ayrshire
Dean Castle & Country Park, Kilmarnock

Fife
Balcaskie House & Gardens, 2m W of Pittenween
Cambo Gardens, 1m S of Kingsbarns
Earlshall Castle & Gardens, 1m E of Leuchars
Falkland Palace & Gardens, 11m N of Kirkcaldy
Hill of Tarvit Mansionhouse & Garden, 2m S of Cupar
Kellie Castle & Garden, 3m N of Pittenween
Sir Douglas Bader Garden for the Disabled, Duffus Park

Highland
The Achiltibuie Hydroponicum
Balmacara Estate & Lochalsh Wood land Garden, Kyle of Lochalsh
Dunrobin Castle, Gardens & Museum, Golspie, Sutherland
Dunvegan Castle, Isle of Skye
Inverewe Garden, by Poolewe
Oldwick Castle, Wick

Moray
Brodie Castle, 4m W of Forres

Perth & Kinross
Bell's Cherrybank Gardens, Perth
Blair's Castle, 7m NNW of Pitlochry
Branklyn Garden, Perth
Cluny House Gardens, $3\frac{1}{2}$ m from Aberfeldy
Edzell Castle & Garden, 6m N of Brechin
Magginch Castle Gardens, 10m E of Perth
Scone Palace, 2m NE of Perth

Scottish Borders
Bowhill, 3m W of Selkirk
Dawyck Botanic Garden, Stobo
Floors Castle, Kelso
Kailzie Gardens, 2m E of Peebles

Stirlingshire
Culcreuch Castle & Country Park, Fintry

South Ayrshire
Culzean Castle & Country Park, 4m W of Maybole

West Lothian
Suntrap (Garden) Gogarbank, 6m W of Edinburgh

Walks & Nature Trails

Aberdeenshire
Aden Country Park, Mintlaw
Braeloine Visitor Centre, Glen Tanar, by Aboyne
Bullers of Buchan, Cruden Bay
Forview Nature Reserve, Newburgh

Angus
Monikie Country Park, 10m N of Dundee

Argyll & Bute
Carsaig Arches, on shore 3m W of Carsaig, Isle of Mull
King's Cave, shore, 2m N of Blackwaterfoot
Lauder Forest Walks, 3m S of Strachur, Glenbranter
Puck's Glen, 5m W of Dunoon

Dumfries & Galloway
Caerlaverock National Nature Reserve, S of Dumfries

City of Edinburgh
Cammon Estate, NE off Queensferry Road, Edinburgh

East Ayrshire
Muirshiel Country Park, 9m SW of Paisley

East Lothian
John Muir Country Park, Dunbar

Fife
Scottish Deer Centre, £m W of Cupar

Highland
Abriachan Garden Nursery Walk, Loch Ness
Aultfearn Local Walk, Kiltarlity
Dalabil Glen, between Tarskavaig & Ostair, Isle of Skye
Falls of Foyers Woodland Walks
Farigaig Forest Trails
Forestry Walk, between Ardvasar & Aird of Sleat, Isle of Skye
Glen Affric Forest Walks
Plodda Falls Scenic Walk
Reelig Forest Walks, W of Inverness
The Trotternish Ridge, Isle of Skye

Perth & Kinross
Queen's View Centre, Loch Tummel, 6m NW of Pitlochry
St Cyrus National Nature Reserve, Nether Warburton

Scottish Borders
Jedforest Deer & Farm Park, Camptown
Pease Dean, Nr. Cockburnspath

Stirlingshire
Gartmorn Dam Country Park & Nature Reserve, by Sauchie

Historical Sites & Museums

Aberdeenshire
Aberdeen Maritime Museum - Provost Ross's House
Ballindalloch Castle
Balmoral Castle, Crathie
Braemar Highland Heritage Centre
Brodie Castle, Forres
Castle Fraser, Nr Inverurie
Colgarff Castle, Strathdon
Crathie Church, Crathie
Dallas Dhu Distillery, Forres
Kings College Chapel & Visitor Centre
Provost Skene's House, Aberdeen
St Michael's Cathedral, Old Aberdeen

Angus
Angus Folk Museum, Glamis
Arbroath Abbey
Barrie's Birthplace, Kirriemuir
Glamis Castle, 5m SW of Forfar

Argyll & Bute
Bonawe Iron Works, Nr Taynuilt
David Livingstone Centre, Blantyre
Doon Valley Heritage, 2m S of Patna
Duart Castle, Isle of Mull
Inverary Castle & Gardens
Kilmory Castle Gardens, Lochgilphead
The Old Byrem, Dervaig, Isle of Mull
Rothesay Castle, Isle of Bute
Souter Johnnie's Cottage, Kirkoswald

City of Edinburgh
Craigmillar Castle, 2.5m SE of Edinburgh
Edinburgh Castle
Palace of Holyrood House, Edinburgh

City of Glasgow
The Tenement House, Garnethill

Dumfries & Galloway
Burns House, Dumfries
Caerlaverock Castle, 8m SE of Dumfries
Carlyle's Birthplace, Ecclefechan
Dumfries Museum & Camera Obscura, Dumfries
Maclellan's Castle, Kirkcudbright
Mill on the Fleet Heritage Centre,

Scotland

Gatehouse of Fleet New Abbey Cornmill, 8m S of Dumfries
Sweetheart Abbey, New Abbey
Threave Castle, 3m E of North Berwick

East Ayrshire
Weaver's Cottage, Kilbarchan, 12m SW of Glasgow

East Renfrewshire
Coats Observatory, Paisley

East Lothian
Dirleton Castle & Garden, 7m W of North Berwick
Preton Mill a Phmtassie Doocot, 23m E of Edinburgh
Tantallon Castle, 3m E of North Berwick
The Heritage of Golf, Gullane

Fife
Aberdour Castle
Balgonie Castle, by Markinch
Inchcolm Abbey (via ferry from S Queensferry)
St Andrew's Cathedral
St Andrew's Castle

Highland
Castle Grant, Grantown-on-Spey
Cawdor Castle, 5m N of Nairn
Colbost Folk Musuem, Isle of Skye
Culloden Battlefield, 5m N of Inverness
Dornoch Cathedral
Durness Visitor Centre
Eilean Donan Castle, 9m E of Kyle of Lochalsh
Fort George, 10m W of Nairn
Giant MacAskill Museum, Dunvegan, Isle of Skye
Glen Coe Visitor Centre, 17m S of Fort William
Glenfinnan Monument, Lochaber, 18m W of Fort William
Hugh Miller's Cottage, Cromarty, 22m NE of Inverness
Leckmelm Shrubbery & Arboretum, Nr Ullapool
Lochinver Visitor Centre
Piping Centre, Borreraig, Isle of Skye
Skye Museum of Island Life, Kilmuir, Isle of Skye
Urquart Castle on Loch Ness, Nr Drumnadrochit

Moray
Elgin Cathedral

Perth & Kinross
Atholl Country Collection, Blair Atholl
Black Watch regimental Museum, Balhousie Castle, Perth
Doune Castle, 8m S of Callander
Killiekrankie Visitor Centre, 3m N of Pitlochry
Loch Leven Castle, via ferry from Kinross

Scottish Borders
Dryburgh Abbey, 5m SE of Melrose
Robert Smail's Printing Works, Innerleithen
Hermitage Castle 5m NE of Newcastleton
Jedburgh Abbey
Jim Clark Memorial Trophy Room, Duns
Melrose Abbey
Smallholm Tower, 6m W of Kelso

South Ayrshire
Bachelor's Club (re: Robert Burns), Tarbolton
Burns Cottage & Museum, 2m S of Ayr

South Lanarkshire
Gladstone Court Museum, Biggar
John Buchan Centre, 6m E of Biggar

Stirlingshire
Inchmahoune Priory, Lake of Mentieth
National Wallace Monument, 1 1/2 m NNE of Stirling

West Dunbartonshire
Dumbarton Castle
The Hill House, Helensburgh

West Lothian
Linlithgow Palace
Blackness Castle, 4m NE of Linlithgow

Entertainment Venues

Aberdeenshire
Alford Valley Railway, Alford
Fowlsheugh RSPB Seabird Colony
Glenshee Ski Centre, Cairnwell by Braemar
Holyneuk Bird Park, Nr Macduff
Loch Muick & Lochnagar Wildlife Reserve, Crimond
North East Falconry Centre, Cairnie,

by Huntly
Peterhead Fish Market
Royal Lochnagar Distillery, Crathie
St Cyrus National Nature Reserve, by Montrose
Storybook Glen, Maryculter
Ugie Fish House, Peterhead

Angus
Discovery Point, Dundee

Argyll & Bute
Ardnamurchan Natural History & Visitor Centre, Nr. Glenborrowdale
Antartex Village, Balloch
Balloch Castle Country Park, at S end of Loch Lomond
Glenbart Abbey Visitor Centre, 12m NW of Campbeltown
Glenfinnart Deer Farm, Ardentinny
Inverawe Smokery, Bridge of Awe
Isle of Mull Wine Company, Bunesan
Kelburn Country Centre, between Lairgs & Fairlie
Mull Railway, Craignure
Mull Little Theatre, Dervaig
Tobermory Distillery Visitor Centre

City of Edinburgh
Camera Obscura, Castlehill
Edinburgh Clan Tartan Centre, Leith
Crabbie's Histonc Winery Tour, Great Junction Street
Edinburgh Crystal Visitor Centre, Penicuik
Kinloch Anderson Heritage Room, Leith
National Gallery of Scotland, The Mound
The Scottish Whisky Heritage Centre, Royal Mile

Dumfries & Galloway
Old Blacksmith's Shop Centre, Gretna Green
Robert Burns Centre, Dumfries

Fife
Deep sea World, North Queensferry

Highland
Aviemore Centre
Castle Grant, Grantown-on-Spey
Clan Donald Visitor Centre at Armadale Castle
Dulsie Bridge
Glen Ord Distillery, Muir of Ord
Highland Folk Museum, Kingussie
Loch Ness Centre, Drumnadrochit
Made in Scotland Exhibition of Crafts, Beauly
The Malt Whisky Trail, Speyside
Rothiemurchas Estate, Nr. Aviemore
Skye Oysters, Loch Harport
Speyside Heather Centre, Grantown
Strathspey Steam Railway, Nr. Aviemore
Talisker Distillery, Loch Harport
Torridon Countryside Centre, 9m SW of Aberdeen

North Lanarkshire
The Time Capsule, Monklands, Coatbridge

Perth & Kinross
Beatrix Potter Garden & Exhibition, Brinham
Caithness Glass (Perth), Inveralmond
Crieff Visitors' Centre
Rob Roy & Trossachs Visitor Centre, Callander

Scottish Borders
Borders Wool Centre Nr. Galashiels
Peter Anderson of Scotland Cashmere Woollens Mill & Museum, Galashiels
St. Abb's Head, 2m N of Coldingham

Stirlingshire
Bannockburn Heritage Centre, 2m S of Stirling
Blair Drummond Safari & Leisure Park
Village Glass, Bridge of Allan

Scotland

Outdoors in Scotland

Scotland is synonymous with outdoor sports - golf, sailing, fishing, shooting and deer-stalking. Ideal country for field sports, it nurtured the game of golf - now at least four centuries old. It was the size of the Old Course at St. Andrews which dictated that golf everywhere should be played over nine holes or a multiple of nine.

The Royal and Ancient Club at St. Andrews is golf's ruling body and the democratic nature of the game is reflected in the great number of municipal courses and the low cost of playing.

Scotland has a large network of golf courses. The "Gold Coast" on the west between Troon and Turnberry on the Firth of Clyde has 20 courses in 20 miles. East-coast towns from the Borders to Caithness have fine breezy courses on undulating land among the dunes.

Whatever the origins of golf, Scotland is definitely the home of curling. The roaring game, as it is called from the hum of the polished stones gliding across the ice, was born on frozen Highland lochs.

Native enthusiasts made it a game of skill and exported it to Canada, Switzerland and other lands which now have curling traditions of their own. Most large Scottish towns and a few hotels have their artificial curling rinks, so it is no longer just a winter game.

To see the Scots at play, and enjoying a unique social occasion, go to Loch Leven or the Lake of Menteith after a prolonged January frost, when conditions permit a Grand Match, North versus South, to take place.

Scotland has four ski resorts - Aviemore, Glencoe, Glenshee and the Lecht. The large number of ski shops and instruction schools in Scotland mean snow business is becoming big business. The Cairngorm foothills around Aviemore are well provided with hotels, restaurants and bars with generous après-ski amenities. When conditions are right, some of the best skiing in Europe is to be found in the central Highlands of Scotland.

A fishing rod is part of a boy's heritage in Scotland and country buses are noted for the number of unscheduled stops they make at angling beats. More than three hundred Scottish rivers and numerous lochs are world famous for trout and salmon fishing. Apart from some private beats, fishing is very reasonably priced, occasionally free, and available (even on the celebrated Tweed, Tay or Spey rivers) with a permit from the local hotel, angling/tackle shop or fishing society.

In reservoirs, canals, some rivers and inland lochs, coarse fishing is cheaper, while sea angling from the shore is free on most parts of the coast. Another bonus is Scotland's *Fishing Heritage Trail* which offers touring motorists a choice of scenic and historic routes along the east coast from Eyemouth to Scrabster.

Highland Games staged throughout Scotland include more sporting and spectacular activities. Centuries ago, a Scottish king crossed a fallen enemy's sword with his own and danced a victory jig. That was the origin of the sword dance. The same king kept his soldiers fit by making them run up and down hills, and this is retained in many Highland Games. Ancient Picts improvising hunting dances, raised their arms and pointed their fingers, like antlers, and imitated the movements of a rutting stag. An early Highland fling, perhaps? Later feats of strength were devised by young clansmen: caber-tossing, shot-putting, hammer throwing.

Scotland's other open-air activities include pony trekking - a Highland invention, bird-watching, cycling, canoeing, mountaineering, rock-climbing, sailing and gliding. A sporting paradise, indeed.

Dumfries & Galloway

Turn left at Scotland and you will find yourself in Dumfries and Galloway, an area combining the grandeur of hill, forest and sweeping coastline with an especially mild climate, making it the perfect region for all kinds of holidays. It is ideal car touring country with quiet roads and a host of fascinating byways for you to explore; hill roads, shore roads, forest roads and farm roads ... and it won't take you long to get there. From England the main M6 motorway joins the A74 highway just north of Carlisle. Cross the border at Gretna and you're in Dumfries and Galloway.

While you don't need to leave the main roads to enjoy the area's scenic beauty, it is an ideal refuge for climbers and walkers, and for anyone who enjoys silence, space and solitude. Pony trekking is another excellent way of getting off the beaten track, and you don't need to be an experienced rider to enjoy travelling through the heart of the countryside.

Sparkling clear lochs and rivers and miles of attractive coast make fishing and water sports firm favourites throughout the year. The area offers variety for yachtsmen or anyone who enjoys messing about in boats. Visitors with a taste for exercise may wish to try water skiing, wind surfing or sub aqua. Others may prefer to find a quiet beach in one of the sheltered bays around the coast, soak up the sun and watch the rest of the family getting wet! The beaches offer safe bathing and swimming. The fisherman's paradise provides just the climate for a good day's sport, with game fishing for trout and salmon available at modest cost, and coarse fishing and sea angling growing in popularity every year. Dumfries and Galloway has a tremendous variety of golf courses, with glorious scenery included at no extra cost, and very moderate green fees.

The region's history is rich and fascinating, stretching back to the strange anonymous figures who have left their standing stones, chambered cairns and scattered relics to intrigue us. There are traces of Roman occupation, particularly in the east of the area and, even before St. Columba founded his abbey at Iona, St. Ninian had come to Scotland in the 4th century, making Whithorn a religious centre and place of pilgrimage, and the cradle of Christianity in Britain. The remains of this Priory are well worth a visit, as are other intriguing monuments. At Dundrennan Abbey Mary Queen of Scots spent her last night on Scottish soil before fleeing to England, captivity and execution. Sweetheart Abbey still stands as a memorial to a love story six hundred years old. Here in 1263 the grieving widow of John Balliol (together they founded the Oxford college) had her husband's heart built in over the high altar of the abbey, which became known as "*Dulce Cor*" - "Sweet Heart". In the spectacular Galloway Forest Park stand two memorials to Robert the Bruce, who sheltered in the Galloway hills to pursue guerilla warfare against the English in the fourteenth century. Walk up Glen Trool to one of the Bruce Stones, which commemorates a battle on the hill, and enjoy the lovely view over the wooded banks of the loch. This was never an uneventful part of the world, even when free from wars. The imposing Caerlaverock, Threave and many other castles evoke the dangerous days when ruthless local families like the Douglases and Maxwells fought for domination of the area. The region's history is echoed in the continuing traditions of pageants and festivals. The Common Ridings in towns like Lockerbie and Annan revive times when it was necessary to patrol the boundaries of one's territory, to ward off rival families or English marauders.

The region's musical and literary heritage is similarly kept alive, and can be appreciated during the Arts Festival (May and early June). Scotland's most famous son, Rabbie Burns wrote many of his best-loved songs and poems when he lived in this area. Pay your respects at his house, now a curious museum, and then drink to his memory in his own "local", the still-flourishing Globe Inn. After many years of providing a haven for artists and craftspeople the region must now have more per mile than any other part of Scotland. Most are delighted to welcome visitors to watch them at work. You will find weavers, potters, glass-blowers, toy makers, textile printers, jewellers, woodturners, sculptors, and silk screen printers.

Accommodation is as varied as the scenery. Country house hotels, once private homes, are furnished to preserve their original character. Here you can enjoy a "house party" atmosphere in gracious surroundings, often with a range of leisure pursuits like fishing and golf available in the hotel's grounds or nearby. Dumfries and Galloway takes a pride in the friendliness of its people. Living out of the mainstream of today's hurry-scurry means that locals are happy to spare the time to make visitors feel at home.

DIARY OF EVENTS 2000

January

29 Dec-Jan 1. **Edinburgh's Hogmanay -** the world's largest winter festival.
22. **Scottish Borders National Chase.** Race meeting, Kelso, Scottish Borders.
22. **Robert Burns Day** - celebrations throughout Scotland for national poet.

February

11-13. **Rugby International.** Scotland v Wales, Murrayfield, Edinburgh.
19-March 11 .**Inverness Music Fest ival.** Var. venues.

March

2-4. **Dumfermline Abbey Sound & Light 2000.**
4. **Scotland v France.** Rugby Int'l, Murrayfield, Edinburgh
25. **Millenium Champions Challenge.** Blair Castle. Highland dancing competition.

April

1. **Rugby International.** Scotland v England, Murrayfield, Edinburgh.
8-23. **Edinburgh International Science Festival.** Var.
1-2. City of Dundee **Flower Show**
1-9. **World Curling Cham' ships.** Braehead, Glasgow.
18*. **Scottish Grand National.** Ayr Racecourse.
27-1 May. **Isle of Bute Jazz Festival.** Var. venues, Bute.
29. **Silk Cup Rugby League.** Murrayfield, Edinburgh.

May

7. **Mayfire Festival & Fireworks.** Beltane, Stirling.
26-June 10. **5th Annual Highland Festival.**Thurso & various venues in Highlands
May*. Dundee **Jazz Festival**
26-June 4. **Dumfries & Galloway Arts Festival.** Var. venues throughout D & Gall
27-28. **Angus Show.** Haughmuir, by Brechin.

June

3-5*. **Scotland's National Gardening Show**. Strathclyde Country Park, Glasgow
6-12*. **Isle of Arran Folk Fest -ival.** Var. venues, Isle of Arran
16-22. **St Magnus Festival,** Kirkwall, Orkney.
17-27. **Mass Participation Cycling Event** - var. venues.
24-25. **Royal HighlandShow** Ingliston, Edinburgh.
24-July 3*. **Glasgow International Jazz Festival.** Various venues, Glasgow.

July

July*. **Hebridean Celtic Music Festival**. Var. venues, Stornoway. Isle of Lewis
1-31. **Festival of Scottish Craft** Royal Museum, Edinburgh.
13-16. **World Corporate Games**. Aberdeen.
15. Loch Lomond **Highland Games.**
15. North Uist **Highland Games.**
20-23. **Open Golf Championship.** St Andrew's, Fife.
29-Aug 1*. **Cutty Sark Tall Ships Race.** Greenock, Inverclyde.
22-29 **Cowal Europe**. Dunoon Carnival var. European c'trys
29-7 Aug*. **Edinburgh International Jazz & Blues Festival.** Various venues.

August

4-26. **Edinburgh Military Tattoo.** Edinburgh Castle.
2-12. **International Youth Festival** Aberdeen.
14. **World Pipe Band Championship.** Glasgow.
13-27. **Edinburgh Int'l Film Festival.** Filmhouse Theatre.
13-Sept 2. **Edinburgh International Festival.** Prestigious multi-arts festival.
23-24. **Millennium Highland Gathering & Games Champ'** Muir of Ord, Nr Inverness.

September

1-3. **Flower & Food Festival** Dundee.
2. **Braemar Royal Highland Gathering.** Braemar, Aberdeenshire.
9. **RAF Battle of Britain International Airshow.** Leuchars, Fife.

October

2*. **October Musical Beerfest & Barbecue.** Gatehouse of Fleet, Dumfries-shire.
5-8. **St Giles 2000.** St Giles Cath, Edinburgh.Flower Fest
14-23* **Aberdeen Alternative Festival.** Music, dance, drama
13-21. **Royal National Millennium MOD -** Dunoon, Argyll.

November

5. **Fireworks Display.** Var. venues, Dundee.
25-26. **Dundee Mountain** Film Festival.

**Denotes provisional date*
For further details contact:
The Scottish Tourist Board,
23 Ravelston Terrace, Edinburgh EH4 3EU.
Tel: 0131 332 2433

Ardoe House Hotel

Blairs, South Deeside Road,
Aberdeen AB12 5YP
Tel: (01224) 867355;
Fax: (01224) 861283
E-mail: reservations@ardoe.macdonald-hotels.co.uk
Internet: http://www.macdonaldhotels.co.uk

Built in 1878 in Scottish Baronial style, Ardoe House is situated within its own beautifully landscaped grounds with magnificent views over the river Dee and open countryside. It has the style of an elegant country mansion with all modern comforts. Each bedroom has a pleasant and comfortable atmosphere and the fare available in the hotel's 2 AA Rosette award-winning restaurant will suit even the most critical palate. The hotel's extensive conference and banqueting facilities and its proximity to Aberdeen make it an ideal venue for both business and pleasure and a good base from which to explore North East Scotland. Aberdeen City Centre and Rail Station are only ten minutes away and Aberdeen International Airport 30 minutes. Ardoe is an ideal gateway for touring Royal Deeside with Balmoral only 40 miles upstream. A new fully equipped Leisure and Beauty Centre opens January 2000.

Rates: *Mid-week from £80 single, £90 double.* V
Leisure Breaks*: at weekends & certain mid-week dates accomm. from £130 per person 2-night stay inc dinner, b&b. Third night accom only free to Signpost readers on production of 2000 guide.*

● *114 en suite bedrooms (inc 3 suites) all with colour TV + satellite, direct-dial telephone, hairdryer, laundry/valet service, tea/coffee making facilities, 24-hr room/meal service, music/radio/alarm, trouser press. Non-smoker & disabled rooms*
● *❀❀ Restaurant. A la carte, lunch & special diets available; last orders 9.45. 10 meeting rooms to 500*
● *Croquet, fitness centre, indoor pool, tennis.*
Aberdeen 3 ,Braemar 50, Inverness 112, Edinburgh 125

Maryculter House

South Deeside Road, Maryculter,
Aberdeen AB12 5GB
Tel: (01224) 732124;
Fax: (01224) 733510
E-mail: maryculter.house.hotel@dial.pipex.com
Website: http://www.macdonaldhotels.co.uk

One of the most attractive small hotels I have stayed at, Maryculter is situated on the banks of the river Dee, built on the site of a preceptory of the Knights Templar and dating from the 13th century. Many of the original features can still be traced inside the walled churchyard in the hotel grounds. The last owner of the property, Sir Cosmo Duff Gordon, in 1935 was one of the few male survivors of the Titanic. All 23 bedrooms are individually furnished. Dining areas include the Poachers Pocket for snacks, the Cocktail Bar, built above the cellars, and the main Priory Restaurant where the cuisine is traditional Scottish with French influences. Maryculter is an ideal hideaway for that special short break or longer holiday, being ideally situated for golf, shooting, fishing and country walks.

Rates: *Single (room only) from £65; double from £90.* ***Bargain Breaks:*** *at weekends from £60 per person per night inc. breakfast & house dinner ★ Sunday night accommodation complimentary to SIGNPOST readers.★* V

● *23 en suite bedrooms with colour TV + satellite, direct-dial telephone, hairdyer, laundry/valet service, music/radio/alarm, trouser press.*
● *4-course Table d'hôte dinner £31.50; lunch & special diets available; last orders 9 pm. AA ❀ food*
● *Fishing, riding, shooting, golf nearby.*
● *Open all year. Major credit cards accepted.*
Aberdeen 8, Dundee 59, Edinburgh 122.

Scotland

Norwood Hall Hotel

Garthdee Road, Cults,
Aberdeen AB15 9FX
Tel: (01224) 868951;
Fax: (01224) 869868
E-mail: reservations@norwood-hall.co.uk

Built in 1887 on the site of Pitfodels Castle, this Victorian Mansion House standing in seven acres of its own wooded grounds has been fully restored to its former glory, combining traditional elegance and warmth with the comforts of a modern house. It is an ideal base for visiting Aberdeen (only three miles away) and Royal Deeside, famed for its fishing and golf courses. A magnificent carved oak staircase leads to the 21 bedrooms, whose décor and facilities match those of a four-star hotel. The restaurant, which has been awarded an AA rosette, has all the rtadition and grandeur of a country house, with its tapestry walls, carved ceilings nd antique paintings. Here you can sample some of the finest Scottish cuisine. Alternatively you can dine in the comfort of the Georgian lounge which offers lunches and suppers daily.

Rates: *Single with breakfast from £70; double with breakfast from £90.* V
Bargain Breaks: *Weekends £120 per couple per night, dinner, bed & breakfast. Stay Fri & Sat & stay Sunday night free*

- *21 en suite bedrooms with TV, telephone, hairdryer, laundry/valet service, tea/coffee making facilities, music/radio/alarm clock.*
- *A la carte £27; lunch & special diets available; last orders 9.30 pm. AA Rosette. Car parking for 60*
- *Four meeting/function rooms, capacity to 350.*
- *Open all year. All major credit cards accepted.*

Balgonie Country House Hotel

Braemar Place, Ballater,
Aberdeenshire AB35 5NQ
Tel & Fax: (013397) 55482

One of the most attractive small hotels it has been my pleasure to visit. The Edwardian-style country house is set in 4 acres of mature gardens, commanding superb views westward to Glen Muick and *Dark Lochnagar.* Each of the comfortable bedrooms is named after a fishing pool on the banks of the Dee. As befits a previous Caithness Glass / Taste of Scotland Prestige Award Winner, the two AA rosette dining-room is at the heart of the Balgonie experience. It offers the best of local produce: salmon from the river, game from the hill, beef from the field and seafood from the North Sea. In the heart of Royal Deeside, Balgonie is convenient for visiting Balmoral (open May-July) and as a centre for the famed Whisky and Castle trails as well as for walking, golf, fishing, shooting and ski-ing in winter.

Rates: *Single inc breakfast from £65; double from £110. Visa, Amex, JCB, Diners, M'card.* V

- *9 en suite bedrooms with colour TV, radio, direct-dial telephone, hairdryer.*
- *4-course tdh dinner £28.50. Lunch & special diets available. Last orders 2100. Car parking 16*
- *Croquet. Golf & tennis 1 m. Riding, fishing 10 m*
- *Open February-December.*

Balmoral 7, Aberdeen 42, Perth 67, Edinburgh 111, London 483.

Stakis Craigendarroch Hotel & Country Club

Braemar Road, Ballater, Royal Deeside, Aberdeenshire AB35 5XA
Tel: (013397) 55858; Fax: (013397) 55447
E-mail: enquiries@craigendarroch. stakis.co.uk
Internet: http: / / www.stakis.co.uk

This was my first visit to Craigendarroch and I was not disappointed. Built in 1891 for the Keiller (marmalade) family of Dundee and located in the heart of Royal Deeside, the hotel is still first and foremost a country retreat, retaining all its original charm and character, yet with 4-star facilities. Set in 29 acres of woodland, it overlooks the river Dee, the forest of Balmoral and the peak of Lochnagar. The magnificent oak panelled hallway with its fine staircase leads to 45 individually furnished bedrooms, each with every modern facility and comfort. Dining is one of the pleasures of Craigendarroch. A choice of restaurants offers superb food and excellent service: the *Oaks* modern cuisine in a formal setting; the *Clubhouse* brasserie snacks and meals; the *Study* a cosy haven for that pre-dinner drink. The Country Club and Sporting Estate has activities for all, including a *Clarins* Health & Beauty parlour and timeshare opportunities, with children well catered for. General Manager Andrew Murphie and his friendly staff will make your stay a memorable one.

Rates: *Single room with breakfast from £95; double inc. breakfast from £130.* V
Bargain Breaks: *2 nights min, dinner, b & b £75 per person per night. Other breaks available throughout the year - contact hotel for details.*

- *45 en suite bedrooms, all with telephone, TV + video & satellite, hairdryer, laundry/valet service, tea/coffee making facilities, 24 hr room/ meal service, radio/alarm clock, trouser press.*
- *Table d'hôte Oaks restaurant £27.50; Clubhouse £20. A la carte, lunch & special diets available; last orders 10 pm.*
- *Acorn Club for children; crèche; parking for 100.*
- *Full business services inc. 3 meeting rooms to 110*
- *Billiards/snooker, fitness centre, indoor games, jacuzzi/sauna, squash, indoor swimming pool, tennis, barber shop/(Clarins) beauty clinic, dry ski slope. Golf, shooting, riding nearby*
- *Open all year. All major credit cards accepted*

Balmoral 7, Aberdeen 42, Perth 67, Edinburgh 111

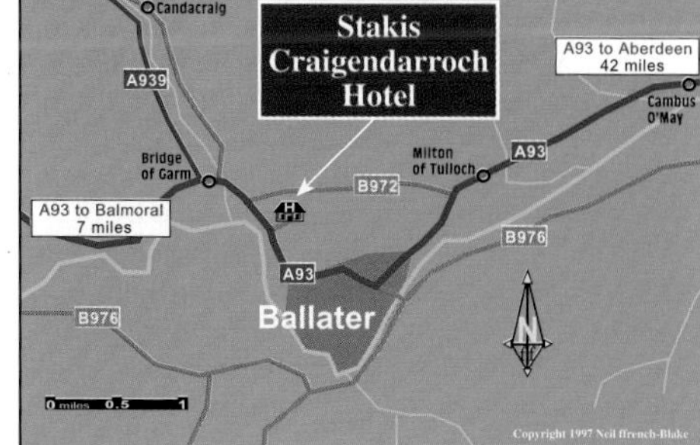

Raemoir House Hotel

Raemoir, Banchory,
Aberdeenshire AB31 4AD
Tel: (01330) 824884; Fax: (01330) 822171
E-mail: raemoirhse@aol.com

Raemoir House Hotel stands in the middle of a 3500 acre estate, sheltered by the Hill of Fare which rises some 1500 foot behind it. It is situated on Royal Deeside, an area noted for its picturesque scenery, numerous castles, golf courses and hill walking. The original house of Raemoir, dating from the 16th century, known as the 'Ha' Hoose, where Mary, Queen of Scots is said to have rested after the Battle of Corrichie, now makes a popular annex adjacent to the hotel. The coach house and stables have also been converted into luxury self-contained suites. The main mansion dates from 1750. It is sumptuously furnished with antiques and tapestries and a feature is the oval ballroom dining room, whose walls are covered in Victorian velvet brocade. Each bedroom is different, with the style in many cases reflecting the name of the room. One, the Old English Room, has a 500-year old four poster. Raemoir's proximity to Aberdeen, coupled with its peaceful rural setting, make it an ideal venue for both a leisure break or a business conference or corporate entertainment day.

***Rates:** Single with breakfast from £60; double with breakfast from £80.* V

- *20 en suite double and twin bedrooms with TV, telephone, hairdryer, laundry/valet service, tea/coffee making facilities,radio/alarm & trouser press*
- *Four superb self-catering apartments.*
- *3 course table d'hôte dinner £27.50; lunch & special diets available; last orders 9 pm.*
- *Two meeting/function rooms, capacity up to 50.*
- *Croquet, 9-hole pitch n putt course, jogging track, exercise room, sauna/sunbed, tennis court, private helipad. Skirmishing, orienteering, off road driving, golf, salmon fishing, clay pigeon shooting and stalking can be arranged locally.*
- *Open all year. All major credit cards accepted.*

Aberdeen 16½, Ballater 26, Braemar 43, Glasgow 151, Edinburgh 114.

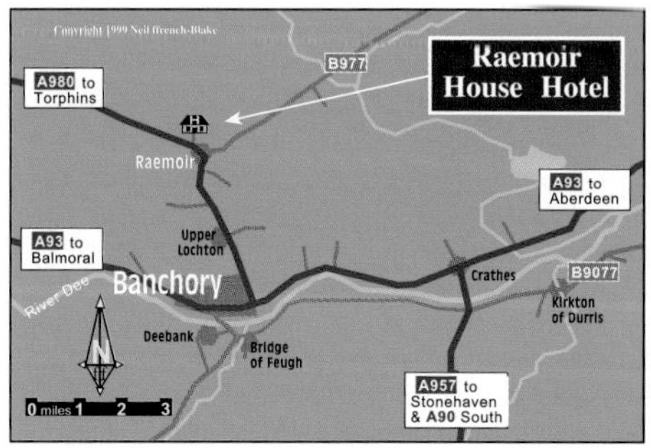

Thainstone House Hotel & Country Club

Inverurie, Aberdeenshire AB51 5NT
Tel: (01467) 621643; Fax: (01467) 625084 STB Highly Commended. Taste of Scotland. AA ★★★★ RAC

Set in 40 acres of lush meadowland, the original Thainstone was burned by Jacobites in the 18th century. The Thainstone of today dates from the early 19th century and combines stately elegance with all the modern comforts of a luxurious 20th century hotel. A grand portal introduces you to the majestic galleried reception area on the way to your individually furnished bedroom which has nice extra touches like a decanter of sherry and Scottish shortcake awaiting you. The main restaurant *Simpsons* has two AA rosettes. In a sumptuous Georgian setting you can enjoy some of the most exciting menus in the North of Scotland. Situated between Inverness and Aberdeen, the hotel is well placed for visiting the North of Scotland's prehistoric stone circles, whisky distilleries and castles.

Kintore 4, Aberdeen 14, Inverness 90, Edinburgh 147

Rates: *Single with breakfast from £80; double with breakfast from £95.* V
Bargain Breaks: *weekends 2 nights dinner bed & breakfast £72 per person per night min. two-night stay inc. full use of Country Club.*

- *48 en suite bedrooms all with colour TV+ satellite, telephone, hairdryer, laundry/valet service, tea/coffee making facilities, music/radio/alarm clock, trouser press. Non smoker bedrooms available.*
- *Table d'hôte £29.95; à la carte, lunch & special diets available; last orders 9.30 pm. ✪✪ Restaurant*
- *Business services inc. 5 meeting rooms to 350.*
- *Country Club with indoor pool, gym, jacuzzi/sauna, jogging track. Golf, riding, fishing nearby.*
- *Open all year. All major credit cards accepted.*

Kirkton House

Darleith Road, Cardross G82 5EZ
Tel: (01389) 841951;
Fax: (01389) 841868
E-mail: info@kirktonhouse.co.uk;
Internet: www.kirktonhouse.co.uk

Kirkton House is an old 18/19th century farmhouse hotel enjoying panoramic views of the river Clyde, set in open countryside, yet only 40 minutes from Glasgow city centre. It is also convenient for touring Loch Lomond and the Trossachs. The 12th century Kirkton Chapel is next door and Charles Rennie Mackintosh's Hill House is four miles away. Stewart and Gillian Macdonald moved here in 1984 after a lifetime of working abroad and have been welcoming guests like friends of the family ever since. Kirkton has a reputation for high, yet unpretentious, standards, good food and cosiness. Guests mingle in the sitting room before dinner, which is served by oil lamplight at individual tables. Local beef, venison and sole are specialities and Gillian's home made puddings are renowned.

Rates: *Single with breakfast from £40; double with breakfast from £59.* V

- *6 en suite bedrooms (2 ground floor) with TV, telephone, hairdryer, laundry service, iron, tea/coffee making facilities, radio/alarm clock.*
- *Table d'hôte £19.50; à la carte, sandwich lunch & special diets available; last orders 7 pm.*
- *Children and pets welcome. Facilities for disabled*
- *Golf one mile; fishing seven. Car parking for 12.*
- *Closed Dec/Jan. All major credit cards accepted.*

Helensburgh 5, Loch Lomond 10, Glasgow 17, Edinburgh 63.

Killiechronan House

Aros, Isle Of Mull, Argyll PA72 6JU
Tel: (01680) 300403; Fax: (01680) 300463

What more picturesque and quiet rural setting than at the head of Loch na Keal, on the west side of Mull? When I was there, a stag was leisurely cropping the grass in the garden, not the least worried by my photographing him. Killiechronan House is part of the beautiful 5000 acre Killiechronan Estate, with its own fishing and pony trekking facilities, and arrangements for stalking can easily be made. There are five miles of coastline along the north side of the Loch, and, of course miles of seldom used, single track roads. The hotel is easily accessible from the mainland, only 14 miles from the ferry terminal at Craignure, and forty minutes from Oban. The house was tastefully refurbished and redecorated in 1995, to the same standard as the Leroy family's other hotel at Oban (*page 207*). The warm and cosy décor of both the lounge and drawing room is most welcoming, with open log fires on colder days. In overall charge are Patrick Freytag, a very experienced chef of traditional Scottish cuisine, using fresh local produce and Donna McCann, who presides over the front of house.

Rates: *Dinner, room and breakfast from £62.00 per person.* ***Minibreak*** *(min. 2 nights) from £59 per person. STB Four Star.*
AA ❁ for food. A special weekly rate is available allowing consecutive nights to be spent at two of the Leroy hotels, with at least two nights being spent at Killiechronan.

- *6 en suite bedrooms, all with direct dial telephone and radio.*
- *Last dinner orders 8. 00 p.m, special diets; dogs accepted.*
- *Sea bathing; sailing/ boating; pony trekking; shooting/fishing; stalking by arrangement; golf five miles.*
- *Hotel closed from October 31st-1st March. Mastercard, Visa, Amex & Switch accepted.*

Salen 2, Craignure 14, Tobermory 15, Iona 35, Edinburgh 130.

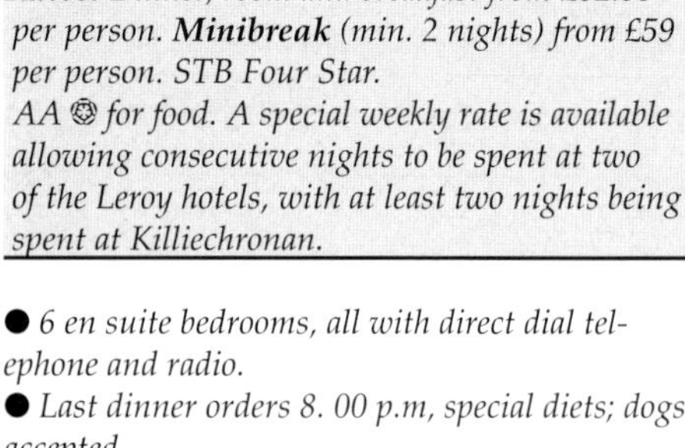

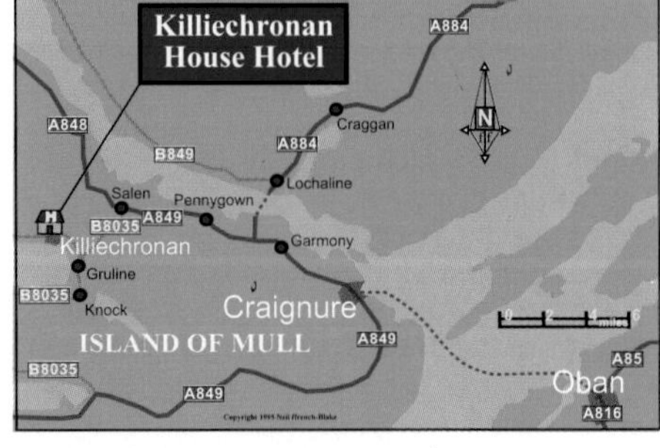

The Manor House

Gallanach Road, Oban, Argyll PA34 4LS
Tel: (01631) 562087; Fax: (01631) 563053

For peace and quiet within walking distance of the bustle of Oban, I recommend the elegant little Manor House Hotel. Built beside the sea on the tip of the bay, it enjoys unrivalled views over the harbour, the adjacent islands and the mountains beyond. The hotel is owned by the Leroy family, who also own Killiechronan House on the Isle of Mull (*see facing page*), and is supervised by their manager, Gabriel Wijker. It provides a high standard of hospitality, service, comfort, and good food. The house is furnished in keeping with its dignity and age, offering pretty, well appointed bedrooms and an elegant drawing room. The parlour and well furnished cocktail bar, with large windows overlooking the bay, make a pleasant spot for an aperitif or bar lunch. The dining room, which has an excellent reputation locally, glows with silver in the candlelight. The chef offers a tempting menu of Scottish and continental cuisine, specializing in local fish dishes and game in season. A good jumping off point for fishing, exploring the scenic West Coast, Mull or for visiting other islands and places of interest.

Rates: *Dinner, room and breakfast per person from £48 (low season) - £76 (high season) inc. VAT. Weekly from £322 (low season) to £490 (high season).*

- *11 en suite bedrooms, all with telephone, colour TV and full central heating.*
- *Bar lunches; diets; AA ®® for food. STB★★★★*
- *Sea bathing; sailing and boating ½ mile; indoor heated swimming pool, sauna and solarium, golf, each within 2 mile radius; helipad.*
- *Closed Monday & Tuesday from mid-November to February (exc. Xmas/New Year); dogs allowed.*
- *Amex, Mastercard and Visa cards accepted.*

Fort William 50, Glasgow 96, Dundee 116, Inverness 118, Edinburgh 123, London 489.

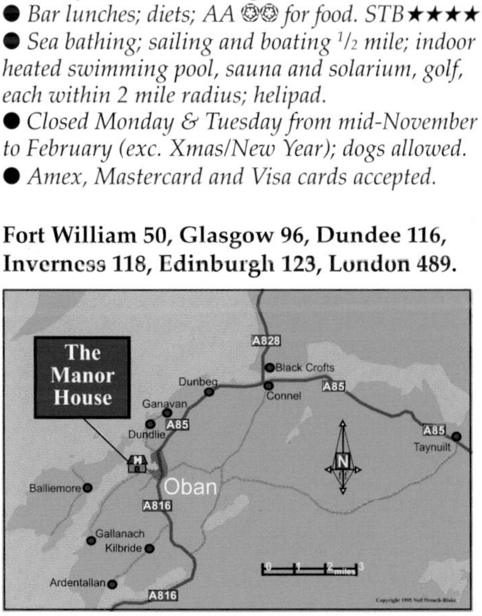

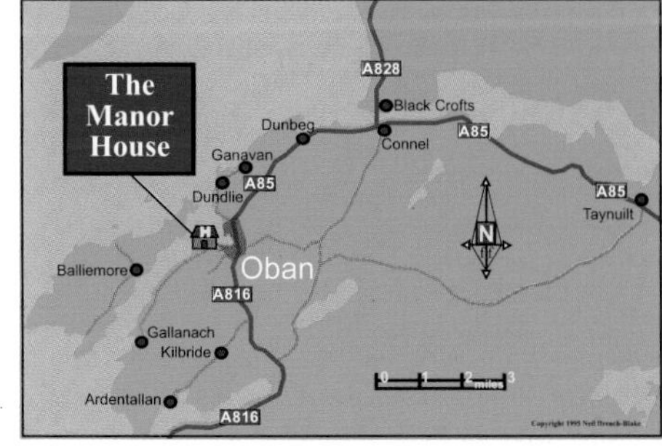

Dungallan House Hotel

Gallanach Road, Oban, Argyll PA34 4PD
Tel: (01631) 563799; Fax: (01631) 566711

Superbly situated overlooking Oban Bay and with magnificent views to the West and North, Dungallan House has seen some changes since building was started in 1868. It was originally a stone built family home, then a rehabilitation nursing home in the Great War. Called up again in the 1939-1945 war, it was the headquarters of the Operational Signals Squadron for the Flying Boat Base. Owners George and Janice Stewart took over in 1995 and have instituted a major programme of refurbishment since then. Janice presides in the kitchen and her skill has been recognised by the award of an AA rosette. She specialises in local produce, particularly fish and shellfish. Oban is an excellent base for touring with Mull, Iona, Staffa and Fort William all within a day's excursion. Return in the evening to welcoming log fires, fine cuisine, a good range of single malts and the cosy, family atmosphere of the hotel.

***Rates**: Single room with breakfast from £40; double inc. breakfast from £80. Master, Euro & Visa acc'd.*

Fort William 50, Glasgow 96, Inverness 118, Edinburgh 123

● *13 bedrooms, 11 en suite, with colour TV, hairdryer, laundry service. Car parking for 15.* V
● *Table d'hôte dinner £25. A la carte, lunch (booked) & special diets available. Last orders 2030.*
● *Sailing, sea/river bathing. Gym, fishing, golf nearby. 2 meeting rooms 30/15. Closed Nov & Feb*

Stonefield Castle Hotel

Tarbert, Loch Fyne, Argyll PA29 6YJ
Tel: (01880) 820836; Fax: (01880) 820929

Stonefield, tastefully converted from a 19th century castle, is charmingly situated on a peninsula separating the isles of Jura and Islay from Arran. It has panoramic sea views and its gardens are known for some of the finest rhododendrons in Britain, azaleas and other exotic shrubs that flourish in the mild west coast climate. Bedrooms are spacious and comfortable; those in the older part of the house being traditional, whilst those in the newer wing are more contemporary in style. There is a large cocktail bar, lounge-hall, library and drawing room. The dining room, which enjoys stunning views, offers interesting table d'hôte menus, using local produce wherever possible. The accompanying wine list satisfies every taste and pocket. Most traditional outdoor pursuits are available nearby and ferry trips to Arran, Gigha, Islay, Mull and Iona, together with the Mull of Kintyre, are all within reach. STB ★★★★.

***Rates:** Dinner, bed & breakfast from £69-89 dinner, b & b per person per night.* V
***Bargain Breaks:** Very special offers of up to 30% off normal tariff available at certain times.*

● *33 bedrooms (32 en suite), all with colour TV, direct dial telephone, room service, lift.* ● *Open all year.*
● *Table d'hôte and à la carte dining; bar lunches and special diets available.* ● *Snooker, fishing, sea bathing, sailing/boating. Clay shooting, golf ,riding nearby.* ● *All major credit cards accepted.*
Lochgilphead 12, Campbeltown 38, Oban 51, Glasgow 95, Edinburgh 135.

Creggans Inn

Strachur, Argyll PA27 8BX
Tel: (01369) 860279; Fax: (01369) 860637
E-mail: info@creggans-inn.co.uk

The Creggans Inn is now run by Sir Charles and Lady Deborah Maclean. Lady Maclean (of cookbook fame), Sir Fitzroy's widow, still keeps an eye on the cuisine and chooses the décor. Sir Charles has continued the Creggans' tradition of receiving guests as 'one of the family' and that, together with the food and stunning position, is why people from all over the world keep on coming back to this tranquil lochside inn. I was impressed by the homely public rooms, the candlelit dining-room with view of the loch and the character and furnishing of the gabled rooms and passages. After a superb fish and beef dinner, I enjoyed a dram of the hotel's own Malt Whisky *Old MacPhunn*. Next morning in the breakfast room I studied the many famous tributes and photographs from past guests - Sir Winston Churchill, Mrs Rockefeller, David Puttnam, Joanna Lumley and Michael Caine, to name but a few. Loch Fyne is prime hiking country and there are nature and woodland trails on the Strachur Estate and the adjoining Argyll Forest Park. Inveraray Castle is across the loch. Brown trout can be caught on the estate lochan; the hotel can arrange clay pigeon shooting and off-road driving. Golf, sailing, stalking, salmon fishing and rough shooting are available in season. Creggans is a superb spot for a break at any time of year.

Rates: *Single room inc breakfast from £59; double from £95.* V
Bargain Breaks: *Off-season two-night breaks available £59 per person per night, dinner, b & b.*

- *17 en suite bedrooms with TV, radio, direct dial telephone, hairdryer, laundry service, tea/coffee making facilities.*
- *Table d'hôte 3 courses £23.50; à la carte, lunch & special diets available; last orders 9 pm. AA ✪ Restaurant.*
- *Pool, fishing, loch bathing, massage, clay shooting, stalking available. Golf & riding 20 miles.*
- *Business services inc. 2 meeting rooms up to 100 capacity. AV equipment. Car parking for 40.*
- *Open all year. Major credit cards accepted.*

Inveraray 19, Dunoon 19, Glasgow 59, Oban 59, Campbeltown 85, Edinburgh 101.

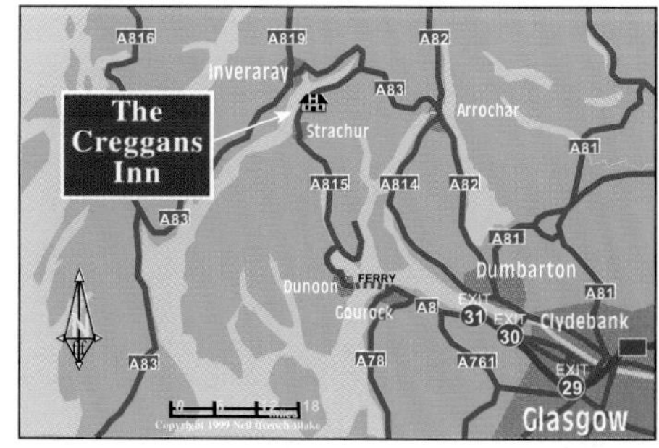

Balcary Bay Country House Hotel

Auchencairn, Nr. Castle Douglas,
Dumfries & Galloway DG7 1QZ
Tel: (01556) 640217/640311
Fax: (01556) 640272

A winding lane leads from Auchencairn to this enchanting hotel, which has views over Balcary Bay to Hestan Island and the Solway Firth. The hotel stands in three acres of its own grounds on a safe beach. Its cuisine has an excellent local reputation, specialities including Galloway beef, Balcary Bay salmon, West Coast Scallops and grilled wild boar sausages. At lunchtime the conservatory offers a lighter alternative or sandwicjes can be served in the lounge. Bedrooms are spacious, airy and quiet, either overlooking the bay or the quiet land-side garden. Each has a welcoming tartan teddy bear! The area is rich in shoreline and forest walks, five golf courses are nearby as are numerous National Trust houses and gardens. This relatively undiscovered area of southwest Scotland is warmed by the Gulf Stream and remains mild all year round.

***Rates**: Single with breakfast from £59; double from £104* **V** *. **Spring & Autumn Breaks**: 4th March-20th May (exc. Easter) and 1st Oct-mid Nov 2 days from £52 pp per night, dinner, b&b; 4 days from £50 pppn; 7 days from £44 pppn.*

● 17 en suite bedrooms, all with TV, telephone, radio & TV, hairdryer, tea/coffee making facilities. Trouser press, iron, drying room on request. ● 4 cse tdh dinner £24.75. A la carte & lunch available.; last orders 8.30 pm. ● Children welcome. Baby listening. Dogs welcome. ● Open March-mid Nov. Major credit cards accepted.

Dalbeattie 7, Dumfries 21, Gatehouse 19, Glasgow 90, Edinburgh 91.

Corsemalzie House Hotel

Port William, Newton Stewart,
Wigtownshire DG8 9RL
Tel: (01988) 860254;
Fax: (01988) 860213

Superb example of a 19th century Scottish country mansion of classic proportions and character, the hotel is set in 47 acres of mature gardens and woodland in an area of unspoiled natural beauty. Cuisine features 'Taste of Scotland' and 'Taste of Burns Country' cooking, both using fresh local produce. The hotel has exclusive salmon and trout fishing rights on a 4 1/2 mile stretch of the river Bladnoch, five miles of salmon and trout fishing on the river Tarff and trout fishing on the Malzie burn, which runs through the hotel grounds. Rough shooting is available in season and golf can be arranged on two local courses. Wigtown is fast becoming the antiquarian book capital of Scotland, having no less than 17 bookshops. This charming small hotel lies on the narrow B 7005. It is signed after Bladnoch coming from the east and by Alticry off the A747 coast road if approaching from the west.

***Rates:** Single inc breakfast from £39; double from £78. Spring & Autumn breaks available.* **V**

● 14 en suite rooms with radio/TV, telephone, hairdryer, laundry, tea/coffee making, safe.
● Open 1st Mar-mid Jan. Visa, Mastercard, Amex, Switch accepted. Parking for 35.
●Tdh til 9pm £22. Marquee receptions up to 200.
● Croquet, fishing, jogging, game shooting. Golf, riding, tennis nearby

Wigtown 6, Newton Stewart 13, Stranraer 20, Edinburgh 114.

Greywalls Hotel

Muirfield, Gullane, East Lothian
EH31 2EG
Tel: (01620) 842144; Fax: (01620) 842241

This lovely hotel enjoys views over the Firth of Forth and Muirfield golf course. Its architecture, history, atmosphere and award-winning restaurant combine to make a stay at Greywalls a very pleasurable experience. The then holiday home was created by the architect of New Delhi, Sir Edwin Lutyens, in 1901 and later the leading Scottish architect Sir Robert Lorimer added a wing, making Greywalls a unique co-operation between two eminent designers, as well as being the only complete Lutyens house in Scotland. The beautiful walled garden has been attributed to Gertrude Jekyll. One famous visitor was King Edward V11 and his outside lavatory is now transformed into a charming bedroom aptly named the *King's Loo*. Greywalls became a hotel in 1948 and the same family, which has now owned it for over seventy years, continue to impart the atmosphere of a private house to their guests. This shows in the bedrooms and the wood panelled library with its open fire - probably one of the finest rooms in this home from home. The bar is cosy and the sun room a delight. A new chef arrived to preside over the acclaimed restaurant in 1998. The kitchen produces modern British cuisine using the best of Scottish produce. The cool green dining-room overlooks Muirfield golf course. Greywalls is a perfectly enchanting place and the hotel's particular magic has few equals.

Rates: *Single room including breakfast from £100; double room with breakfast from £170.00.* V
Leisure Breaks: *Spring & autumn breaks available.*

- *23 en suite bedrooms with satellite TV, radio and direct-dial telephone, hairdryer, laundry service.*
- *Last orders for dinner 21.00. Meeting room with capacity for 20 guests; secretarial services.*
- *Golf, tennis (hard court & grass court), croquet. Airport pick-up. Ample car parking.*
- *Open April-October. Major credit cards accepted.*

Haddington 7½, Edinburgh 18, Berwick-upon-Tweed 45, Glasgow 62, London 377.

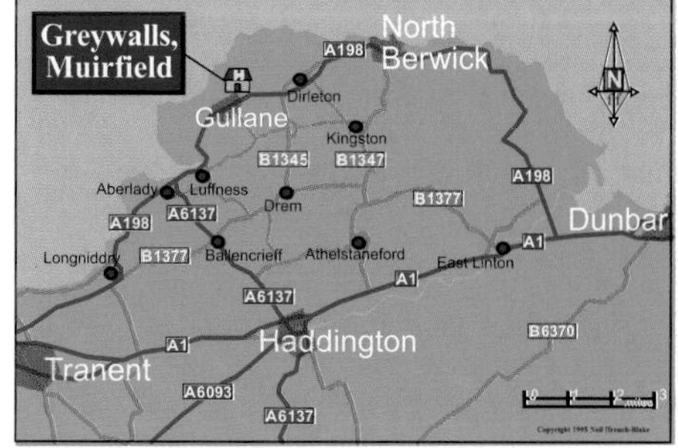

The Woodside Hotel

High Street, Aberdour, Fife KY3 0SW
Tel: (01383) 860328; Fax: (01383) 860920

The Woodside is undergoing a face-lift after its acquisition in 1999 by Stewart and Lesley Dykes. They have appointed Gerard Boylan (ex Loch Torridon) as their chef and memorable dishes include brill with scallop and crab, monkfish and finest Scottish beef, all using fresh local produce. I enjoyed its character, exemplified by its history and its facilities. The hotel was built in 1873 by the Greig brothers, whose great-grandfather founded the Russian navy. Original oil paintings of both brothers hang in the foyer. As for the facilities: The Clipper Bar is one of the most unusual in Scotland featuring antique stained glass and panelling from the famous Orient line vessel *Orontes*. The lovely bedrooms have been completely redecorated, each one individual in style and featuring a clan, and there is a superb suite as well. The village, dominated by its 14th Century castle, is a gem offering the freshness of the seaside, the tranquillity of the country, a picturesque old harbour and the prettiest railway station in Britain (£4 day return to Edinburgh) - and there is golf and many other attractions in the area. The personality of the Woodside, so perfectly matched by the character of the village, guarantees a most enjoyable stay.

Rates: *Single room with breakfast from £55.* V
Double room including breakfast from £70.
Leisure Breaks: *Please 'phone for current offers.*

- *20 en suite bedrooms with colour TV, direct-dial telephone, hairdryer, trouser press, laundry service, non-smoker bedrooms, tea/coffee making facilities.*
- *Last orders for dinner 21.30 hrs. Special diets available.*
- *Business services including meeting room with 50 guest capacity. Beauty salon adjacent.*
- *Car rental. Car parking 40 cars. Pets welcome.*
- *Open all year. Main credit cards accepted.*

Dunfermline 7½, Edinburgh 17, Kincardine 17, Kinross 13, London 392 .

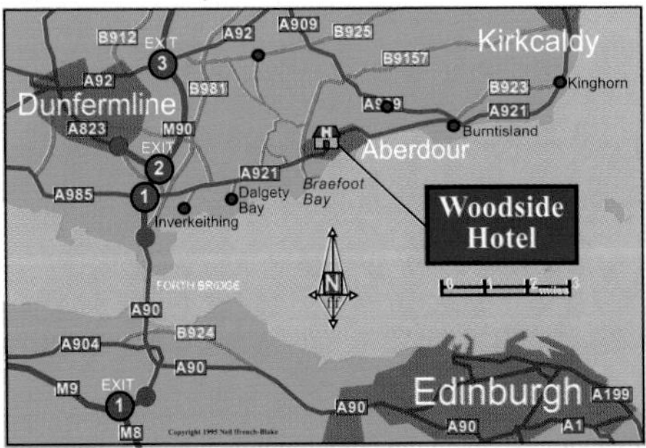

Balbirnie House

Balbirnie Park, Markinch, Glenrothes,
Fife KY7 6NE
Tel: (01592) 610066; Fax: (01592) 610529

A delightful Georgian house dating from 1777, Balbirnie is now a quite unique multi-award winning hotel which combines understated luxury with superb service and outstanding value. Bedrooms are large and luxurious, furnished with antiques and with many fine touches: a welcome letter from the family owners, a decanter of sherry, 20" TV, bathrobes, welcome fruit and 'tablet' and many trappings of a luxury hotel. At dinner my locally caught *fruits de mer* main course was excellent and throughout we were looked after by friendly, but not over-solicitous, staff. Afterwards we relaxed with a Malt in the Library Bar. At lunchtime there is the less formal *Gamekeeper's Inn*, a country-style bistro. The hotel is the centrepiece of a 416-acre park featuring specimen trees and a rare collection of rhododendrons. There is a par 71 golf course in the park (the hotel was named *Golf International Hotel of the Year* in 1998) and other activities are on offer in the grounds. For the year 2000 the hotel is building on a state-of-the-art banqueting venue and conference centre with capacity for 250 delegates. Balbirnie is an exceptional haven for those on business or pleasure wanting easy access to Edinburgh (half an hour away), Perth, the Fife coast and golf courses.

Rates: *Single room inc. breakfast from £120; double from £180.*
Pampered Weekend Breaks: *dinner, b&b+tea £85 pppn sharing.* ***Golf Breaks*** *from £110 ppp night.*

- *30 en suite bedrooms with radio/TV + SKY, telephone, hairdryer, laundry, tea/coffee making, 24-hr room service, trouser press.*
- *Table d'hôte dinner £23.50; lunch & special diets available; last orders 9 pm.*
- *Golf (71 par own course), snooker, clay pigeon shooting, off track driving, motor racing, croquet, jogging at hotel. Squash, game shooting, riding nearby. Ample car parking.*
- *Conferences to 250. A/V material available.*
- *Open all year. Major credit cards accepted.*

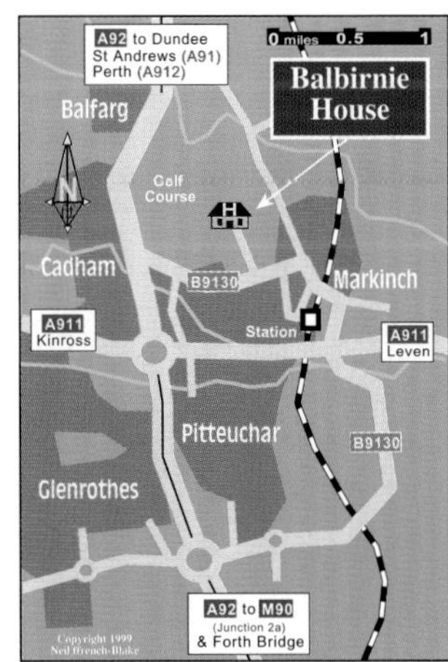

Glenrothes 2, Perth 23, St Andrews 20, Dundee 26, Stirling 37, Edinburgh 35.

Corrour House Hotel

Inverdruie, by Aviemore, Inverness-shire, Highland PH22 1QH
Tel: (01479) 810220;
Fax: (01479) 811500

Looking for somewhere peaceful away from the bustle of Aviemore, I was fortunate to find Corrour House, set in 4 acres of garden with magnificent views of the Cairngorms. Built as a Victorian Dower House, it is now run by David and Sheana Catto. The eight airy bedrooms are prettily decorated. Downstairs there is a cosy cocktail bar and large comfortable sitting room. Dinner is freshly cooked daily using Scotland's abundant larder. The hotel is a member of Taste of Scotland & Scotch Beef Club. The whole house is 'bright as a pin' with an atmosphere that is at once warm, friendly, slightly formal and very Scottish. The Aviemore Centre is nearby and in winter, the hotel can arrange 5 and 7 night ski-ing packages. In summer the hotel is an ideal centre for walking, golf, watersports, fishing, birdwatching and riding. The Whisky Trail, castles, wildlife parks, heritage sites and garden centres are also all within easy reach.

Rates: *Room and breakfast fm £37.50 per person. Dinner, bed & breakfast from £60 per person.* V
Bargain Breaks: *3 days, d,b&b for £165; 7 days £349. Winter tariff also available. STB ★★★★.*

- *8 en suite bedrooms with television, telephone, radio, tea/coffee making facilities.*
- *Table d'hôte dinner £22.50, 7-8.30pm.*
- *Walking, golf, fishing, ski-ing, birdwatching, riding, shooting, watersports, leisure centre nearby.*
- *Closed November & December, but office open for enquiries. Major credit cards accepted.*
- *Children welcome. Pets by arrangement.*

Aviemore 1, Inverness 30, Perth 85, Aberdeen 90, Edinburgh 128.

Ashburn House

20 Achintore Road, Fort William, Highland PH33 6RQ
Tel / Fax: (01397) 706000
E-mail: ashburn@scotland2000.com
Internet: www.scotland2000.com / ashburn

Ashburn House is an exceptional country house with rooms, situated on the A82 southern approach to the town. It is on the shores of Loch Linnhe and looks onto the Ardgour Hills, yet is only five minutes from the town centre. After a day's hill walking, Munro bagging, sightseeing, castle hunting or monster spotting, you can relax in Ashburn's conservatory and watch the sun go down over the loch. Ashburn is famous for its breakfasts, starting with *Lite Uachdar* (creamy porridge) then offering the choice, among others, of Lochaber Haggis, grilled Mallaig kippers and *Aran Ugh Marag Meas* (Fried Egg Bread & Fruit Pudding), complemented by 'melt in the mouth' scones. From the hall the magnificent barley twist pine staircase leads up to the five bedrooms, individually designed and appointed to the highest stándard. Two other bedrooms are on the ground floor.

Rates: *Room and breakfast from £35 per person inc.VAT low season; from £40 per person high season. Other terms on application. Non smoking.*

- *4 double en suite bedrooms, three singles, television, tea/coffee making, hairdryer, radio/alarm, laundry service. Public telephone box in hotel.*
- *Golf, fishing, climbing, sailing nearby.*
- *No restaurant. Ample car parking.*
- *Open all year. Major credit cards accepted.*
- *Airport pickup, car rental can be arranged.*

Glencoe 15, Mallaig 45, Oban 45, Inverness 65, Glasgow 100, Edinburgh 140.

Culloden House Hotel

Inverness, Highland IV2 7BZ
Tel: (01463) 790461); Fax: (01463) 792181
USA Toll-free fax: 1-800-373 7987;
E-mail: info@cullodenhouse.co.uk;
Website: www.cullodenhouse.co.uk

Culloden House is a handsome Adam style Georgian country house with a tradition of lavish hospitality stretching back hundreds of years. Bonnie Prince Charlie spent his last night before the fateful Battle at Culloden House. Today the long serving Scottish resident staff are on hand at all times to extend a warm welcome to all visitors - *Ceud Mi'le Fai'lte!* The house is decorated with magnificent Adam plasterwork and fireplaces and furnished to the highest standard. Every bedroom is individually decorated, many with fireplaces and four-posters and come with every luxury. The newly refurbished *Tartan Wing* and the *Garden Pavilion* in the grounds offer the discerning guest suite and junior suite accommodation. Dinner is announced by a piper on the lawn and prepared by award-winning chef Michael Simpson. A private dining room is also available. The extensive wine cellar is complemented by a large selection of single malt whiskies. Leisure facilities include a two-tee, net golf driving range and there are plans for a spa development. Situated in 40 acres of elegant lawns and parkland, just 3 miles from the centre of Inverness, Culloden represents the highest standards in Highland hospitality.

Rates: *Room and breakfast from £190.00 (one single room - £145).* ***Bargain breaks*** *- November 1st -April 30th - rates on application.*

● *28 en suite bedrooms, all with direct dial telephone, TV (+satellite), tea/coffee making, laundry service, music/radio/alarm, trouser press, hairdryer. Eight non-smoking rooms inc 4 junior suites in Garden Pavilion. Car parking for up to 60 cars.*
● *Table d'hôte 4 cse dinner £35; à la carte, lunch & special diets catered for; last orders 9 pm.* ⚘ ⚘ *AA Restaurant. Meeting room up to 28 delegates*
● *Tennis, sauna, croquet, boules, golf net driving tee at hotel. Shooting, fishing, 4x4 off-road driving by arrangement. Golf, watersports nearby.*
● *Open all year. Major credit cards accepted.*

Inverness 3, Airport 5, Nairn 13, Aberdeen 104, Dundee 131, Edinburgh 158, London 532

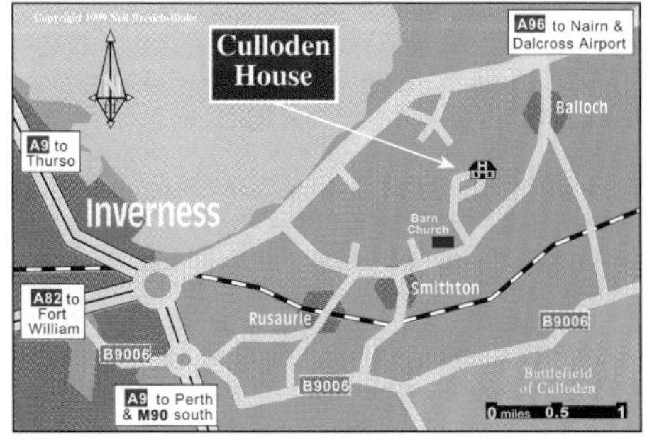

Rosedale Hotel

Portree, Isle Of Skye,
Highland IV51 9DB
Tel: (01478) 613131;
Fax: (01478) 612531

The Rosedale is a family run hotel with magnificent views. It was originally a row of William IV cottages adjacent to the harbour in old Portree. It now occupies nearly all of one side of the waterfront and looks out across the Sound of Raasay to the Isle beyond. An interesting feature is the first floor restaurant, which gives a unique view of fishermen unloading the day's catch, some of which you may find on the next day's menu! Tony Parkyn supervises the cuisine, using as much local produce as possible, and the restaurant maintains its AA Rosette and Taste of Scotland Award amid other plaudits. A good selection of Highland malt whiskies is available in the friendly bar, including the locally distilled *Talisker.* The comfortable guest lounge help you relax and plan the next day's sightseeing. Portree as the capital of Skye is a natural focal point - the scenery is spectacular with dramatic skylines and impressive views.

Rates: *Room and breakfast from £35 per person inc.VAT. Other terms on application.*
Bargain Breaks: *Skye Explorer holiday rates available for stays of 3 days or more from £50 per day.*

● *23 en suite bedrooms (7 ground floor) with television, telephone, radio, tea/coffee making; + 3 twin en suite rooms in nearby Beaumont House.*
● *Boating; tennis, swimming pool, squash and golf nearby; fishing by arrangement; open air parking.*
● *Open all year. Visa & Mastercard accepted.*
Kyle of Lochalsh 34, Invermoriston 90, Fort Augustus 97, Edinburgh 237

Corriegour Lodge Hotel

Loch Lochy, by Spean Bridge,
Inverness-shire, Highland IV51 9DB
Tel: (01397) 712685; Fax: (01397) 712696
E-mail: info@corriegour-lodge-hotel.co.uk
Website: corriegour-lodge-hotel.com

I was pleased to return to Corriegour Lodge, one of my favourite Highland hotels, to meet new owners Christian and Ian Drew. Corriegour sits in 9 acres of mature woodland and garden, with a spectacular waterfall and burn running through it, and overlooks Loch Lochy. Formerly a Victorian hunting lodge, it enjoys one of the finest settings on the Great Glen. Christian and son and chef Ian place great emphasis on guests' relaxation and comfort. Each bedroom is individually decorated and most have loch views. Stripped pine and log fires in the public rooms create an atmosphere of cosy warmth. The Loch View Conservatory Restaurant gives a splendid panorama. The area is a paradise for nature lovers and walkers. Ben Nevis is nearby and boat hire, pony trekking, mountain bike hire are all available in the vicinity. The self-catering Corriegour Cottage, sleeping 4, is in the grounds. *"Better food than the top restaurants in London and a view to die for."* - Daily Mirror

Rates: *Single room and breakfast from £43.50; double from £87. Major credit cards accepted.* V
Bargain Breaks: *Special rates available for two nights or more. Special Spring/Autumn and Winter Breaks available - rates on application.*

● *9 en suite bedrooms with television, hairdryer, tea/coffee making, safety deposit box. Separate self-catering cottage (rates on demand). Sorry, no pets.*
● *Table d'hôte 5-cse dinner from £29.50; lunch by arr't; special diets catered for; last orders 8 pm.*
● *Private fishing school & jetty; private beach. Skiing 9 miles, walking, climbing, sailing nearby .*
● *Open February to November and Dec 27-Jan 3.*
Spean Bridge 5, Ft William 17, Ft Augustus 17, Inverness 47,Edinburgh 140

The Lodge on the Loch Hotel

Onich, by Fort William, Highland PH33 6RY
Tel: (01855) 821582; Fax: (01855) 821463
E-mail: reservations@freedomglen.co.uk
Internet: www.freedomglen,co.uk

The Lodge on the Loch is the flagship hotel of the Freedom of the Glen family-owned hotel group (*see map below*). From the moment you step over the threshold you will be impressed by the warmth and friendliness of this hotel. The reception 'hatch' is discreetly curtained over in the evenings. The lounge, restaurant and many bedrooms overlook Loch Linnhe to the distant hills of Morvern and Mull - one of the finest panoramas in Scotland. Palm trees grow in the sheltered grounds and wild rhododendrons flourish on Gulf Stream-warmed hillsides. Ongoing refurbishment is creating a number of romantic luxury rooms with jacuzzi baths for two, in-room entertainment systems and a host of individual touches. The lochview restaurant offers five-course dinners, carefully hand cooked by award winning chefs, using the freshest local produce. After a day's sightseeing or walking, guests will be drawn to the intimate Cocktail Bar to sample a Malt Whisky and choose from the discerning wine list. The Lodge on the Loch is small enough to guarantee individual attention and is an unrivalled haven of comfort, seclusion and serenity, from which to explore the West Highlands.

Rates: *Single/double room, dinner, bed & breakfast & afternoon tea from £75.50 (low season) to £85.50 (high season).* ***Bargain breaks*** *-three nights b & b £99 per person; dinner +£15 per pers.* V

● *18 en suite bedrooms, all with direct dial telephone, colour TV, hairdryer, laundry service, radio/alarm clock, tea/coffee making, trouser press*
● *4-course table d'hôte dinner £29.50; soup & sandwich lunch available; special diets catered for. Last orders 9pm.*
● *Complimentary use of indoor pool & leisure centre at relaxed & friendly Isles of Glencoe sister hotel - 6m; riding & shooting ten miles. Children under 12 not encouraged.*
● *Hotel closed 7 November-23 Dec and 9 Jan-30 March. Mastercard, Visa, Switch cards accepted.*

Ballachulish 4, Fort William 10, Oban 43, Crianlarich 48, Glasgow 84, Edinburgh 116.

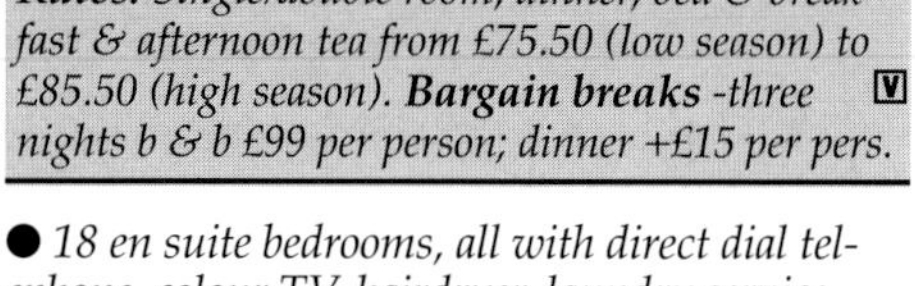

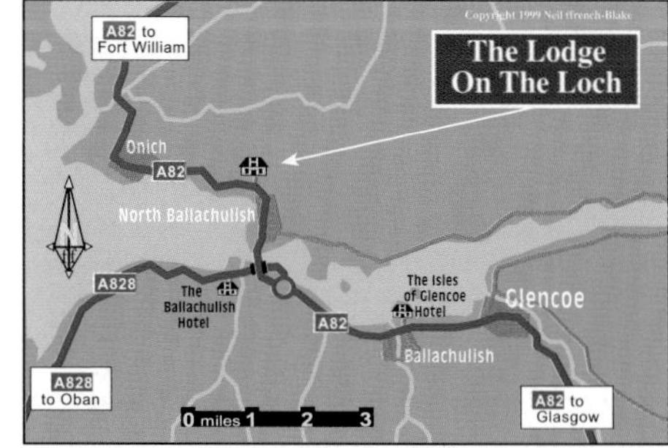

Eddrachilles Hotel

Badcall Bay, Scourie, Sutherland IV27 4TH
Tel: (01971) 502080; Fax: (01971) 502477

Rates: *Room and breakfast from £38.00; dinner, room and breakfast from £49.00. Prices include VAT.* ***Bargain breaks*** *- reduced rates available on stays of 3, 6 or 10 days.*

The Eddrachilles commands a fine position, overlooking the sea with mountains behind it. Inside, the hotel is clean, bright and comfortable, with many of the windows having a sea view, thanks to the foresight of Mr. and Mrs. Alasdair Wood, who have restored and extended this old building, and are kind and hospitable hosts. The logistics of providing food and drink in these remote parts makes the discovery of an à la carte and table d'hôte menu, together with an interesting wine list, a pleasant surprise. The emphasis is on home cooking, using fresh and seasonal ingredients. Hill lamb, venison and seafood are the local delicacies. The north of Scotland is unique; its remote and untouched beauty cannot be described in a few words. You can explore it from quiet, single-track roads, or, for the more energetic, there are numerous scenic walks and climbs. Nearby Handa Island is famous as a bird sanctuary, and boat trips across the short stretch of water can be made from Tarbet. When returning to Eddrachilles after a tiring day of exploration, you can always be assured of warmth, comfort and good food.

- *11 en suite bedrooms (4 on ground floor), all with direct dial telephone and TV.*
- *last orders for dinner 8. 00 p.m; bar lunches available; special diets by arrangement.*
- *Children of 3 years and over welcome.*
- *Sailing/boating; fishing.*
- *Hotel closed Nov.-Feb. inclusive. Mastercard and Visa credit cards accepted.*

Ullapool 40, Thurso 95, Inverness 98, Edinburgh 245, Glasgow 266, London 620.

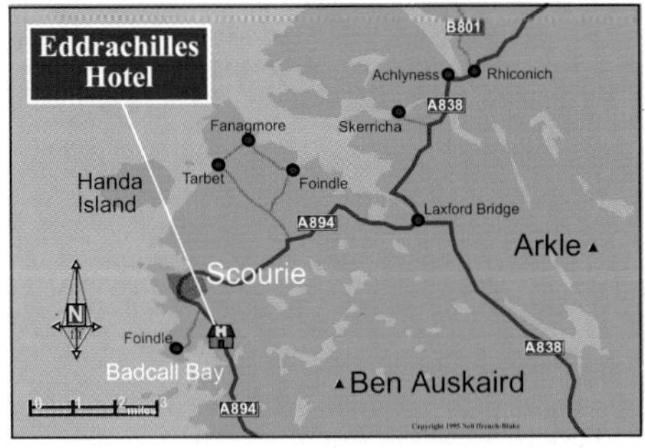

The Strathaven Hotel

Hamilton Road, Strathaven,
Lanarkshire ML10 6SZ
Tel: (01357) 521778;
Fax: (01357) 520789
E-mail: sthotel@globalnet.co.uk

The Strathaven was built by Robert Adam Jnr in 1797 for a Glasgow merchant. It retains many of the original features and is Grade B listed. It is now owned and managed by the Macintyre family. With the recent addition of the 12-room extension, with rooms restfully decorated in two-colour pine, Strathaven is the area's premier hotel. Bedrooms have welcome fruit baskets, a private minibar and bathrooms have power showers and a range of toiletries. For wedding receptions, the hotel can cater for 180, but these need to be booked well in advance. Strathaven is a small market town with its own castle and links with the music-hall artist, Sir Harry Lauder. The hotel is well located for touring Central Scotland, being just 30 minutes for the centre of Glasgow and 45 minutes from Edinburgh.

***Rates:** Single inc breakfast from £69; double from £85.*
***Weekend Breaks** £89 per person for two nights,d, b&b.*

M74 (Junc 8) 5, Hamilton 8, Glasgow 12, Edinburgh 32

- *22 en suite rooms with colour TV + satellite, telephone, hairdryer, tea/coffee making, minibar, radio/alarm, trouser press. Non-smoker bedrooms.*
- *3 course table d'hôte dinner £19.50. A la carte, lunch & special diets available. Last orders 2130.*
- *Golf, watersports, sailing, shooting, squash, tennis and riding nearby. Car parking for 80.*
- *Major credit cards accepted. Open all year.* V

Craigellachie Hotel of Speyside

Craigellachie, Speyside,
Banffshire, AB38 9SR
Tel: (01340) 881204;
Fax: (01340) 881253
E-mail: sales@craigellachie.com
Website: www.craigellachie.com

A true haven of Highland hospitality at the centre of the world - for malt whisky! The fabulous new master rooms and mini suites all have a view over the river Spey. I was impressed by five-star touches such as a wine decanter, a *hand-written* welcome card from the manager and a printed card of the day's TV programmes. My *medaillons* of duck was excellent, prepared by the team of award winning chefs whose menus change daily. I could not compete however with some of the *aficionados* who had sampled 40 malts at a sitting in the internationally famous Quaich Bar. Winner of the prestigious *Glenmorangie Hotel Bar of the Year* award, it has one of the largest selections of drinking malt whiskies **in the world** and is recognised as *the* place to drink *the* drink. Aberdeen & Inverness airports are each around an hour's scenic drive away.

***Rates:** Single inc breakfast from £84.50; double from £99.* STB ★★★★
***Special Breaks** from £57.50 pppn, dinner,b&b.*

- *16 standard rooms; 6 master rooms, 4 mini-suites, all en suite with radio/TV, telephone, hair-dryer, laundry, tea/coffee making, trouser press.*
- *Fixed price dinner to 22h00 £27.50.* AA ⊛⊛ Food.
- *Snooker, indoor games, gym, tennis. Walking, shooting (clay and game), cycling, fishing & golf nearby. Whisky distillery and castle tours nearby.*
- *Open all year. Major credit cards accepted.*

Elgin 12 (station), Grantown-on-Spey 23, Inverness 53, Aberdeen 58, Edinburgh 190.

Monachyle Mhor

Balquhidder, Lochearnhead,
Perthshire FK19 8PQ
Tel: (01877) 384622;
Fax: (01877) 384305
E-mail: monachylemhorhotel@balquhidder.freeserve.co.uk

An absolutely enchanting place, six miles up Loch Voil west of Balquhidder, in whose church Rob Roy is buried and where chamber music concerts are now held on Summer Sunday evenings. Our inspector was torn between keeping Monachyle a secret for his private enjoyment or bringing it to the attention of discerning Signpost readers. Owned by the Lewis family, son Tom is in charge of the much acclaimed kitchen. Specialities include Scottish West Coast Lemon Sole, Mallaig Scallops and Perth- shire beef. Puddings are home made and our fluffy scrambled egg and smoked salmon breakfast, with fresh scones, was equally memorable. Bedrooms and public rooms are furnished like a private house. Small wonder that Scots come from as far away as Glasgow to sample the peace and quiet and good food here.

Rates: *Single room with breakfast from £50. Dble inc. breakfast from £65. Visa, Mastercard accepted*

● *10 en suite bedrooms, 8 with colour TV, all with telephone, hairdryer, tea/coffee making facilities, music/radio/alarm clock. Non smoker bedrooms available. Two self-catering cottages.*
● *Table d'hôte £30; à la carte, lunch & special diets available; last orders 8.45 pm. ◎◎ Restaurant*
● *No pets or disabled facilities.* ● *Open all year.*
● *2000 acre estate. Private fishing, red deer stalking and grouse moor in season. Loch bathing.*

Callander 17, Lochearnhead 10, Glasgow 53, Edinburgh 62

Loch Rannoch Hotel & Highland Resort

Kinloch Rannoch, Perthshire
PH16 5PS.Tel: (01882) 632201;
Fax: (01882) 632203

Loch Rannoch is unusual in Signpost, as it consists of a quality furnished 19-bedroom hotel, complemented by 85 one to three bed-roomed luxury holiday exchange lodges, situated amongst some of the most spectacular scenery of Perthshire. Originally used in the late 19th century as a hunting lodge, the hotel retains its style and character, with splendid furnishings and Highland landscapes. The Ptarmigan Restaurant sources the region's finest produce - wild vension, Perthshire lamb, Tay salmon and West Coast seafood in a mouth-watering combination of French-influenced cuisine and 'Taste of Scotland' dishes. A less formal atmosphere prevails in the Rannoch Larder. For relaxation after a busy day, the Schiehallion Bar, with its selection of over 40 malts, is ideal. The hotel specialises in conferences, weddings and tailored sporting packages.

Pitlochry 20, Aberfeldy 20, Lochearnhead 40, Edinburgh 88

Rates: *Single room with breakfast from £55. Dble inc. breakfast from £90. Credit cards accepted.* 🅅
Bargain Breaks: *Weekends and certain midweek dates accomm from £130 pp two night stay inc. d,b&b. Third night accomm free to Signpost readers on production of 2000 Guide.Open all year.*

● *19 en suite bedrooms with colour TV, telephone, hairdryer, tea/coffee making facilities, radio/alarm, trouser press. Non smoker bedrooms available.*
● *Table d'hôte £20.95; lunch & special diets available; last orders 9 pm. Car parking for 120.*
● *Snooker, fishing, indoor games, jogging track, watersports, sauna, sailing, squash, indoor pool, tennis, gorge walking, loch bathing.*

Ballathie House Hotel

Kinclaven by Stanley, Perthshire PH1 4QN
Tel: (01250) 883268; Fax: (01250) 883396

Tranquillity, warmth, comfort and style are the hallmarks of Ballathie House Hotel, set on the banks of the river Tay in its own 1500-acre estate. The house dates from 1850. The original public rooms are eloquently furnished with antiques. The bedrooms, which underwent redecoration in 1999, are each different and bear the name of Scottish cities and regions: *Argyll, Oban* etc. All bathrooms now have power showers as well as baths; one is even in a turret! Ballathie's chef, Kevin MacGillivray was named Scottish chef of the year in 1999 and has just published his second recipe book. In addition two of Ballathie's sous-chefs won *Salon Culinaire* Silver Medals. One of Kevin's award-winning specialities is *Rosemary skewered quail breast in honey and sesame seeds on an artichoke and summer truffle risotto.* Perthshire is renowned for its wide range of sporting facilities, from salmon fishing to golf, hill-walking to shooting. Ballathie offers access to all these and has special facilities for fishermen. The estate provides 1500 acres of low ground and woodland for the sportsman whilst the gentler pursuits of tennis and croquet are available in the grounds.

Rates: *Single room and breakfast from £70; double room with breakfast £140.* V
Bargain breaks*: Any 2-day break from £80 per person per night, dinner, bed & breakfast.*

- *28 en suite bedrooms (1 suite), all with colour TV + satellite, direct-dial telephone, hairdryer, laundry/valet service, radio/alarm clock, trouser press, tea/coffee making facilities. Car parking for 100.*
- *5-course table d'hôte dinner £30; lunch & special diets available; last orders 9 pm. AA ⚙⚙ Restaurant*
- *Business services inc. one meeting room for 16.*
- *Croquet, fishing, putting green, tennis, shooting from hotel. Golf, riding, squash , sauna, swimming pool nearby.*
- *Children welcome; baby listening.*
- *Open all year. All major credit cards accepted.*

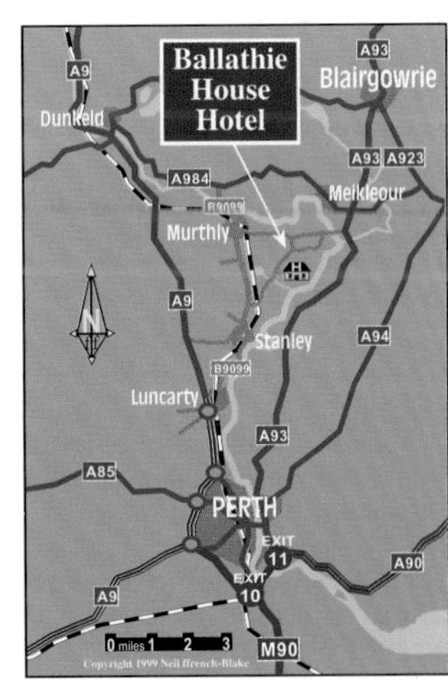

Blairgowrie 5, Perth 12, Dundee 17, Pitlochry 20, Aberfeldy 25, Glasgow 69, Edinburgh 53.

The Four Seasons Hotel

St Fillan's, Perthshire PH6 2NF
Tel: (01764) 685333; Fax: (01764) 685444
Website: http://www.thefourseasonshotel.co.uk

Andrew Low, an experienced local hotelier, bought the Four Seasons in 1999 and is busy bringing the standard of public and bedrooms up to that of the acclaimed AA two-rosette restaurant. The hotel has its own jetty and slipway on Loch Earn and St Fillans is an excellent centre for sailing and watersports. It also has its own 9-hole golf course and this part of Perthshire is superb walking country. Ben Vorlich, a 3000+ ft Munro, can be approached from the south side of the loch. The Four Seasons has two restaurants: the acclaimed *Meall Reamhar* (High Hills), which specialises in local 'Taste of Scotland' dishes such as Seared Islay Scallops, Saddle of Rannoch Venison, Highland Guinea Fowl, West Coast Halibut and Aberdeen Angus fillet steak and the less formal Tarken Room. As well as the main hotel, there are six smart chalets in the grounds, providing privacy for couples with one or two children. The Four Seasons provides a wonderful base for exploring Perthshire and the Heart of Scotland.

Rates: *Single occupancy from £36; double/twin rooms from £72.* V
Bargain breaks*: 3 nights for the price of two on dinner, b & b basis, acc. to season & availability.*

- *12 en suite bedrooms, all with colour TV, direct-dial telephone, hairdryer, laundry service, radio/alarm clock, trouser press, tea/coffee making facilities. Non-smoker rooms available.*
- *Table d'hôte £23.95; lunch & special diets available; last orders 9.30 pm. AA ⚘⚘ Restaurant*
- *Two meeting rooms, capacity 40. Airport pickup by arrangement. Car parking for 30 cars.*
- *Fishing, sailing, bathing from hotel. 9-hole golf course one mile; watersports one mile.*
- *Open Easter to Jan 3rd. Credit cards accepted.*
- *Directions. On A85 Lochearnhead-Crieff road at west end of St Fillans Village.*

Perth 30, Stirling 30, Glasgow 56, Edinburgh 65

Dalmunzie House Hotel

Spittal O'Glenshee, Blairgowrie,
Perthshire PH10 7QG
Tel: (01250) 885224; Fax: (01250) 885225
E-mail: dalmunzie@aol.com

If you are looking for perfect peace and quiet or for a sporting holiday, this impressive country house, hidden away in the hills, is an excellent venue. Dalmunzie has been in the Winton family for many years, and is now looked after by Simon and Alexandra, whose care and attention result in a well run house, personal service, and a happy atmosphere. The sitting rooms, cosy cocktail bar and spacious bedrooms are all in excellent decorative order, well furnished and comfortable, and log fires and central heating ensure warmth in every season. In the dining room, the varied table d'hôte dishes are well cooked and feature traditional Scottish fare, which is accompanied by a carefully chosen wine list. This family owned sporting estate can organise almost any shooting holiday, whilst other field sports, trout fishing, walking and climbing also await you here. Dalmunzie have their own 9 hole golf course available for guests. Nearby Glenshee offers well organised skiing for all abilities, and for those wishing to explore on wheels, there are quiet roads and much to see.

Rates: *Room and breakfast from £43 per person, weekly rates from £390 per person, full board.* V
During the ski season, dinner, bed and breakfast from £50-£60.
Bargain breaks*: From Jan-April 2 nights from £100 & 5 nights from £220. From April-October 3 nights from £180.*

- *18 bedrooms (1 for the disabled, 16 en suite), lift.*
- *Last dinner orders 8.30 p.m.; light bar lunches; special diets on request. Restaurant AA rosette.*
- *Children welcome; dogs accepted; conferences to 20.*
- *Games room; bar billiards; 9 hole golf course; tennis; shooting/fishing (trout/salmon, own rainbow trout stocked loch); skiing in Glenshee; pony trekking; mountain bikes.*
- *Closed December. Mastercard & Visa accepted.*

Perth 35, Dundee 37, Braemar 15, Blairgowrie 20, Edinburgh 78, London 453.

Scotland

Ardeonaig Hotel

South Loch Tay Side,
Perthshire FK21 8SU
Tel: (01567) 820400;
Fax: (01567) 820282
Internet:
http: / / www.ardeonaighotel.co.uk

The Ardeonaig Hotel is none other than a pure haven for the visitor and sportsman alike. It is situated amongst breathtaking scenery. Within a 25 minute drive, there are golf courses at Killin, Kenmore and Aberfeldy. This secluded 17th century inn has its own salmon fishing rights on the Loch, with its own boat and rod and drying room. Guests can also fish for salmon on the River Tay, and excellent stalking can be arranged. The tasty Scottish cuisine is created from the freshest of local produce, and is complemented by a good selection of international wines. The Ardeonaig boasts a cheery bar, which offers some of the best Scottish malts, a cosy sitting room, and a second floor library with wonderful views over Loch Tay and the hills of Ben Lawers. I can recommend a stay at the Ardeonaig either for the sporting facilities or purely for a spate of peace and relaxation.

Rates: *Room & breakfast from £48.50; dinner, room and breakfast from £73.50. Prices inc. VAT.*

- *14 en suite bedrooms (5 ground floor), all with tea/coffee making facilities.*
- *Last orders for dinner 8.30 p.m; special diets; dogs most welcome; conferences max. 16; public telephone box in hotel.*
- *Own harbour and boats; shooting/fishing; riding nearby; limited service in the winter.*
- *Switch, Delta, Access & Mastercard accepted.*

Perth 50, Stirling 50, Edinburgh 72, London 445.

Peebles Hotel Hydro

Peebles EH45 8LX
Tel: (01721) 720602;
Fax: (01721) 722999
E-mail: reservations@peebleshydro.co.uk

Situated high above the east end of Peebles with superb views across to the river Tweed is the Hydro - the ultimate Scottish Borders experience. Dating from 1907 the magnificent Edwardian building has one of the most impressive staircases in Scotland.

The accommodation is of a high standard and includes family rooms. There are two restaurants: the main dining room offering the best of Scottish traditional fare and international dishes and, new this year, *Lazels*, bistro-style, and open 1030-1800. There is also a new children's dining room. The Hydro is a resort in itself, with many sporting facilities under one roof. It is also well placed for exploring the whole gamut of Scottish history, with castles, abbeys, stately homes and battlefields nearby and Edinburgh only 30 minutes away.

Galashiels 18, Glasgow 49, Edinburgh 22.

Rates: *Room & breakfast from £65 single, £100 double. All major credit cards accepted.*
Bargain Breaks: *Many special breaks on application*

- *133 en suite bedrooms, all with radio/TV, direct dial telephone, hairdryer, laundry service, tea/coffee making facilities, 24-hr room/meal service, trouser press. Bedrooms for disabled available. Open all year.*
- *Tdh dinner from £22.50. A la carte, lunch & special diets available. Last orders 9. 00 p.m. Car parking 200.*
- *Business services inc 7 meeting rooms, 28-450.*
- *Billiards/snooker, fishing, gymnasium, indoor games jacuzzi, massage, sauna, solarium, badminton, indoor pool, tennis, riding, beauty salon, hairdresser.*
- *Switch, Delta, Visa & Mastercard accepted.*

Dryburgh Abbey Hotel

St Boswell's, Melrose TD6 ORQ
Tel: (01835) 822261; Fax: (01835) 823945
E-mail: enquiries@dryburgh.co.uk

Dryburgh Abbey is owned and managed by the Grose family, who also own Thurlestone in Devon, another Signpost hotel. I was very impressed by Dryburgh. It sits atop a hill rising above the Tweed in an area of outstanding natural beauty. The ruins of Dryburgh Abbey, Sir Walter Scott's last resting place, are in the grounds. Inside the hotel is comfortable without frills or fuss. Yet everything you want for a relaxing stay is here: spacious bedrooms named after salmon flies: *Silver Wilkinson, Hairy Mary, Roger's Fancy*; two dining-rooms, the Tweed Restaurant, overlooking the river, or the Courtyard Bar bistro. Menus change daily to reflect the abundance and quality of local produce. From freshly caught salmon to haggis in a whisky cream sauce or roast rack of border lamb, all meals are prepared with style and imagination. The wine list boasts over 150 vintages. Dryburgh is very popular for business events and there was a wedding going on when I stayed. What a romantic start to married life! As well as being able to arrange shooting in season, the hotel can book salmon or trout fishing on 14 beats of the Tweed. There are 14 golf courses nearby, plenty of sites of interest and an indoor pool in the hotel.

***Rates:** Single room & breakfast from £38; double inc. breakfast from £76.* V
***Bargain Breaks:** Dinner, bed & breakfast from £49 per person 5th Dec-16 March. Weekend breaks.*

- *38 en suite bedrooms, all with colour TV, telephone, hairdryer, laundry service, tea/coffee making facilities, 24-hr room/meal service, trouser press, radio/alarm clock. Deluxe, half-tester, four-poster and tower suites also available. Facilities for the disabled.*
- *Table d'hôte 4-cse dinner £26. A la carte, lunch & special diets available. Last orders 9.15 pm.*
- *Business services inc 2 meeting rooms 20/150 cap*
- *Car parking for 100. Airport pickup by arrang't*
- *Croquet, fishing, shooting, indoor swimming pool, tennis. Golf 3m, riding 4m, off-road driving 25m.*
- *Open all year. Visa, Master, Amex cards accepted*

Melrose 4, Hawick 17, Newcastle-upon-Tyne 66, Glasgow 79, Edinburgh 39.

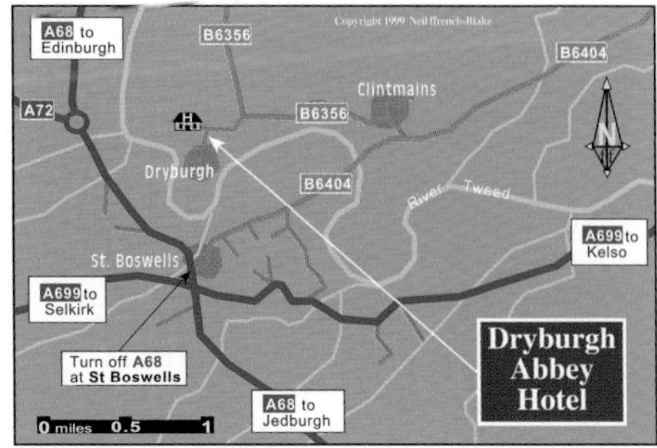

Culcreuch Castle & Country Park

Fintry, Loch Lomond, Stirling & Trossachs, Stirlingshire G63 OLW
Tel: (01360) 860555; Fax: (01360) 860556
Website: http://www.culcreuch.com

Tucked away in spectacular scenery is the historic 13th century Culcreuch Castle, offering elegant family-run accommodation within a tranquil 6000-acre parkland estate. Log fires, cosy Dungeons Bar, candlelit dinners and four-poster beds welcome visitors from all over the world to one of the most romantic venues in Scotland. Cuisine is based on traditional Scotish fayre using locally produced ingredients and is complemented by a well-stocked and interesting wine cellar. Fishing is available on the estate and shooting and deerstalking can be arranged in season. The estate is rich in plant, bird- and wildlife and the surrounding fells offer excellent walking. There are a wealth of visitor attractions in the area. Our location is rural but not isolated. The fresh air of the countryside, coupled with good food and the unique warmth of welcome and hospitality found in a home from home environment, make Culcreuch a most conducive spot for shedding the cares of modern life and for completely relaxing.

Kippen 8, Aberfoyle 14, Stirling 16, Glasgow 20, Edinburgh 52.

Rates: *Single room & breakfast from £85; double fm £130. Visa, Switch, Mastercard, Amex accepted*
Bargain Breaks: *Up to 40% disc. on midweek breaks.*

● *10 en suite bedrooms, all with TV, telephone, hairdryer, laundry service, tea/coffee making, music/alarm clock, safety deposit box, trouser press. Non-smoker/disabled bedrooms available. Open all year.* V

● *Fishing, fitness centre, jogging track, shooting, walking, squash. Golf/Riding 5/6m. 3 meeting rooms - cap. 110*

Forest Hills Hotel

Kinlochard, Aberfoyle,
Stirling FK8 3TL
Tel: (01877) 387277;
Fax: (01877) 387307

Dominated by the towering bulk of Ben Lomond to the Northwest and on the banks of Loch Ard at the edge of the Trossachs, Forest Hills offers everything for a memorable holiday. I was particularly attracted by the setting - 25 acres of landscaped gardens and woodland with rushing burns, winding pathways and breathtaking scenery. The original house dates from Edwardian times and boasts some fine wood panelling in the lobby. The Garden Restaurant features the best of local produce prepared in the traditional manner by award-winning chefs. For less formal dining there are grills in the Bonspiel Cafe / Bar. For that relaxing pre-dinner drink, there is the piano bar with log fires in winter and superb views in summer. Nearly every sporting activity is available in the purpose built Leisure Centre or in the immediate vicinity.

Rates: *Room & breakfast from £63 single; £95 double. Open all year. Credit cards accepted.* V
Bargain Breaks: *Min. 2-night stay, dinner,b&b from £55 pppn.*

● *56 en suite bedrooms, all with colour TV, telephone, hairdryer, laundry service, tea/coffee making facilities, trouser press.*

● *Table d'hôte 4-cse dinner £26.95. A la carte, lunch & special diets available, Car parking for 70*

● *Billiards/snooker, croquet, fishing, gymnasium, indoor games, jacuzzi, jogging track, massage, sauna, solarium, shooting, squash, indoor swimming pool, tennis. Golf 5 m, riding 2m.*

Stirling 23, Glasgow 26, Perth 40, Edinburgh 57.

The Lake Hotel

Port of Menteith, Stirlingshire FK8 3RA
Tel: (01877) 385258; Fax: (01877) 385671

The Lake Hotel stands right on the shore of the Lake of Menteith, with the most panoramic views spread before it. Graeme and Rosaleen Mc Conachie bought the Lake Hotel earlier in 1999 and are polishing this gem of a hotel, whilst not neglecting their local clientèle. The hotel was recently renovated in keeping with the style of the building. The bedrooms are comfortable and individual, many overlooking the lake. There is a smart cocktail lounge for browsing over menus and this leads to the star feature of the hotel - the two AA rosette lakeside conservatory restaurant. Here head chef Stuart Taylor presides over a daily changing menu of freshly prepared dishes such as honey glazed breast of Barbary duck with a creamed leek risotto and soy sauce or grilled fillets of red mullet garnished with smoked salmon. The mood created here, candle-lit and with soft piano music in the background, is romantic indeed.
The Lake Hotel is a good centre for touring the Trossachs and there are several attractions nearby: Inchmahome Priory on the lake itself , where both Mary Queen of Scots and Robert the Bruce sheltered, nearby Loch Lomond, Doune Castle and Motor Museum, Stirling Castle and the Campsie Fells.

Rates: *Dinner, bed & breakfast per person from £48 low season - £96 high season, inc VAT & service; weekly rate from £290 low season to £458 high season.* V
Bargain Breaks: *Low season £44 pppn min. two nights inc. dinner, b &b; high season £70 pppn.*

- *16 en suite bedrooms, all with radio/colour TV, direct-dial telephone, tea/coffee making, room service*
- *AA ❀❀ restaurant. Lunch & special diets available. Last orders 8.30 pm.*
- *Children over 8 welcome; dogs by arrangement.*
- *Golf, riding and fishing available nearby.*
- *Hotel closed after Sunday lunch til Tuesday evening November-March (exc. Xmas & New Year)*
- *Amex, Switch, Visa & Mastercard accepted.*
- *STB ★★★★ Highly Commended.*

Stirling 18, Glasgow 30, Edinburgh 40, Perth 50, Oban 84, London 410.

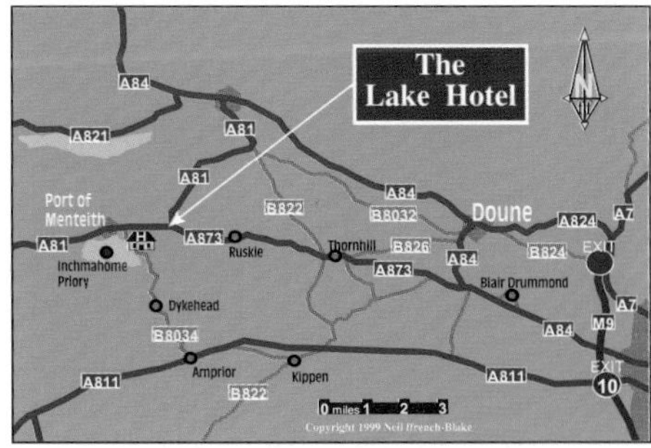

Inchyra Grange Hotel, Leisure Club & Restaurant

Grange Road, Polmont, Falkirk,
Stirling FK2 OYB
Tel: (01324) 711911; Fax: (01324) 716134

Situated just off the M9 Motorway, Inchyra Grange was originally a period manor house which has been developed into a fine hotel meeting the demands of the most discerning leisure or business traveller. It stands in 44 acres of private grounds. The Priory restaurant has recently been extended to create a number of semi-private areas. The chef serves a daily changing menu, according to local availability. Light, less formal meals are available in the Pelican Leisure Club Restaurant. Most of the main attractions of Central Scotland are within a day's touring - St Andrews and East Lothian for golf, Loch Lomond and the Trossachs for scenery, Stirling Castle and Bannockburn for history, Glasgow and Edinburgh for culture and Glengoyne or Glen Turret to experience the Water of Life (whisky).

Rates: *Single (room only) from £80; double (room only) from £90.* ***Bargain Breaks:*** *1.11.99-31.3.00 Min 2 nights stay £47.50 pppn b&b; £65 pppn d,b&b*

● *109 en suite bedrooms inc 2 suites, all with radio/ TV+ satellite, telephone, hairdryer, laundry service, minibar, trouser press, tea/coffee making, 24-hr room service. Non-smoker & disabled bedrooms available.* ● *Tdh til 2130 £31. A la carte, lunch & diets available. AA ® Restaurant.* ● *Gymnasium, jacuzzi, massage, sauna, indoor pool, tennis. Golf adjacent; riding locally.* ● *Business services inc 7 meeting rooms to 500.* ● *Open all year. All credit cards accepted.*

Houstoun House Hotel & Country Club

Uphall, West Lothian
EH52 6JS
Tel: (01506) 853831;
Fax: (01506) 854220

The old tower of Houstoun House, which forms its redoubt, dates from the 17th century. Today this tower, the adjacent manor house (*The Women House*) and the *Steading*, together with some new buildings, have all been sympathetically combined to form the 4-star Hotel & Country Club. For that pre-dinner drink or nightcap the *Vaulted Bar* has a selection of around 100 single malt whiskies, including some of 'cask strength'. The hotel has two restaurants: *Pelegrinos*, an Italian bistro situated in the Leisure Club and the main Dining Room which has been created from a combination of the Great Hall, Drawing Room and Library and which has two AA rosettes. Standing in 20 acres of parkland and close to Edinburgh Airport, Houstoun, with its many activities, is ideal for a business or leisure stay.

Rates: *Single, room only from £120; double from £140.* ***Bargain Breaks:*** *1.11.99-31.3.00 Min 2 nights stay fm £58 pppn b&b; £80 pppn d,b&b.* V

● *72 en suite rooms inc 1 suite, all with radio/colour TV + satellite, direct-dial telephone, hairdryer, laundry service, tea/coffee making, 24-hr room service, bathrobe, iron, trouser press. Non-smoker and disabled rooms available. Open all year* ● *Table d'hôte & à la carte ®® restaurant. Lunch & special diets available. Last orders 2130. Italian Bistro.* ● *9 Conference rooms to 350 pax. Parking for 200.* ● *Croquet, gymnasium, massage, sauna, indoor pool, tennis, beauty salon, dance studio. Golf and riding adjacent.* ● *Major credit cards accepted.*

Moët & Chandon - **Signpost** *exclusive champagne partner.*

Guernsey

The Channel Island of Guernsey - a veritable haven for the holidaymaker. A modern airport, excellent harbour, hotels and guest houses with every amenity. A thriving tourist industry which encourages and welcomes visitors, and rewards them with all the comforts associated with up-to-date civilised living.

But existing alongside the evidence of today's lifestyle are customs and traditions that have resisted change. Large chunks of Guernsey's intricate and chequered history blend harmoniously with the present. This is all part of Guernsey's unique character; the present is built around the past rather than unceremonously trampling upon it.

For the visitor who is ignorant of Guernsey's history, it would seem also that the island cannot decide whether it is French or British! In St. Peter Port, for example, street names are displayed in both English and French, and the town retains a definite air of an ancient Norman seaport. Now and again throughout the island, one can catch snatches of conversations spoken in Guernsey *patois*, which the uninitiated could forgivably mistake for French.

The French/British connection is in itself unusual. Geographically closer to France, but essentially a "British" Island, Guernsey was once under the domination of the Norman dukes, who in turn were vassals of the French king. William II of Normandy, crowned William I of England in 1066, established the connection with England and subsequent events have established the Channel Islands as part of the dominion of the Kings of England, but never part of their kingdom.

An air of the past, a French flavour - the visitor cannot ignore these influences. St. Peter Port, a flourishing commercial centre with its busy harbour, still preserves its past identity, with its buildings of traditional Guernsey granite and its unspoilt skyline. And from the castle ramparts throughout the summer season booms the noonday gun, after a ceremony that is fascinating to witness.

Guernsey has many unique attractions for the visitor. The Little Chapel is the smallest chapel in the world, and lavishly decorated with pottery and shells, has room for only five people inside. Victor Hugo, the famous French author, lived in exile for 15 years on Guernsey, and his house is an extravagant monument to his life and work. Guernsey has a host of museums, a butterfly centre, zoo, aquarium, craft centre and a variety of fascinating archaeological sites as well as a fine leisure centre which caters for all the main sports. Add to this Guernsey's spectacular cliff walks and beautiful countryside and the visitor will find that all tas-tes are catered for.

As is to be expected, Guernsey is famed for a number of traditional dishes and delicacies, not the least of which is the *Guernsey Gache,* a sort of fruit loaf still popular on the island. It can be purchased in a number of shops, and many people have their own, special recipes, but perhaps the most intriguing place to purchase it is in the Old Guernsey Market, held on Thursdays in St. Peter Port. Traditionally dressed stall holders sell all manner of island-produced wares from freesia corms, to the beautifully made, oiled-wool Guernseys for which the island is so famous.

St Peter Port

There is much to fascinate the holidaymaker in Guernsey; one could spend many return visits delving into traditions, customs and folklore alone. The islanders, proud of their heritage and keen to share it, afford the warmest of welcomes to every visitor.

Channel Islands

Historic Houses, Gardens & Parks

Candle Gardens, St Peter Port, G'y
Castle Cornet & Maritime Museum, Guernsey
Eric Young Orchid Foundation, Trinity, Jersey
Fantastic Tropical Gardens, St. Peter's Valley, Jersey
Grande Marais Koi Farm, Vale, G'y Howard David Park, St. Helier, Js'y
Jersey Flower Centre, St. Lawrence
Jersey Lavender Farm St. Brelade
La Mare Vineyards, St. Mary, Jsy
La Seigneurie, Island of Sark Samares Manor, St Clement, Jsy
St. Ouen's Manor Grounds, St Ouen, Jersey
Saumarez Manor, St Martin's, Guernsey
Specialist Gardens at Castle Cornet, Guernsey
Sunset Carnation Nurseries, St. Ouen's Bay, Jersey

Walks & Nature Trails

Grandes Rocques, Guernsey
Guided nature walks - Jersey's Coastal Walks:
i) Grosnez to Sorel
ii) Sorel to Bouley Bay
iii) Bouley Bay to St. Catherine's
Le Catioroc Nature Trail & L'Eree
Port Soif Nature Trail, Guernsey
Shingle Bank Portinfer, Guernsey
The Saumarez Nature Trail& Park Walk, starting at Cobo Bay, Guernsey
St Peter Port to St Martin's Point Walk, Guernsey

Historical Sites & Museums

La Valette Underground Military Museum, St. Peter Port, Guernsey
German Occupation Museum, St. Peter Port, Guernsey
Guernsey Aquarium, Havelet Bay
Guernsey Museum & Art Gallery, St Peter Port
National Trust of Guernsey Folk Museum, Saumarez Park

Fort Grey Shipwreck Museurn, St. Saviours, Guernsey
Battle of Flowers Museum, St Ouen, Jersey
Elizabeth Castle, St Aubin's Bay, Jersey
Faldouet Dolmen, Gorey, Jsy
German Underground Hospital, St. Lawrence, Jersey

Grosnez Castle & La Pinacle, Les Landes, Jersey
Hamptonne Country Life Museunn, St. Lawrence, Jersey
The Hermitage St Helier, Jersey
La Hougue Bie, Grouville, Jersey
Island Fortree Occupation Museum, St. Helier, Jersey
Jersey Motor Museum
The Living Legend, St Peter, Jersey
Mont Orgueil Castle, Gorey, Jersey
The Pallot Heritage Steam Museum, Trinity, Jsersey
St. Peter's Bunker Museum, St. Peter, Jersey

Entertainment Venues

Fort Regent Leisure Centre, St Helier, Jersey
Guernsey Bird Sanctuary, St Andrew's
Jersey Butterfly Centre, St Mary
Jersey Shire Horse Farm & Museum, St Ouen
Jersey Pottery, Gorey Village
Jersey Zoo, Trinity
Le Friquet Butterfly Centre, Castel, Guernsey
Oatlands, Guernsey's craft Centre, St Sampson's

Channel Islands

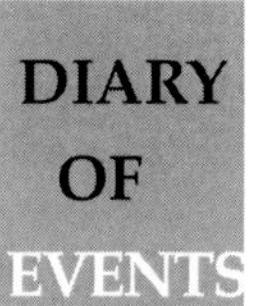

February

20-26. **Jersey Chess Festival**
Feb-Mar. **Guernsey Eisteddfod Festival.** Beau Sejour Centre, St Peter Port

March

11-17*. **English Bridge Union Bridge Week.** Guernsey

April

April. **Guernsey Fesatival of Food and Wine** leading to....
21-24. **Guernsey Salon Culinaire.** Displays by visiting & local chefs; competitions.
21-24. **Guernsey Easter Runs.**
21-24. **Guernsey Easter Hockey Festival.**
6-9. **Jersey Jazz Festival.**

May

9. **Liberation Day.** Celebration of the liberation of Guernsey from German occupation.St PP
13-21. **International Food Festival,** Jersey .

June

8-9. **Floral Guernsey Show.** Cambridge Park, St Peter Port
11. **Guernsey Classic Vehicle Club Summer Show,** Sausmarez Park, St Martins, Gnsy.
25-July 1. **Guernsey Square Dance Festival.**

July

1. **North Regatta.** St Sampson's Harbour, Guernsey.
3. **Le Viaer Marchi.** Trad'l festival with songs, dance, arts etc. Sausmarez Park, Guernsey.
11-15. **Jersey Garden Festival.**
4. **American Car Club Show,** Guernsey.
July / Aug. **Valestock 2000.** Guernsey's biggest outdoor music festival.
July. **Rocquaine Regatta,** Rocquaine Bay, St Pierre du Bois, Guernsey.
22-29. **St Peter Port Carnival** Guernsey.
31-Aug 6*. **Alderney Week.** Carnival Time in Alderney.

August

10-11. **Jersey Battle of Flowers.**
28.**10th Guernsey Custom & Classic Bike Show.** Mont Herault, St Pierre du Bois.
19. **Lions Club Donkey Derby.** Guernsey.
23-24. **North Show/Battle of Flowers.** Saumarez Park, Gnsy.
18. **Jersey Summer Flower Show.**

September

2-5. **Jersey Film Festival.**
Sept*. **29th Guernsey Int'l Air Rally,** Guernsey Airport.
14*. **Battle of Britain Air Display.** Over St Peter Port, Guernsey &over St Aubins Bay, Jersey.
18-26*. **English Bridge Union Congress,** St Pr Port, Guernsey

October

6-8. **Guernsey Real Ale & Cider Festival.**
5-8. **World Music Festival.** (25th anniversary) Jersey.
15-21*. **26th Int'l Chess Festival** Peninsula Hotel, Vale, Guernsey

**dates to be confirmed*
For further details contact:

TOURIST BOARDS

States of Guernsey Department of Tourism and Recreation, PO Box 23, St. Peter Port, Guernsey, Channel Islands GY1 3AN. Tel: 01481 723552
Jersey Tourism. Liberation Sq, St Helier, Jersey E1 1BB, Channel Islands. Tel: 01534 500700

Jersey

The island of Jersey has something to offer everyone, but there's a lot more for children than just the obvious attractions of sun, sea and sand. Its wealth of sporting facilities, historic sites and animal centres make it an ideal spot for family holidays, and even offer children and parents the chance to get away from each other once in a while.

If you really can't bear to tear yourself away from the sea, there are all kinds of watersports available around the island and Jersey Tourism can provide a comprehensive list of surfing, sailing and water-ski clubs.

But if the children want to go it alone, there's no need for parents to worry. *The Wind & Water Windsurfer School* at St. Aubin offers a 5-hour windsurfing course for beginners from the age of nine upwards, using a small lightweight rig for younger pupils. Tuition is by fully qualified instructors.

Youngsters who prefer riding a horse to a surfboard are well catered for by the island's numerous riding stables, several of whom are also pleased to welcome unaccompanied helpers. Prices average £9 an hour for a hack, £10-12 for a lesson and hard hats can usually be provided, so there's no need to squeeze one into the hand-luggage.

A number of sports centres and pleasure parks offer a variety of activities from weight-training to table tennis, go-karts to snooker, but perhaps the best known of them all is Fort Regent - the huge sports and leisure complex housed in the Napoleonic fortress overlooking St. Helier.

When the family is tired of having fun and fancies a little gentle education, there is no shortage of historical sites to interest visitors of all ages. Elizabeth Castle in St. Aubin's Bay was begun in the reign of Queen Elizabeth I and has been re-

fortified throughout the centuries right up until the First World War. Open only during the summer months, the castle is reached across the bay from St. Helier by an amphibious vehicle service using a World War II landing craft.

Even older - a mere 5,000 years - is the 40ft mound of the Neolithic tomb at La Hougue Baie in Grouville. Here you can walk right inside the ancient burial chamber, visit the railway exhibition and the agricultural museum, or just relax in the wooded park.

Those who like natural history will enjoy a visit to the Kempt Tower Interpretation Centre on the Five Mile Road at St. Ouen. A converted Martello tower, it contains displays and artefacts relating to the special characteristics of Jersey's "mini national park". Open every afternoon from June to September.

Animal lovers of all ages are well catered for on the island. Heatherbrae Farm in St. John offers visitors the chance to learn all about milk production and watch the 50-strong herd of pure bred Jersey cows during afternoon milking. There's also a fascinating Shire Horse Farm in St. Ouen and, for the very large to the very small, a butterfly farm at the Haute Tombette.

Finally, no animal lover can afford to miss the unique collection of endangered species at the Jersey Wildlife Preservation Trust established 33 years ago by naturalist Gerald Durrell in Trinity.

Jersey may measure a mere nine miles by five, but it is packed with interesting things to see and do - for the young in years and the young at heart!

La Favorita Hotel

Fermain Bay, Guernsey GY4 6SD
Tel: (01481) 235666; Fax: (01481) 235413
E-Mail: info@favorita.com
Internet: http://www.favorita.com

The warmth of the welcome from proprietors Helen and Simon Wood and their staff sets the tone for your stay at La Favorita. Nothing will be too much trouble to ensure that you have a relaxed and memorable stay at this one time country house, now a fully licensed successful hotel which combines original character and charm with modern extensions and facilities. Set in the attractive wooded valley that leads down to Fermain Bay and within walking distance of St Peter Port, the hotel enjoys beautiful views over the valley and sea. The 37 bedrooms are comfortable with all modern amenities and the restaurant has a good reputation for traditional English cooking. As a less formal alternative the Coffee Shop serves snacks and lighter meals. The other public rooms and extensive leisure facilities make La Favorita a veritable 'favourite' for a relaxing break in whatever season. The hotel can also help with travel arrangements, car hire and in pointing out to visitors the many delights of the island.

Rates: *Single room inc. breakfast from £46; double room with breakfast from £77.* **Romantic Breaks** *including travel, car hire, champagne and roses from £190 (2 nights).* V

● *36 en suite non smoking bedrooms (inc 5 family rooms), all with colour TV, radio, hairdryer, laundry/valet service, tea/coffee making, baby listening.*
● *4-cse table d'hôte menu £14.75; à la carte, lunch & special diets available; last orders 9 pm.*
● *Meeting room to 80; car parking for 30; airport pickup by arrangement. Facilities for the disabled.*
● *Indoor swimming pool, jacuzzi, sauna. Fishing, sea, sailing, clay shooting, tennis, riding and walking all nearby.*
● *Open April-November. Visa, Amex, Diners, Mastercard accepted.*

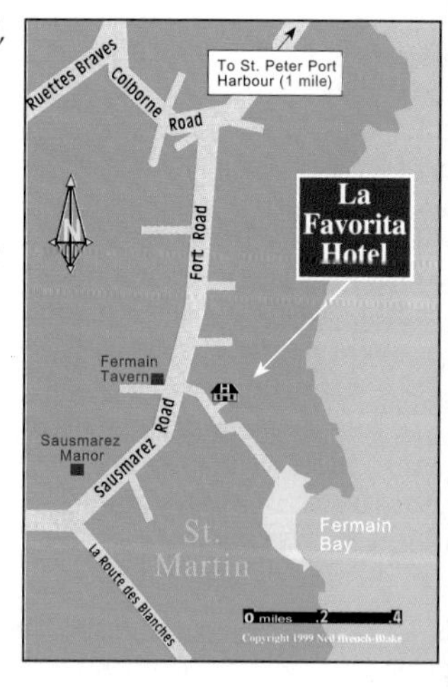

St Peter Port 2miles.

Bella Luce Hotel & Restaurant

Moulin Huet, St. Martins, Guernsey
GY4 6EB
Tel: (01481) 238764; Fax: (01481) 239561

The Hotel Bella Luce is a former 12th century manor house that is attractive both inside and out. There is an abundance of flowers, from the sweet peas lining the swimming pool, to the wonderful hanging baskets on the walls. The Proprietor, Richard Cann, and his staff take great pride in running this hotel to ensure their guests' maximum contentment. All the public rooms are well furnished and very comfortable. The lounge bar, with its oak beamed ceiling, has a warm and friendly atmosphere, and is the ideal place in which to enjoy either a drink or a dish chosen from the extensive bar lunch menu. The freshly prepared food served in the restaurant is excellent, with a delicious choice of dishes from either the table d'hôte or à la carte menus. To accompany these, there is a comprehensive wine list to suit all palates. The hotel is well located in a peaceful and tranquil setting in St Martin's just two miles from the beautiful "capital" of Guernsey, St. Peter Port, with the island's magnificent cliffs and coastal scenery providing breathtaking views.

Rates: *Room and breakfast £30-£53.50; dinner, room and breakfast £44-£67.50.*
Bargain breaks *available 1st November-1st April, £28 pppn for b & b.*

- *31 en suite bedrooms (3 ground floor), all with direct dial telephone and TV+ SKY; room service; baby listening.*
- *Last orders for dinner 9.45p.m.; bar meals; special diets.*
- *Children welcome; dogs accepted at management's discretion.*
- *Outdoor heated swimming pool; sauna; solarium.*
- *Open all year; major credit cards accepted.*

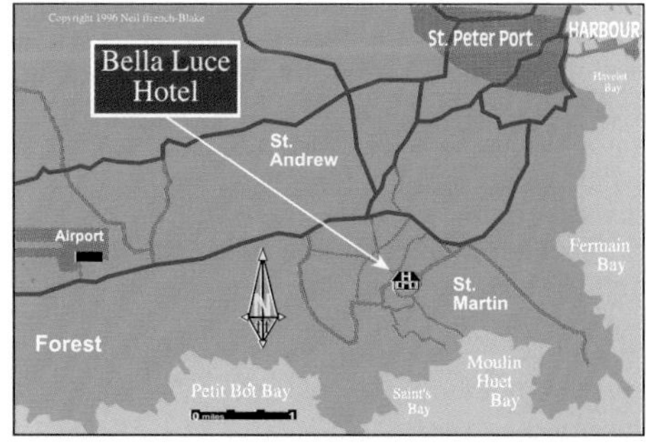

The Duke of Richmond Hotel

Cambridge Park, St Peter Port,
Guernsey GY1 1UY
Tel: (01481) 726221; Fax: (01481) 728945
E-mail: duke@guernsey.net;
Internet: http//accom.guernsey.net/duke

Rates: *Single room with breakfast from £55; double room with breakfast from £75.* V
Bargain Breaks: *Discounts of 10% for weekends. Terms inclusive of flights & ferries can be arranged.*

Situated opposite Cambridge Park and overlooking the picturesque capital of St Peter Port, the Duke of Richmond Hotel is well located for both holiday maker and business visitor alike. It stands on the site of *Grovers* Hotel, established in 1790, of which the third Duke of Richmond, Master of Ordnance from 1781 to 1795, was a patron. This well run hotel prides itself on courteous, attentive service and standards throughout hold the keynote of comfort. Seaview and penthouse rooms benefit from stunning views. The Saumarez Cabin - with its unique ship's cabin motif, the Victoriana Bar with its period atmosphere, and the restaurant with its pastel decor are all full of style. Presentation and service is first class. Groups and private functions can be well catered for in the ballroom and other flexible rooms. An attractive sun terrace and pool are set in the grounds with extra leisure and sports facilities at Beau Séjour nearby. The Duke of Richmond is an ideal base from which to explore the enchanting island of Guernsey and the cobbled streets of St Peter Port and its shopping centre, which are within easy reach.

- *75 en suite bedrooms with satellite TV, direct-dial telephone, hairdryer, laundry service, tea/coffee making facilities, radio alarm clock, safety deposit box, 24-hour room service, trouser press; non-smoker rooms available.*
- *Table d'hôte £15; à la carte, lunch & special diets available; last orders 9.30 pm.*
- *Business centre inc. meeting rooms to 36 people.*
- *Outdoor swimming pool.*
- *Open all year. All major credit cards accepted.*

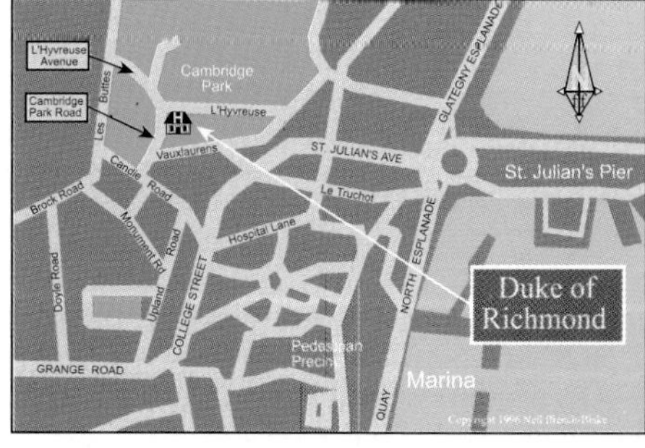

The Old Government House Hotel

Ann's Place, St. Peter Port, Guernsey
GY1 4AZ
Tel: (01481) 724921; Fax: (01481) 724429

Within the heart of St. Peter Port, enjoying breathtaking views, the location of the OGH (as it is affectionately known) is the perfect setting for a holiday or business break on Guernsey. Once the official residence of the Island's Governors, the Hotel has served visitors since 1858 and is today a gracious blend of old and new, offering the highest standard of accommodation and with all bedrooms' colour schemes complementing the character of the hotel. You may enjoy a quiet drink amongst the portraits of former governors in the Governors' Bar before adjourning to the Regency Restaurant - one of the island's finest with à la carte, table d'hôte and themed gourmet menus being offered, accompanied by Chateau and Estate bottled wines from an excellent list. The Centenary is one of three bars - each with their own personality - and light lunches can be taken there, or at the relaxing poolside outdoors. The OGH is quite simply a very good hotel - to be recommended whatever the reason for your stay.

Rates: *Single room including breakfast from £75.00. Double room with breakfast from £115.00.* V

- *71 en suite bedrooms with satellite TV, direct-dial telephone; hairdryer, trouser press, laundry service, tea/coffee making facilities. Disabled access to most rooms.*
- *Last orders for dinner 21.30 hrs. Special diets available. A la carte restaurant.*
- *Fishing, fitness centre, massage, golf, watersports, riding, sauna, squash, tennis all can be arranged nearby.*
- *Three conference rooms to capacity of 225 guests. AV equipment and full secretarial service. Car rental. Car parking for 25 cars.*
- *Open all year. All major credit cards accepted.*

The White House Hotel

Herm Island, via Guernsey GY1 3HR
Tel: (01481) 722159; Fax: (01481) 710066

Herm is a 20-minute boat journey from Guernsey and is the smallest of the Channel Islands. There are no cars and Herm's magic starts to work as soon as you are greeted on the quayside: the pretty harbour houses the island's three shops and the Ship Inn. Nearby is the castellated manor, where the owners of the island, the Heyworths, live and where you will find the island's school and 10th century chapel. There are bracing cliff walks and beautiful unspoiled beaches, wild flowers and clear landscapes for painting. As the gentle chugging of a tractor heralds the arrival of your luggage, you know the White House Hotel is special. After all, how many hotels can boast an island as their garden, a harbourside setting and such spectacular sea views? Where else could you enjoy shellfish so fresh that the oyster beds can be seen from your table in the award-winning restaurant? Tradition is cherished at the White House Hotel. You are assured of a warm welcome and friendly service from Sue Hester and her staff. In the 38 delightful bedrooms, you'll find private bathrooms and baby listening but no televisions, clocks or telephones. Children have always been welcome, with a popular high tea for junior diners. The hotel encourages you to unwind and the island is perfect for that away-from-it-all break.

Rates: *Dinner, bed & breakfast from £58 per person per night. Saturday night gourmet menu.* V
Bargain Breaks: *Bluebells in Bloom Spring Break to end-May (exc Easter) £125 pp two nights inc boat fare, 75cl of wine & flowers.*

● *38 en suite bedrooms with hairdryer, radio, baby listening, tea/coffee making. Non-smoker bedrooms available.*
● *Last orders for dinner 9 pm. Special diets and lunch available.*
● *Croquet, fishing, tennis, bathing, sailing, outdoor swimming pool.*
● *Open April 2-Oct 10th. Amex, Visa, Master-, Euro and Switch accepted.*

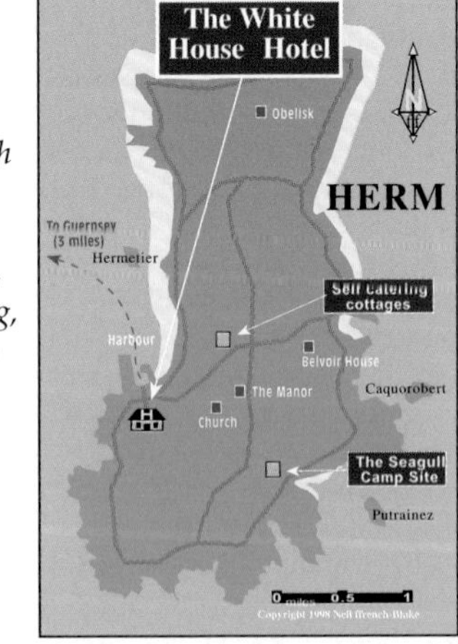

The Moorings Hotel & Restaurant

Gorey Pier, Jersey JE3 6EW
Tel: (01534) 853633; Fax: (01534) 857618
E-mail: Casino@itl.net

I have been wining and dining here for over 25 years and I share in the view of its popularity which causes it to be a frequent meeting place for local residents. Joyce McMinnies, the wife of the founder of SIGNPOST also spent several happy holidays here. Its position is unique and bridges time. Overlooked by an Elizabethan castle, floodlit at night, the Moorings provides a haven for those who enjoy good food and wine combined with an individual and sensitive service in homely and comfortable surroundings. The quayside outside is often thronged with shoppers plying its quaint arcade of shops. The pretty harbour, once the centre of Jersey's oyster industry, is alive with colour and movement throughout the day. Several times each day ferries arrive and depart for local French ports. This is a great centre not only for shopping but also for walking, cycling, golf, sailing and many other holiday pursuits. In many ways Gorey retains the relaxed and festive atmosphere of a seaside fishing port at the turn of the century. You will enjoy your holiday here - the ambience and location are unsurpassed.

Rates: *Single room including breakfast from £35. Double room with breakfast from £70.00.* **V**
Winter Breaks *available 1st Nov-31st March. Full Christmas programme inc. hire car. Details on application.*

- *17 en suite bedrooms with TV, direct-dial telephone; hairdryer, trouser press, muisc/radio/ alarm clock, tea/coffee making facilities.*
- *Restaurant, two bars + lounge; last orders for dinner 10.15 pm; A la carte, lunch & special*

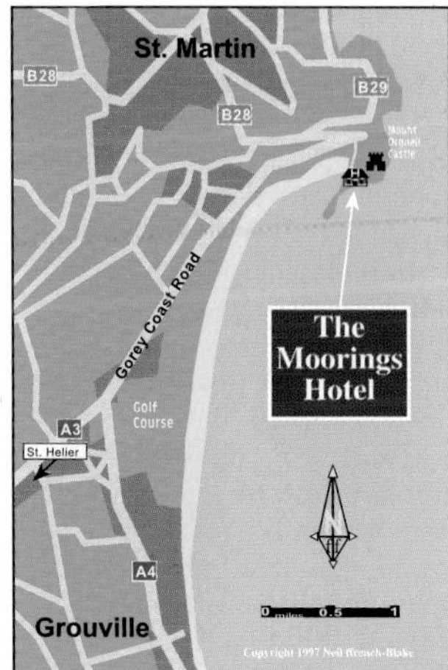

- *Fishing, golf, watersports, riding, sailing/ boating, outdoor swimming pool, tennis nearby.*
- *Business services. Car rental.*
- *Open all year. Visa, Mastercard, Amex, Switch accepted.*

Sea Crest Hotel

Petit Port, St Brelade's, Jersey JE3 8HH
Tel: (01534) 746353; Fax: (01534) 747316
E-mail: seacrest@super.net.uk

The Sea Crest is well known in Jersey as one of the best places to wine and dine, a reputation totally justified by table d'hôte and à la carte cuisine of the highest standard, a wine list extensive in its quality and an environment enhanced by new décor and contemporary British art on the walls. However, set in attractive gardens with a private swimming pool in the secluded and picturesque bay of Petit Port, the Sea Crest is more than just a restaurant....its seven en suite bedrooms are most comfortable, with hand made English furniture and attractive French material. Each has modern amenities including a small refrigerator in which fresh milk is placed each morning. Such thoughtfulness is typical of owners Julian and Martha Bernstein, who, with their helpful staff, will endeavour to make your stay memorable.

***Rates**: Single room with breakfast from £72; double inc. breakfast from £104.* V

● *7 en suite bedrooms each with colour TV, direct-dial telephone, safe, mini-fridge, hairdryer, laundry service, tea/coffee making facilities.* ● *Table d'hôte fm £20.50. A la carte, lunch & special diets available. Ample car parking.* ● *Outdoor swimming pool.* ● *Closed January.* ● *Visa, Amex, Switch accepted.*

Directions: A13 to St Brelade, then B44 Rte du Petit Port towards La Corbière. Hotel on right.

Greenhills Country Hotel & Restaurant

St Peter's Valley, Jersey JE3 7EL
Tel: (01534) 481042;
Fax: (01534) 485322
E-mail: greenhills@messages.co.uk

What a discovery! This 17th century country house is one of the most delightful small hotels in Jersey. Set in award winning gardens and nestled attractively in the tranquil heart of St Peter's Valley, the hotel has retained its character and features to ensure that guests experience the unique atmosphere and intimacy of a period country house. The 25 comfortable and traditionally styled bedrooms have a 'cottagey' atmosphere but with all modern amenities. Cuisine is British with continental influences, the accent being on fresh local seafood. Add to this comfortable public rooms and a sheltered swimming pool and you have a perfect hideaway. Personal and unpretentious hospitality from owner Peter Bromley and his staff will ensure that you'll want to keep the Greenhills secret to yourself!

***Rates:** Single room with breakfast from £48; double inc breakfast from £96.* V

● *25 en suite bedrooms (inc one suite), all with colour TV+satellite, radio, direct-dial telephone, hairdryer, laundry servicve, trouser press, safe.* ● *4 cse table d'hôte from £17. A la carte, lunch & special diets available. Last orders 9.30 pm* ● *Conference room & car parking for 40. Airport pickup by arrangement.* ● *Open Easter-24th October.* ● *Major credit cards accepted. Directions: From St Helier take A1, then A11 to St Peter's Valley. 4 miles out turn rt on C112; hotel signed on left.*

The Lobster Pot

L'Etacq, St Ouen, Jersey JE3 2FB
Tel: (01534) 482888; Fax: (01534) 485584

With a breathtaking vista over the unspoiled sands of St Ouen's Bay, this 17th-century granite farmhouse has long been a favourite restaurant with locals and visitors alike. Under the new owners, the Restaurant, Bar, Kitchen and Residents' Lounge have been tastefully refurbished to give a new feel. Although known to specialise in seafood, the restaurant also offers a wide variety on the à la carte menu, under the new innovative chef, Gerard Le Miere. The hotel and restaurant are wonderfully light, fresh and airy, and provide a relaxed and peaceful atmosphere all year round. Mountain bikes can be arranged for the more adventurous visitor. The hotel is situated in the tranquil north-western corner of the Island, and has winding cliff paths leading from its door, while still only a minute's walk from the beach. The area enjoys fantastic sunsets and an abundance of wildlife unique to this part of the island. The Lobster Pot is a choice haven away from the crowds, yet close enough to all Jersey's attractions and only a twenty minute drive from St Helier.

***Rates:** Double room with Continental breakfast from £49 per room; single occupancy from £29.*

- *12 en suite bedrooms, with colour TV + video/satellite, direct-dial telephone, hairdryer, tea/coffee making facilities, trouser press, room service, CD/radio/alarm clock.*
- *Separate lunch and evening menus; à la carte and regular specials.*
- *Beach and cliff paths adjacent. Golf, riding two miles; many other activities within 5 miles.*
- *Airport pickup; car parking for 50, car rental.*
- *Business services inc two meeting rooms to 100.*
- *Open March-1st Jan. Visa, Mastercard, Switch accepted.*

Hotel Petit Champ

Sark, Channel Islands GY9 0SF
Tel: (01481) 832046; Fax: (01481) 832469
E-mail: hpc@island-of-sark.co.uk
Internet: http://www.island-of-sark.co.uk

The island of Sark is truly unique. It retains a feudal constitution dating back to the reign of Elizabeth I, has its own government, no income tax and is home to just 550 residents. It is also a natural, car free and tranquil retreat for people who enjoy beautiful walks, breathtaking scenery and a refreshing break from the modern world. The Hotel Petit Champ is a reflection of all that with its secluded position and views to the sea. Here, under the expert supervision of the resident proprietors Chris and Caroline Robins, is a true gem of an hotel with a country house atmosphere and 16 cosy en suite bedrooms, some of which have balconies. There are three sun-lounges as well as a peaceful library lounge. Drinks before dinner are taken in the intimate bar and then guests repair to the candlelit restaurant renowned for its good cuisine with local lobster and crab dishes as specialities. A solar heated swimming pool nestles in the natural setting of an old quarry and forms a perfect sun trap. The Hotel Petit Champ, set in the island magic of Sark, is truly enchanting and the spell draws visitors back for holidays year after year.

***Rates:** Single room including breakfast and dinner from £47.50. Double room with breakfast and dinner from £45.50 per person.* V

- *16 en suite bedrooms. Hairdryers available.*
- *5-course table d'hôte dinner £17.95; à la carte, lunch & special diets available. Last orders 20.30.*
- *Putting green and solar heated outdoor swimming pool, garden walks, boat trips. Nearby sea fishing, tennis, billiards, badminton.*
- *All-inclusive holidays with travel available.*
- *Open Easter to early October. Mastercard, Visa, Switch, Amex & Diners Card accepted.*

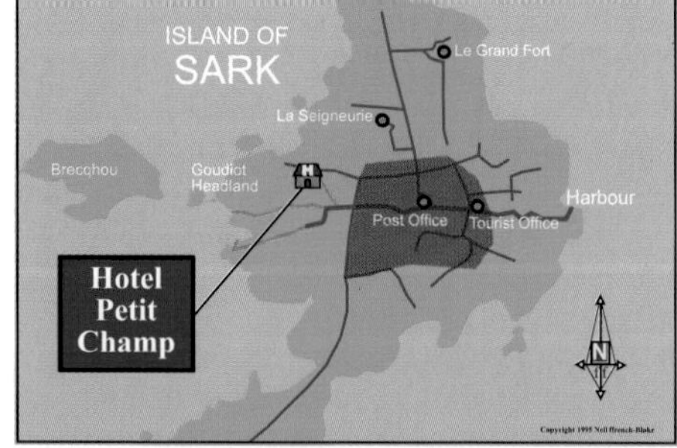

Houses, Gardens & Parks

Andress House, Co Armagh
The Argory, Co Armagh
Castle Coole, Co Fermanagh
Castle Ward, Co Down
Cratlow Woods House, Co Down
Downhill, Londonderry
Florence Court, Co Fermanagh
Gray's Printing Press, Strabane, Co Tyrone
Hezlett House, Co Londonderry
Mount Stewart House, Garden & Temple
Rowallane Garden, Saintfield, Down
Springhill, Moneymore, Co Londonderry
Templetown Mausoleum, Co Antrim
Wellbrook Beetling Mill, Cookstown, Co Tyrone

Historical Sites & Museums

Carrickfergus Castle, Carrickfergus, Co Antrim
City Hall, Belfast
Devenish Island, Lough Erne
Giant's Causeway, Nr Coleraine, Co Antrim
Glen of Glenariff, NE of Ballymena
Slieve Gullion, Newry, Co Down
Stormont Castle, Belfast
Ulster Museum, Belfast

DIARY OF EVENTS

January

4. **New Year Viennese Concert.** Ulster Orch Box Office, Belfast.
21-23. **Millennium Festival of Billiards.** Bangor Reading Rooms, Co Down.
20-23. **Holiday World.** Kings Hall, Balmoral, Belfast.

February

7-13. **Ulster Motor Show 2000.** Kings Hall, Belfast
28-Mar 4. **Opera Northern Ireland Spring Season.** Grand Opera House, Belfast

March

14-21. **Celtic Spring Festival.** St Patricks Week.Var.Londonderry
13-17. **St Patrick's Day Celebrations.** Armagh, Newry, Ballymena, Downpatrick.
23-April 2. **Between The Lines 2000.** Int'l literary festival. Crescent Arts Centre, Balfast.

April

14-15. **Coleraine Int'l Choral Festival.** Int'l choirs, University of Ulster, Coleraine.
15-23. **World Irish Dancing Championships.** Waterfront Hall, Belfast.
26-30. **Festival of Culture & Sport** Ballymoney Borough.
29-30. **City of Belfast Flower Show.** Barnett Park, Belfast.

May

1-2. **Belfast Marathon.** City Ctre
6. **Millennium Lord Mayor's Show.** Parade thru streets Belfast
10-12. **Balmoral Show 2000.** Agricult'l/entertainment event, Balmoral Showgrounds, Belfast.
12. **Millennium Tattoo.** Royal British Legion marches, Banbridge
13. **Coca-Cola North-West 2000** Motorcycle races, Portstewart.
20-June 4. **Belfast Summerfest 2000.** Entertain't. Var ven, Belfast

June

3-24. **Castleward Opera.** 18 perfs, Strangford, Co Antrim.
9-11. **Jazz & Blues Festival,** Limavady, Co Derry.
17-21. **Irish Amateur Close Cham -pionship.** Royal Portrush G Cb
23-25. **Lough Erne Millennium Regatta.** Lower Lough Erne.
24. **Festival of Air & Sea.** Air show, Bangor Bay, Co Down.

July

10-15. **North of Ireland Amateur Open Golf Champ'ship.** Royal Portrush, Causeway Coast
17-23. **City of Belfast International Rose Week.** Dixon Park.
19. **Ulster Motorcycle Grand Prix.** Dundrod Circuit.

August-November

28-29 Aug. **Oul' Lammas Fair.** Ireland's oldest traditional fair. Ballycastle.
1-3 Sept. **Appalachian & Bluegrass Music Festival.** Ulster-American Folk Park, Belfast.
26 Sept-1 Oct. **Aspects Irish Lit' Festival.** Bangor Heritage Centre.
27 Oct-12 Nov. **(21st) Belfast Festival at Queens.** Queens University, Belfast.

For further information, contact:
The Northern Ireland Tourist Board
St Anne's Court, 59 North Street
Belfast BT1 1NB
Tel: (01232) 231221; Fax: (01232) 240960

Historic Houses, Gardens & Parks

Annes Grove Gardens, Castletownroche
Ayesha Castle, Killiney, Co Dublin
Bantry House, Bantry, Co Cork
Birr Castle Demesne, Co Offaly
Blarney Castle & Blarney House, Blarney, Co Cork
Bunratty Castle & Folk Park, Bunratty, Co Clare
Carrigglass Manor, Longford, Co Longford
Castletown House, Cellbridge, Co Kildare
Cloghan Castle, Banagher, Co Clare
Colnalis House, Castlerea, Co Roscommon
Craggaunowen - The Living Past - Kilmurry, Co Clare
Dunguaire Castle, Kinvara, Co Galway
Dunloe Castle Hotel Gardens, Beaufort, Killarney, Co Kerry
Emo Court, Portlaoise, Co Leix
Fernhill Garden, Sandyford, Co Dublin
Fota Wildlife Park, Fota Island, Carrigtwohill, Co Cork
Glin Castle, Glin, Co Limerick
GPA Bolton Library, Cashel, Co Tipperary
Japanese Garden, Tully, Co Kildare
Johnstown Castle Demesne, Wexford, Co Wexford
The James Joyce Tower, Sandycove, Co Dublin
The John F Kennedy Arboretum, New Ross, Co Wexford
Knappogue Castle, Quin, Co Clare
Kylemore Abbey, Kylemore, Conne mara, Co Galway
Lismore Castle, Lismore, Co Water ford
Lissadell, Sligo
Lough Gur Visitor Centre, Lough Gur, Co Limerick
Lough Rynn Estate & Gardens, Mohill, Co Leitrim
Malahide Castle, Malahide, Co Dublin
Mount Congreve Gardens, Nr. Waterford
Mount Usher Gardens, Ashford, Co Wicklow
Muckross House & Gardens, Killarney, Co Kerry
National Botanic Gardens, Glasnevin, Dublin 9
Newbridge House, Donabate, Co Dublin
Phoenix Park, Dublin
Powerscourt Gardens & Waterfall, Enniskerry, Co Wicklow
Powerscourt Townhouse Centre, 59 South William St, Dublin 2
Riverstown House, Glanmire, Co Cork
Royal Hospital, Kilmainham, Co Dublin
Russborough, Blessington, Co Wicklow

Slane Castle, Slane, Co Meath
Strokestown Park House, Strokestown, Co Roscommon
Swiss Cottage, Chir, Co Tipperary
Thoor Ballylee, Gort, Co Galway
Timoleague Castle Gardens, Bandon, Co Cork
Tullynally Castle, Castlepollard, Co Westmeath

Historical Sites & Museums

Augustinian Priory (14thC), Kells, Co Kilkenny
Blarney Castle & Stone, Co Cork
Castle (State Apartments), Dublin
Christ Church Cathedral, Dublin
Cliffs of Moher & O'Brien's Tower, Lahinch, Co Clare
Glengarrif, 8m N of Bantry, Co Cork
Grianan of Eilach Fort, 18m NE of Letterkenny, Co Galway
Jerpoint Abbey ruins, 12m SE of Kilkenny, Co Kilkenny
Lough Corrib/Claregalway, Gal way, Co Galway
Lough Gill/Lough Colgath, Sligo, Co Sligo
Lynch's Castle, Galway, Co Galway
Mellifont Abbey, Drogheda, Co Louth
Monasterboice, Drogheda, Co Louth
Monastic City/St Kervin's Church, Glendalough, Co Wicklow
Municipal Art Gallery/Hugh Lane Gallery, Dublin
Museum of Modern Art, Kilmainham, Dublin
National Gallery, Dublin
National Museum, Dublin
Ring of Kerry, Killarney, Co Kerry
St Ann's Shandon Church, Cork
St Canice's Cathedral, Kilkenny, Co Kilkenny
St Patrick's Rock (Rock of Cashel), Co Tipperary
Sheehans Pt, remains of Carhan House, Waterrville, Co Kerry
Timoleague Franciscan Abbey, Courtmacsherry, Co Cork
Trinity College Library, Dublin
Tulla Church, 10m E of Ennis, Co Clare
Writers' Museum, Dublin

DIARY OF EVENTS

February

5*Rugby International: Ireland v France. Landsdowne Road, Ballsbridge, Dublin 4

March

7-16*. **Dublin Film Festival.** Various cinemas in Dublin.
17-19. **St Patrick's Festival.** Nationwide (Day = 17th)
24-26*. **Galway International Set Dancing Festival.** Through the streets & shops of Killarney, Co Kerry.
25-April 2*.**World Irish Dancing Championships.** West County Hotel, Ennis, Clare

April

1. **Rugby World Cup 2000. Wales v Ireland.** Dublin
26-30. **Cork International Choral Festival.** City Hall, UCC, Triskel Arts Centre.
28-May 1. **Heineken Kinsale Sevens by the Sea**, Kinsale Rugby Club, Kinsale, Cork

May

1-3*.**West of Ireland Amataur Open Golf Championship.** Inniscrone, Co Sligo.
4-7. **Murphy's International Mussel Fair.** Bantry, Co Cork.
11-14. **Galway Early Music Festival - Volta 2000.** Cork.
12-July 9*. **Co Wicklow Gardens Festival.** Throughout Co Wicklow, south Co Dublin, Co Carlow & North Co Wexford.
13-21. **South of Ireland Bridge Congress,** Killarney, Co Kerry
19-21. **Irish Amateur Open Golf Championship,** Royal Dublin GC, Co Dublin.

June

1-2. **Irish Seniors Amateur Open Golf Championship.** Westport, Co Mayo.
1-6. **Murphy's Int'l Comedy Festival.** Var. venues, Kilkenny
3-5. **East of Ireland Open Golf Championship,** Co Louth.
RDS, Simonscourt Pav. Dublin 4
16-18. **D unlavin Festival of Arts.** Market House, Dunlavin, Co Wicklow.

July

1-8. **Willie Clancy Summer Sch,** Milton Malbay,Co Clare
7-12. **Galway Film Fleadh.**Town Hall Theatre, Galway City.
16-23.**Longford Summer Music Festival.** VarVenues, Longford

August

9-13*. **Kerrygold Horse Show** RDS Showground, Dublin 4.
10-12. **Puck Fair.** Irish Festival, Killorglin, Co Kerry.
18-22.**Rose of Tralee Int'l Fest -ival.** Festival Dome, Tralee.

September

13-Oct 30*. **Waterford Int'l Festival of Light Opera.** Theatre Royal, Waterford.
27-Oct 1. **Irish Antique Dealers Fair**, RDS, Ballsbridge, Dunlin 4.

October

2-14. **Dublin Theatre Festival.** Major theatres, Dublin
8-15. **Cork Int'l Film Festival.** Cork Opera House etc, Cork.
19-Nov 5. **Wexford Festival Opera,** Theatre Royal Wexford.
28-30. **Kinsale Fringe Jazz Festival.** Var. venues, Kinsale,Cork
30. **98FM Dublin City Marathon**, Dublin.
Provisional dates.

Republic of Ireland

**Provisional dates.*
For further information, contact:
Bord Fáilte (Irish Tourist Board), Baggot Street Bridge, Dublin 2.
Telephone: 1 676 5871 / 6024000
Fax: 1 475 8046

Circuit of Ireland

Ireland is roughly 300 miles long from the north coast of Donegal to the south coast of County Cork and about 170 miles wide from Dublin on the east coast to the west coast of County Mayo. Dublin and Belfast have fine airports. Car ferries run from Holyhead to Dun Laoghaire, Fishguard to Rosslare, Swansea to Cork, and Stranraer in Scotland to Larne in Northern Ireland. In recent years they have all been modernised. Efficient and helpful car hire firms operate in the principal cities and even in a small town one may well alight on an efficient service station if your own car needs attention.

One of the most attractive reasons for choosing Ireland as a country for scenery, sport and ports of call, is the freedom of its roads. They are not infested by monster juggernauts, exasperating queues and long delays at junctions. So the driver proceeds in peace enjoying the view of the country without wondering if he's likely to be mown down by some rushing madman. Be warned, 'though, that road surfaces are not always as smooth as in Britain, so cars tend not to live to a ripe old age.

Ireland, North or South, has a huge choice for people of varied interests. Fishing, of course, the Dublin Horse Show, racing, splendid golf courses, unpolluted sands, ancient relics, and all sorts of magnificent coastal scenery like the tremendous Cliffs of Moher on the west coast, Blarney Castle near Cork where you can kiss the stone and supposedly be rewarded with exceptional eloquence. The Giant's Causeway, easily reached from Portrush in County Antrim, and its thousands of basalt columns which are certainly one of the most curious geological formations in the world. As a similar formation is found in the Scottish Island of Staffa on the west coast of Scotland, it has been suggested that these formations may extend and meet under the Irish Sea. These wonders are only a tiny list of the strange collection of objects, some of which were in existence thousands of years ago.

Now a few hints on how to see the West of Ireland. Whether you start from Dublin, Rosslare or Cork, from a viewing point it's better to follow the sun round, in other words left handed keeping to the coast. Starting at Rosslare you can visit the famous crystal glass factory at Waterford; in nearby Middleton, the home of Irish whisky, you can tour a distillery. Wexford has a famous Opera Festival and Heritage Park, bringing Irish history to life. County Cork and County Kerry are generally reckoned to provide the finest and most varied scenery. Cork is Ireland's second city, home of *Murphy's* stout and the famous jazz festival. The road from Cork gives one a taste of the mountains ahead, Killarney follows, a veritable wonderland of mountains and lakes many with odd names like the *MacGillicuddy Reeks* 3,414' which include the highest peaks in Ireland. There are first class hotels in the town and several most excellent ones a few miles west. One could spend a fortnight exploring this wonderful and beautiful area alone.

From Killarney to Waterville, a noted fishing town with several first class and friendly hotels. Limerick and Galway are the main cities of Ireland's West Coast; the latter famous for its annual Race Meeting and Oyster Festival. In nearby Connemara you will find the world famous marble, and see the equally famous wild Connemara ponies. Next to County Mayo where the soft pastel shades of the mountains and clouds appeal to the artist and photographer. In the Oughterard, Clifden, Newport and Westport area have some charming family run hotels of special merit.

Southwest of Westport the 2,510' high hump of *Croagh Patrick* (near Knock) attracts yearly pilgrimages up its stony flanks and unfortunately now is apt to be trippery with tourists sometimes outnumbering pilgrims. County Donegal is famed for its Atlantic Drive and has one of the least polluted coasts in Europe.

From here one turns east into Londonderry and then to Portrush and its golf courses and the Giant's Causeway near Bushmills. The Antrim coast road south to Belfast affords sea and land views while a more exciting hilly road from Bally Castle takes in Carrick-a-Rede whose cliffs and suspension bridge are well worth a visit. In Dungannon you can visit and purchase the famous Tyrone Crystal.

'or private accommodation in London, Signpost also recommends Uptown Reservations – *see page 65*

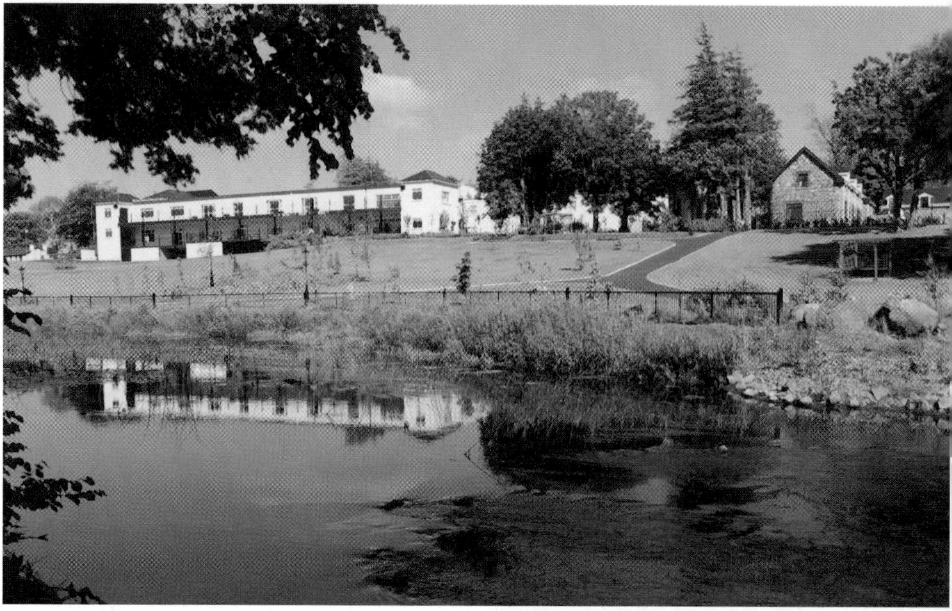

Dolmen Hotel

Kilkenny Road, Carlow
Tel: (0503) 42002; Fax: (0503) 42375
E-mail: reservations@dolmenhotel.ie
Internet: http://www.dolmenhotel.ie

Nestled along the scenic banks of the river Barrow and set in 20 acres of landscaped beauty is the Dolmen Hotel. It stands on the site previously occupied by Belmont House. This was pulled down in the 1960s but the former stables and staff quarters have been converted into ten one-bedroom lodges which are ideal for sporting enthusiasts - individuals or families who want to enjoy golfing nearby or fishing on the hotel's private stretch of the river Barrow but retain some privacy. The Dolmen is a little over one hour's drive from Dublin, Rosslare or Waterford car ferries and two hours from Shannon Airport. Carlow is known as the Celtic centre of Ireland, because of the profusion of neolithic and early Christian sites in the vicinity. The Dolmen is an excellent base from which to explore south-east Ireland with golfing, walking, garden visiting and canal cruising all nearby. The hotel is also popular for weddings and business meetings.

Kilkenny 24, Wexford 44, Waterford 46, Dublin 49.

Rates: *Single room with breakfast from £48.50; double from £79.* **V** ***Bargain Breaks:*** *Jan-April & Oct-Dec weekends 2 x b & b + dinner £89 per person; midweek 3 x dinner, b & b from £150 per person; May-Sept as above 2 nights from £119/3 nights from £179 per person.*

● *40 en suite double/twin rooms & 10 River Court Lodges, all with colour TV, direct-dial telephone, hairdryer, laundry service, trouser press. Non-smoker & disabled rooms available.*

● *Table d'hôte £18.95; à la carte, lunch & special diets available. Last orders 9.30 rest't/10.30 grill.*

● *Full business services inc 5 meeting rooms to 1200. Car parking for 450.*

● *Fishing from hotel's river. Tennis, riding, golf, sailing, clay shooting, squash all within 2 miles.*

● *Open all year exc. Xmas Day;*

● *Visa, Amex, Diners, Mastercard accepted.*

Please note that when dialling into the Republic of Ireland from the UK or USA, numbers should be prefaced by +353, and the first zero

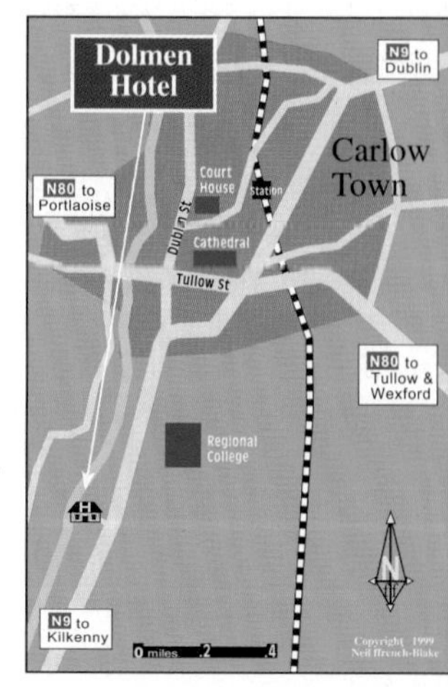

Dromoland Castle

Newmarket-on-Fergus, Co Clare
Tel: (061) 368144; Fax: (061) 363355
E-mail: sales@dromoland.ie
Internet: http://www.dromoland.ie

There are several reasons to relax and luxuriate in Dromoland Castle, one of the most famous baronial castles in Ireland. It was once the home of Ireland's Celtic High Kings - The O'Briens. It sits in 370 acres of parkland and is naturally imposing - yet it is one of Europe's leading hotels. Open log fires, attentive and friendly staff , family portraits and antique furniture create an ambience of warmth and relaxation. The luxurious bedrooms are spacious and beautifully decorated with fine views over the lake or the grounds. Dine in style in the high-ceilinged Earl of Thomond dining room of fine china, crystal and white linen tablecloths. The quality classical cuisine offered through a variety of dishes includes delicious *Taste of Ireland* fare. The hotel has every leisure facility including an 18-hole golf course, full health & beauty spa with indoor swimming pool, fishing, boating and delightful walled gardens. Dromoland also has excellent conference facilities and is well placed for excursions to local places of interest like Bunratty Folk Park. It is just eight miles from Shannon International Airport.

Rates: *From IR£140 to IR£810.* V
Bargain Breaks: *Nov 1-March 31: two nights b & b + one dinner IR£240 per person sharing weekends; IR£180 per person sharing midweek.*

- *100 en suite double/twin rooms, all with colour TV+ satellite, direct-dial telephone, hairdryer, laundry service, trouser press, safety deposit box. Non-smoker & disabled bedrooms available.*
- *Table d'hôte £40; à la carte, lunch & special diets available. Last dinner orders 9.30*
- *Full business services inc. four meeting rooms with capacity to 400. Car parking for 400 cars.*
- *Billiards/snooker, fitness centre, indoor games, newsstand, beauty salon, indoor pool, fishing, boating, tennis, clay pigeon shooting. Horseriding nearby.*
- *Open all year. Major credit cards accepted.*

Shannon 8, Ennis 8, Limerick 15, Dublin 136.

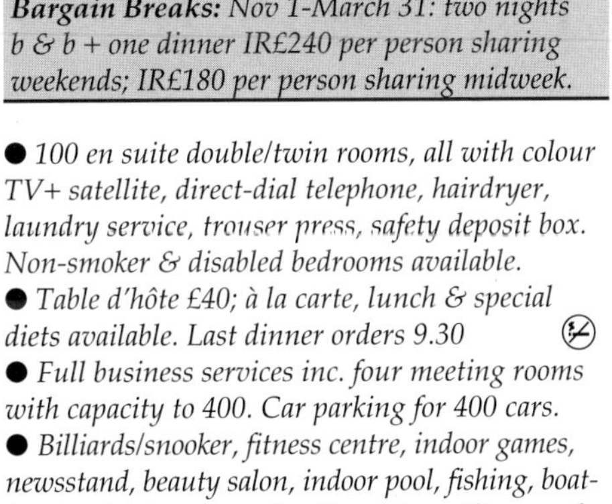

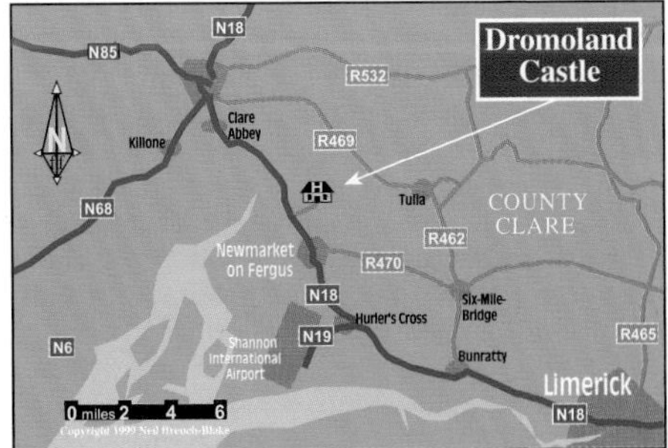

Halpins Hotel

Erin Street, Kilkee, Co Clare
Tel: (065) 905 6032;
Fax: (065) 905 6317
E-mail: halpins@iol.ie

Halpins Hotel, which has recently been refurbished and upgraded, offers quality, comfort and good food with an excellent tradition of personal service. Its open hearth fires and friendly old world bar provide a warm welcome for the weary traveller. The hotel enjoys a fine reputation and its *Vittles* restaurant is well known throughout the county. Lighter meals are available from the Cellar menu. The picturesque Victorian resort of Kilkee has frequently won the EU Blue Flag Award for its clean beaches. This small townhouse hotel in the centre of Kilkee is personally run by Pat Halpin and his charming staff. It is a sister property to the Merrion Hall and Aberdeen Lodge hotels in Dublin 4. Those looking for a relaxing environment for a business or leisure stay will be well looked after at Halpins.

Rates: *Single room with breakfast from IR£40;* V *double inc. breakfast from IR£70.* ***Bargain Breaks:*** *2 nights b&b + one dinner from £99 pp.*

- *12 en suite bedrooms with colour TV, direct-dial telephone, hairdryer, laundry service, tea/coffee making facilities, 24-hr room service, radio.*
- *A la carte restaurant; lunch & special diets available; last orders 10 pm. Meeting room to 50 people*
- *18-hole golf course adjacent to hotel; beach nearby*
- *Open all year. All major credit cards accepted.*

Kilrush 8, Ennis 35, Limerick 58, Dublin 109.

Seaview House Hotel

Ballylickey, Bantry, Co Cork
Tel: (027) 50073 / 50462;
Fax: (027) 51555

This delightful country house hotel stands in its own wooded grounds close to the Ballylickey Bridge over the river Ouvane, commanding views of Bantry Bay and the distant mountains. Locally and further afield, Seaview is renowned for its comfort and cuisine. Owner Kathleen O'Sullivan has doubled the hotel in size without forgoing the friendly welcome and personal service for which the house is so well known. She is an accomplished cook and the cuisine has been recognised by several awards including two AA rosettes. Bedrooms are furnished with antiques and there is a cottage and a small lodge in the grounds for family occupation if required. Ballylickey is an ideal centre for touring the peninsulas of West Cork and Kerry. There are two golf courses nearby as well as other activities in the vicinity.

Rates: *Single room with breakfast from IR£60;* V *double from IR£100.* ***Bargain Breaks:*** *on request.*

- *17 en suite bedrooms with satellite TV, hairdryer, tea/coffee making facilities. Facilities for disabled.*
- *Table d'hôte dinner £25. A la carte & special diets available. Last orders 9 pm.*
- *Open 15 March-15 November. All major credit cards accepted.*

Bantry 3, Killarney 45, Cork 55, Dublin 216.

V after prices = hotel accepts £5 off vouchers from Signpost readers - see back of this book.

Emmet Hotel

Emmet Square, Clonakilty, West Cork
Tel: (023) 33394; Fax: (023) 35058
E-mail: emmethotel@eircom.ie

The new Emmet Hotel is situated in a very picturesque Georgian square in the bustling West Cork town of Clonakilty, overall winner of the *National Tidy Towns Competition 1999*. The central location just off the main street makes the Emmet hotel the ideal base for touring, sightseeing, holidaying or for business purposes. It has recently been refurbished to a very high standard. The decor is tasteful and fits the relaxed atmosphere of this very homely hotel. All food is cooked to order using the best local fresh produce, organically farmed where possible. The bistro and bar menus offer a variety of enticing ideas and flavour. Emmet Square itself has an interesting background. It was laid out between 1785 and 1810 and called originally Shannon Square. It has housed a classical school, a meeting house for Plymouth Brethren, a constabulary barracks, a glebe and a gentleman's club. Its most famous resident was Michael Collins, who lived at No 7. Clonakilty is a good centre for touring Cork and Kerry. Local attractions include beach fishing, pony trekking, golf and a model railway village opened in 1995.

Rates: *Single room inc. breakfast from IR£35; double room inc. breakfast from £65.* V
Bargain Breaks: *Midweek packages available low season; weekends in low season. Details on appli cation.*

- *20 en suite bedrooms, all with air-conditioning, colour TV+ satellite, direct dial telephone, hair-dryer, laundry/valet service, tea/coffee making facilities, safety deposit box.*
- *Table d'hôte dinner £18.20; à la carte, lunch & special diets available.*
- *Two meeting rooms, capacity 120. Airport pickup*
- *Indoor swimming pool, fitness centre 500 metres; fishing, golf, sea/river bathing, watersports, sailing, riding nearby.*
- *Open all year. All major credit cards accepted.*

Cork Airport 31, Cork 32, Dublin 193.

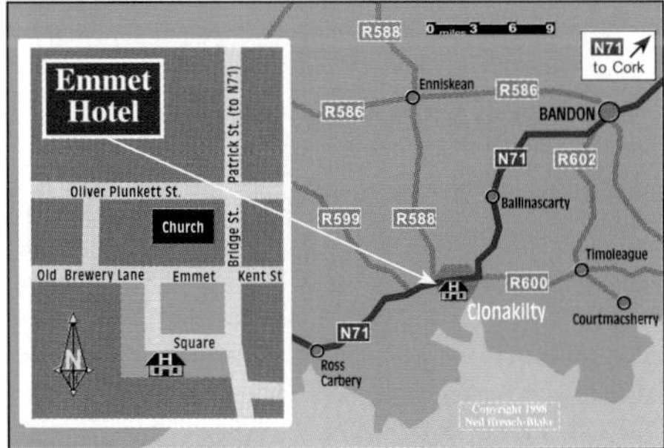

Ireland

Hayfield Manor Hotel

Perrott Avenue, College Road, Cork
Tel: (021) 315600;
Fax: (021) 316839
E-mail: enquiries@hayfieldmanor.ie
Internet: http://www.hayfieldmanor.ie

Situated in two acres of mature gardens adjacent to University College, Cork, this hotel is a haven of tranquillity, yet just a mile away from the bustle of the city centre. The blend of country house atmosphere with the comfort, standards and facilities of a first class international hotel is a product of genius. Elegant bedrooms, overlooking the gardens, are matched by luxurious marble bathrooms with bathrobes and baskets of toiletries. The gourmet cuisine of the Manor Room restaurant is well known locally and the atmosphere, with piano accompaniment, is intimate and warm. With its excellent leisure and business facilities, Hayfield is a first class base, providing a relaxing aura of quiet efficiency.

***Rates**: Single room with breakfast from £140; double room from £180.*

- *87 en suite bedrooms (15 suites) with aircon, satellite TV, telephone, hairdryer, laundry/valet service, 24-hr room service, radio, safe, trouser press, iron + board.*
- *Table d'hôte dinner £35; à la carte, lunch & special diets available; last orders 9.30 pm.*
- *Full business serviecs inc 7 meeting rms to 100.*
- *Indoor pool, jacuzzi, massage. Fishing, jogging, sailing, squash/tennis nearby.*
- *Open all year. Major credit cards accepted.*

Castlehyde Hotel

Castlehyde, Fermoy, Co Cork
Tel: (025) 31865; Fax: (025) 31485
E-mail: cashyde@iol.ie

A beautifully restored 18th century courtyard situated in the Blackwater Valley of North Cork. Set in secluded woodland that borders the Blackwater River, this hotel c aptures the atmosphere that must have been prevalent 250 years ago. The original features have been retained, the hotel being contained within the outbuildings - 14 bedrooms and five cottage suites. The restaurant and its conservatory overlook the lawn as they lie in the shade of the oak and ash trees bordering the lawn. Indoors one can relax and unwind in the lounge or library, or by the fire. Proprietors Helen and Erik Speekenbrink are experienced hotel managers who will point you in the direction of the best golf courses (8 are near the hotel), fishing or hill walking nearby. Historical sites abound in the vicinity and the sea is close at hand. Hospitality, excellent service and tranquillity can be savoured here in historic surroundings.

Mallow 19, Cork 22, Waterford 61, Dublin 133

***Rates:** Single room with breakfast from £75; double room inc. breakfast from £95. **Bargain Breaks:** 2 nts b & b weekends + 1 dinner in Mermaids Restaurant, golf or horse riding fm £120 pp* V

- *19 en suite bedrooms (inc cottage suite for 5) all with colour TV + satellite, telephone, radio, hairdryer, tea/coffee making. Non-smoker rooms avail.*
- *Fishing, golf, bathing, riding, squash within 5 m.*
- *Open all year. All major credit cards accepted.*

Maryborough House Hotel

Maryborough Hill, Douglas, Cork
Tel: (021) 365555; Fax: (021) 365662
E-mail: maryboro@indigo.ie
Internet: http://www.maryborough.ie

The Maryborough is a charming old world mansion at the centre of natural parkland with majestic oaks, rhododendrons and an outstanding collection of shrubs and plants. Every room has views of these outstanding gardens. The 18th century core building has been restored to preserve all the original Georgian features: high stuccoed ceilings, gracious curved staircases with antique furniture to match. The Garden Room connects the old mansion with the new wing and leads to the 21st century amenities - banqueting and conference areas, state-of-the-art leisure club, swimming pool, and to the contemporary restaurant which serves an exciting mixture of modern flavours and styles, created where possible from fresh local produce. Douglas is a pleasant suburb of Cork, handy for the airport and ferry port , close to the city centre and road network, yet Maryborough provides an oasis of old world elegance, mixed with new world efficiency. A good business or holiday hotel for those embarking on a tour of southwest Ireland.

Rates: *Single room inc. breakfast IR£99-150; double room inc. breakfast from £110-220.* V
Bargain Breaks: *Weekend breaks - 2 nights b&b + 1 dinner from £110 per person sharing.*

- *79 en suite bedrooms, all with colour TV+ satellite, direct dial telephone, hairdryer, laundry/ service, tea/coffee making facilities, 24-hr room service, trouser press. Non-smoker and disabled bedrooms available*
- *Table d'hôte dinner £21; à la carte, lunch & special diets available. Last orders 10 pm.*
- *Six meeting rooms, capacity 5-500. Airport pickup. Car parking 300. Car rental.*
- *Billiards/snooker, croquet, gymnasium, jacuzzi, massage, sauna, indoor swimming pool, tennis. Fishing, golf, watersports, sailing, riding nearby.*
- *Closed 24-26 Dec. All major credit cards accepted*

Cork 3, Airport 5, Killarney 51, Dublin 157.

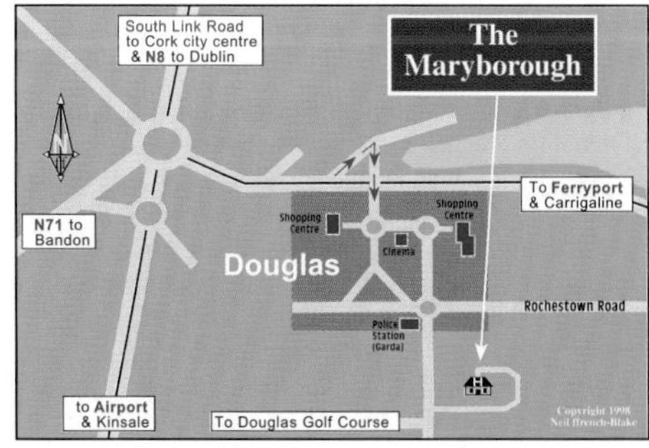

Innishannon House Hotel

Innishannon, Co. Cork
Tel: (021) 775121; Fax: (021) 775609
E-mail: innishannon@tinet.ie

Back in 1720, when a wealthy farmer had his home built half a mile from the village of Innishannon, he could hardly have imagined that over 250 years later it would be a delightful country house hotel offering world class hospitality. Innishannon House Hotel is only 15 minutes from Cork airport but the setting is as romantic as you could wish, with gardens running down to the river Bandon where salmon and trout fishing as well as boating are available free to guests. All the bedrooms overlook this rural idyll and they in turn are full of personality, being individually decorated and furnished with antiques. They vary in size, from smaller dormer rooms to spacious ones on the first floor and the vast suite with its period bathroom. My walk round the public rooms was also an experience. A pleasant sunny drawing-room with a corner bar gives on to a separate 'snug' and the whole is decorated with verve using idiosyncratic modern paintings juxtaposed with traditional Irish landscapes. The new chef de cuisine is Pearse O'Sullivan, the son of the house, and the restaurant has won several awards including two AA rosettes 1993 through 1999 for "culinary excellence". In 1998 the hotel was the only Irish hotel in 50 worldwide to win the *Insider Award* from Holiday / Travel Magazine USA. The Innishannon is a hotel to be savoured for its character and the quality of its hospitality.

***Rates:** Single room including breakfast from IR£75; double room with breakfast from IR£99; Garden Suite £250.* V
***Leisure Breaks**: Any two nights b&b plus one table d'hôte dinner from £95 pp sharing; Jan-Mar, November and sometimes April, May, Oct. Dec.*

- *14 en suite bedrooms with radio and colour TV; direct-dial telephone, hairdryer, laundry service; non-smoker rooms; disabled facilities.*
- *Last dinner orders 21.30.*
- *Fishing & boating from the hotel's grounds. Golf, riding, shooting, squash and tennis all nearby.*
- *Meeting room with 150 capacity; AV equipment & secretarial services. Safe deposit box. Car parking 100 cars.*
- *Open all year. All major credit cards accepted.*

Cork 14, Killarney 46, Bandon 4½, Dublin 175.

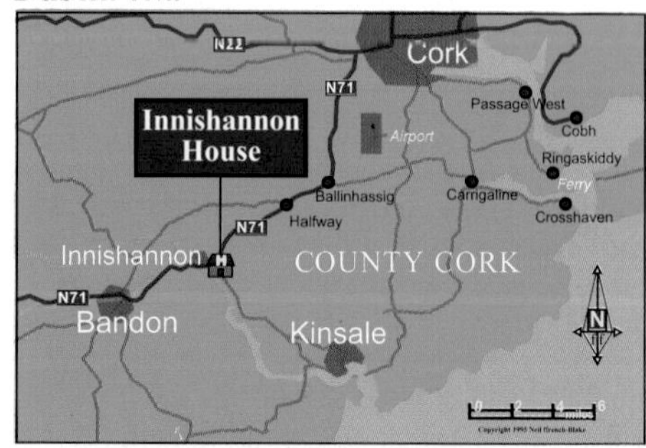

Ballymaloe House

Shanagarry, Co Cork
Tel: (021) 652531; Fax: (021) 652021

Ballymaloe is a large family farmhouse, still with its 14th century keep, situated on a 400-acre farm 20 miles east of Cork city. It has become well known throughout the British Isles and the USA for the high standard of its accommodation and cuisine. To stay here is to savour all the charm of Irish country living at its best, as exemplified by the spacious public rooms graced by modern Irish paintings and in particular by the large comfortable drawing room where you can relax in front of a roaring log fire. The bedrooms are full of character and are cosy, traditionally furnished or more modern depending whether they are in the main "home" or in one of the outbuildings. The Ballymaloe Cookery School in Shanagarry, the restaurant in the Crawford Art Gallery in Cork City are both run by members of the Allen family, as is the excellent craft shop at Ballymaloe itself. The cuisine in the hotel has won many plaudits. Vegetables are home grown on the farm and fish is fresh from Ballycotton nearby. Nor should you miss the most genuine Irish breakfast you are likely to sample. There is beautiful country to explore nearby: sandy coves, hills to climb, golf courses to play and houses and gardens to visit. But Ballymaloe is the jewel in the crown of this lovely region with the warmth and welcome of a home creating a carefree, smiling hotel.

***Rates:** Double/twin room including breakfast IR£140-£170. **Bargain Breaks:** Nov-March 2 nts dinner, b & b fm £145 per person.* V

● *33 en suite bedrooms all with radio and colour TV+satellite, direct-dial telephone, hairdryer, laundry service, iron, room safe. Rooms for the disabled*
● *Table d'hôte £34.50; lunch & special diets available; last orders 21.30. Car parking for 200.*
● *Croquet, miniature golf, swimming pool, children's play area. Fishing, watersports, sea bathing, riding, tennis, golf courses nearby. Baby sitting.*
● *Closed Dec 24-26. Major credit cards accepted.*

Cork 25, Waterford 64, Limerick 91, Dublin 163

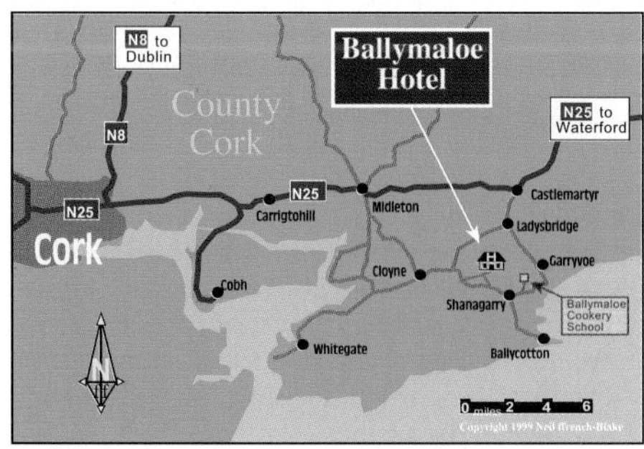

Fort Royal Hotel

Rathmullen, Co Donegal.
Tel: (074) 58100; Fax: (074) 58103
E-Mail: fortroyal@eircom.net

A beautiful situation by the shoreline of Lough Swilly, Co. Donegal's great sea lake, gives Fort Royal natural advantages - not only fine views and invigorating air but a magnificent sandy beach for swimming and watersports. Built in 1819, the house is set in 18 acres of lawn and woodland overlooking the sea with easy access to miles of sandy beach. Long shadows stretching gently across the lawns in early evening settle the peace and tranquillity that make Fort Royal a place apart. The hotel is in the careful hands of Ann, Robin and Tim Fletcher whose warmth and hospitality will ensure your stay is a memorable one. Enjoy their greeting, the comfort of their rooms, the quality of their food (two AA rosette cuisine)- many of the herbs and vegetables used in the kitchen are grown in the hotel's own walled gardens - and the variety of their wine list. And welcome to the peace of Donegal. Glenveagh National Park is a short drive from the hotel. Their magnificent gardens and castle perched on the Lough's edge should not be missed. Fishing for wild brown trout and sea trout is available in the Lough.

Rates: *Single room with breakfast from £45; double room inc. breakfast from £100.* V
Bargain Breaks: *Midweek 3 days, dinner b & b from £185 per person; weekend breaks 2 days b & b + 1 dinner from £110 per person.*

● *15 en suite bedrooms with colour TV, direct-dial telephone.*
● *4-course table d'hôte dinner £25; special diets & bar lunch available; last orders 8.45 pm. AA* ❁❁
● *Croquet, tennis, squash, par 3 9-hole golf course at hotel. Fishing, 18-hole golf, swimming, watersports, sailing nearby. Riding 10 miles.*
● *Open 1st April - 1st November. Visa, Amex, Mastercard, Diners credit cards accepted.*

Letterkenny 15, Londonderry 36, Donegal 45 , Dublin 165.

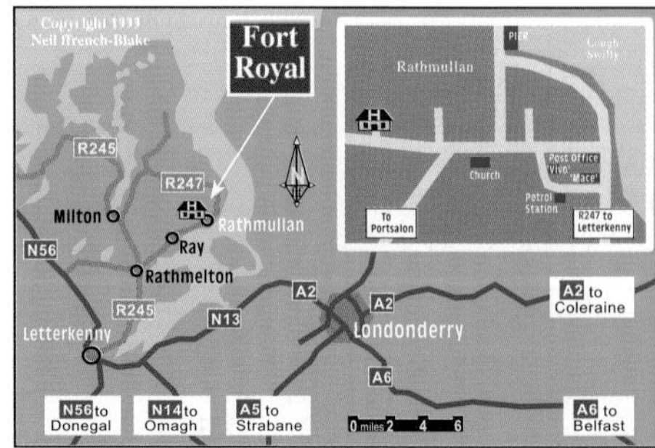

Please note that when dialling into the Republic of Ireland from the UK or USA, numbers should be prefaced by +353, and the first zero

Castle Grove Country House & Restaurant

Ballymaleel, (off Ramelton Road), Letterkenny, Co Donegal.
Tel: (074) 51118; Fax: (074) 51384

Castle Grove is a fine Georgian house, set in its own estate and approached by a mile long drive through parkland. It overlooks Lough Swilly and boasts a quietness and quality of life that is rare in most parts of the world today. Bedrooms are individually decorated and the restaurant specialises in seafood and the best of Irish food, accompanied by an excellent cellar. The house exudes the warmth and comfortable informality of a private home. Nearby is Glenveagh National Park, whose magnificent park and castle are open to the public, and Churchill Art Gallery. There are 3 local 18-hole golf courses and fishing, shooting and riding are all available in the area.

Rates: *Single room inc. breakfast IR£45-55; double room IR£80-100; suites IR£150-200.* V
Leisure Breaks: *Midweek 2nights b&b + 1 dinner £95 pp sharing; weekend £105 pp. Exc July/Aug.*

- *14 en suite bedrooms with direct-dial telephone, hairdryer, laundry service, radio/alarm, trouser press. Colour TV & minibar on request. Non-smoker rooms available.*
- *Tdh dinner til 2130 £20; à la carte, lunch & diets available. Car parking for 25. Meeting room for 20.*
- *Golf, fishing, tennis, riding nearby. Watersports 12 m*
- *Open Jan-22 Dec. Major credit cards accepted.*

Letterkenny 2½, Londonderry 22, Donegal 30, Dublin 159

Richmond House

Cappoquin, Co Waterford
Tel: (058) 54278; Fax: (058) 54988
Internet: http://www.amireland.com/richmond

This elegant 4 star 18th century Georgian Country House stands in private parkland half a mile from the picturesque village of Cappoquin. Of "Olde Worlde" charm and character, yet with every comfort for the discerning guest, Richmond House is furnished throughout with beautiful furniture and antiques. The main drawing room leads to a conservatory overlooking the garden where you can have a quiet drink before dinner. Relax in total tranquillity in front of log fires and treat yourself to a gourmet meal in our award winning, fully licensed restaurant. One of its three rooms is set aside as 'honeymooners' corner'. The son of the house, Swiss-trained Paul and his wife Clare, preside over a menu which is not only popular locally but enjoys international recognition. This is the ideal location for walking, fishing, golfing or touring the Southeast and the hotel is recommended in all good travel guides.

Rates: *Single room with breakfast from IR£60; double room with breakfast from IR£90.*

- *9 en suite bedrooms with colour TV, direct-dial telephone, hairdryer, trouser press, tea/coffee making facilities.*
- *Table d'hôte dinner £30. A la carte & diets available. Last dinner orders 9 pm.*
- *Fishing, golf & riding within 3 miles.*
- *Open February 14 to December 23rd.*
- *Visa, Amex, Diners & Mastercard accepted.*

Directions: On the N57 Lismore-Dungarvan road.
Cork 31, Waterford 40, Rosslare 90, Dublin 136

Aberdeen Lodge

53-55 Park Avenue, off Ailesbury Road, Ballsbridge, Dublin 4
Tel: 01 283 8155; Fax: 01 283 7877
E-mail: aberdeen@iol.ie

Aberdeen Lodge shares its neighbourhood with the world's embassies who have chosen Ballsbridge, the most exclusive area of Dublin, for its convenience to the city centre. Large well kept gardens surrounding grand mansions give the area an air of refined exclusivity. Aberdeen Lodge shares all these privileges. Standards are high and the rooms are large in this restored Edwardian house. Comfort combines with all the facilities required to make an enjoyable stay. This property has all to offer that one would expect of a private hotel. There are two four poster rooms and two suites with period furniture and whirlpool spas. Fine cuisine is served in the restaurant which overlooks landscaped gardens and cricket grounds. Aberdeen Lodge is well reviewed by leading guides and can match the qualities of city centre hotels but adds to them a quieter location and great value. It is seven minutes away from the city centre by DART (Dublin Area Rapid Transport) and is a good base for exploring the sights of the city. Sister property of Merrion Hall (*see page 239*).

Rates: *Single room including breakfast from IR£70; double IR£90.* V
Leisure Breaks: *Two nights b & b from 1R£90 per person sharing.*

- *17 rooms (inc 2 suites), all with airconditioning, colour TV+satellite, direct-dial telephone, hairdryer, laundry service, tea/coffee making facilities, radio, trouser press. Non-smoker rooms avail.*
- *A la carte restaurant, open lunch & dinner; special diets catered for; last orders 10 pm.*
- *Residents may use local leisure centre with swimming pool sauna, jacuzzi and gym. Gardens.*
- *Business services inc. 2 meeting rooms up to 50.*
- *Car parking. Car rental & airport pick-up by arrangement.*
- *Open all year. All major credit cards accepted.*

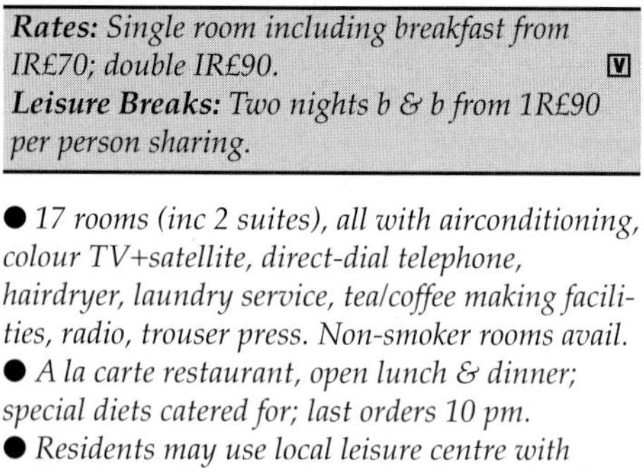

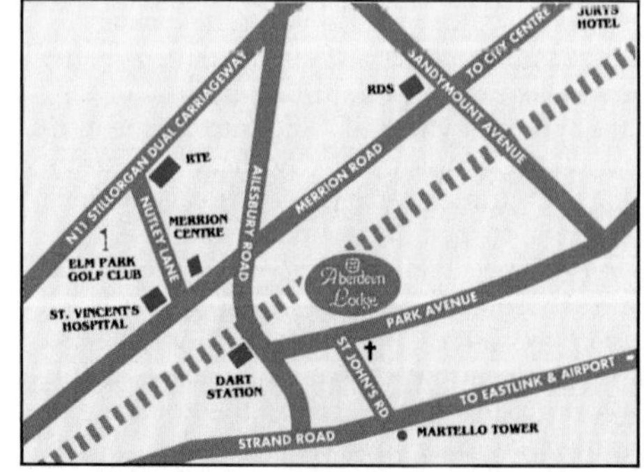

Please note that when dialling into the Republic of Ireland from the UK or USA, numbers should be prefaced by +353, and the first zero

Beaufort House and Serviced Apartments

25 Pembroke Park. Ballsbridge, Dublin 4
Tel: (00353-1) 6689080;
Fax: (00353-1) 6609963

Beaufort House will most probably become your 'home away from home' whilst in Dublin. Your host, Rosemary Nevin, has created a lovely relaxed atmosphere - the rooms are individually and thoughtfully furnished, the decor sympathetic, bright, cosy and comfortable. All guestrooms have PC modem points, yet are graced with original fireplaces and old world elegance. Breakfasts are a house speciality, offering crêpes suzette and home-made bread. Afternoon tea is available and light meals are served until 10.30 pm in the conservatory. The house is only minutes' walk to Dublin's busy financial and entertainment centre and all guests have access to private leisure facilities. As an alternative to the hotel, try one of the elegant serviced apartments. All have personal phone/fax & answering service, housekeeping, dry cleaning and reception facilities. Beaufort Performance Car Rental is also available from the same premises, so you can treat yourself to another bit of escapism!

***Rates**: Single inc. 4-course breakfast IR£45-85; double with breakfast IR£55-160.* V*
***Leisure Breaks:** Winter 2-night breaks from £50 per person. Also luxury weekends incorporating sports car rental or chauffeur driven, theatre, restaurant and private table reservations.*
*(*Please quote Signpost at time of booking)*

- *9 en suite bedrooms with colour TV, direct-dial telephone, hairdryer, laundry service, tea/coffee making, music/radio/alarm clock, safety deposit box, trouser press & iron. Non-smoker & disabled bedrooms available. Modem points in bedrooms.*
- *Car parking -5. Car rental. Airport pickup.*
- *Leisure Centre available nearby. Golf one mile.*
- *Open all year. Visa, Mastercard, Diners, Amex credit cards accepted.*

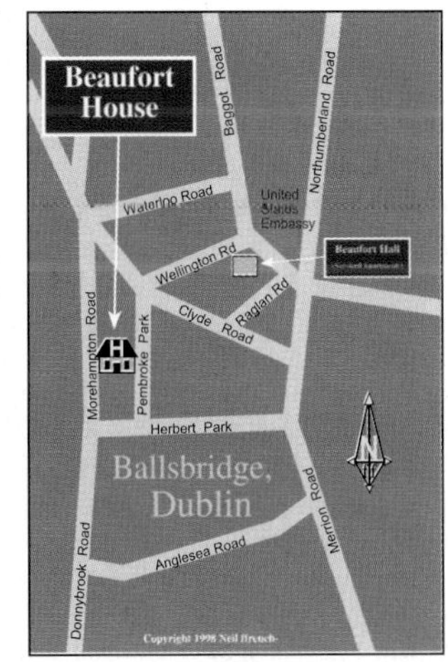

Longfields Hotel

10 Fitzwilliam Street Lower, Dublin 2
Tel: (00353-1) 676 1367;
Fax: (00353-1) 676 1542
E-mail: LFIELds@indigo.ie

The Georgian Doors of Dublin are an established visual attraction in souvenir poster form. A prime example is No 10 Fitzwilliam Street Lower, part of the longest unbroken line of Georgian houses in Ireland and home to Longfields, one of Dublin's most distinguished small hotels. A quiet haven for the visitor, Longfields is an ideal base for forays into the capital's prime shopping streets, such as Grafton Street, for bargain hunting in antique and curio shops, for cinemas and theatres and for Dublin's numerous art galleries and museums - all are within easy walking distance. The city's main burgeoning Bohemian quarter of Temple Bar is ten minutes' walk, as are St Stephen's Green and Trinity College. Attention to detail and personal service are the hallmarks of Longfields. This is seen in the elegantly furnished bedrooms and reception area and perhaps best exemplified in the restaurant. Affectionately known as *No 10* to the business lunch set and to Dubliners dining out, it has received excellent reviews.

***Rates**: Single room inc. breakfast from £95; double room inc. breakfast from £140.* V
***Bargain Breaks**: Midweek & weekend pack ages available in low season. Details on application.*

- *26 en suite bedrooms (inc 2 mini-suites) all with colour TV, direct-dial telephone, hairdryer, laundry/valet service, radio/alarm clock.*
- *Table d'hôte dinner £30; A la carte, lunch & special diets available. Last orders 10 pm.*
- *Street parking - ask porter.*
- *Closed 24-26 Dec. Major credit cards accepted.*

Merrion Hall

54/56 Merrion Road, Ballsbridge,
Dublin 4
Tel: (01) 668 1426/1825; Fax: (01) 668 4280
E-mail: merrionhall@iol.ie

When awards are given there is always a lurking danger of complacency setting in - but in so far as Merrion Hall, an RAC property of the year, is concerned, the reverse applies. This impeccably maintained private hotel is situated in the embassy district, close to its sister property Aberdeen Lodge, and specialises in providing an exceptionally warm and welcoming ambience where nothing is too much trouble for the friendly and welcoming staff. There are five four-poster rooms and two suites with period furniture and whirlpool spas. The attractive dining room, overlooking a pretty garden, is bright and airy. Yet my favourite room was the larger of the drawing rooms which is naturally homely and nicely furnished with a welcoming glowing fire providing the centrepiece. At Merrion Hall you start your day fully refreshed for it has won awards for its breakfasts too. The menu is a full page of fresh and home-made fare and, to do full justice to it and to this charming private hotel, you will need to stay for quite a few days, which would be a very happy experience. Total refurbishment was undertaken in 1997 and bedroom suites were added.

Rates: *Single room including breakfast from IR£70; double room with breakfast from IR£90.* V
Leisure Breaks*: 2 nights from IR£90.00 per person sharing with breakfast.*

- *25 en suite bedrooms (inc 2 suites) with satellite TV; direct-dial telephone, fax & modem facilities, hairdryer, laundry service; tea/coffee making facilities, mineral water, room service, clothes press, bathrobes.*
- *No restaurant*
- *Leisure centre nearby with gym, pool, gym, sauna, jacuzzi.*
- *Car parking - 12 cars. Gardens*
- *Open all year.*
- *All major credit cards accepted.*

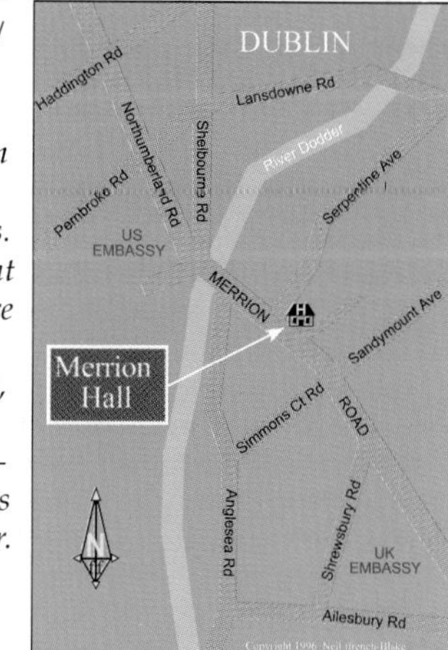

Merrion Hotel

Upper Merrion Street, Dublin 2
Tel: (00353-1) 6030600; Fax: (00353-1) 6030700. E-mail: info@merrionhotel.com

The Merrion, Dublin's most luxurious five-star luxury hotel is a member of the Leading Hotels of the World. Accolades include Fortune Magazine (USA)'s *Best Hotel Room in Dublin* award, The American Academy's *Five Star Diamond Award* and most recently in the 1999 Robb Report's annual *Best of the Best*, the Merrion was voted the third best boutique hotel in the world. Situated in the centre of Dublin opposite the Irish Parliament, the hotel is created from four Grade I listed Georgian townhouses and a contemporary Garden Wing arranged around two 18th Century style gardens. Stunning Georgian interiors provide the perfect backdrop to Ireland's most impressive private art collection. *Mornington's Brasserie* serves exciting contemporary cuisine with an Irish flair while *Restaurant Patrick Guilbaud* offers gourmet dining. Lord Mornington's former wine vault has become *The Cellar Bar* and there is also *No 23* for that more intimate drink. The Tethra Spa offers an 18-metre swimming pool and state of the art Leisure Club.

Rates: *Single room including breakfast from IR£225; double room with breakfast from IR£260.*
Leisure Breaks: *The Merrion Getaway - one night in a luxurious double room, full Irish breakfast + a bottle of champagne on arrival- IR£195 per couple.*

- *145 en suite bedrooms (inc 20 suites) with AC, colour TV+satellite, telephone/fax/ISDN lines, hairdryer, laundry/valet service, minibar, 24-hr room/meal service, radio/alarm clock, safety deposit box, trouser press. Non-smoking & disabled bedrooms available.*
- *A la carte lunch/dinner £13 2-cse/£16 3-cse; special diets available. Last orders 10.30 pm.*
- *Business services inc. 6 meeting rooms, cap. 60.*
- *Indoor swimming pool, steam room, gymnasium & spa treatment rooms. Fishing, golf, watersports, sailing, shooting, squash, tennis, riding nearby. Beauty salon. Car rental. Car parking for 60.*
- *Open all year. Visa, Amex, Diners cards accepted*

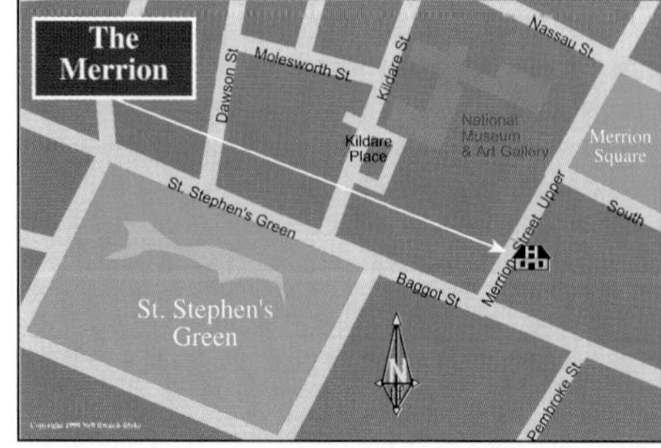

Number 31

31 Leeson Close, Dublin 2
Tel: (00353-1) 676 5011; Fax: 676 2929
E-mail: NUMBER31@iol.ie

The brochure for No 31 describes it as *'one of Dublin's best-kept secrets'*, and your inspector has to agree that he was immensely surprised and delighted by the location, standard of accommodation and welcome which all guests receive. An award winning guesthouse in the heart of Georgian Dublin, it is the former home of leading architect Sam Stephenson. Set almost in the epicentre of Dublin, St Stephen's Green, owners Deirdre and Noel Comer have made No 31 into a haven of quiet good taste, tranquillity and greenery. There are 18 en suite bedrooms, all large, comfortable and spacious. The beds are firm and comfortable and the furnishings blend with the house, long lined expensive curtains covering the Georgian windows. Being so central, Number 31 does not provide dinner, but a breakfast the size of many dinners, with excellent fresh ground coffee. The helpful staff will park your car for you, relieving you of the worry of clampers and ever vigilant wardens. No 31 is extremely comfortable, quiet and a great find in central Dublin. Children over the age of 10 are welcome. Parents with younger children may be worried about the abundance of fine furniture and paintings. No 31 is within walking distance of Dublin's art galleries, fashionable shops, museums and top restaurants.

Rates: *Single room including breakfast from £85; double room with breakfast from £90-130.* **V**

● *20 en suite bedrooms (inc 2 suites) all with colour TV, direct-dial telephone, hairdryer, safety deposit box, tea/coffee making facilities. Non-smoking bedrooms available.*

● *Car parking for 16.*

● *Children over 10 welcome.*

● *Open all year. Visa, Amex, Mastercard accepted.*

Glenogra House

64 Merrion Road, Dublin 4.
Tel: (01) 668 3661; Fax (01) 668 3698
E-mail: glenogra@indigo.ie

Seamus and Cherry McNamee have very carefully developed an ideal guesthouse with 13 beautifully furnished rooms. A finely appointed Edwardian residence opposite the Royal Dublin Society (RDS) and Four Seasons Hotel, it is close to the city centre, bus routes and the Sandymount DART station, and minutes walk from the US embassy and many fine restaurants. Breakfast has always been regarded as the essential foundation for a good day by the hosts and afternoon tea by the fire is just what is needed after a day's shopping or sightseeing in central Dublin. Bedrooms are smartly decorated in harmony with the period residence. Glenogra is a Four Star Irish Tourist Board guesthouse, ideal for business or leisure travellers looking for good value near to the centre of Dublin.

Rates: *Single room inc. breakfast IR£45-55. Double room with breakfast IR£65-75.* ***Bargain breaks:*** *3 day midweek special fm £90 per person.*

- *13 en suite bedrooms with radio, colour TV+ satellite, direct-dial telephone, hairdryer, laundry service, non-smoker bedrooms, trouser press.*
- *Airport pick-up and car rental by arrangement.*

Portmarnock Hotel & Golf Links

Strand Road, Portmarnock,
Co Dublin
Tel: (00353-1) 8460611;
Fax: (00353-1) 8462442;
Internet: http://www.portmarnock.com

Originally owned by the Jameson (whisky) family, the Portmarnock is now an international hotel with an 18-hole golf course designed by Bernhard Langer and covering 180 acres. It occupies a peaceful, quiet location just 11 miles from Dublin city centre and four from the airport. Nearby are miles of sandy beaches. Other sports like archery or quad bikes are equally on offer near the hotel. All bedrooms overlook either the sea or the golf course. The *Osborne* restaurant has an excellent choice of international cuisine and a good selection of wines. The less formal *Links* restaurant caters for golfers and locals alike.

Rates: *Single room inc. breakfast from IR£140. Double room with breakfast IR£205.*
Bargain breaks: *2 nights b&b, one round of golf, one dinner £199 per person sharing (subj. avail'y)*

- *103 en suite bedrooms with radio, colour TV + satellite, telephone, hairdryer, laundry service, minibar (exec. rms), 24-hr room service, safety deposit box. Non-smoker rooms available.*
- *2 restaurants. Special diets available. Last orders 10 pm. Ample car parking.*
- *Own 18-hole golf course. Archery, quad bikes, sailing, riding, clay pigeon shooting nearby.*
- *Full business services including 5 meeting rooms to total capacity 350.*
- *Open all year. Mastercard, Visa, Amex, Diners credit cards accepted.*

Finnstown Country House Hotel

Newcastle Road, Lucan, Co Dublin
Tel: (01) 628 0644; Fax: (01) 628 1088
E-mail: manager@finnstown-hotel.ie
Internet: http://www.finnstown-hotel.ie

Only eight miles for Dublin, Finnstown represents the best in country house hotels. Set in 45 acres of woodland, it is one of finest established Manor Houses in County Dublin. The old world charm greets you as soon as you enter. From the sculpted ceiling to the majestic staircase, you'll be aware of a tradition of style and elegance. The public rooms retain the atmosphere of the old house whilst the bedrooms have all the facilities of a modern hotel. The restaurant has a good local reputation with an extensive wine list. Finnstown will particularly appeal to golfers - there is an excellent 9-hole course and the golf annexe of Studio Suites is particularly designed for the enthusiast as each has a patio opening out onto the edge of the course, affording easy access and a fine panorama. Finnstown offers a wide range of recreational activities as well as executive suites for business meetings. Its location so close to Dublin makes it an ideal jumping-off point for an Irish holiday.

***Rates:** Single room inc. breakfast from IR£94; Double room with breakfast from IR140.* V
***Bargain Breaks:** 2 nights bed & breakfast + one dinner from IR£147 per person.*

- *51 en suite bedrooms with radio, colour TV+ satellite, telephone, hairdryer, laundry service, trouser press , tea/coffee making facilities. Non-smoker & disabled bedrooms available.*
- *5-course table d'hôte dinner £24; lunch & special diets available; last orders 9.30 pm.*
- *Business centre inc. 5 meeting rooms to 100.*
- *Billiards, croquet, fitness centre, golf, indoor games, indoor swimming pool, tennis, Turkish baths. Sailing, fishing & riding 12 miles.*
- *Open all year. Visa, Amex, Diners, Mastercard accepted.*

Lucan 1, Dublin City Centre 8, Airport 12.

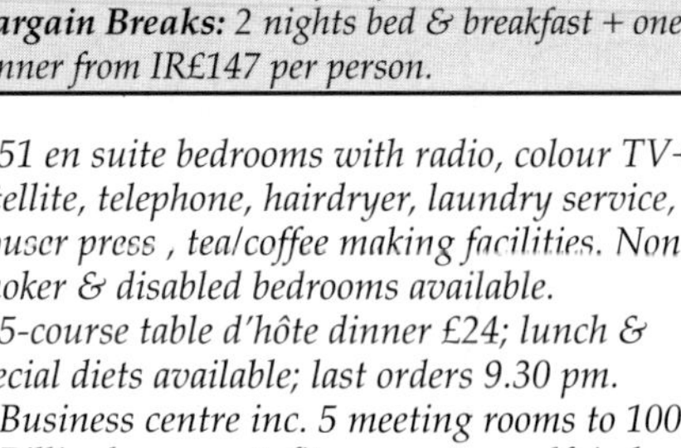

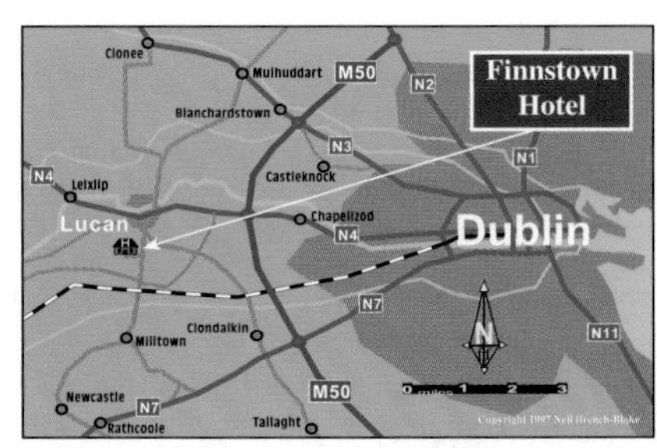

ote that when dialling into the Republic of Ireland from the UK or USA, numbers should be prefaced by +353, and the first zero omitted.

Ardagh Hotel & Restaurant

Ballyconneely Road, Clifden, Co. Galway
Tel: (095) 21384; Fax (095) 21314
E-mail: ardaghhotel@tinet.ie
Internet: http://www.commerce.ie/ardaghhotel

Stephane and Monique Bauvet add gallic flair to this simple family run hotel which is situated beside the road, close to lovely, sandy beaches and the excellent Connemara Golf Club. It is a quiet place and unpretentious but with two features of remarkable quality in its restaurant and the bedrooms. The first floor dining room enjoys beautiful views over Ardbear Bay and Monique creates the most delicious fare from local produce with lobster and seafood generally being a speciality, complemented by locally grown vegetables. The wine list is good as well. In addition there's a comfortable bar downstairs where pub lunches are served and the home-made soup is lovely. The Ardagh has two pleasant lounge areas for relaxation but it was the family rooms which impressed me as being amongst the best I have ever seen. Twin beds for the children are set aside in an alcove slightly separated from the rest of the room. There is plenty of space for them to play too - and colour TV and sea views. The rooms reflect the whole ambience of the Ardagh as being clean, comfortable and friendly. It is a charming hotel for a leisurely holiday.

***Rates:** Double room for 2 persons from IR£95* V

- *21 en suite bedrooms with TV.*
- *Billiards/ snooker. Squash one mile. Watersports three miles. Riding five miles. Golf (10 miles) by arrangement with hotel.*
- *Open end March - November.*
- *All major credit cards accepted.*

Ballyconneely 5, Oughterard 32, Westport 43, Galway 49, Dublin 168.

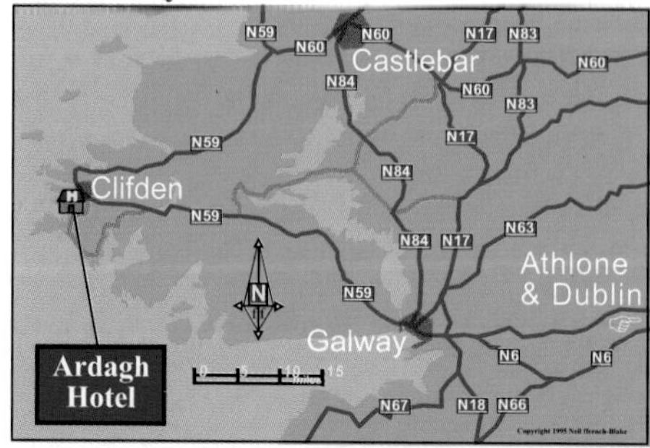

St Clerans

Craughwell, Co Galway
Tel: (091) 846555; Fax: (091) 846600
E-mail: stcleran@iol.ie
Internet: http://www.merv.com/stclerans

St Clerans is the former home of the film director John Huston. It was bought in 1997 by the American hotelier Merv Griffin, who has luxuriously refurbished it to 21st century standards, providing stunning yet intimate accommodation in an impressive Georgian mansion. All 12 de luxe guestrooms have been individually decorated with a blend of luxury, tradition and imagination, best described as *contemporary colours and materials with a classical touch.* All the bedrooms are named rather than numbered, to reflect the unique character, atmosphere and style of each unit. The guest rooms feature period furnishings and décor, deluxe bathrooms, two-line telephones, CD players, modem links and personalised suite stationery. The dining room is in keeping with the rest of the house - unique, furnished with care and exuding a wonderful relaxed atmosphere in which to enjoy the meals. As their brochure says *'the fresh Galway air gives one an appetite that is best satisfied by fresh Galway produce....'*

St Clerans is set in 45 acres of parkland with woods, stream and lake. Hunting can be arranged in season ('Galway Blazers Country'). For luxury in a small intimate historic house, St Clerans is hard to beat.

***Rates:** Single/double with breakfast £170-£260.*

- *12 en suite bedrooms all with TV+ satellite, radio, telephone, hairdryer, laundry service; safety deposit box, modem, CD players. Rooms for disabled available. Airport pickup & car rental by arr't*
- *Table d'hôte £38 7-9 pm; special diets available.*
- *Fishing, shooting, riding & hunting, massage on site. Swimming & watersports within 12 miles.*
- *Open February-December. Major credit cards exc. Diners accepted*

Loughrea 7, Galway 15, Limerick 53, Dublin 120.

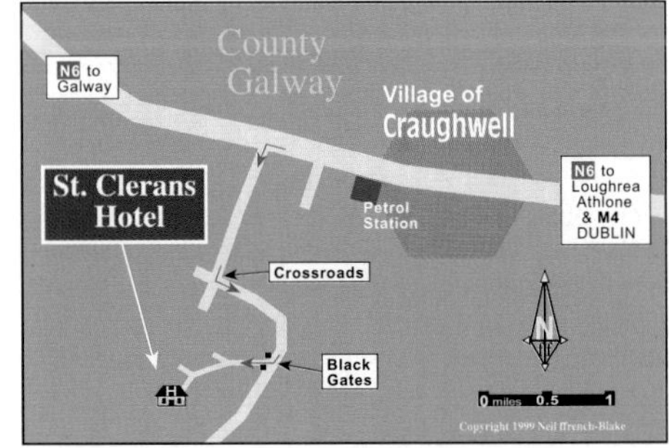

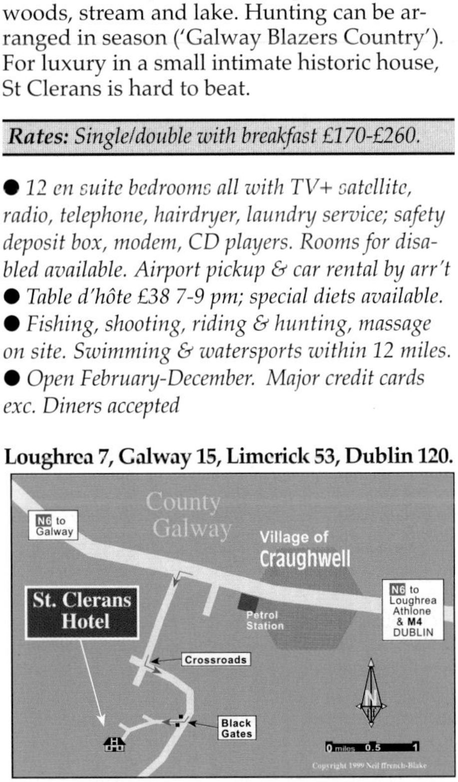

Ballynahinch Castle Hotel

Ballynahinch, Recess, Co Galway
Tel: (095) 31006; Fax: (095) 31085
E-mail: bhinch@iol.ie
Internet: http://www.commerce.ie/ballynahinch

Ballynahinch Castle is set in the heart of Connemara and stands proud and majestic overlooking the famous salmon river of the same name. The castle has been intertwined in the history of Connemara and its people for many centuries from the days of the O'Flaherty Chieftains, Grace O'Malley, Humanity Dick Martin and HRH the Maharajah Ranjitsinji. The hotel has a charm which can best be described as casual country elegance. Open log fires glow in the reception rooms and all the visitor's needs are attended to by friendly, professional staff. Soft, restful colour schemes in the bedrooms harmonise with the natural charm of the surroundings. Local fresh produce is used to create culinary delights for the dining room with its panoramic view of the river. The Castle is surrounded by 350 acres of woods, rivers and lakes, offering miles of scenic walks. Ballynahinch fishery is world renowned as one of the finest salmon and sea trout rivers in Ireland. Casting tuition is available and fishing is reserved for hotel guests. What better way to spend a day than to tempt an eager salmon with a cast fly? The Castle also has 13000 acres of wonderful driven woodcock shooting. The beauties of Connemara are on the doorstep, if you can tear yourself away from the Castle. It has an aura of its own which few forget and many return for.

Rates: *Single with breakfast from £72; double with breakfast from £104.* **V**
Bargain Breaks*: 2 nts weekends pp sharing b & b + 1 dinner from £119; weekdays from £99.*

- *40 en suite bedrooms (inc. 3 suites) all with TV+ satellite, radio, telephone, hairdryer, laundry service; non-smoker bedrooms available.*
- *Table d'hôte £27.50; à la carte, pub lunch & special diets available; last orders 9 pm.*
- *Fishing, shooting, tennis, walks on site. Golf, bathing, sailing, riding within 12 miles.*
- *Closed 20-26 Dec & Feb. Major credit cards acc'd*

Clifden 8, Galway 42, Dublin 179.

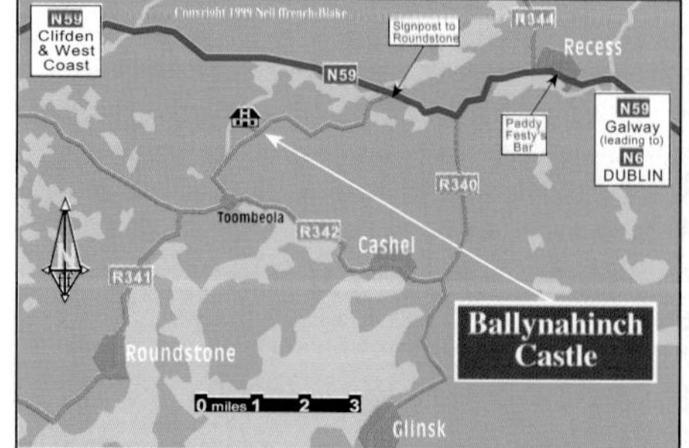

Ross Lake House

Rosscahill, Oughterard,
Co Galway
Tel: (091) 550109;
Fax: (091) 550184

Ross Lake House is a wonderful restored Georgian house set in the magnificent wilderness of Connemara, battleground of the O'Flahertys and the De Durgos (now Burkes) of ancient times. The house stands serenely in its estate of woods and gardens beckoning the world weary with its own refreshing charm. The Georgian theme is carried throughout the furnishings, fittings and fabrics from the top of the house to the front door. From the moment you arrive, your hosts Elaine and Henry Reid will make you feel at home. The intimate bar is ideal for a pre-dinner drink. A high quality Irish menu is delightfully prepared and presented featuring a tempting variety of fresh produce from the nearby Connemara hills, streams and lakes, as well as fish from the Atlantic. Ross Lake House, the best kept secret in Connemara, awaits your discovery.

Rates: *Single with breakfast £40-60; double inc. breakfast £72-100.* ***Bargain Breaks****: On application*

- *13 en suite bedrooms, with colour TV + satellite, telephone, hairdryer, laundry service, tea/coffee making, safe.*
- *A la carte dinner - last ordersr 9 pm. Lunch & special diets available.*
- *Fishing, golf, bathing, watersports, sailing, tennis riding all nearby.*
- *Open mid-March-31st October. Credit cards accepted. Car rental/airport pickup by arrangement.*

Galway 17, Clifden 32, Westport 40, Dublin 149

The Rosegarden Guesthouse & Restaurant

Kenmare, Co Kerry
Tel: (00353) 64 42288;
Fax: (00353) 64 42305
E-mail: rodegard@iol.ie
Internet: http://www.europa.com/rosegarden

The Rosegarden is within walking distance of Kenmare - a busy market town full of interesting little shops - on the N70 (Ring of Kerry). Peter and Ingrid Ringlever have custom built a charming guesthouse and surrounded it with a lovely rosegarden. The interior is bright and spotlessly clean with cheerful blue and yellow curtains and table mats. The rooms are all en suite with showers and have all modern facilities. Peter's restaurant cum bistro was packed on the evening I stayed there with both tourists and locals - always a good sign! They had fresh fish, shellfish, lamb and a dish of the day on the menu and very good it was too. Peter and Ingrid run their guesthouse with cheerful, welcoming, calm efficiency. An excellent budget choice.

Rates: *Single room inc. breakfast from IR£32.50; double room inc breakfast from IR£45.* ***Bargain Breaks:*** *3-day special: 3 x b&b + dinner £120 per person. 7-day special: 7 x b&b + dinner £250.*

- *8 en suite bedrooms with power showers, telephone, colour TV+satellite, hairdryer, tea/coffee making, radio, safety deposit box. Car parking 25.*
- *A la carte restaurant. Last orders 9 pm*
- *Fishing, golf, watersports, sailing, swimming pool, tennis, riding, seafari (seals & birds) nearby.*
- *Open 1 April-Oct 31. Credit cards accepted.*

Killarney 20, Bantry 25, Cork 58, Dublin 210.

Dingle Skellig Hotel

Dingle Peninsula, Co. Kerry
Tel: (00353) [0] 66 915 1144;
Fax: (00353) [0] 66 915 1501
E-mail: dsk@iol.ie
Interent: http://www.dingleskellig.com

Dingle Skellig Hotel overlooks Dingle Bay and, wherever you look, you can see the sea - either at first hand or in the numerous seascapes or murals in the hotel! The hotel has a magic feeling of space, tranquillity and friendliness. During my stay, the staff were, without exception, polite, cheerful and welcoming. The food was delicious - there was a choice of six main courses, three of them seafood, my steamed John Dory on a bed of spinach being memorable. The hotel is built on three floors with families on the middle floor and couples and individuals on the third floor where all rooms have personal videos and CD players. All rooms have views of either the sea or mountains and gardens. The 4-star hotel has first class conference and leisure facilities. The Dingle Peninsula offers all sorts of activities: hill walking, trips to the Blasket Islands, climbing, fishing, abseiling, shopping in Dingle and much more. There is golf at Ceann Sibeal - the most westerly course in Europe. You will enjoy this complete 'hotel experience' as much as I did. Watch out for *Fungi* - Dingle's friendly dolphin - you may well glimpse him from a window!

Rates: *Single room inc. breakfast from IR£57; double inc. breakfast from IR£95.* V
Bargain Breaks: *Winter Specials from £95 pp for 2 nts b&b + one dinner. Golden Breaks available. Winter midweek specials from £135 pp - 3 nts b&b + 2 dinners. Midweek Golf Specials from £155 pp - 3 nts b&b, 2 dinners + 2 rounds golf.*

● *116 en suite bedrooms, all with radio, colour TV+ satellite, telephone, hairdryer, laundry, tea/coffee making, 24-hr room service, safe. Non-smoker and disabled bedrooms available.*
● *Fitness centre/gym, indoor games, jacuzzi, sea bathing, massage, solarium/steam room, indoor swimming pool, boat trips. Sailing, riding, fishing 1m; golf 10m. Car parking - 120.*
● *Business services inc 3 meeting rooms to 250*
● *Open Feb-Dec. All major credit cards accepted*

Tralee 30, Killarney 40, Limerick 95, Dublin 216.

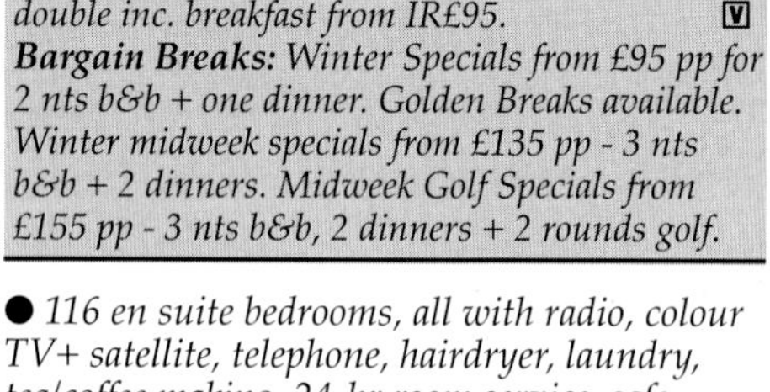

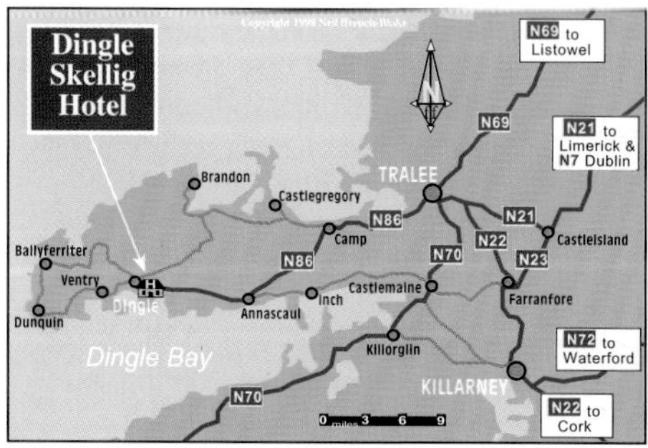

Cahernane House Hotel

Killarney, Co. Kerry
Tel: (064) 31895;
Fax: (064) 34340
E-mail: cahernane@tinet,ie
Internet: http://www.cahernane.com

The last quarter mile approach to the Cahernane House Hotel is through a tunnel of greenery which frames its long private drive - an approach that helps the visitor to adjust to a slower, sweeter tempo in tune with the hotel's tranquillity. Formerly the residence of the Earls of Pembroke, the present house dates from 1877 and, in addition to the impressive and comfortable reception rooms with log fires, it features many grandly spacious furnished bedrooms, together with an extension that has been designed to blend with its older sister. There are two dining rooms, the Herbert and the Pembroke Rooms - and a charming cellar bar by an impressive wine cellar with 300 well judged bins. Outside and locally there is fishing, walking, tennis and golf on Killarney's world famous championship courses. Also the scenic charms of lovely Lough Leane - the principal lake in Killarney's glittering necklace, where the wise old peaks of Mangerton, Tove and McGillycuddy seem to gaze down on their own reflections with satisfaction.

Rates: *Single room with breakfast from £80; double inc. breakfast from £110.* V
Bargain Breaks: *April & Oct £70 per person, dinner b & b; May-Sept £80 pp d, b & b; two nights d, b & b pp £130-160.*

- *48 en suite bedrooms, all with satellite TV, telephone, radio, hairdryer, laundry service, safety deposit box. Non-smoker bedrooms available.*
- *3-cse table d'hôte £29; à la carte, lunch & speciaol diets available; last orders 9.30 pm.*
- *Business services inc. meeting room for 30. Airport pickup, car parking for 60, car rental, barber shop, newsstand.*
- *Fishing, tennis on site. Golf, riding, shooting, inddor pool, squash within 3 miles. Sailing 13m.*
- *Open April-November 1. Visa, Amex, Diners, Mastercard accepted.*

Tralee 15, Kenmare 24, Cork 54, Dublin 189.

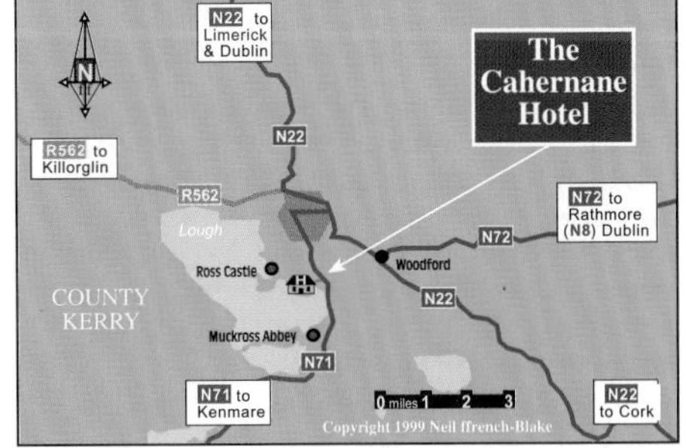

Ireland

Hotel Europe

Killarney, Co. Kerry
Tel: (064) 31900; Fax: (064) 32118

This 5-star hotel overlooks Killarney's lakes and mountains. There are superb views from the restaurant where the most delicious Irish and international cuisine can be enjoyed, with local fish, lobster and smoked salmon as specialities. The hotel is the right choice for an active holiday. Some of Ireland's most beautiful and famous golf courses are within easy reach. The ideal place to relax after an invigorating day exploring southwest Ireland.

Rates: *Single room with breakfast from IR£104; double room with breakfast from IR£124.* V

● *197 en suite bedrooms, 8 suites, all with satellite TV, direct-dial telephone, hairdryer, laundry service, 24-hour room service.* ● *Table d'hôte dinner £29; à la carte, lunch & special diets available; last orders 9.30 pm.*
● *Billiards/snooker, fishing, golf adjacent, indoor swimming pool, fitness centre, free riding, boating, indoor tennis. Watersports & squash nearby. Shooting by arrangement.*
● *Open March - November.All credit cards accepted exc JAC.*

Hotel Ard Na Sidhe

Caragh Lake, Killorglin, Co. Kerry
Tel: (066) 979105; Fax: (066) 979282

At Ard Na Sidhe (*The House of the Fairies*), one is a guest in an elegant country house, furnished with valuable antiques and warmed by open fires. Built in 1880 with fabulous award-winning gardens sloping down to the lake, the house offers a tranquillity rarely found today. You can read, go for walks, paint, dream or simply 'switch off' in this idyllic setting. For the more energetic, there are 9 golf courses within a 30-mile radius and fishing and hill trekking nearby. Any visit to the south west and the Ring of Kerry would be incomplete without staying here for at least a couple of days to recharge the batteries.

Rates: *Single room with breakfast from IR£75; double room with breakfast from IR£124.* V

● *17 en suite bedrooms, 2 suites, all with telephone, hairdryer.*
● *Table d'hôte dinner IR£29. Special diets available; last orders 9.00 pm*
● *Open May - October.All credit cards exc. JAC accepted.*

Hotel Dunloe Castle

Killarney, Co. Kerry
Tel: (064) 44111; Fax: (064) 44583

A modern hotel set in the most fabulous gardens leading to the ruins of the old castle itself. The park is host to a remarkable award-winning botanical collection of rare flowers and plants as well to grazing Hafflinger horses. The surrounding countryside is famous for walking, fishing and riding, with tennis and swimming on the premises and a golf course opposite the hotel. What could be more satisfying than relaxing here in the gourmet restaurant after a day of sporting activity in one of Ireland's loveliest spots?

Rates: *Single room with breakfast from IR£104; double room with breakfast from IR£124.* V

● *102 en suite bedrooms, one suite, all with satellite TV, direct-dial telephone, hairdryer, laundry service, 24-hour room service.* ● *Table d'hôte dinner £29; lunch & special diets available; last orders 9.30 pm.* ● *Free river fishing, golf adjacent, jogging track, riding, indoor swimming pool, indoor tennis. Historical gardens, sailing, squash nearby. Shooting by arrangement.* ● *Open May - October. All credit cards exc JAC*

The Bianconi

Annadale Road, Puckfair,
Killorglin, Kerry
Tel: (066) 976 1146;
Fax: (066) 976 1950

I had received many recommendations about the Bianconi. Reports spoke of a high standard of cuisine, a vibrant but relaxed atmosphere and comfortable bedrooms with the facilities a weary traveller might need. They were right! The Bianconi is located on the banks of the river Laune in the centre of Killorglin - a well known tourist area on the Ring of Kerry. Consequently you need to book ahead particularly in high season. Ray Sheehy, the owner, together with his brother Rick, own and manage this very popular country inn. Dinner is served in The Art Gallery Restaurant, so called as the works of local artists adorn the walls. Cuisine is traditional Irish with French influences; there is an excellent selection of fish, local vegetables and irresistible desserts. After dinner a nightcap at the bar, with a piano tinkling in the background, provides a good opportunity to meet the locals! There are many and varied activities in the area: golf, salmon fishing, deer stalking, and, of course, hill walking. All can be arranged through the Bianconi management. For good value, comfort and charming, helpful staff, the Bianconi is an excellent stopping off point on the ring of Kerry.

Rates: *Single room with breakfast from IR£45; double from IR£65.* V

- *16 en suite bedrooms, with colour TV+ satellite, direct-dial telephone, laundry service, hairdryer, tea/coffee making facilities, safety deposit box.*
- *3-course table d'hôte dinner £20. A la carte, lunch & special diets available. Last orders 9 pm.*
- *Fishing, sailing, golf, shooting, tennis, riding, walking, deer stalking all nearby. Ample parking.*
- *Airport pickup, car rental by arrangement.*
- *Open all year. Credit cards accepted.*

Killarney 9, Limerick 63, Cork 63, Dublin 204.

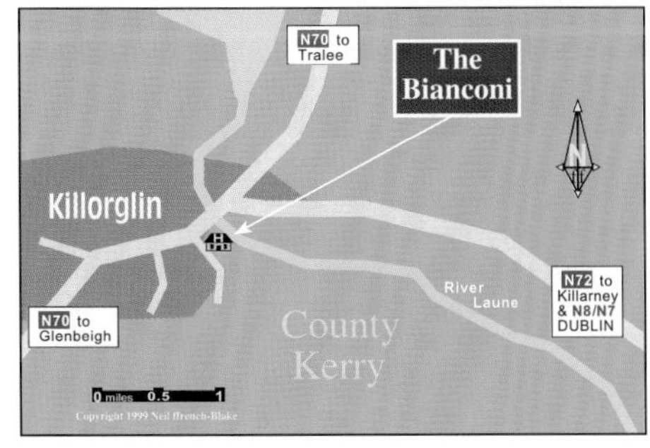

Carrig House Country House & Restaurant

Caragh Lake, Killorglin, Ring of Kerry
Tel: 00353 (0) 66 976 9100;
Fax: 00353 (0) 66 976 9166

Once you leave the main road, you know you are heading somewhere special. You are about to discover one of the best kept secrets in Ireland. This charming and meticulously restored Victorian residence has a sense of timelessness about it. It is perched on the shores of Lake Caragh in Kerry with some of the cleanest air in Europe, beautiful gardens and spectacular views across the still waters to the Kerry mountains. The restaurant overlooks the lake and serves the freshest Irish food with salmon and trout from the lake, succulent Kerry lamb from the hill, wild game and organic vegetables from the hotel's own garden. Frank Slattery is a most welcoming host and Mary has done a wonderful job with the decor and with fresh flowers in all public rooms. This area of Kerry has sailing, climbing, golf, archaeological sites and some of the best walks in the southwest within easy reach. Carrig only opened in 1997 but has already established a considerable reputation. Be sure to reserve well in advance as its popularity can only grow.

Rates: *Single room with breakfast from IR£68; double from IR£92.* V
Bargain Breaks: *On application.*

- *9 en suite bedrooms (one suite) with colour TV, direct-dial telephone, radio/alarm clock, hairdryer, tea/coffee making facilities.*
- *Extensive table d'hôte and à la carte dining; special diets available. Last dinner orders 21.00 hrs*
- *Rock climbing, sailing, golf, cycling, canoeing, fishing, boating walking all nearby.*
- *Closed 24-26 Dec, Jan & Feb. Car parking for 20*
- *Visa, Mastercard, Diners credit cards accepted.*

Killorglin 3, Killarney 16, Limerick 66, Cork 66, Dublin 207

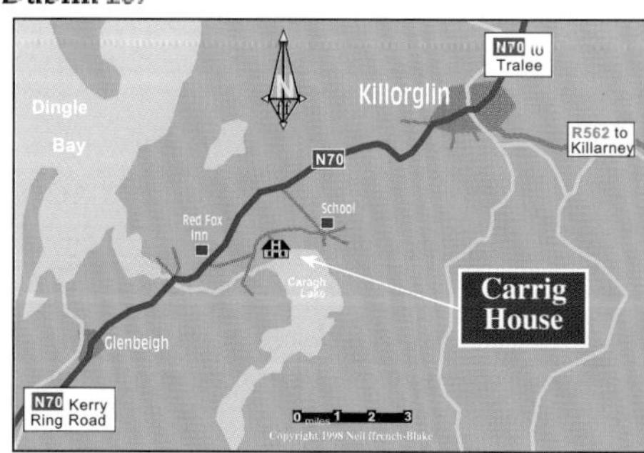

Brandon Hotel

Princes St, Tralee, Co. Kerry
Tel: (066) 712 3333; Fax: (066) 712 5019

The Brandon is one of Tralee's oldest established hotels, situated in the centre of town. Being one of Tralee's largest hotels, the Brandon is frequently host to corporate conferences and large groups. But this should not discourage the individual traveller or family. The Brandon has the air and tranquillity of a comfortably run establishment that knows its business and looks after each guest as an individual. There is a fully equipped leisure centre with a beauty salon including even a hydrotherapy bath. The Galleon Restaurant has been highly acclaimed for its imaginative menus. Situated at the foot of the Slieve Mish mountains, Tralee has a superb range of visitor attractions, leisure activities and outdoor pursuits. It is a paradise for touring and rambling. At night its pubs and restaurants come alive to give you a true Irish welcome. Reasonably priced, the Brandon offers the traveller good accommodation, excellent facilities, a renowned restaurant and the lively Fiddlers Bar - all located in the centre of Tralee. A recommended stop over location on the way to the Dingle peninsula.

Rates: *Single with breakfast from £58; double inc breakfast from £90.* V
Bargain Breaks: *On application.*

- *186 en suite bedrooms, all with colour TV+ satellite, direct-dial telephone, hairdryer, laundry/ valet service, minibar (Regent rooms),tea/coffee making, radio/alarm clock, safe, trouser press. Non-smoker and disabled bedrooms available.*
- *A la carte restaurant, last orders 9.45 pm; lunch & special diets available.*
- *Full business services inc. 7 meeting rooms to 400; car parking for 450; airport pickup and car rental by arrangament.*
- *Gym/fitness centre, jacuzzi, massage, sauna, indoor pool, beauty salon. Tennis, riding, fishing one mile. Golf, watersports, sailing six miles.*
- *Open all year. All major credit cards accepted.*

Killarney 20, Limerick 64, Cork 74, Dublin 185.

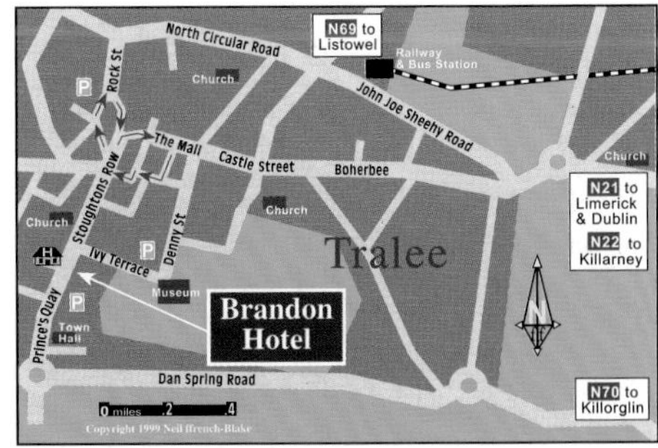

Meadowlands Hotel

Oakpark, Tralee, Co Kerry
Tel: (066) 718 0444; Fax: (066) 718 0964
E-mail: medlands @iol.ie

A charming and intimate hotel set in a quiet corner of Tralee in its own three acres of landscape gardens. It is fast gaining a reputation for excellent accommodation, service and good food. Open fires are a feature throughout the hotel. Hotel proprietor Paddy O'Mahoney owns his own fishing boats, so the *An Pota Stóir* Restaurant is guaranteed the freshest of locally caught seafood and shellfish within hours of the boat's landing! The restaurant is unique with its own character and charm, set on two levels and with clever use of colour, tile and timber throughout. The Meadowlands is an ideal base for touring the Dingle peninsula, Ring of Kerry, Killarney Lakes and West Cork. There are many golf courses nearby. Tralee itself is renowned for its hospitality and as a tourist centre. Its famous Rose of Tralee festival is the highlight of the town's activities. Other local attractions include The Aqua Dome at Ballyard, Ireland's largest indoor water world leisure complex with Tralee Steam Railway adjoining.

***Rates:** Single room with breakfast from IR£60. Double inc. breakfast £90-120.*
***Leisure Breaks**: 2 nts, b & b + 1 dinner £110-115; 3 nts b & b + 2 dinners £162-185; 7 nts b & b £266-315; 7 nts dinner, b & b £434-490. All rates nett per person sharing. Single supplement +£15 pn.*

● *27 en suite bedrooms (3 suites) with radio, satellite TV, airconditioning, direct-dial telephone; hairdryer, laundry service, trouser press. Non-smoker and disabled bedrooms available.*
● *Table d''hôte £25; à la carte, lunch & special diets available; last orders 9.15 pm. Car parking 120.*
● *Full business services inc. meeting room to 30*
● *Indoor pool, fitness centre/gym 1/2 mile; watersports 2m, riding 5m, golf 10m, fishing 7m*
● *Closed 24/25 Dec. All major cards accepted.*
Killarney 20, Lim erick 64, Cork 74, Dublin 185.

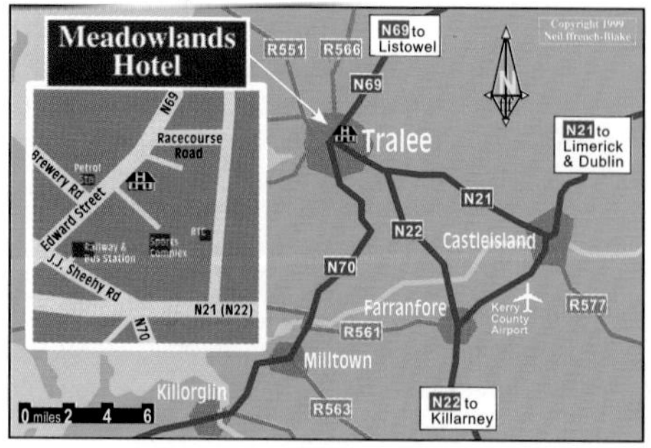

Dowdstown Hotel

Straffan Road, Maynooth, Co Kildare
Tel: (01) 628 5002; Fax: (01) 628 9781
E-mail: manager@dowdstownhotel.ie

Dowdstown was a former stud farm that has been cleverly converted into a modern hotel utilising the yard to form a central quadrangle with the main hotel complex and bedrooms located on four sides of the square. The elegant Courtyard Restaurant is the perfect place to entertain or be entertained. Cuisine is Irish and International with an extensive wine list. A carvery lunch is available daily and there is also an evening bar menu. The Horseshoe Bar has a large collection of memorabilia on that most famous of Irish racehorses - Arkle, who is buried nearby. Bedrooms are comfortable and include three family apartments. The hotel can also cater for weddings or conferences of up to 200 people. Maynooth has an abundance of sights - Co Kildare being the centre of the Irish bloodstock industry. There are many stud farms nearby and the Irish National Stud is at Kildare Town. Dowdstown is convenient for Dublin City Centre (20 minutes) and for the airport (25 minutes) and is thus a good starting or finishing point for an Irish holiday.

***Rates:** Single room with breakfast from £59; double room inc. breakfast from £79.*
***Bargain Breaks:** Details on application.*

- *22 en suite bedrooms (inc 3 family suites), all with airconditioning, colour TV+satellite, direct-dial telephone, hairdryer, laundry service, tea/coffee making facilities, wake-up call service, safety deposit box, trouser press. Non smoker and disabled bedrooms available.*
- *Table d'hôte £25; à la carte, lunch & special diets available; last orders 2130.*
- *Fishing, golf,shooting,tennis, riding nearby.*
- *Busines services inc 2 meeting rooms 20-100.*
- *Airport pickup & car rental by arrangement*
- *Open All Year (exc Xmas Day). Major credit cards accepted.*

Naas 7, Dublin Airport 20, Dublin Centre 17.

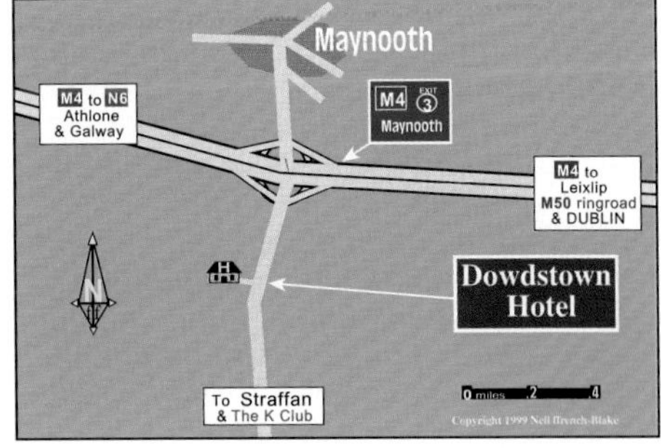

Ashford Castle

Cong, Co. Mayo
Tel: (092) 46003; Fax: (092) 46260

This splendid place is situated in acres of gardens and parkland on the shores of Lough Corrib, and to come here is to visit a stately home with suits of armour, fine furnishings and beautiful paintings set amidst rooms decorated with rich panelling and lit by chandeliers, Here too you can relax in the conservatory or the Dungeon Bar, where you will be entertained in the evening by harpist, pianist or folk singer. There are two elegant restaurants in character with the hotel - the main George V Room and the intimate à la carte Connaught Room. The food is superb as you would expect, with ample use of the local produce of fish and lamb. The bedrooms, including several suites, and the bathrooms are both very large - they have been refurbished to a de luxe standard having all luxuries and facilities - plus lovely views over the lake. Ashford Castle offers countless leisure activities including its own 9-hole golf course and fully equipped gym. Nothing has been overlooked in the efforts to please guests - it is the sort of place that exists in dreams but this is a reality and to stay here is a very pleasurable experience.

***Rates:** Single room with breakfast from £175; double room with breakfast £195.* V
***Bargain Breaks:** From £240 pp sharing, 2 nights b& b + 1 dinner 1.11.99-22.12.99 and 3.1.00-31.3.00.*

- *83 en suite bedrooms with TV+satellite, direct-dial telephone, hairdryer, trouser press, laundry service, safety deposit box, 24-hour room service.*
- *Table d'hôte fm £24. A la carte, lunch & special diets available; last orders 9.30 pm.*
- *Business centre inc. conference room, cap. 110.*
- *Billiards/snooker, fitness centre/gym, jacuzzi, jogging track, massage, sauna, 9-hole golf on site. Fishing, 18-hole golf, riding, clay shooting, tennis, cruising & archery can be arranged.*
- *Open all year. All major credit cards accepted.*

Headford 10, Galway 28, Ballina 49, Dublin 160.

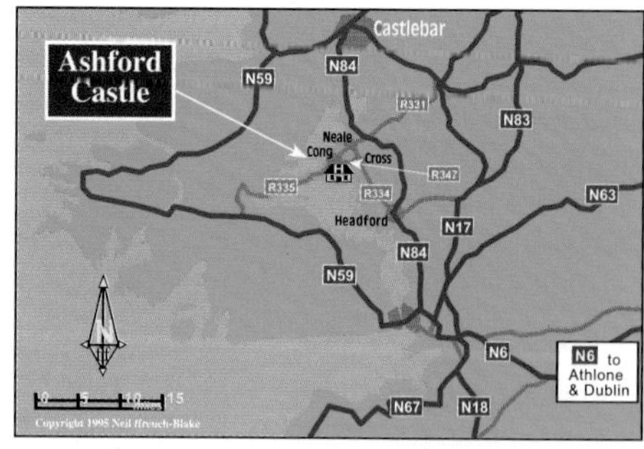

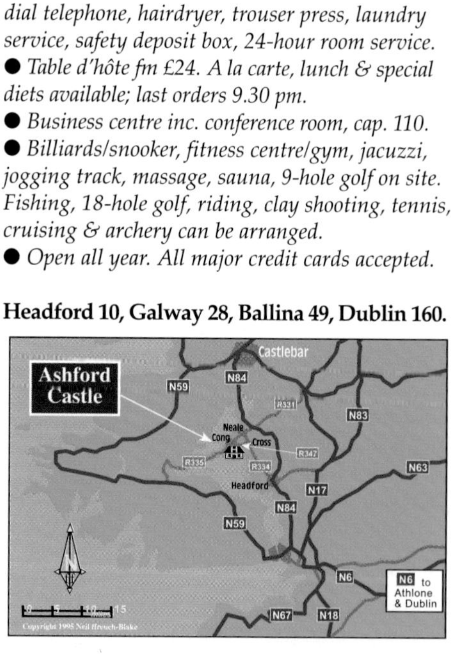

Kinnitty Castle

Kinnitty, Birr, Co Offaly
Tel: (0509) 37318; Fax: (0509) 37284
E-mail: kinnittycastle@tinet.ie

The history and background of Kinnitty Castle is like a short history of Ireland. It has its roots in fable, has frequently succumbed to attack and has risen with pride from its own ashes. The present phoenix arose after destruction in 1929. Why is Kinnitty such a centre of interest? The answer can be found by simply visiting this resplendent Gothic edifice standing in woodlands on the slopes of the Slieve Bloom Hills. First the sheer size and beauty of the estate is enough to engender four of the seven deadly sins; secondly its strategic position in the centre of Ireland, $1^1/_2$ hours from Dublin, Limerick and Galway; thirdly - its wealth of wildlife and game make it a paradise for almost every country pursuit; and there is now a fourth attraction - a dedication to good food and wine. The hotel has recently undergone a £3 million refurbishment which puts it among Ireland's leading luxury hotels. An elegant restaurant offers gourmet cuisine and equestrian holidays, from pony trekking to fox hunting, are a speciality. Other field sports, miles of woodland trails and golf & fishing nearby make Kinnitty a real country hideaway that will particularly appeal to the overseas visitor.

Rates: *Single room with breakfast £95; double room inc. breakfast £160.* V
Bargain Breaks: *weekends 2 nights b & b + 1 dinner pp sharing from £175; midweek from £155 pp.*

- *37 en suite bedrooms (inc 4 four-posters), all with direct-dial telephone, hairdryer, 24-hr room service, radio/alarm clock.*
- *Table d'hôte dinner £28. Light lunches & vegetarian options available; last orders 9.30 pm.*
- *Full business services inc. conference rooms to 250*
- *Jacuzzi, massage, sauna, shooting, tennis, riding, hunting, archery, quad bikes at hotel. Fishing and golf nearby. Airport pickup on request.*
- *Open all year. Major credit cards accepted*

Birr 8, Athlone 28, Limerick 58, Dublin 79.

The Horse and Jockey Inn

A8 Main Road, Nr. Thurles, Co Tipperary
Tel: (0504) 44192; Fax: (0504) 44747
E-mail: horseandjockeyinn@tinet.ie
Internet: http://www.horse-jockey-inn.htm

If you are at all interested in equestrian sports, be it racing, hunting or just hacking or if you just appreciate the beauty of horses, then this is the place for you! This inspector has to confess that he had driven past the Horse & Jockey many times without entering..... now that he has, he will return time and time again. The visitor should not be put off by the location of the Horse & Jockey on a great traditional crossroads of Ireland, North / South and East / West. It has been trading for over 250 years. Recently the owner, a quiet and charming soul, has refurbished the whole building - adding on bedrooms to create a blend of luxury and unspoiled friendliness. My room was very comfortable, and the bathroom had big brass taps, fluffy white towels and many little luxuries. I spent a long time looking at the many equestrian pictures and memorabilia on the walls of the public rooms. Well known jockeys and trainers gaze down from the dining room walls - Mick Kinane, Enda Bulga, Charlie Swan, Jamie Spenser and Aidan O'Brien to name just a few. You might even find yourself sitting next to one of them as several of Ireland's leading racecourses, training yards and studs are nearby. There are books and old photographs to look at in the hotel's comfortable sitting rooms. There is even an hotel shop with designer clothes, local pottery and jewellery.

***Rates:** Single room inc. breakfast from IR£45; double inc. breakfast from IR£75.* V

● *33 en suite rooms with direct-dial telephone, satellite TV, hairdryer, laundry service, tea/coffee making, radio/alarm clock, safe, trouser press. Non-smoker and disabled bedrooms available.*
● *A la carte restaurant; lunch & special diets available. Last orders 9.45 pm. Hotel shop.*
● *Open all year. All major credit cards accepted.*
Thurles 5, Cashel 9, Limerick 47, Dublin 87.

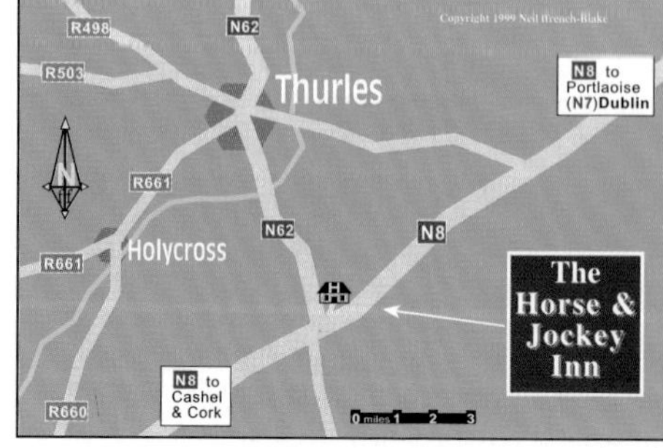

Crookedwood House

Crookedwood, Mullingar,
Co. Westmeath
Tel: (044) 72165; Fax: (044) 72166
E-mail: cwoodhse@iol.ie
Internet: http://www.iol.ie~cwoodhse

Noel and Julie Kenny started at Crookedwood in 1989 running a restaurant, which through necessity blossomed into a restaurant and guesthouse. Bedrooms are generous in size and provide every hotel convenience. The restaurant is cosy and intimate in what used to be the old wine cellars and Noel is a fine chef, having won several awards including the *Egon Ronay Irish Beef Award* in 1996. He makes skilled use of local meat, game and venison, accompanied by home-grown fresh vegetables and an extensive wine list. Crookedwood used to be the Taghmon Parish Rectory and stands next door to the 15th-century Taghmon Church overlooking Lough Derravaragh. Other historic sites in the vicinity include Tullynally Castle, Multyfarnhan Franciscan Friary and Fore Abbey. Otherwise fishing, golf and horse riding are available nearby and the staff will be pleased to advise visitors on the best local walks, golf courses, fishing rivers and lakes to explore in order to work up a good appetite for dinner! Crookedwood offers splendid food in a glorious setting. Small wonder the Irish Times wrote: *"Well worth a trip to the Midlands"*

Rates: *Single inc. breakfast from IR£32.50; double from IR£45.* V

- *8 rooms, all non-smoking & en suite, with colour TV, direct-dial telephone, hairdryer.*
- *Table d'hôte dinner £25. A la carte, lunch & special diets available. Last orders 9 pm.*
- *Private dining room 10-30 persons. House open Tuesday-Saturday and Sunday lunch.*
- *Golf, riding, fishing, tennis, croquet nearby.*
- *Open all year. Major credit cards accepted.*

Mullingar 6, Longford 25, Cavan 27, Drogheda 33, Dublin 55.

<u>*Directions:*</u> *Coming from Dublin, take 3rd exit on Mullingar bypass (signed Castlepollard) - drive to Crookedwood Village. Turn right at the Wood Pub, 2 km further you will see the house.*

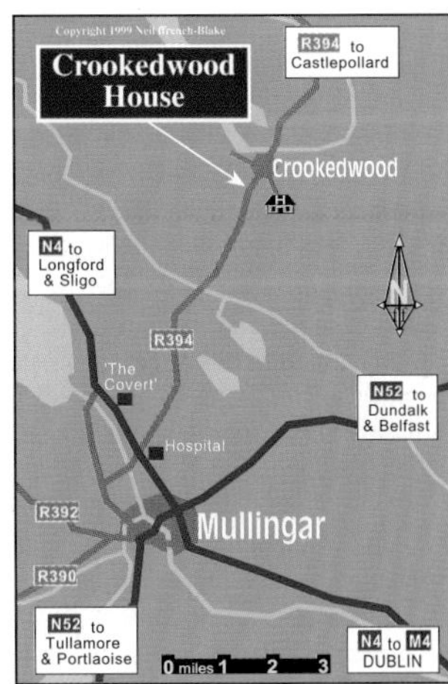

Rathsallagh Country House & Golf Club

Dunlavin, Co. Wicklow
Tel: (+353) 45 403112; Fax: (+353) 45 403343
E-mail: info@rathsallagh.com
Internet: http://www.rathsallagh.com

The approach to Rathsallagh is a long drive bisecting the golf course. Happily there are cattle grids whose rattle reminds golfers to give way to cars when making their swings! Rathsallagh was converted from a Queen Anne stable block into a comfortable country house with bags of charm and character. It sits in 530 acres of mature parkland. Joe and Kay O'Flynn will make you feel at ease with all home comforts and excellent food prepared from local ingredients, where possible. Breakfast is special at the house - there are big enticing silver domes on the sideboard and bread is home made. Indeed Rathsallagh has won the National Breakfast Award three times. The golf course was designed by Peter McEvoy and Irish professional Christy O'Connor and is laid out to 252 acres of lush parkland, with mature trees, natural water hazards, USGA-specification greens and a gently rolling landscape, belying its age. Rathsallagh is only an hour's drive from Dublin. It makes the perfect spot for a peaceful holiday for golfer and non-golfer alike.

Rates: *Single room inc. breakfast IR£95-110; double inc. breakfast £210.* V
Bargain Breaks: *Two nights dinner, b&b £219-£269 pp sharing. Same with 2 rounds of golf £254-£304. Midweek from £180 pp sharing.*

- *17 en suite bedrooms all with colour TV, direct-dial telephone, hairdryer, laundry service, tea/coffee making. Non-smoker & disabled rooms available.*
- *Table d'hôte dinner from £35; lunch & special diets available. Last orders 9 pm.*
- *Business services inc 3 meeting rooms, cap. up to 100. Airport pickup; car rental by arr't. Car parking*
- *Billiards/snooker, croquet, golf, indoor games, massage, sauna, clay shooting, indoor pool, tennis, archery. Fishing, riding locally.*
- *Open all year exc. 23-27 Dec.*
- *All major credit cards accepted.*

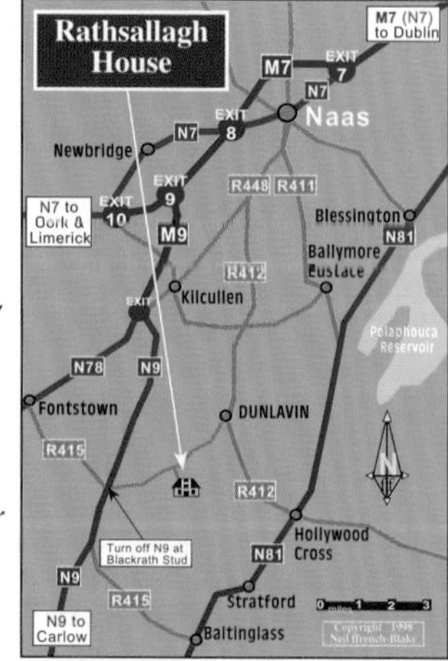

Humewood Castle

Kiltegan, Co. Wicklow
Tel: (+353) 508 73215; Fax: (+353) 508 73382; E-mail: Humewood@iol.ie

Humewood is indeed a fairytale castle with battlements and granite towers. It is not an hotel but a private house and sporting estate. Guests are invited to bring guns, jodhpurs, fishing tackle and hiking boots for an exceptional sporting stay. Shooting is allowed in Ireland on Sundays and the pheasant and duck shooting season can be extended till February 15th. Trail riding is on the doorstep and a day's hunting with the Kildare can be arranged. Trout and pike fishing is from four lakes on the estate. Any feeling one might have on entering of an austere or intimidating castle is immediately banished by the warm, welcoming, family atmosphere inside. Humewood was completed in 1870 for Hume Dick, MP for Co Wicklow. Each piece of furniture fits the period. I particularly admired the four-poster beds. Each bedroom has its own theme. Food is delicious and served in one of the two dining rooms. Humewood has been awarded the American Five Star Diamond Award twice - in 1997 and 1998. The castle can accommodate small conferences and banquets for up to 80.

***Rates:** Single room inc. breakfast from IR£200; double from IR£280; suite from IR£420.*

- *13 en suite bedrooms, all with colour TV+ satellite, direct-dial telephone, hairdryer, laundry service. All bedrooms non-smoking.*
- *Table d'hôte dinner £45. Lunch & special diets available.*
- *Business services inc. meeting room to 20. Receptions up to 80 seated/120 cocktail. Car parking.*
- *Snooker, croquet, fishing, jogging track, massage, clay (20+ traps) and game shooting, polo, riding, 3-day event course, trail riding, hunting, bike riding, hill walking, falconry. Golf 20 miles.*
- *Open all year. Mastercard, Visa, Amex accepted.*

Baltinglass 6, Carlow 20, Wicklow 30, Dublin 40.

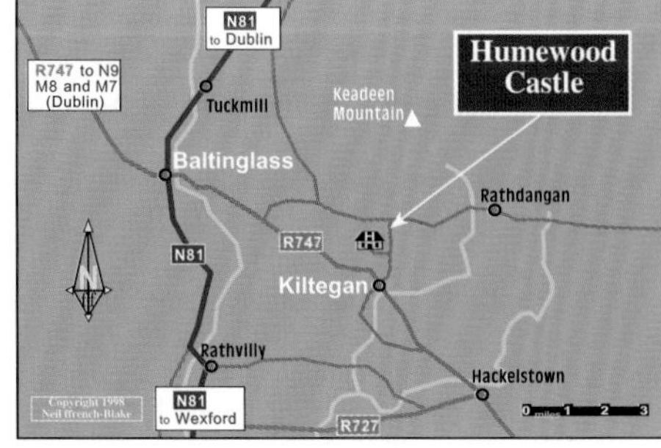

Signpost and Ireland

The founder of Signpost, W G McMinnies, travelled extensively in Ireland, and, although Ireland was not included in the first 1935 edition, he dedicated a special edition to the country in 1950 (see cover illustration on right). Thereafter Ireland was included until the early eighties, then there was a break until the 1996 edition. Now we are pleased to report that some 20% of all our pages are devoted to Hibernia. We thought readers would be interested to read the extracts below from the 1950 edition as well as to see entries from two hotels who have featured both in the first Irish edition and in this Diamond Jubilee Edition.

In 1950 Great Britain was still in the throes of rationing, so that the grandfather of the present publisher wrote: "*My three-week tour cost £10-12 a week, staying at the best hotels... Remember that food is not subsidised in Eire...A butcher I picked up told me that the country was overflowing with meat and bacon and he couldn't understand why Britain did not take more, and that the oat crop was so large that the surplus was fed to animals...this seems as strange as the fact that Eire has ample petrol and that such things as sweets, tobacco and drink are all easily obtainable.*"

As to finding his way around..." *Instructions on finding the way, generally with an airy wave of the hand 'keep switching off' or 'keep straight on to the left'. Often I was told to turn right, while my informant waved his left hand to make sure I understood.*" There are tales of Ireland's most unorthodox hotel-keeper, Major Dermot Freyer of the then Corrymore House Hotel on Achill Island, County Mayo, who charged guests a few shillings if he liked them or even nothing at all if they helped by chopping wood or doing a job in the house, or a guinea if he didn't like them! But then, as his successors are today, Mr McMinnies was everywhere made to feel most welcome and was bowled over by the charm of the country and its people. This he communicated to his readers and we hope we may emulate him today.

Top: Parknasilla Great Southern Hotel in 1950. See page 261 for today's hotel.
Below: Cover of the 1950 SIGNPOST to Ireland, featuring the editor.

Telephone : Sneem 3 — 67

Cö. Kerry (E), Park-nasilla

ON THE NORTH BANK OF KENMARE RIVER ESTUARY.

Kenmare 19½, Sneem 2½, Killarney 30.

(For position see map on page 8, square B.7).

THIS Great Southern Railway hotel is indeed fortunate in its setting for behind it are luxuriantly wooded hills, and great spreads of rhododendrons, eucalyptus, rose and pine trees and semi-tropical flowers of many kinds. In front sea and river merge, promontories, scores of islets accessible by bridge or boat and distant coastline bewildering the onlooker as to which is mainland and which is not. Out of this famous and lovely setting rises a fine 100 room stone-built hotel recently enlarged. Judging by the gaily coloured crowd and the buzz of conversation in the cocktail bar before lunch, a good time was being had by all. And there is no doubt that the place lays itself out to maintain the party spirit for they dance every night and people soon get together for expeditions, fishing, picnics, bathing, boating, walking and so on. Tennis and golf are available too on the spot. I enjoyed my lunch served by attractive maids in buff aprons and port coloured uniform. Bedroom equipment and detail work were entirely satisfactory. Daily from 35/-. Other Great Southern hotels at Killarney, Mallaranny, Galway, Sligo and Kenmare.

Telephone : Office, Portmarnock 16 ; Visitors, Portmarnock 50 — 53

Co. Dublin (E), Nr. Dublin, Portmarnock Country Club.

ON THE COAST BETWEEN HOWTH AND MALAHIDE.

Dublin 11, Howth 6, Malahide 2.

(For position see map on page 7, square I.7).

MR. J. P. GALVIN and his good wife, who incidentally at one time ran the best hotel in Vienna, were both wise and fortunate to take over this millionaire's home from the Irish Tourist Board. And being keen and competent hotelkeepers they have naturally endowed this beautifully appointed place with food, service and facilities to match its quality. Before looking round let me say that the house lies alongside the famous golf course and a wonderful stretch of sand and bathing beach. There is a longish view south towards Dublin and Ireland's Eye while at hand is a sheltered and semi-tropical garden where you can laze at your leisure. And now for the inside. Here there is the immediate appeal of spacious and well proportioned apartments, soft colour scheming and really comfortable detail work. There's a fine dining room where I enjoyed a first-class dinner. In my bedroom the lighting over bed and shaving mirror was excellent, the bed cosy and the appointments delightful and complete. The fresh cork carpeted bathroom provided almost boiling water and was a joy to use. All this inevitably produces a feeling of well-being, nay even of opulence, in the heart of a visitor. In conclusion please note that you can use the place though it is called a Country Club and that there's no nonsense like there is in Britain about having to join before you get a drink. Weekly 10-15 gns. according to season.

***Right:** Portmarnock Golf & Country Club in 1950. See page 252 for today's hotel.*
***Below:** 'Obstacles to enforce a reduced speed limit at the bridge near Yougal, Co Cork' 1950*

SPORTING AND CONFERENCE FACILITIES

Sporting and conference facilities to be found at *Signpost* hotels are tabulated on the following pages. This section is arranged by regions within England, Wales, Scotland, the Channel Islands and Ireland and by counties within each country.

KEY

- ● Facilities available at hotel
- ❍ Facilities available within five miles of the hotel
- ✪ Special arrangements can be made by the hotel

TRADE DESCRIPTIONS ACT 1968
The facilities in italics in each hotel entry are submitted each year to us by hotels but the comments on each hotel are the personal opinion of a member of the Signpost team as he or she found it. Due to a number of factors such as changes in management or chefs, we are unable to guarantee that the visitor will find any particular hotel in the exact state that our inspectors found it or will have the same opinion of it. We are therefore not responsible for eventual disappointment but we try to include in the book a wide range of hotels and we sincerely hope that guests will agree with our inspectors' choice. Please use the Report Forms on the following page if you would like to make any particular comments.

PRICES. Please note that the prices quoted to us by establishments listed in this book date, in most cases, from mid-1998 and are liable to amendment by the hotels without prior notice.

Page	Other	Watersports	Tennis	Swimming pool	Squash/badminton	Shooting	Sea/river bathing	Sauna/solarium	Sailing/boating	Riding	Massage	Jogging track	Jacuzzi/whirlpool	Indoor games	Golf	Gym/fitness centre	Fishing	Croquet	Conferences	Billiards/snooker
ENGLAND - The West Country																				
CORNWALL																				
6 Royal Duchy Hotel, Falmouth				●		○	●	●	○	○					✪		○			●
7 Greenbank Hotel & Retreat, Falmouth	Diving, yacht cahrters							●	●	○							●		●	●
8 Meudon Hotel, Mawnan Smith		○	○		○		●		○	○					✪		●			●
10 Polurrian Hotel, Lizard Peninsula			●	●	●	○	●	●	○				●	●	○	●	○		●	●
11 Coombe Farm, Nr. Looe		○	○	○	○										○					●
12 Hannafore Point, West Looe	Hydrotherap, diving	○		●	●			●	○		✪			●	○	●	○		●	
14 Crantock Bay Hotel, Newquay		●	●	●	○		○	●	○	○		●	●	●	✪	●	○	●	●	●
15 Cross House Hotel		○							○	○	○				○		○			
16 Port Gaverne Hotel, Port Isaac							●		○	○					○		○			
17 Trevaunance Point Hotel, St Agnes		●					●			○	●				○		●			
18 Carlyon Bay Hotel, St Austell		○				○			○	●					●		○		●	●
19 Boskerris Hotel, St Ives	Putting green		○	●			○		○						○					
20 The Garrack Hotel, St Ives		○	○	○	○	○		●		○			●		○	●	○		●	
21 Alverton Manor, Truro			○	○	●	○		○	●	○	○				●	○		○	●	●
DEVON																				
22 The Berry Head Hotel, Brixham	Boules		○	○	○	○	●		○	○					○		○		●	
23 Quayside Hotel, Brixham																			●	
24 Hoops Country Inn, Bideford		○	●	○		○	○		○	○		●	●		○		○	●	●	●
25 The Cottage Hotel, Hope Cove							●		●					●	○				●	
26 Buckland-tout-Saints, Kingsbridge	Helipad		○		○	✪	○		○	○								●	●	
27 Thurlestone Hotel		✪	●	●	●	✪		●	○	○	●		●	●	○	●	✪	●	●	●
28 Collavon Manor, Okehampton	Bowls				●													●		
30 Bolt Head Hotel, Salcombe	Private moorings		○	●					●								●			
31 Tides Reach Hotel, Salcombe		●	○	●	●		●	●	●	○	●				○	●	●			●
32 Saunton Sands Hotel, Saunton Sands			●	●	●	●	●	●	●	●					○		●		●	●
34 The Victoria Hotel, Sidmouth	Putting	✪	●	●	○		●	●	●	○			●				✪		●	●
35 Royal Glen Hotel, Sidmouth	Surfing		○	●			●								○					
36 The Osborne Hotel, Torquay	+Indoor pool. Putting lawn	○	●	●			○	●							○		○		●	●
37 Woolacombe Bay Hotel, Woolacombe	Short mat bowls, yacht		●	●		○	●	●	●	○			●		●	●	○		●	●
38 Kitley House, nr Plymouth		○	○		○	●	●		○	○		●			○	●	●		●	

SOMERSET																				
40 Hunstrete House, Chelwood, Nr Bath		●	●													●	●			
41 Walnut Tree Hotel, Bridgwater		●											●							
42 Bindon Country House Hotel, Wellington		●	●	○		○					○				○		●	●		
Central Southern England																				
BERKSHIRE																				
46 The Swan Diplomat, Streatley-on-Thames		●		○	●	○		●			○	✪	●		○		●	○		Bike hire, beautician
DORSET																				
47 Manor Hotel, Dorchester		●				○					○			●						
48 Knoll House Hotel, Studland Bay				○	●	●	●	●			○	○	●	●			●	●		Windsurfing
50 Manor House Hotel, Studland Bay						○					●	○		○				●		
HAMPSHIRE																				
51 Tylney Hall, Hook	●	●	●		●	○	●	●	●		○	●		●		●	●	○		+ Indoor pool.
52 Royal Hotel, Winchester	●		○							○							○			
WILTSHIRE																				
53 Beechfield House, Melksham		●	●	●		○					○				○	○	●	○		
London &The South-East																				
EAST SUSSEX																				
74a Little Hemingfold Hotel, Battle		●	●	●		○					○	●				○	●	●		Boules
68 Grand Hotel, Eastbourne	●	●		○	●	○		●		●	○	○	●	●	○	○	●	●	○	+ Indoor pool
69 Lansdowne Hotel, Eastbourne	●	●				○	●													Putting, bridge
70 Ashdown Park Hotel, Forest Row	●	●	●		●	●		●	●	●	○		●				○	●		
71 Beauport Park, Hastings		●				●					●						●	●		
72 Flackley Ash Hotel, Peasmarsh		●	●		●	○		●					●				●			Putting green
KENT																				
74b Thanington Hotel, Canterbury	●																●			
75 Walletts Court, Nr. Dover			●	●		○								○						
76 Stade Court, Hythe	○	●	○		○	○	○	○		○		●	○	●		○		○		
SURREY																				
77 Coulsdon Manor, Coulsdon		●			●	●							●			●		●		
78 Chase Lodge, Kingston-upon-Thames		●			○	○					○					○	○	○		
80 Oatlands Park Hotel, Weybridge		●	●		●															

Page	East of England BEDFORDSHIRE 85 The Woburn Arms	HERTFORDSHIRE 87 Redcoats Farmhouse Hotel, Hitchin	LINCOLNSHIRE 88 Kenwick Park Hotel, Louth	NORFOLK 90 Links Country Park Hotel, Cromer	91a The Hoste Arms, Burnham Market	91b Elderton Lodge, Thorpe Market	SUFFOLK 92 Wentworth Hotel, Aldeburgh	93 The Angel, Bury St Edmunds	94 Hintlesham Hall, Nr Ipswich	95 Bedford Lodge Hotel, Newmarket	96 The Swan, Southwold	The Heart of England DERBYSHIRE 104 Riverside House Hotel, Ashford-in-the-Water	106 The Peacock Hotel, Rowsley	GLOUCESTERSHIRE 107 The Swan Hotel, Bibury	109 Burleigh Court, Minchinhampton	110 Hare & Hounds, Westonbirt
Other						Helipad			Beauty salon, cookery	Beauty salon					Putting green	
Watersports	○				○			○								
Tennis		○	●	●	○		○		●		○				○	●
Swimming pool			●	●					●	●					●	
Squash/badminton			●				○		○						○	●
Shooting					○	○			●			○		○		
Sea/river bathing				●	○		●		●							
Sauna/solarium			●	●					○	●						
Sailing/boating					○		○		○		○				●	
Riding	○			●	○	○		○	●		○	○		○		
Massage			●						●							
Jogging track									●							
Jacuzzi/whirlpool			●						●	●						
Indoor games			●												●	
Golf	○		●	●		○	○	○	●		○			○	○	○
Gym/fitness centre	○		●						●	●						
Fishing								○	○		○	○	●	●		
Croquet									●		●					●
Conferences	●	●	●	●	●	●	●	●	●	●				●		●
Billiards/snooker			●						●							●

LEICESTERSHIRE																				
111 Stapleford Park, Nr. Melton Mowbray			●	○		○			●	●	●				●			○		Falconry
NOTTINGHAMSHIRE																				
113 Langar Hall, Langar		●		●		○														
114 The Old England. Nr. Newark		●		○		○									○					
WARWICKSHIRE																				
115 Stratford Victoria, Stratford-upon-Avon		●			●			●												
WORCESTERSHIRE																				
116 The Dormy House, Broadway	●	●	●	●	●	●	●		●		●	●	●		●			●		
117 Cottage in the Wood, Malvern Wells		●				○					○				○	○				
The North West																				
CHESHIRE																				
122 Sutton Hall Hotel, Macclesfield		●				○					○							○		
CUMBRIA																				
123 Rothay Manor Hotel, Ambleside		●		○	○							○						○		
124 Wateredge Hotel, Ambleside		●		●	○							●		●						
125 Appleby Manor Country House Hotel	●	●		○	●	○	●	●			○		●			○	●			
126 Armathwaite Hall, Bassenthwaite Lake	●	●	●	●	●	○		●	●	●	●		●		●		●	●		Falconry
127 Graythwaite Manor Hotel, Grange-o-Sands	●	●				○					○						○	●		
128 Netherwood Hotel, Grange-over-Sands		●		○	●						○	●	●	●	○	○	●	○		
129 Dale Head Hall Lakeside Hotel, Keswick		●		●	○	○						●			●	○		●		
130 Hilton Keswick Lodore Hotel, Keswick	●		✪	●	○					○	○	●			●	●	●			
131 Scafelll Hotel, Nr. Keswick				○		✪					●	○		○				✪		
132 Sharrow Bay Country House Hotel, Ullswater		●		●		○					○	●		●						
134 Old Church Hotel, Watermillock				●							○	○							○	
135 Cedar Manor Hotel, Windermere		●		○	○	✪					○				✪			○	○	
137 Linthwaite House Hotel, Windermere		●		●		○					○	○	○	○						Golf practice hole, par3
138 Old Vicarage Country House Hotel, Witherslack				○		○					○	○			○	○		●		
LANCASHIRE																				
139 Chadwick Hotel, Lytham St Annes		●		●	●	○	●	●			○	○	●			○	●	○		
Yorkshire & the North East																				
Co. DURHAM																				
146 Headlam Hall Hotel	●	●	●	●	●						○		●		●		●	●		

(Hotels not listed have not informed us of sporting/conference facilities) Page No	**NORTHUMBERLAND** 147 Waren House, Bambergh	**NORTH YORKSHIRE** 148 Aldwark Manor Golf Hotel, Nr. York	149 Bolton Abbey, Skipton	150 Balmoral Hotel, Harrogate	151 Simonstone Hall, Hawes	152 Wrangham House Hotel, Hunmanby	154 Lastingham Grange Hotel, Kirkbymoorside	155 Millers House Hotel, Middleham	156 Solberge Hall, Northallerton	157 Dunsley Hall, Whitby	158 Judges Lodging Hotel, York	**WALES** **GLAMORGAN** 164 St Mellons Hotel, Cardiff	**GWYNEDD** 165 Trefeddian Hotel, Aberdovey	166 Bontddu Hall Hotel, Nr. Dolgellau	**MONMOUTHSHIRE** 167 Glen-Yr-Afon House, Usk	**PEMBROKESHIRE** 170 St Brides Hotel, Saundersfoot	171 Warpool Court Hotel, St David's	**POWYS** 171 Gliffaes Country House Hotel, Nr. Crickhowell
Other					Paragliding								Pitch n putt. Play area		Gliding, grass ski-ing			Hang gliding nearby
Watersports	●												●			●		
Tennis	○		●	✪					○	●		●	●				●	●
Swimming pool			●	○						●		●	●			●	●	
Squash/badminton								○				●				○		
Shooting		✪			●				●				●			○		
Sea/river bathing	●		●					○		○			●	○			●	
Sauna/solarium			●	●						●		●	●				●	
Sailing/boating										○	○		●			○	○	○
Riding	○	✪		○			○	○	○	○			○	○				○
Massage			●									●						
Jogging track																		
Jacuzzi/whirlpool			●									●						
Indoor games													●					
Golf	○	●		○		○	○	○	○	○	○	○		○	○	○	○	○
Gym/fitness centre			●	○						●		●					●	
Fishing		✪	●		●				○	○			○		○	●		●
Croquet			●							●					●			●
Conferences	●	●	●	●	●	●			●	●	●	●			●	●		●
Billiards/snooker													●					●

SCOTLAND																				
ABERDEENSHIRE																				
179a Ardoe House, Aberdeen		●	●	○	●	○					○				✪			●		
179b Maryculter House, Aberdeen	○	●		○	○	○					○				○	○	○	○		
180a Norwood Hall, Aberdeen		●																		
180b Balgonie Country House Hotel, Ballater			●			○												○		
181 Stakis Craigendarroch, Ballater	●	●		●	●	●	●	●			○		●		●	●	●	●		Dry ski slope,timeshares
182 Raemoir House, Banchory		●	●	○		●			●									●		Helipad
183a Thainstone House, Inverurie	●	●		✪	●	○		●	●		✪		●		●		●			
ARGYLL & BUTE																				
184 Killiechronan House, Isle of Mull				●		○					●	●		●	●					Stalking by arrangement
185 The Manor House, Oban					○	○						○	○	●			○			
186a Dungallan House Hotel, Oban		●		○	○	○						●		●						
186b Stonefield Castle Hotel, Tarbert		●		●		○					○	●	●		○		●			
187 Creggans Inn, Strachur	●	●		●						●				●	●					
DUMFRIES & GALLOWAY																				
188a Corsemalzie House Hotel, Newton Stewart		●	●		●									●			✪			
188b Balcary Bay, Auchencairn						○								●						
EAST LOTHIAN																				
189 Greywalls Hotel, Gullane		●	●			○												●		
FIFE																				
190 The Woodside Hotel, Aberdour						○							●							
191 Balbirnie House, Glenrothes	●	●	●			●					○				○	○				
HIGHLAND																				
192a Corrour House, Aviemore				●	○	●					●				●				●	Ski-ing nearby
192b Ashburn House, Fort William				●	○	○					○	●	○			○		○		Climbing, walking
193 Culloden House, by Inverness			●	●		●			●		●	●	●	●	●			●	○	
194a Rosedale Hotel, Isle of Skye				✪		○						●		●				○		
194b Corriegour House, Loch Lochy				●								✪			✪				●	
195 Lodge on the Loch, Onich				●	○												○			Highland Mysteryworld
196 Eddrachilles Hotel, Scourie				●								●								
LANARKSHIRE																				
197a Strathaven Hotel, Strathaven		●				●					●	●			●	●		●	●	

(Hotels not listed have not informed us of their sporting/conference facilities)

Page No.	Other	Watersports	Tennis	Swimming pool	Squash/badminton	Shooting	Sea/river bathing	Sauna/solarium	Sailing/boating	Riding	Massage	Jogging track	Jacuzzi/whirlpool	Indoor games	Golf	Gym/fitness centre	Fishing	Croquet	Conferences	Billiards/snooker
MORAY																				
197b Craigellachie Hotel, Speyside	Cycling nearby		●			○								●		●	○			●
PERTH & KINROSS																				
198a Monachyle Mhor, Balquhidder	Farm nearby					●	●					●					●			
198b Loch Rannoch Hotel, Kinloch Rannoch	Gorge walking, timeshares	●	●	●	●	○	●	●	●			●		●			●			●
199 Ballathie House Hotel, Kinclaven by Stanley						●									●		●	●	●	
200 Four Seasons Hotel, St Fillans		○					●		●						○		●		●	
201 Dalmunzie House Hotel, Spittal of Glenshee	Ski-ing nearby		●			●									●		●		●	
202a Ardeonaig Hotel, South Loch Tay					●			●	○					●		●		●		
SCOTTISH BORDERS																				
202b Peebles Hydro Hotel, Peebles			●	○	●			●		●	●	●	●	●	○	●	●		●	●
203 Dryburgh Abbey, St Boswell's				○		○		○		○					○		●	●	●	
STIRLINGSHIRE																			●	
204a Culcreuch Castle, Fintry					●	●						●			○	●	●		●	
204b Forest Hills Hotel, Aberfoyle		●	●	○	●	●	●	●	●	○	●	●	●	●	○	●	●	●	●	●
205 Lake Hotel, Port of Menteith						○				○					○		○			
206a Inchyra Grange, Falkirk			●	●				●		○	●		●		○	●			●	
WEST LOTHIAN																				
206b Houstoun House Hotel, Uphall	Beautician. Dance studio		●	○				●		○	●				○	●		●	●	
CHANNEL ISLANDS																				
212 La Favorita, Guernsey		○	○	●		○	○	●		○			●				○		●	
213 Hotel Bella Luce, Guernsey				●				●											●	
214 Duke of Richmond Hotel, Guernsey				●																
215 Old Government House Hotel, Guernsey		○	○	●	○			○		○	○				○	○	○	○	●	○
216 The White House, Herm			●	●			●		●								●	●		
217 The Moorings Hotel & Restaurant, Jersey		●	●	●					●	●					●		●			
218a The Sea Crest, Jersey				●																
219 The Lobster Pot, Jersey	Mountain bikes							○		○					○					
220 Hotel Petit Champ, Sark	Putting green		○	●										○			○			○

IRELAND																				
CO CARLOW																				
226 Dolmen Hotel, Carlow		●		●		○					○	○		○	○	○		○	○	
CO. CLARE																				
227 Dromoland Castle, Newmarket-on-Fergus	●	●		○	●	○	●			●	○				○			○		Beauty salon
228a Halpins Hotel, Kilkee		●		○		○														
CO. CORK																				
229 Emmet Hotel, Clonakilty		●		○	○	○					○	○		○			○		○	
230a Hayfield Manor, Cork				○				●	○		○	○				○	●	○		
230b Castlehyde Hotel, Fermoy		●		○		○					○			○		○				
231 Maryborough House, Douglas	●	●	●	○	●	○		●		●	●	○	●		✪	✪	○	●	○	Scuba diving. Sailing courses
232 Innishannon House, Innishannon		●		○		○					○	○			○	○		○		
233 Ballymaloe House, Shanagarry		●	●	●		●					●			●			●	●	●	Cookery school
CO. DONEGAL																				
234 Fort Royal Hotel, Rathmullen				●		●						●		●		●		●	●	
235aa Castle Grove Hotel, Letterkenny		●		○		○					○				○			○		
CO. DUBLIN																				
236 Aberdeen Lodge, Dublin 4		●		○	●	○		●			○	○		○			○	○	○	
239 Merrion Hall, Dublin 4		●		○	●	○		●			○	○		○				○	○	
240 Merrion Hotel, Dublin		●		○	●	○				●	○	○	●		○	○	○	●	○	
242b Portmarnock Golf & Country Club, Co Dublin		●				●					○			○	○				○	
243 Finnstown Hotel, Lucan		●	●	○	●	●	●			●			●				●	●		Turkish baths
CO. GALWAY																				
244 Ardagh Hotel & Restaurant, Clifden	●					✪					○					○			○	
245 St Cleran's Hotel, Craughwell		●		●		●				●	●			○	●				○	
246 Ballynahinch Castle, Recess		●	●	●											●			●		350 acre gardens
247a Ross Lake House, Oughterard				●		●					●	●		●				●	|	
CO. KERRY																				
248 Dingle Skellig Hotel, Dingle		●		○	●		●	●		●	○	●	●	●			○		○	*Fungi* trips. Island trips
249 Cahernane House Hotel, Killarney				●		○					●	●		●	●	●	●	●	●	
250 Hotel Dunloe Castle, Killarney				●		●			●		●	○			✪	○	●	○		Gardens
250 Hotel Europe, Killarney	●			●	●	●					●	●			✪	○		●	○	
251 The Bianconi, Killorglin		●		●		○					●	●			●	●		●	●	

(Hotels not listed have not informed us of their sporting/ conference facilities)

Page No.	252 Carrig House, Killorglin	253 Brandon Hotel, Tralee	254 Meadowlands Hotel, Tralee	**CO. KILDARE** 255 Dowdstown Hotel, Co Kildare	**CO. MAYO** 256 Ashford Castle, Cong	**CO. OFFALY** 257 Kinnitty Castle, Birr	**CO. WATERFORD** 256b Richmond House, Cappoquin	**CO. WESTMEATH** 259 Crookedwood House, Mullingar	**CO. WICKLOW** 260 Humewood Castle, Kiltegan	261 Rathsallagh House, Dunlavin
Other	Windsurfing				Archery	Quad bikes archery			Bike riding, polo, hunting	Archery
Watersports			○	✪						
Tennis		○		✪	✪	●	○	●		●
Swimming pool		●	○							
Squash/badminton										
Shooting	●			○	✪	●		○	●	●
Sea/river bathing	●									
Sauna/solarium					●	●				●
Sailing/boating	●									
Riding	○	○	○	○	✪	●	○	○	●	○
Massage					●	●			●	●
Jogging track					●				●	
Jacuzzi/whirlpool		●			●	●				
Indoor games										●
Golf	○			✪	●	○	○	○		●
Gym/fitness centre		●	○		●	●				
Fishing	●	○		✪	✪	○	○	●	●	○
Croquet								●	●	●
Conferences	●	●	●	●	●	●			●	●
Billiards/snooker					●		●		●	●

LOCATION INDEX ENGLAND

THE WEST COUNTRY

CENTRAL SOUTHERN ENGLAND

ALPHABETICAL INDEX OF HOTELS

Other Signpost Approved Partners

For a chance of winning a FREE weekend in a luxury SIGNPOST Country House Hotel for two people, simply answer the following ten ROYAL questions, all of whose answers can be found in *Signpost,* and complete the tie-breaker.

1. *Which West Country hotel is built on an estate once owned by the Saxon King Athelstan?*

....

2. *Which city is reputed to house King Arthur's Round Table?*

....

3. *Which hotel was formerly the estate of the Celtic High Kings, the O'Briens?*

....

4. *Which islands are part of the dominions of the Kings of England, but not part of their kingdom?*

....

5. *Which Irish hotel was once the home of HRH the Maharajah Ranjitsinji?*

....

6. *On the site of which hotel did Bonnie Prince Charlie spend a fateful night?*

....

7. *Which Scottish hotel has a bedroom known as* The King's Loo?

....

8. *Which hotel near London was built for an earlier Duke and Duchess of York?*

....

10. *On which West Country hotel's golf course did Edward VIII used to play when Prince of Wales?*

....

Tie breaker: *The following hotel is my favourite in the Signpost collection because...(max 40 words),*

....

....

Hotel:

....

Continue on a separate sheet if necessary

Please see overleaf for conditions and address panel.

Conditions

1. This competition is not open to employees of hotels reviewed in this book, nor to employees or agents of Priory Publications Ltd, W Foulsham & Co Ltd, Pelican Publishing Co, USA, nor to travel agents.

2. This form must be returned to Priory Publications Ltd by 30th June 2000.

3. Priory Publications Ltd reserve the right to choose the hotel at which the weekend is to be spent. The month of August is excluded. The prize will not have a value of less than £200 but money may not be claimed in lieu. The weekend must be taken during 2000.

4. The first twenty runners-up will receive a FREE second copy of this guidebook.

5. The publisher's decision is final. It is regretted that no correspondence concerning returned forms can be entered into.

Cut out and send to SIGNPOST/Premier Hotels Competition Dept at Priory Publications Ltd., FREEPOST NH0504, Brackley, Northamptonshire NN13 5BR, UK *(No stamp required within UK*

Signature ....

Name ....

Address ....

....

Date ....

£5

OUCHER

ff accommodation when
voucher is presented at
blishments with [V] printed
heir prices in Signpost 2000
over for conditions)

GUIDE TO PREMIER HOTELS AND ACCOMMODATION IN GREAT BRITAIN AND IRELAND

S

Signpost

SELECTED PREMIER
ESTABLISHMENT
2000

£5

VOUCHER

£5 off accommodation when
this voucher is presented at
establishments with [V] printed
by their prices in Signpost 2000
(see over for conditions)

GUIDE TO PREMIER HOTELS AND ACCOMMODATION IN GREAT BRITAIN AND IRELAND

S

Signpost

SELECTED PREMIER
ESTABLISHMENT
2000

£5

VOUCHER

ff accommodation when
voucher is presented at
blishments with [V] printed
heir prices in Signpost 2000
over for conditions)

GUIDE TO PREMIER HOTELS AND ACCOMMODATION IN GREAT BRITAIN AND IRELAND

S

Signpost

SELECTED PREMIER
ESTABLISHMENT
2000

£5

VOUCHER

£5 off accommodation when
this voucher is presented at
establishments with [V] printed
by their prices in Signpost 2000
(see over for conditions)

GUIDE TO PREMIER HOTELS AND ACCOMMODATION IN GREAT BRITAIN AND IRELAND

S

Signpost

SELECTED PREMIER
ESTABLISHMENT
2000

£5

VOUCHER

off accommodation when
voucher is presented at
blishments with [V] printed
heir prices in Signpost 2000
over for conditions)

GUIDE TO PREMIER HOTELS AND ACCOMMODATION IN GREAT BRITAIN AND IRELAND

S

Signpost

SELECTED PREMIER
ESTABLISHMENT
2000

£5

VOUCHER

£5 off accommodation when
this voucher is presented at
establishments with [V] printed
by their prices in Signpost 2000
(see over for conditions)

GUIDE TO PREMIER HOTELS AND ACCOMMODATION IN GREAT BRITAIN AND IRELAND

S

Signpost

SELECTED PREMIER
ESTABLISHMENT
2000

£5

VOUCHER

off accommodation when
voucher is presented at
blishments with [V] printed
heir prices in Signpost 2000
over for conditions)

GUIDE TO PREMIER HOTELS AND ACCOMMODATION IN GREAT BRITAIN AND IRELAND

S

Signpost

SELECTED PREMIER
ESTABLISHMENT
2000

£5

VOUCHER

£5 off accommodation when
this voucher is presented at
establishments with [V] printed
by their prices in Signpost 2000
(see over for conditions)

GUIDE TO PREMIER HOTELS AND ACCOMMODATION IN GREAT BRITAIN AND IRELAND

S

Signpost

SELECTED PREMIER
ESTABLISHMENT
2000

CONDITIONS

1. £5 off vouchers are only accepted for hotel accommodation at full tariff rate for the room and season, not against already discounted tariffs such as *Bargain Breaks.*
2. Only one voucher per person or party per stay can be presented.
3. Hotels should be informed when a booking is made that a Signpost £5 discount voucher will be presented in part payment.
4. Only Signpost hotels with [V] printed by their prices will accept these vouchers.
5. A copy of Signpost 2000 must be produced when this voucher is used.
6. This voucher may not be accepted at Christmas, Easter or other times of peak occupancy in individual hotels.
7. This voucher is valid until 31st December 2000.

CONDITIONS

1. £5 off vouchers are only accepted for hotel accommodation at full tariff rate for the room and season, not against already discounted tariffs such as *Bargain Breaks.*
2. Only one voucher per person or party per stay can be presented.
3. Hotels should be informed when a booking is made that a Signpost £5 discount voucher will be presented in part payment.
4. Only Signpost hotels with [V] printed by their prices will accept these vouchers.
5. A copy of Signpost 2000 must be produced when this voucher is used.
6. This voucher may not be accepted at Christmas, Easter or other times of peak occupancy in individual hotels.
7. This voucher is valid until 31st December 2000.

CONDITIONS

1. £5 off vouchers are only accepted for hotel accommodation at full tariff rate for the room and season, not against already discounted tariffs such as *Bargain Breaks.*
2. Only one voucher per person or party per stay can be presented.
3. Hotels should be informed when a booking is made that a Signpost £5 discount voucher will be presented in part payment.
4. Only Signpost hotels with [V] printed by their prices will accept these vouchers.
5. A copy of Signpost 2000 must be produced when this voucher is used.
6. This voucher may not be accepted at Christmas, Easter or other times of peak occupancy in individual hotels.
7. This voucher is valid until 31st December 2000.

CONDITIONS

1. £5 off vouchers are only accepted for hotel accommodation at full tariff rate for the room and season, not against already discounted tariffs such as *Bargain Breaks.*
2. Only one voucher per person or party per stay can be presented.
3. Hotels should be informed when a booking is made that a Signpost £5 discount voucher will be presented in part payment.
4. Only Signpost hotels with [V] printed by their prices will accept these vouchers.
5. A copy of Signpost 2000 must be produced when this voucher is used.
6. This voucher may not be accepted at Christmas, Easter or other times of peak occupancy in individual hotels.
7. This voucher is valid until 31st December 2000.

CONDITIONS

1. £5 off vouchers are only accepted for hotel accomm tion at full tariff rate for the room and season, not agai already discounted tariffs such as *Bargain Breaks.*
2. Only one voucher per person or party per stay can b presented.
3. Hotels should be informed when a booking is made Signpost £5 discount voucher will be presented in par payment.
4. Only Signpost hotels with [V] printed by their prices accept these vouchers.
5. A copy of Signpost 2000 must be produced when thi voucher is used.
6. This voucher may not be accepted at Christmas, Eas other times of peak occupancy in individual hotels.
7. This voucher is valid until 31st December 2000.

CONDITIONS

1. £5 off vouchers are only accepted for hotel accomm tion at full tariff rate for the room and season, not agai already discounted tariffs such as *Bargain Breaks.*
2. Only one voucher per person or party per stay can b presented.
3. Hotels should be informed when a booking is made Signpost £5 discount voucher will be presented in part payment.
4. Only Signpost hotels with [V] printed by their prices accept these vouchers.
5. A copy of Signpost 2000 must be produced when thi voucher is used.
6. This voucher may not be accepted at Christmas, Eas other times of peak occupancy in individual hotels.
7. This voucher is valid until 31st December 2000.

CONDITIONS

1. £5 off vouchers are only accepted for hotel accommo tion at full tariff rate for the room and season, not agai already discounted tariffs such as *Bargain Breaks.*
2. Only one voucher per person or party per stay can b presented.
3. Hotels should be informed when a booking is made a Signpost £5 discount voucher will be presented in pa payment.
4. Only Signpost hotels with [V] printed by their prices w accept these vouchers.
5. A copy of Signpost 2000 must be produced when this voucher is used.
6. This voucher may not be accepted at Christmas, East or other times of peak occupancy in individual hotels.
7. This voucher is valid until 31st December 2000.

CONDITIONS

1. £5 off vouchers are only accepted for hotel accommo tion at full tariff rate for the room and season, not agai already discounted tariffs such as *Bargain Breaks.*
2. Only one voucher per person or party per stay can b presented.
3. Hotels should be informed when a booking is made Signpost £5 discount voucher will be presented in part payment.
4. Only Signpost hotels with [V] printed by their prices w accept these vouchers.
5. A copy of Signpost 2000 must be produced when this voucher is used.
6. This voucher may not be accepted at Christmas, East other times of peak occupancy in individual hotels.
7. This voucher is valid until 31st December 2000.

If you have stayed in an hotel which is not yet featured in SIGNPOST and you think it merits an inspection for possible future inclusion, please send one of the forms below in confidence (no stamp necessary) to Signpost, Priory Publications Ltd, FREEPOST NH0504, Brackley, Northamptonshire NN13 5BR

I would like to recommend the under-mentioned hotel for possible inclusion in the next edition of SIGNPOST - the premier hotel guide to the British Isles.

Name of hotel____________________

____

City/Town______________________

My name______________________

My address____________________

____

____

____

I certify that I have no connection of any sort with the management or owners of the above hotel

Signed____ Date______________

GUEST RECOMMENDATION FORM

I would like to recommend the under-mentioned hotel for possible inclusion in the next edition of SIGNPOST - the premier hotel guide to the British Isles.

Name of hotel____________________

____

City/Town______________________

My name______________________

My address____________________

____

____

____

I certify that I have no connection of any sort with the management or owners of the above hotel

Signed____ Date______________

GUEST RECOMMENDATION FORM

I would like to recommend the under-mentioned hotel for possible inclusion in the next edition of SIGNPOST - the premier hotel guide to the British Isles.

Name of hotel____________________

____

City/Town______________________

My name______________________

My address____________________

____

____

____

I certify that I have no connection of any sort with the management or owners of the above hotel

Signed____ Date______________

GUEST REPORT FORM

Cut out and send the enclosed form (no stamp necessary) to Signpost, Priory Publications Ltd, FREEPOST NH0504, Brackley, Northamptonshire NN13 5BR

I have stayed in the below mentioned hotel, recommended by SIGNPOST, and would make the following comments: *(Continue overleaf if necessary)*

NAME OF HOTEL TOWN

REPORT

I certify that I have no connection with the management or owners of the hotel and I understand that my report will be treated in the strictest condidence.

Name:..Date..

Address:.. SIG

GUEST REPORT FORM

Cut out and send the enclosed form (no stamp necessary) to Signpost, Priory Publications Ltd, FREEPOST NH0504, Brackley, Northamptonshire NN13 5BR

I have stayed in the below mentioned hotel, recommended by SIGNPOST, and would make the following comments: *(Continue overleaf if necessary)*

NAME OF HOTEL TOWN

REPORT

I certify that I have no connection with the management or owners of the hotel and I understand that my report will be treated in the strictest condidence.

Name:..Date..

Address:.. SIG96/2

If you have stayed in an hotel which is not yet featured in SIGNPOST and you think it merits an inspection for possible future inclusion, please send one of the forms below in confidence (no stamp necessary) to Signpost, Priory Publications Ltd, FREEPOST NH0504, Brackley, Northamptonshire NN13 5BR

I would like to recommend the under-mentioned hotel for possible inclusion in the next edition of SIGNPOST - the premier hotel guide to the British Isles.

Name of hotel____________________

____

City/Town______________________

My name________________________

My address______________________

____

____

____

I certify that I have no connection of any sort with the management or owners of the above hotel

Signed____Date______________

GUEST RECOMMENDATION FORM

I would like to recommend the under-mentioned hotel for possible inclusion in the next edition of SIGNPOST - the premier hotel guide to the British Isles.

Name of hotel____________________

____

City/Town______________________

My name________________________

My address______________________

____

____

____

I certify that I have no connection of any sort with the management or owners of the above hotel

Signed____Date______________

GUEST RECOMMENDATION FORM

I would like to recommend the under-mentioned hotel for possible inclusion in the next edition of SIGNPOST - the premier hotel guide to the British Isles.

Name of hotel____________________

____

City/Town______________________

My name________________________

My address______________________

____

____

____

I certify that I have no connection of any sort with the management or owners of the above hotel

Signed____Date______________

GUEST REPORT FORM

Cut out and send the enclosed form (no stamp necessary) to Signpost, Priory Publications Ltd, FREEPOST NH0504, Brackley, Northamptonshire NN13 5BR

I have stayed in the below mentioned hotel, recommended by SIGNPOST, and would make the following comments: *(Continue overleaf if necessary)*

NAME OF HOTEL TOWN

REPORT

I certify that I have no connection with the management or owners of the hotel and I understand that my report will be treated in the strictest condidence.

Name:...Date..

Address:.. SIC

GUEST REPORT FORM

Cut out and send the enclosed form (no stamp necessary) to Signpost, Priory Publications Ltd, FREEPOST NH0504, Brackley, Northamptonshire NN13 5BR

I have stayed in the below mentioned hotel, recommended by SIGNPOST, and would make the following comments: *(Continue overleaf if necessary)*

NAME OF HOTEL TOWN

REPORT

I certify that I have no connection with the management or owners of the hotel and I understand that my report will be treated in the strictest condidence.

Name:...Date..

Address:.. SIG96/2

MAPS

The following section contains road maps of the British Isles and a plan of Central London.

Numbers in black ovals denote page numbers of SIGNPOST hotels. Turn to these pages for full details of hotels in areas where you are looking for accommodation.

Only major roads are shown and we therefore recommend that travellers also use a comprehensive road atlas when travelling “off the beaten track”. Of course we hope that our individual hotel location maps will help.

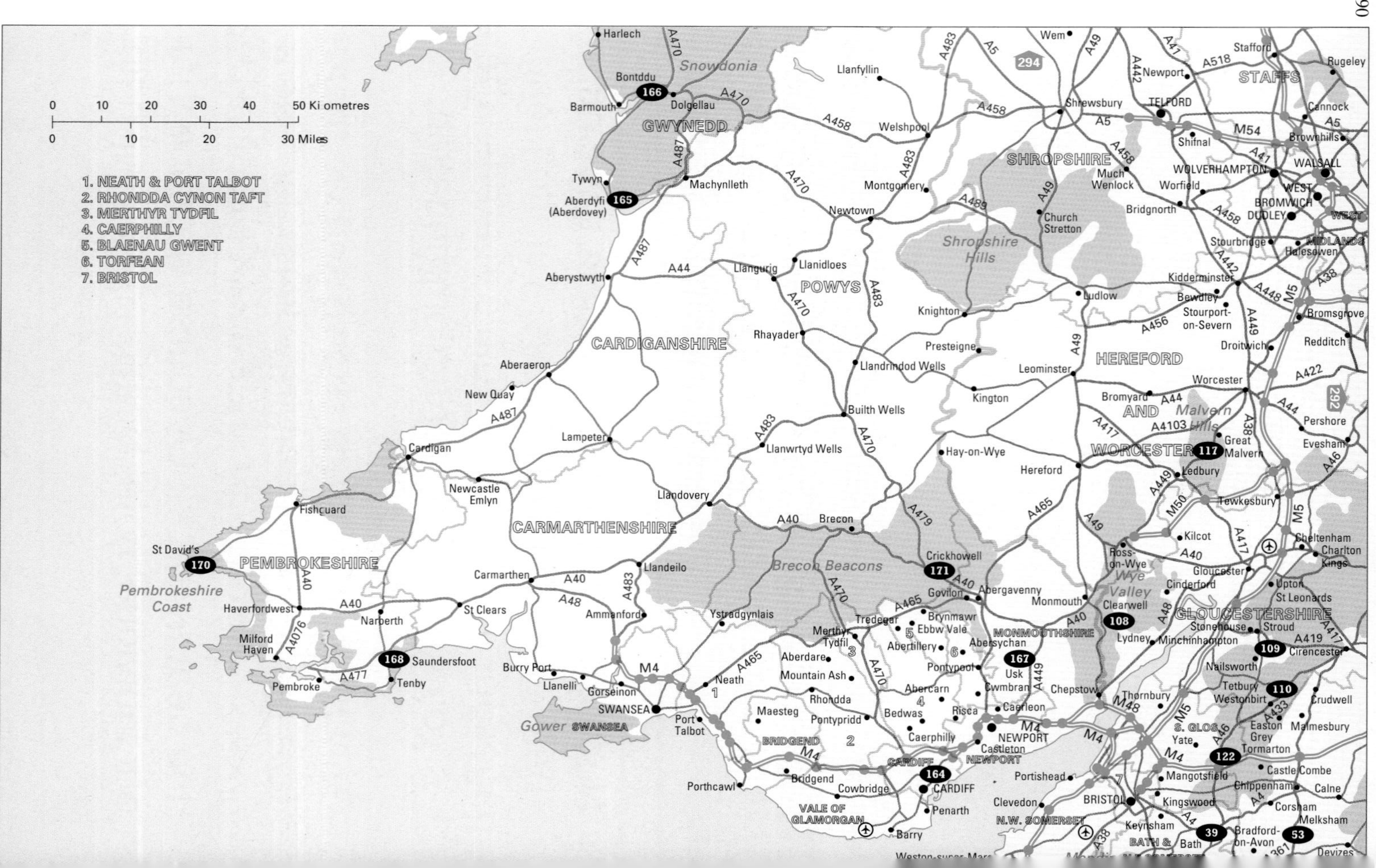

0 10 20 30 40 50 Kilometres
0 10 20 30 Miles
1. NEATH & PORT TALBOT
2. RHONDDA CYNON TAFT
3. MERTHYR TYDFIL
4. CAERPHILLY
5. BLAENAU GWENT
6. TORFEAN
7. BRISTOL
Harlech
Snowdonia
Bontddu
Barmouth
Dolgellau
GWYNEDD
Tywyn
Aberdyfi (Aberdovey)
Machynlleth
Llanfyllin
Welshpool
Montgomery
Newtown
Llanidloes
Llangurig
POWYS
Aberystwyth
CARDIGANSHIRE
Rhayader
Aberaeron
New Quay
Lampeter
Cardigan
Newcastle Emlyn
Fishguard
St David's
PEMBROKESHIRE
Pembrokeshire Coast
Haverfordwest
Milford Haven
Pembroke
Narberth
Saundersfoot
Tenby
St Clears
Carmarthen
CARMARTHENSHIRE
Llandovery
Llandeilo
Ammanford
Burry Port
Llanelli
Gorseinon
SWANSEA
Gower
Port Talbot
Neath
Ystradgynlais
Llanwrtyd Wells
Builth Wells
Llandrindod Wells
Brecon
Brecon Beacons
Crickhowell
Govilon
Abergavenny
Tredegar
Brynmawr
Ebbw Vale
Merthyr Tydfil
Aberdare
Mountain Ash
Abertillery
Abersychan
Pontypool
Abercarn
Rhondda
Pontypridd
Maesteg
Bedwas
Risca
Caerphilly
BRIDGEND
Bridgend
Porthcawl
Cowbridge
VALE OF GLAMORGAN
Barry
Penarth
CARDIFF
NEWPORT
Castleton
Caerleon
Cwmbran
Usk
MONMOUTHSHIRE
Chepstow
Monmouth
Hay-on-Wye
Hereford
HEREFORD
Kington
Presteigne
Knighton
Shropshire Hills
Leominster
Ludlow
Church Stretton
SHROPSHIRE
Much Wenlock
Bridgnorth
Shrewsbury
Wem
Newport
TELFORD
Shifnal
Worfield
WOLVERHAMPTON
WEST BROMWICH
DUDLEY
WEST MIDLANDS
WALSALL
Brownhills
Cannock
Stafford
STAFFS
Rugeley
Stourbridge
Halesowen
Kidderminster
Bewdley
Stourport-on-Severn
Droitwich
Bromsgrove
Redditch
Worcester
Bromyard
WORCESTER AND
Malvern Hills
Great Malvern
Pershore
Evesham
Ledbury
Tewkesbury
Cheltenham
Charlton Kings
Kilcot
Ross-on-Wye
Wye Valley
Gloucester
Cinderford
Clearwell
Lydney
Upton St Leonards
GLOUCESTERSHIRE
Stonehouse
Stroud
Minchinhampton
Cirencester
Nailsworth
Tetbury
Westonbirt
Crudwell
Easton Grey
Malmesbury
Thornbury
S. GLOS
Yate
Tormarton
Castle Combe
Mangotsfield
Chippenham
Calne
Corsham
Melksham
Portishead
Clevedon
N.W. SOMERSET
BRISTOL
Kingswood
Keynsham
BATH &
Bath
Bradford-on-Avon
Devizes
M4
M5
M50
M48
M54
A40
A44
A470
A483
A487
A49
A5
292
294

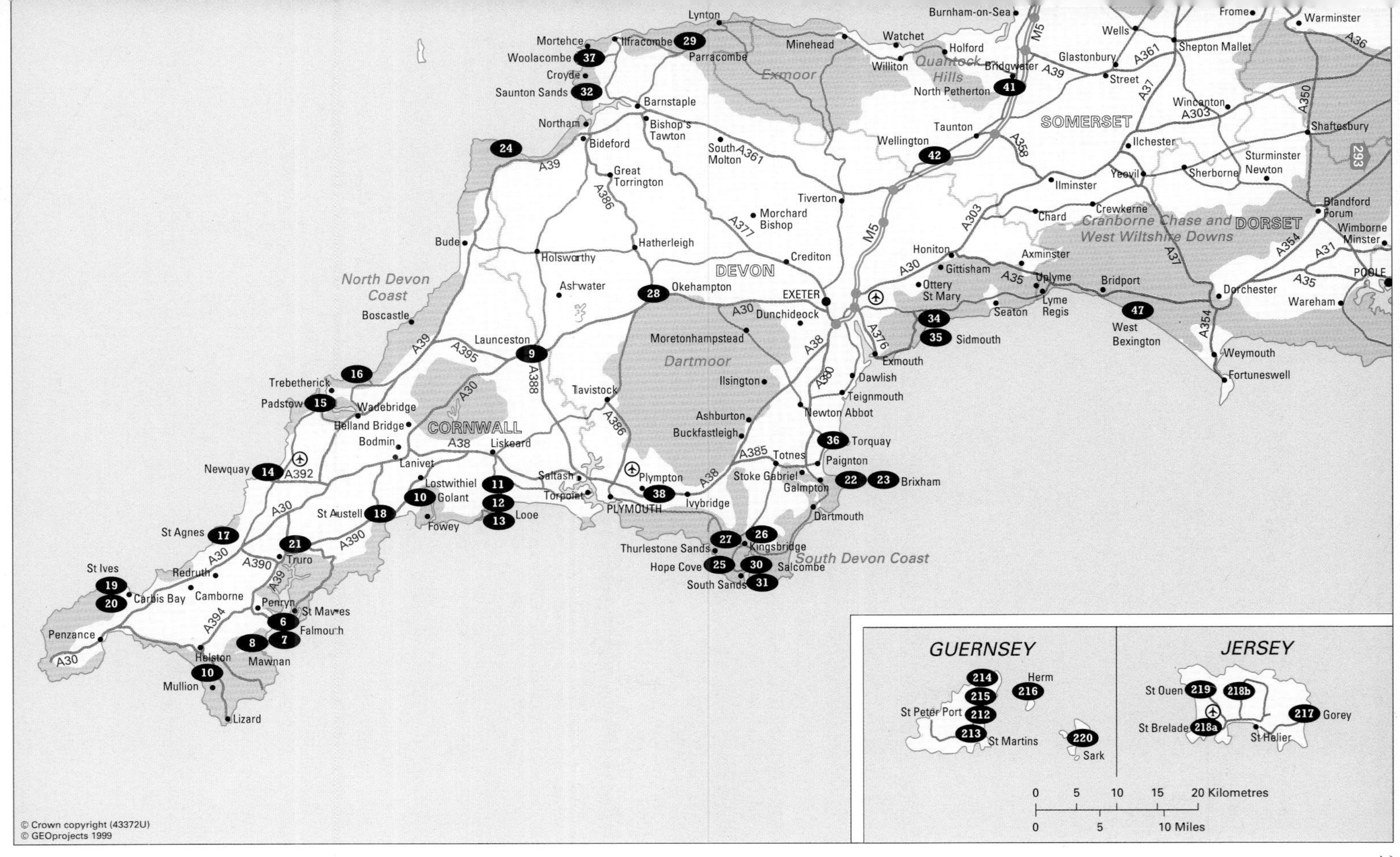
SOMERSET
DEVON
CORNWALL
DORSET
Cranborne Chase and
West Wiltshire Downs
Exmoor
Quantock Hills
Dartmoor
North Devon Coast
South Devon Coast
293
Warminster
Frome
Shaftesbury
Blandford Forum
Wimborne Minster
POOLE
Wareham
Sturminster Newton
Shepton Mallet
Wincanton
Sherborne
Dorchester
Weymouth
Fortuneswell
Wells
Glastonbury
Street
Ilchester
Yeovil
Crewkerne
Ilminster
Chard
Axminster
Uplyme
Lyme Regis
Bridport
West Bexington
Burnham-on-Sea
Bridgwater
Holford
North Petherton
Taunton
Wellington
Watchet
Williton
Minehead
Honiton
Gittisham
Ottery St Mary
Seaton
Sidmouth
Exmouth
Dawlish
Teignmouth
Newton Abbot
Torquay
Paignton
Brixham
Dartmouth
Galmpton
Stoke Gabriel
Totnes
Kingsbridge
Salcombe
South Sands
Hope Cove
Thurlestone Sands
Ivybridge
Plympton
PLYMOUTH
Buckfastleigh
Ashburton
Ilsington
Moretonhampstead
Dunchideock
EXETER
Crediton
Tiverton
Morchard Bishop
South Molton
Okehampton
Hatherleigh
Great Torrington
Bishop's Tawton
Barnstaple
Bideford
Northam
Ilfracombe
Mortehoe
Woolacombe
Croyde
Saunton Sands
Lynton
Parracombe
Holsworthy
Ashwater
Tavistock
Saltash
Torpoint
Launceston
Liskeard
Looe
Lostwithiel
Golant
Fowey
Lanivet
Bodmin
Bude
Boscastle
Wadebridge
Helland Bridge
Trebetherick
Padstow
Newquay
St Austell
Truro
St Mawes
Falmouth
Penryn
Mawnan
St Agnes
Redruth
Camborne
Helston
Mullion
Lizard
Carbis Bay
St Ives
Penzance
GUERNSEY
JERSEY
St Peter Port
St Martins
Herm
Sark
St Ouen
St Brelade
St Helier
Gorey
0 5 10 15 20 Kilometres
0 5 10 Miles
© Crown copyright (43372U)
© GEOprojects 1999

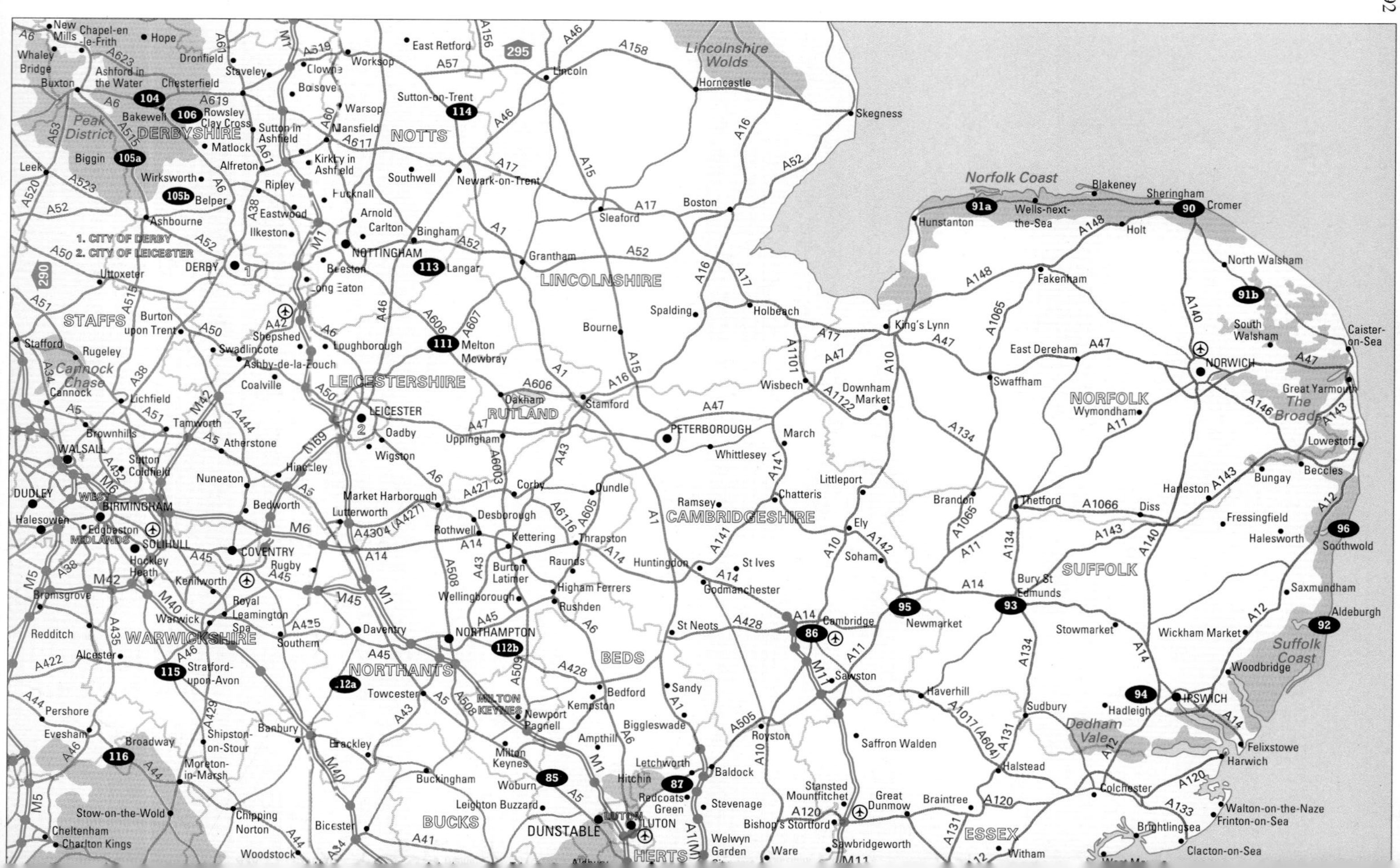
Norfolk Coast
Hunstanton
Wells-next-the-Sea
Blakeney
Sheringham
Cromer
Holt
North Walsham
South Walsham
Caister-on-Sea
Great Yarmouth
The Broads
Lowestoft
Beccles
Bungay
Southwold
Halesworth
Fressingfield
Saxmundham
Aldeburgh
Suffolk Coast
Woodbridge
Felixstowe
Harwich
Walton-on-the-Naze
Frinton-on-Sea
Clacton-on-Sea
Brightlingsea
Colchester
Dedham Vale
Hadleigh
IPSWICH
Wickham Market
Harleston
Diss
NORWICH
NORFOLK
Wymondham
Fakenham
East Dereham
Swaffham
King's Lynn
Thetford
Brandon
SUFFOLK
Bury St Edmunds
Stowmarket
Sudbury
Halstead
Witham
ESSEX
Braintree
Great Dunmow
Haverhill
Saffron Walden
Newmarket
Ely
Soham
Littleport
Downham Market
Cambridge
Sawston
Stansted Mountfitchet
Bishop's Stortford
Sawbridgeworth
Ware
Royston
Baldock
Stevenage
Welwyn Garden
Letchworth
Hitchin
Redcoats Green
LUTON
HERTS
DUNSTABLE
Woburn
Leighton Buzzard
Milton Keynes
Ampthill
Biggleswade
Sandy
Bedford
Kempston
BEDS
St Neots
St Ives
Godmanchester
Huntingdon
Ramsey
CAMBRIDGESHIRE
Chatteris
March
Wisbech
Whittlesey
PETERBOROUGH
Holbeach
Spalding
Boston
Skegness
Lincolnshire Wolds
Horncastle
Lincoln
Sleaford
LINCOLNSHIRE
Bourne
Stamford
Grantham
Oundle
Thrapston
Corby
Kettering
Raunds
Higham Ferrers
Rushden
Burton Latimer
Wellingborough
Desborough
Rothwell
Market Harborough
NORTHAMPTON
Newport Pagnell
MILTON KEYNES
Towcester
NORTHANTS
Daventry
Brackley
Buckingham
BUCKS
Bicester
Woodstock
Chipping Norton
Banbury
Southam
Rugby
COVENTRY
Royal Leamington Spa
Kenilworth
Warwick
WARWICKSHIRE
Stratford-upon-Avon
Shipston-on-Stour
Moreton-in-Marsh
Stow-on-the-Wold
Cheltenham
Charlton Kings
Broadway
Evesham
Pershore
Alcester
Redditch
Bromsgrove
Halesowen
DUDLEY
WALSALL
BIRMINGHAM
WEST MIDLANDS
Edgbaston
SOLIHULL
Hockley Heath
Sutton Coldfield
Tamworth
Atherstone
Nuneaton
Bedworth
Hinckley
Lutterworth
LEICESTER
Oadby
Wigston
Uppingham
Oakham
RUTLAND
Melton Mowbray
LEICESTERSHIRE
Loughborough
Long Eaton
Shepshed
Ashby-de-la-Zouch
Coalville
Swadlincote
Burton upon Trent
Lichfield
Brownhills
Cannock
Cannock Chase
Rugeley
Stafford
STAFFS
Uttoxeter
Ashbourne
DERBY
1. CITY OF DERBY
2. CITY OF LEICESTER
Belper
Ilkeston
Eastwood
Ripley
Alfreton
Wirksworth
Matlock
Bakewell
Rowsley
Clay Cross
DERBYSHIRE
Peak District
Biggin
Leek
Buxton
Whaley Bridge
New Mills
Chapel-en-le-Frith
Ashford in the Water
Hope
Chesterfield
Dronfield
Staveley
Bolsover
Clowne
Worksop
Warsop
Mansfield
Sutton in Ashfield
Kirkby in Ashfield
Hucknall
Arnold
Carlton
NOTTINGHAM
Beeston
Bingham
Langar
Southwell
NOTTS
Sutton-on-Trent
Newark-on-Trent
East Retford

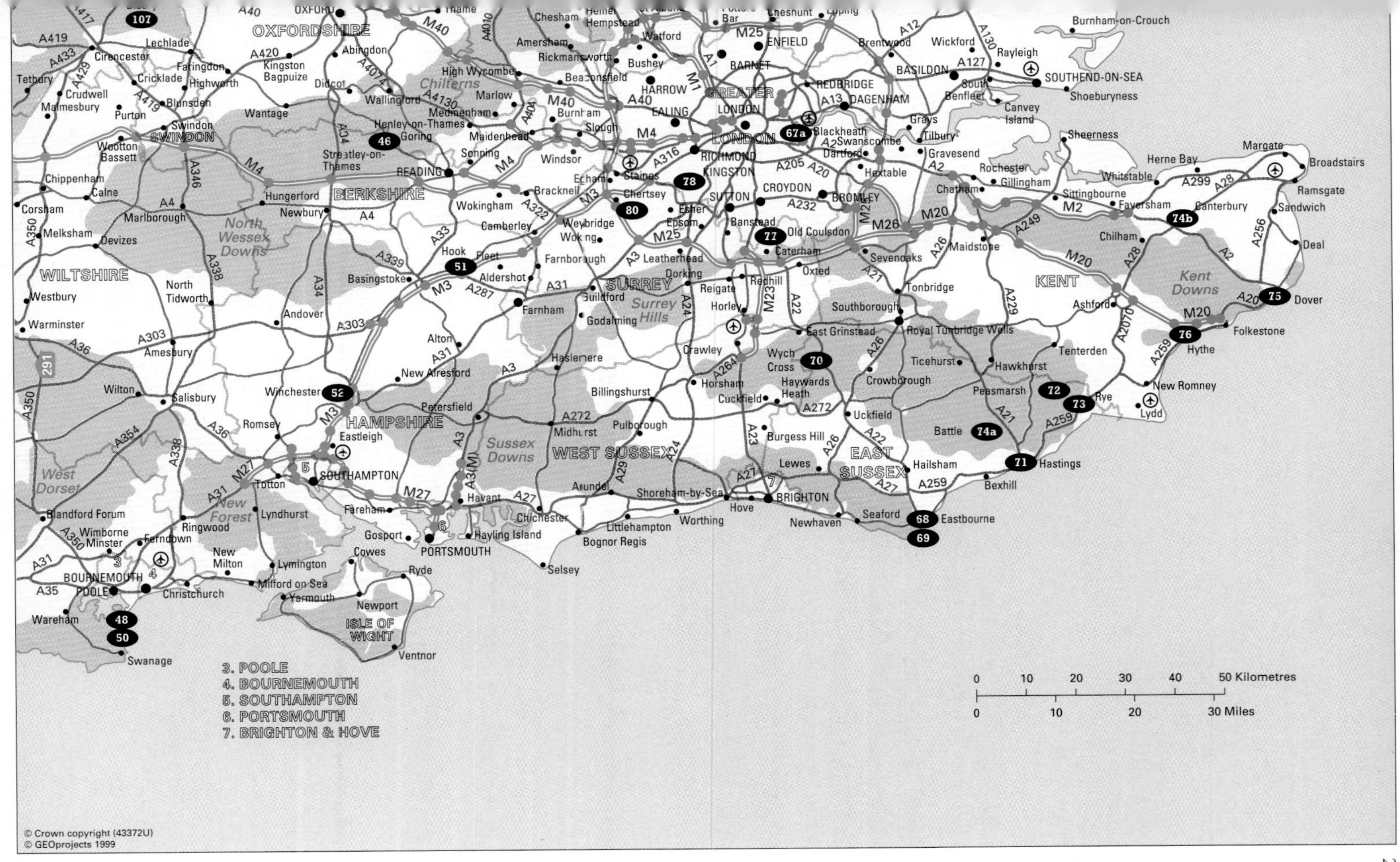
OXFORDSHIRE
BERKSHIRE
WILTSHIRE
HAMPSHIRE
SURREY
WEST SUSSEX
EAST SUSSEX
KENT
GREATER LONDON
ISLE OF WIGHT
Chilterns
North Wessex Downs
Surrey Hills
Kent Downs
Sussex Downs
New Forest
West Dorset
OXFORD
READING
SWINDON
SOUTHAMPTON
PORTSMOUTH
BRIGHTON
BOURNEMOUTH
POOLE
LONDON
SOUTHEND-ON-SEA
BASILDON
Margate
Broadstairs
Ramsgate
Sandwich
Deal
Dover
Folkestone
Hythe
New Romney
Lydd
Rye
Hastings
Bexhill
Eastbourne
Seaford
Newhaven
Lewes
Hove
Worthing
Littlehampton
Bognor Regis
Selsey
Chichester
Hayling Island
Havant
Gosport
Fareham
Cowes
Ryde
Newport
Ventnor
Yarmouth
Lymington
Milford on Sea
Christchurch
Swanage
Wareham
Canterbury
Whitstable
Herne Bay
Faversham
Ashford
Tenterden
Maidstone
Rochester
Chatham
Gillingham
Sevenoaks
Tonbridge
Royal Tunbridge Wells
Crawley
Horsham
Guildford
Winchester
Salisbury
Basingstoke
Newbury
Andover
Farnham
Windsor
Slough
Henley-on-Thames
Marlow
High Wycombe
Wokingham
Bracknell
Marlborough
Devizes
Chippenham
Warminster
Westbury
3. POOLE
4. BOURNEMOUTH
5. SOUTHAMPTON
6. PORTSMOUTH
7. BRIGHTON & HOVE
0 10 20 30 40 50 Kilometres
0 10 20 30 Miles
© Crown copyright (43372U)
© GEOprojects 1999

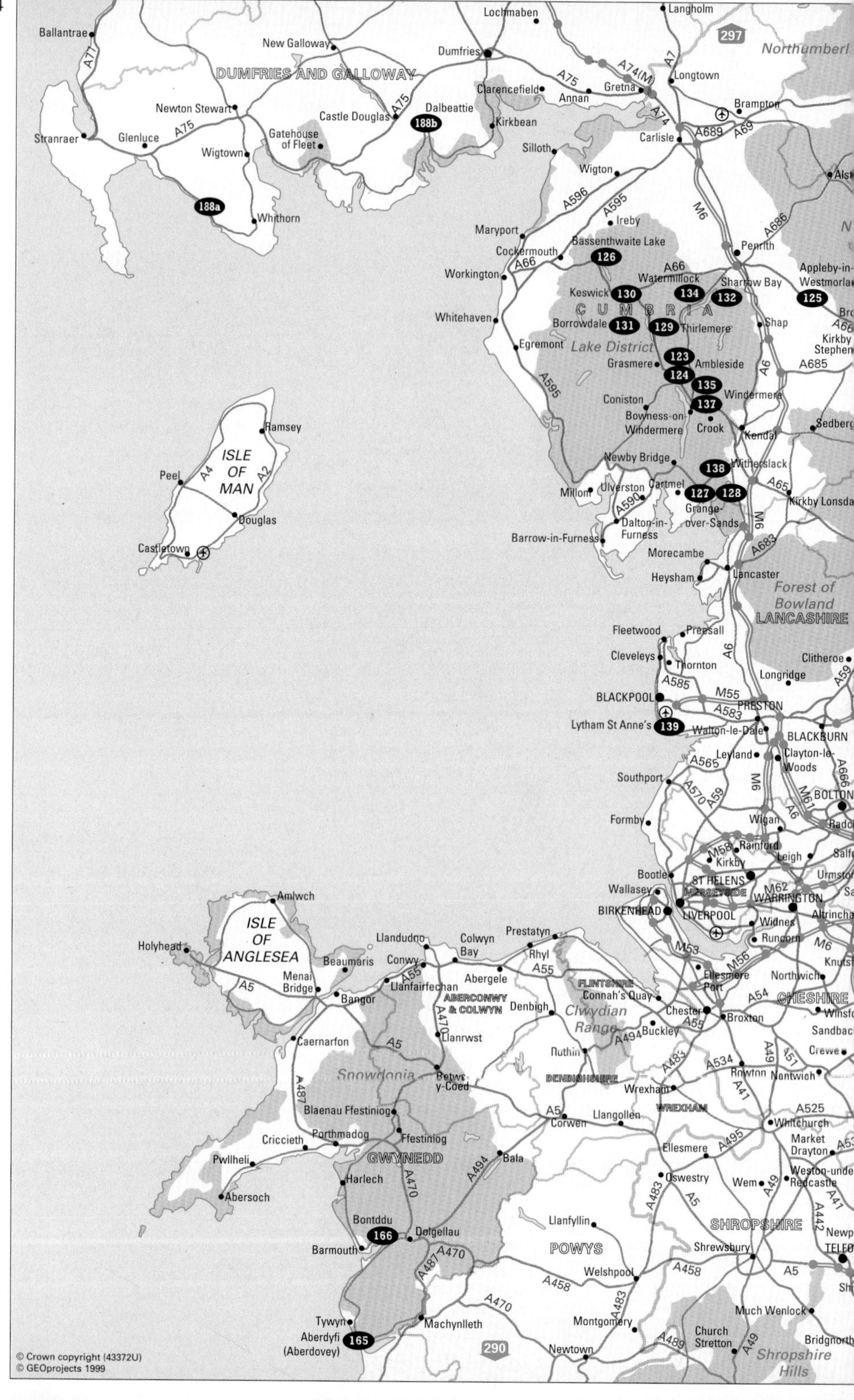
Lochmaben
Langholm
297
Northumberl
Ballantrae
A77
New Galloway
Dumfries
DUMFRIES AND GALLOWAY
A74(M)
A7
Longtown
A75
Gretna
Clarencefield
Annan
Brampton
Newton Stewart
Castle Douglas
A75
Dalbeattie
188b
Kirkbean
A74
A689
A69
Stranraer
Glenluce
A75
Gatehouse of Fleet
Carlisle
Wigtown
Silloth
Wigton
Alst
188a
Whithorn
A596
A595
M6
Ireby
A686
Maryport
Bassenthwaite Lake
Penrith
N
Cockermouth
126
A66
A66
Appleby-in-Westmorla
Workington
Watermillock
Sharrow Bay
Keswick
130
134
132
125
C U M B R I A
Whitehaven
Borrowdale
131
129
Thirlemere
Shap
A66
Kirkby Stephen
Egremont
Lake District
123
Grasmere
Ambleside
A685
124
A6
A595
135
Windermere
Coniston
137
Bowness-on-Windermere
Crook
Ramsey
Kendal
Sedberg
ISLE OF MAN
A4
A2
Peel
Newby Bridge
138
Witherslack
A65
Millom
Ulverston
Cartmel
127
128
Kirkby Lonsda
A590
Grange-over-Sands
Douglas
Dalton-in-Furness
M6
Castletown
Barrow-in-Furness
A683
Morecambe
Heysham
Lancaster
Forest of Bowland
LANCASHIRE
Fleetwood
Preesall
Cleveleys
Thornton
A6
Clitheroe
A585
Longridge
A59
BLACKPOOL
M55
PRESTON
A583
Lytham St Anne's
139
Walton-le-Dale
BLACKBURN
A565
Leyland
Clayton-le-Woods
Southport
A570
A59
M6
A666
M61
BOLTON
A6
Formby
Wigan
Radcl
M58
Rainford
Kirkby
Leigh
Salfo
Bootle
ST HELENS
Urmston
Wallasey
MERSEYSIDE
M62
WARRINGTON
BIRKENHEAD
LIVERPOOL
Widnes
Altrinchar
Amlwch
ISLE OF ANGLESEA
Runcorn
Llandudno
Colwyn Bay
Prestatyn
M53
M6
Holyhead
Rhyl
M56
Knutsfo
Beaumaris
Conwy
A55
A55
Ellesmere Port
Northwich
A5
Menai Bridge
Llanfairfechan
Abergele
FLINTSHIRE
Connah's Quay
A54
CHESHIRE
Bangor
ABERCONWY & COLWYN
Denbigh
Clwydian Range
Chester
Broxton
Winsfo
A470
A494
Buckley
A55
Sandbach
Caernarfon
A5
Llanrwst
Ruthin
A483
A534
A49
A51
Crewe
A487
Snowdonia
Betws-y-Coed
DENBIGHSHIRE
Wrexham
Rowton
A41
Nantwich
WREXHAM
A525
Blaenau Ffestiniog
A5
Corwen
Llangollen
Whitchurch
Criccieth
Porthmadog
Ffestiniog
A495
Market Drayton
A53
Ellesmere
Pwllheli
GWYNEDD
Bala
A494
A470
Oswestry
Weston-under Redcastle
Harlech
A483
A5
Wem
A49
A41
Abersoch
A442
Llanfyllin
SHROPSHIRE
Bontddu
Newpo
166
Dolgellau
TELFOR
Barmouth
A470
POWYS
Shrewsbury
A487
A458
A5
Welshpool
A458
Shif
A470
A483
Much Wenlock
Tywyn
Machynlleth
Montgomery
Church Stretton
Bridgnorth
Aberdyfi (Aberdovey)
165
290
Newtown
A489
A49
Shropshire Hills
© Crown copyright (43372U)
© GEOprojects 1999

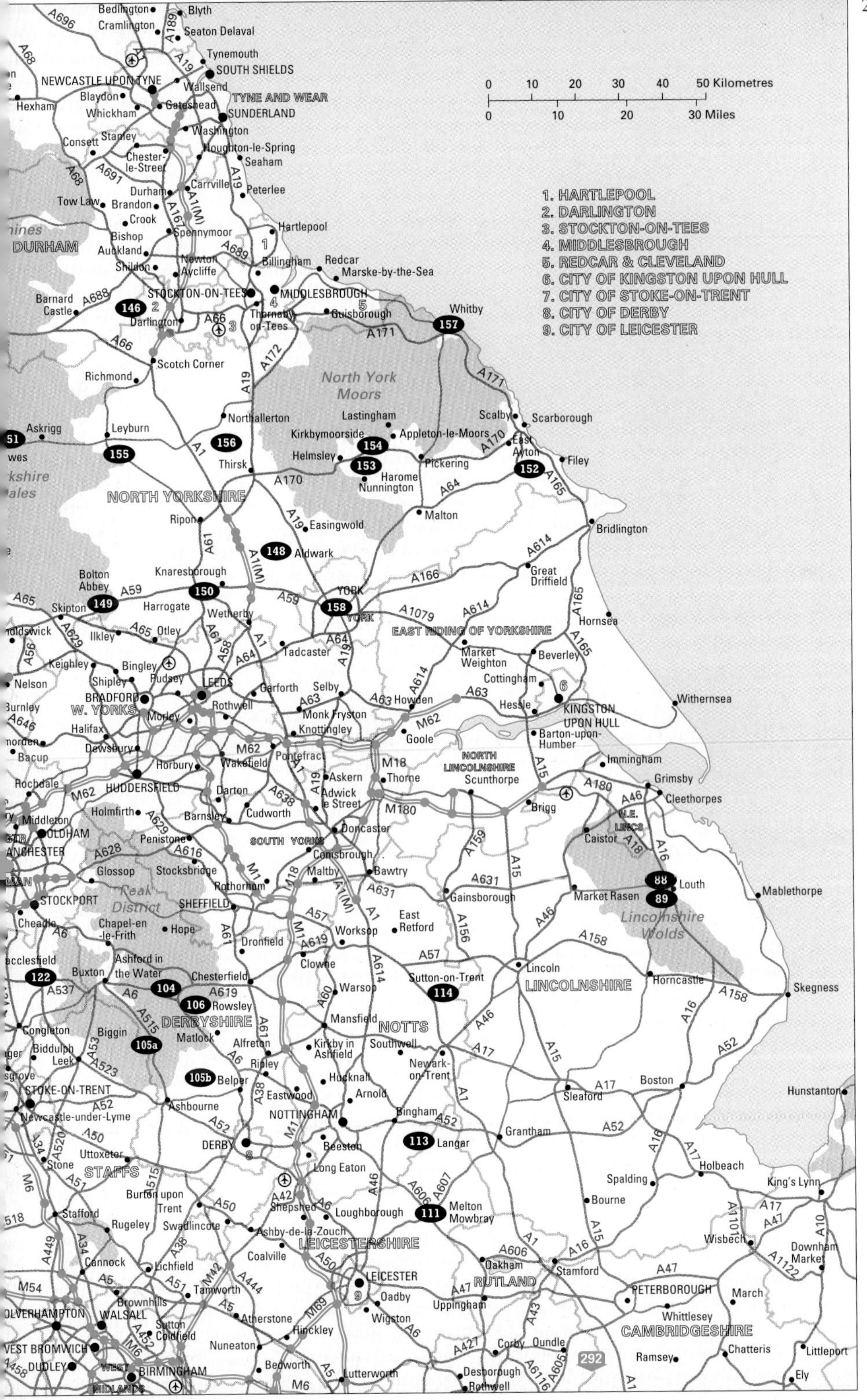
0 10 20 30 40 50 Kilometres
0 10 20 30 Miles
1. HARTLEPOOL
2. DARLINGTON
3. STOCKTON-ON-TEES
4. MIDDLESBROUGH
5. REDCAR & CLEVELAND
6. CITY OF KINGSTON UPON HULL
7. CITY OF STOKE-ON-TRENT
8. CITY OF DERBY
9. CITY OF LEICESTER
Bedlington
Blyth
Cramlington
Seaton Delaval
Tynemouth
SOUTH SHIELDS
NEWCASTLE UPON TYNE
Wallsend
Hexham
Blaydon
Whickham
Gateshead
TYNE AND WEAR
SUNDERLAND
Washington
Consett
Stanley
Chester-le-Street
Houghton-le-Spring
Seaham
Durham
Carrville
Peterlee
Tow Law
Brandon
Crook
DURHAM
Bishop Auckland
Spennymoor
Hartlepool
Newton Aycliffe
Shildon
Billingham
Redcar
Marske-by-the-Sea
Barnard Castle
STOCKTON-ON-TEES
MIDDLESBROUGH
Darlington
Thornaby-on-Tees
Guisborough
Whitby
Richmond
Scotch Corner
North York Moors
Askrigg
Leyburn
Northallerton
Lastingham
Kirkbymoorside
Appleton-le-Moors
Scalby
Scarborough
East Ayton
Helmsley
Pickering
Harome
Nunnington
Filey
Thirsk
NORTH YORKSHIRE
Ripon
Malton
Easingwold
Bridlington
Aldwark
Knaresborough
Great Driffield
Bolton Abbey
Harrogate
Skipton
YORK
Wetherby
Hornsea
EAST RIDING OF YORKSHIRE
Ilkley
Otley
Tadcaster
Market Weighton
Beverley
Keighley
Bingley
Shipley
Pudsey
LEEDS
Garforth
Selby
Cottingham
Nelson
BRADFORD
W. YORKS
Rothwell
Howden
Hessle
KINGSTON UPON HULL
Withernsea
Burnley
Halifax
Morley
Monk Fryston
Knottingley
Goole
Barton-upon-Humber
Dewsbury
Bacup
Wakefield
Pontefract
NORTH LINCOLNSHIRE
Immingham
Horbury
Thorne
Scunthorpe
Grimsby
Cleethorpes
Rochdale
HUDDERSFIELD
Darton
Askern
Adwick le Street
Brigg
Holmfirth
Barnsley
Cudworth
Middleton
OLDHAM
Doncaster
Caistor
Penistone
SOUTH YORKS
Conisbrough
Glossop
Stocksbridge
Maltby
Bawtry
Louth
Mablethorpe
Rotherham
Peak District
STOCKPORT
SHEFFIELD
Gainsborough
Market Rasen
East Retford
Lincolnshire Wolds
Cheadle
Chapel-en-le-Frith
Hope
Worksop
Dronfield
Clowne
Macclesfield
Ashford in the Water
Buxton
Chesterfield
Sutton-on-Trent
Lincoln
Horncastle
Skegness
LINCOLNSHIRE
Warsop
Rowsley
DERBYSHIRE
Mansfield
NOTTS
Congleton
Biggin
Matlock
Alfreton
Kirkby in Ashfield
Southwell
Biddulph
Leek
Ripley
Newark-on-Trent
Belper
Hucknall
Arnold
Boston
Hunstanton
STOKE-ON-TRENT
Eastwood
Sleaford
Ashbourne
Newcastle-under-Lyme
NOTTINGHAM
Bingham
Grantham
DERBY
Beeston
Langar
Uttoxeter
Stone
STAFFS
Long Eaton
Holbeach
Spalding
King's Lynn
Burton upon Trent
Shepshed
Loughborough
Melton Mowbray
Bourne
Stafford
Rugeley
Swadlincote
Ashby-de-la-Zouch
Wisbech
Downham Market
LEICESTERSHIRE
Cannock
Lichfield
Coalville
Oakham
Stamford
LEICESTER
RUTLAND
Brownhills
Tamworth
Oadby
Uppingham
PETERBOROUGH
March
WOLVERHAMPTON
WALSALL
Atherstone
Wigston
Whittlesey
Sutton Coldfield
Hinckley
CAMBRIDGESHIRE
WEST BROMWICH
Nuneaton
Corby
Oundle
Chatteris
Littleport
DUDLEY
WEST MIDLANDS
BIRMINGHAM
Bedworth
Lutterworth
Desborough
Rothwell
Ramsey
Ely

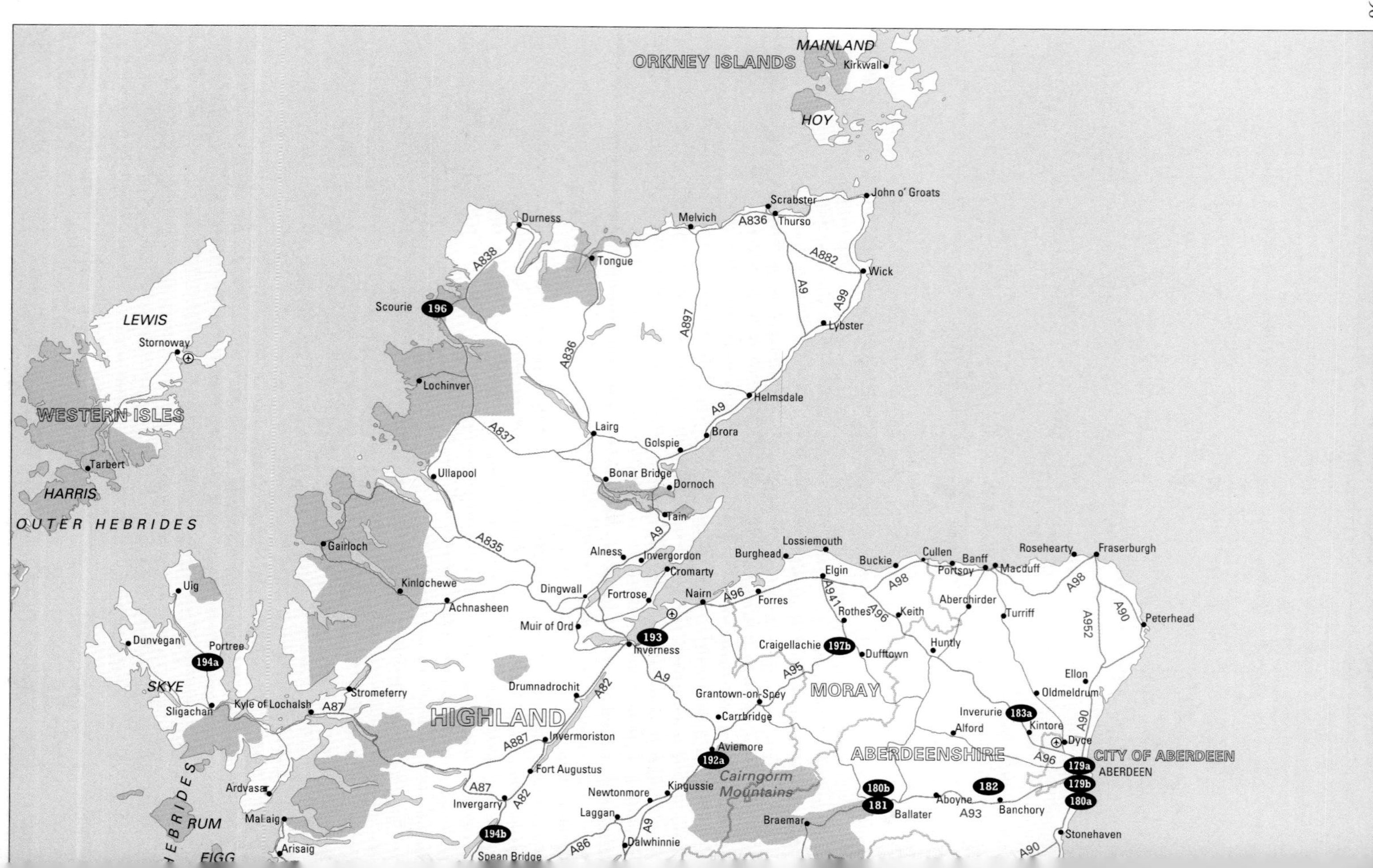
ORKNEY ISLANDS
MAINLAND
Kirkwall
HOY
John o' Groats
Scrabster
Thurso
Melvich
Durness
Tongue
A836
A882
Wick
A9
A99
Lybster
A838
Scourie
196
A897
LEWIS
Stornoway
Lochinver
A836
Helmsdale
WESTERN ISLES
A9
Lairg
Brora
A837
Golspie
Tarbert
HARRIS
Ullapool
Bonar Bridge
Dornoch
Tain
OUTER HEBRIDES
Gairloch
A835
A9
Alness
Invergordon
Cromarty
Lossiemouth
Burghead
Buckie
Cullen
Banff
Portsoy
Macduff
Rosehearty
Fraserburgh
Elgin
Kinlochewe
Dingwall
Fortrose
Nairn
A96
Forres
A941
A98
A98
Achnasheen
Rothes
A96
Keith
Aberchirder
Turriff
A952
A90
Peterhead
Uig
Muir of Ord
193
Inverness
Craigellachie
197b
Dufftown
Huntly
Dunvegan
Portree
194a
Ellon
SKYE
Drumnadrochit
A82
A9
A95
MORAY
Oldmeldrum
Stromeferry
Grantown-on-Spey
Inverurie
183a
Sligachan
Kyle of Lochalsh
A87
HIGHLAND
Carrbridge
Alford
Kintore
A90
Invermoriston
A887
Aviemore
Dyce
ABERDEENSHIRE
CITY OF ABERDEEN
A96
179a
ABERDEEN
192a
Fort Augustus
Cairngorm Mountains
Ardvasar
A87
Newtonmore
Kingussie
180b
182
179b
Invergarry
A82
Aboyne
HEBRIDES
RUM
Mallaig
Laggan
181
Ballater
A93
Banchory
180a
A9
Braemar
194b
A86
Dalwhinnie
Stonehaven
Arisaig
EIGG
Spean Bridge
A90

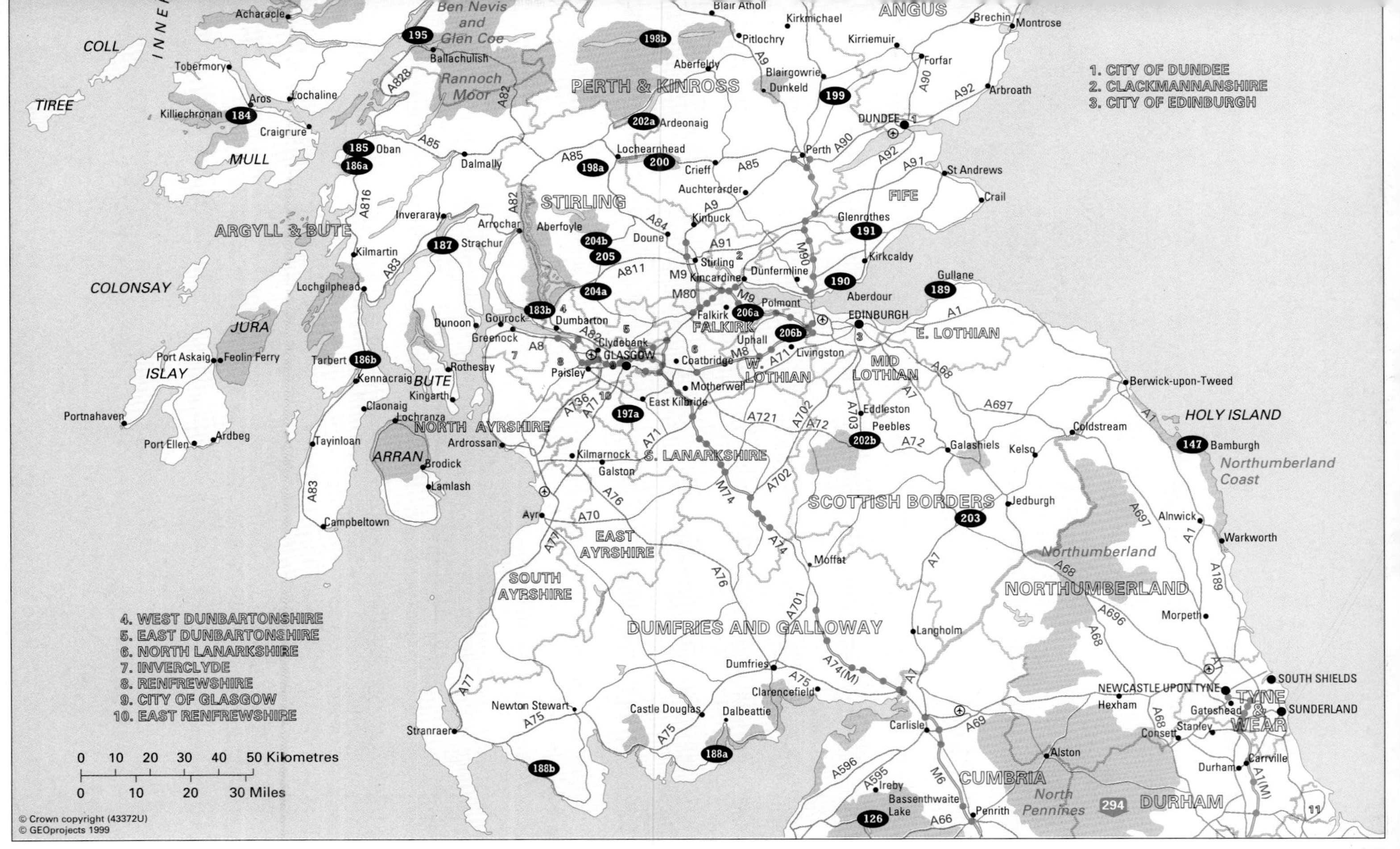
1. CITY OF DUNDEE
2. CLACKMANNANSHIRE
3. CITY OF EDINBURGH
ANGUS
PERTH & KINROSS
STIRLING
ARGYLL & BUTE
FIFE
FALKIRK
E. LOTHIAN
MID LOTHIAN
W. LOTHIAN
NORTH AYRSHIRE
S. LANARKSHIRE
EAST AYRSHIRE
SOUTH AYRSHIRE
SCOTTISH BORDERS
DUMFRIES AND GALLOWAY
NORTHUMBERLAND
TYNE & WEAR
DURHAM
CUMBRIA
COLL
TIREE
INNER
MULL
COLONSAY
JURA
ISLAY
BUTE
ARRAN
HOLY ISLAND
Ben Nevis and Glen Coe
Rannoch Moor
Northumberland Coast
Northumberland
North Pennines
Acharacle
Tobermory
Aros
Lochaline
Killiechronan
Craignure
Oban
Ballachulish
Dalmally
Inveraray
Arrochar
Strachur
Kilmartin
Lochgilphead
Tarbert
Kennacraig
Port Askaig
Feolin Ferry
Portnahaven
Port Ellen
Ardbeg
Tayinloan
Claonaig
Lochranza
Kingarth
Rothesay
Dunoon
Gourock
Greenock
Brodick
Lamlash
Campbeltown
Ardrossan
Aberfoyle
Doune
Lochearnhead
Ardeonaig
Aberfeldy
Blair Atholl
Pitlochry
Kirkmichael
Blairgowrie
Dunkeld
Kirriemuir
Forfar
Brechin
Montrose
Arbroath
DUNDEE
Perth
Crieff
Auchterarder
Kinbuck
Stirling
Kincardine
Dunfermline
Glenrothes
Kirkcaldy
St Andrews
Crail
Aberdour
Gullane
EDINBURGH
Polmont
Falkirk
Uphall
Livingston
Dumbarton
Clydebank
GLASGOW
Paisley
Coatbridge
Motherwell
East Kilbride
Kilmarnock
Galston
Ayr
Eddleston
Peebles
Galashiels
Kelso
Jedburgh
Coldstream
Berwick-upon-Tweed
Bamburgh
Alnwick
Warkworth
Morpeth
Moffat
Langholm
Dumfries
Clarencefield
Castle Douglas
Dalbeattie
Newton Stewart
Stranraer
Carlisle
Ireby
Bassenthwaite Lake
Penrith
Alston
Hexham
NEWCASTLE UPON TYNE
Gateshead
SOUTH SHIELDS
SUNDERLAND
Consett
Stanley
Durham
Carrville
4. WEST DUNBARTONSHIRE
5. EAST DUNBARTONSHIRE
6. NORTH LANARKSHIRE
7. INVERCLYDE
8. RENFREWSHIRE
9. CITY OF GLASGOW
10. EAST RENFREWSHIRE
0 10 20 30 40 50 Kilometres
0 10 20 30 Miles

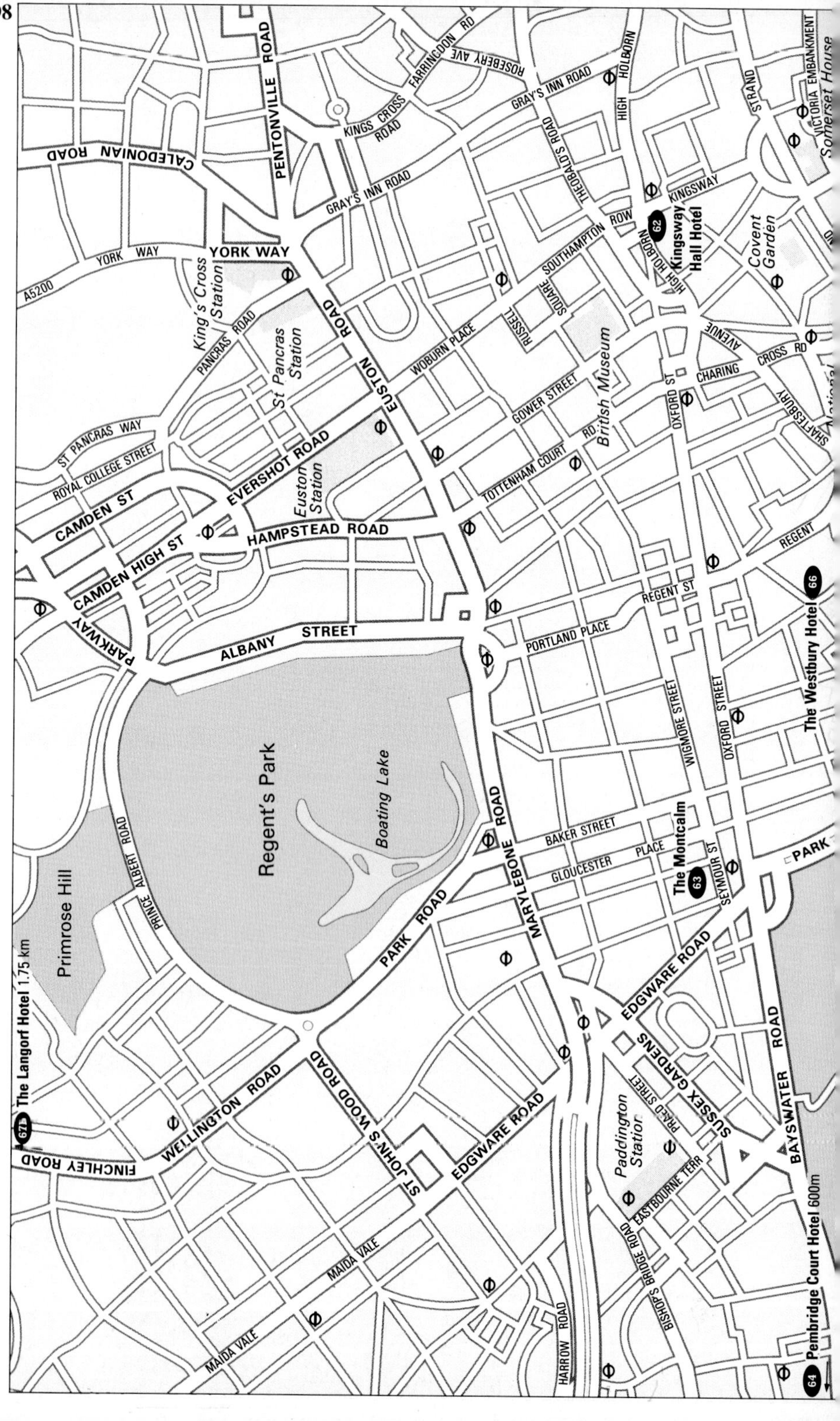

67 The Langorf Hotel 1.75 km
Primrose Hill
FINCHLEY ROAD
PRINCE ALBERT ROAD
PARKWAY
CAMDEN HIGH ST
CAMDEN ST
ROYAL COLLEGE STREET
ST PANCRAS WAY
A5200
YORK WAY
CALEDONIAN ROAD
WELLINGTON ROAD
MAIDA VALE
Regent's Park
ALBANY STREET
HAMPSTEAD ROAD
EVERSHOT ROAD
PANCRAS ROAD
King's Cross Station
YORK WAY
PENTONVILLE ROAD
St Pancras Station
Euston Station
ST JOHN'S WOOD ROAD
Boating Lake
PARK ROAD
EUSTON ROAD
GRAY'S INN ROAD
KINGS CROSS ROAD
FARRINGDON RD
ROSEBERY AVE
WOBURN PLACE
EDGWARE ROAD
MARYLEBONE ROAD
TOTTENHAM COURT RD
GOWER STREET
RUSSELL SQUARE
SOUTHAMPTON ROW
THEOBALD'S ROAD
GRAY'S INN ROAD
HARROW ROAD
GLOUCESTER PLACE
BAKER STREET
PORTLAND PLACE
British Museum
HIGH HOLBORN
Paddington Station
BISHOP'S BRIDGE ROAD
EASTBOURNE TERR
PRAED STREET
SUSSEX GARDENS
EDGWARE ROAD
REGENT ST
62 Kingsway Hall Hotel
HIGH HOLBORN
KINGSWAY
The Montcalm 63
WIGMORE STREET
OXFORD ST
SEYMOUR ST
OXFORD STREET
CHARING CROSS RD
AVENUE
Covent Garden
STRAND
BAYSWATER ROAD
64 Pembridge Court Hotel 600m
PARK
The Westbury Hotel 66
REGENT
SHAFTESBURY
National
VICTORIA EMBANKMENT
Somerset House

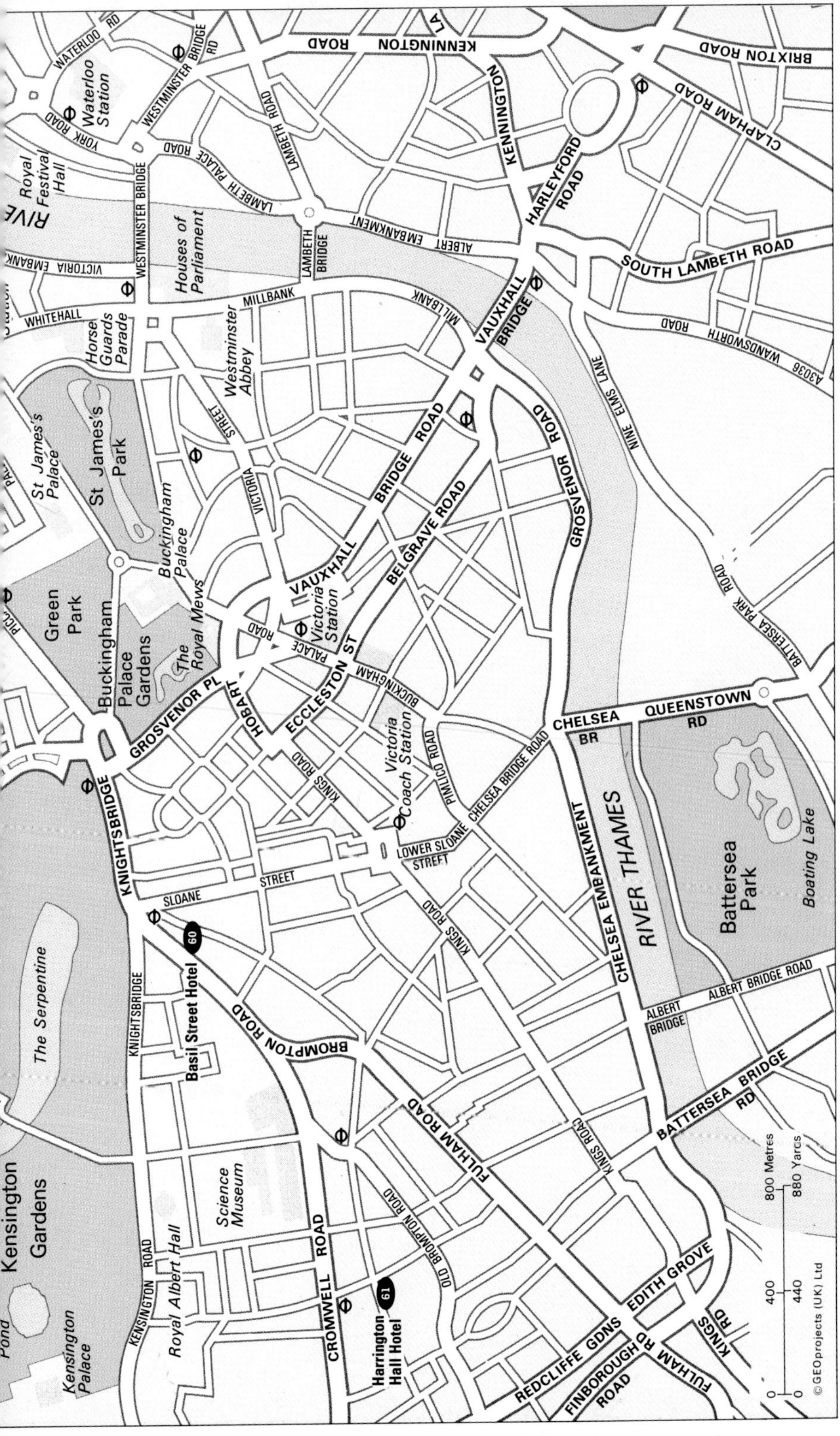

Kensington Gardens
Pond
Kensington Palace
The Serpentine
Royal Albert Hall
Science Museum
KENSINGTON ROAD
KNIGHTSBRIDGE
CROMWELL ROAD
Harrington Hall Hotel
61
BROMPTON ROAD
Basil Street Hotel
60
OLD BROMPTON ROAD
FULHAM ROAD
SLOANE STREET
LOWER SLOANE STREET
KINGS ROAD
REDCLIFFE GDNS
FINBOROUGH ROAD
FULHAM RD
EDITH GROVE
KINGS RD
GROSVENOR PL
HOBART
ECCLESTON ST
BUCKINGHAM PALACE ROAD
Victoria Coach Station
PIMLICO ROAD
CHELSEA BRIDGE ROAD
CHELSEA EMBANKMENT
RIVER THAMES
ALBERT BRIDGE
ALBERT BRIDGE ROAD
BATTERSEA BRIDGE RD
Battersea Park
Boating Lake
CHELSEA BR
QUEENSTOWN RD
BATTERSEA PARK ROAD
GROSVENOR ROAD
BELGRAVE ROAD
VAUXHALL BRIDGE ROAD
Victoria Station
VICTORIA STREET
Green Park
Buckingham Palace Gardens
The Royal Mews
Buckingham Palace
St James's Park
St James's Palace
Westminster Abbey
Horse Guards Parade
WHITEHALL
VICTORIA EMBANKMENT
MILLBANK
Houses of Parliament
WESTMINSTER BRIDGE
LAMBETH BRIDGE
LAMBETH PALACE ROAD
LAMBETH ROAD
ALBERT EMBANKMENT
Royal Festival Hall
RIVER
YORK ROAD
Waterloo Station
WATERLOO RD
WESTMINSTER BRIDGE RD
KENNINGTON ROAD
KENNINGTON LA
HARLEYFORD ROAD
VAUXHALL BRIDGE
SOUTH LAMBETH ROAD
WANDSWORTH ROAD
A3036
NINE ELMS LANE
CLAPHAM ROAD
BRIXTON ROAD
0 400 800 Metres
0 440 880 Yards
©GEOprojects (UK) Ltd

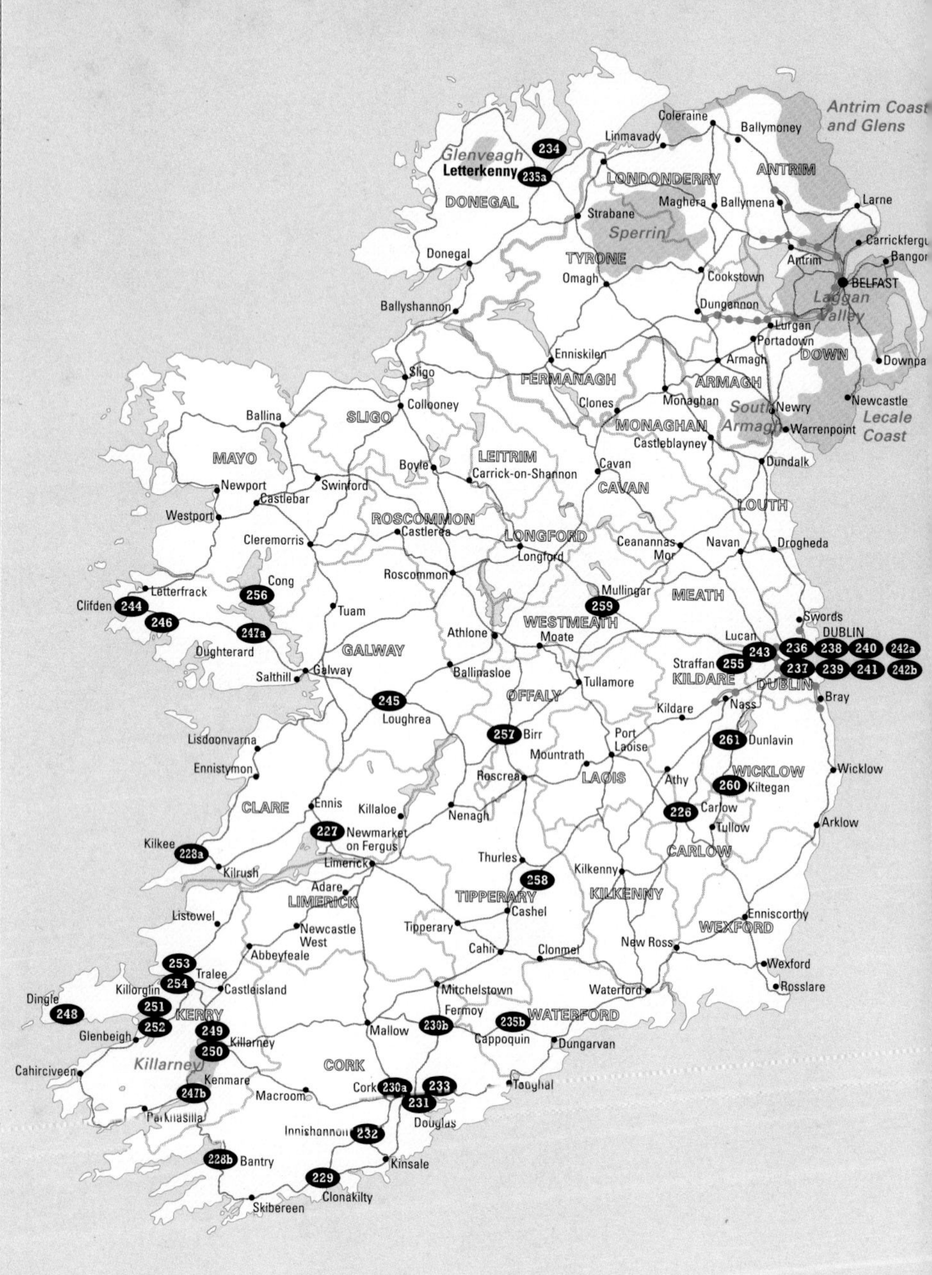
Antrim Coast
and Glens
Coleraine
Ballymoney
Limavady
234
Glenveagh
Letterkenny
235a
LONDONDERRY
ANTRIM
DONEGAL
Maghera
Ballymena
Larne
Strabane
Sperrin
Carrickfergus
TYRONE
Antrim
Bangor
Donegal
Omagh
Cookstown
BELFAST
Lagan
Valley
Ballyshannon
Dungannon
Lurgan
Portadown
DOWN
Enniskilen
Armagh
Downpatrick
Sligo
FERMANAGH
ARMAGH
Collooney
Clones
Monaghan
South
Armagh
Newry
Newcastle
Ballina
SLIGO
MONAGHAN
Warrenpoint
Lecale
Coast
Castleblayney
MAYO
LEITRIM
Cavan
Dundalk
Boyle
Carrick-on-Shannon
Newport
Swinford
CAVAN
Castlebar
Westport
ROSCOMMON
LOUTH
Castlerea
LONGFORD
Ceanannas
Mor
Navan
Drogheda
Claremorris
Longford
Cong
Roscommon
Letterfrack
256
Mullingar
MEATH
Clifden
244
246
Tuam
259
Swords
247a
Athlone
WESTMEATH
DUBLIN
Moate
Lucan
Oughterard
GALWAY
243
236
238
240
242a
Straffan
255
237
239
241
242b
Salthill
Galway
Ballinasloe
KILDARE
DUBLIN
Tullamore
Bray
OFFALY
245
Nass
Kildare
Loughrea
257
Birr
Lisdoonvarna
261
Dunlavin
Port
Laoise
Mountrath
Ennistymon
WICKLOW
Wicklow
Roscrea
LAOIS
Athy
260
Kiltegan
CLARE
Ennis
Killaloe
Carlow
226
Nenagh
Tullow
Arklow
227
Newmarket
on Fergus
Kilkee
228a
Thurles
CARLOW
Limerick
Kilrush
Kilkenny
258
Adare
LIMERICK
TIPPERARY
KILKENNY
Cashel
Listowel
Enniscorthy
Newcastle
West
Tipperary
WEXFORD
Abbeyfeale
Cahir
Clonmel
New Ross
253
Tralee
Wexford
Killorglin
254
Castleisland
Mitchelstown
Waterford
Rosslare
Dingle
251
248
KERRY
Fermoy
WATERFORD
249
230b
235b
252
Glenbeigh
Mallow
Cappoquin
Dungarvan
Killarney
250
Killarney
CORK
Cahirciveen
Kenmare
Cork
230a
233
Youghal
247b
Macroom
231
Parknasilla
Douglas
Innishannon
232
228b
Bantry
Kinsale
229
Clonakilty
Skibereen
0 10 20 30 40 50 Kilometres
0 10 20 30 Miles